READY FOR ANYTHING

READY FOR ANYTHING

The Royal Fleet Auxiliary 1905–1950

Geoff Puddefoot

Seaforth
PUBLISHING

Copyright © Geoff Puddefoot 2010

First published in Great Britain in 2010 by
Seaforth Publishing
An imprint of Pen & Sword Books Ltd
47 Church Street, Barnsley
South Yorkshire S70 2AS

www.seaforthpublishing.com
Email info@seaforthpublishing.com

British Library Cataloguing in Publication Data
A CIP data record for this book is available from the British Library

ISBN 978 1 84832 074 1

Typeset and designed by M.A.T.S. Typesetters, Leigh-on-Sea, Essex
Printed and bound in Great Britain by
CPI Antony Rowe, Chippenham, Wiltshire

Contents

List of Illustrations

(between pages 114 and 115)

PLATE I
The collier *Mercedes*; she was involved in the Admiralty's unsuccessful coaling at sea trials. (National Maritime Museum N4349)
    Mercedes coaling the River class destroyer HMS *Kennet*. (National Maritime Museum N20874)

PLATE II
Petroleum, the first Admiralty tanker to test a RAS(L) rig. (National Maritime Museum N21418)
    First World War RFA officer (Mr A Ballantyne) in working uniform (by courtesy of Mrs Avril Hood)
    Ballantyne in full dress uniform; note the sub-lieutenant RNR rank badge on the sleeve of his jacket (by courtesy of Mrs Avril Hood)

PLATE III
    Thermol, 1911, one of the 2000-ton *Burma* class. (National Maritime Museum G5401)
    Appleleaf, one of the *Trinol* or Fast Leaf class, shown in 1933. (National Maritime Museum N4298)

PLATE IV
Prestol, 1917, of the second 2000-ton class. (National Maritime Museum N4295)
    Delphinula, acquired by the Admiralty in 1918; seen here in 1933. (National Maritime Museum N10699)

PLATE V
Palmol, an early 1000-ton harbour tanker painted in dazzle camouflage, 1918. (National Maritime Museum N4339)
    Petronel, a 500-ton spirit carrier, alongside HMS *Repulse*, 1918. (National Maritime Museum N4346)

PLATE VI
War Diwan in 1936. Built at the end of the First World War, this class was an important element of the inter-war RFA. (National Maritime Museum N4758)
    War Bahadur, showing damage to bridge sustained during storm at sea in January 1938. (National Maritime Museum N10686)

PLATE VII
Oleander, 1922, an inter-war freighting tanker. (National Maritime Museum N4287)
    Broomdale, one of the Dale class of freighting tankers which came into service just before the Second World War. (National Maritime Museum P14197)

PLATE VIII
Bacchus, 1936, an early store ship. (National Maritime Museum P8988)
    Robert Dundas, 1938, one of two coastal store carriers in this class. (National Maritime Museum N4752)

PLATE IX
Inter-war trials: the heavy cruiser HMS *Suffolk* refuelling the destroyer HMS *Verity* by stirrup method. Stirrups on rollers carry the hose suspended below the towline. (National Maritime Museum L3435)
    Stirrup rail and platform. This design was never used at sea because the hose was continually snagged by the rail supports. (National Archives)

PLATE X
Wartime fuelling astern using buoyant hose to supply a destroyer. (National Archives)
    A destroyer refuelling astern. Here the warship has taken position, with the hose in a 'bight', to ease the strain on the refuelling rig. (National Archives)

PLATE XI
Early wooden roller used aboard some convoy escort oilers. (National Archives)
    Hose connector aboard an oiler. (National Archives)
    A later arrangement for oiling at sea aboard convoy escort oilers, with the buoyant rubber hose laid on metal rollers. (National Archives)

PLATE XII
An early experimental method of depth charge transfer. Charges were attached to an oil drum by 30 feet of rope and then tipped over the side. The receiving warship then grappled the drum and pulled the charges aboard. Later methods were less hazardous. (National Archives)
    Brown Ranger. This vessel spent part of the Second World War refuelling Malta-bound convoys (by courtesy of George Mortimore)

PLATE XIII
Fort Dunvegan, one of a class of store ships based on war-standard hulls that served the RFA for many years after 1945 (by courtesy of George Mortimore)
    Oakol, one of the second 1000-ton class of harbour tankers. Crews of these vessels were usually employed on harbour or yard craft agreements (by courtesy of George Mortimore)
    Spalake, 1946, one of the Spa class of water tankers. (National Maritime Museum N16306)

Preface and Acknowledgements

In any book on as extensive a subject as the Royal Fleet Auxiliary, the author's problem is not so much what to include as what to leave out from the vast amount of material the subject encompasses.

I have therefore, once again, included predominantly material, information and personal accounts that reflect the character and development of the Service, rather than introducing strictly technical matters, which have been dealt with exhaustively elsewhere.

As in the previous book, this probably means that some areas are less well and fully documented than would otherwise have been the case. It is, however, my hope that the extensive reference section will serve as an adequate guide to those whose researches require more depth of knowledge than they find available here.

The author would like to acknowledge the help and advice of Captain Shane Redmond OBE RFA (Retd), Gordon Wilson, Martyn Hobbs, George Mortimore, and all of the serving and former members of the RFA, too numerous to name individually who took the time to supply photographs, information and anecdotes, without which this book would not have been possible.

I would also like to acknowledge the help of both Bexley and Dartford Library Services staff and the staff at the National Archive and the National Maritime Museum.

Introduction

Since its creation in 1905, the Royal Fleet Auxiliary has been involved wherever ships of the Royal Navy have seen action.

Supplying the fuel, ammunition and basic necessities of life which keep the ships afloat and operating, the RFA's contribution has gone largely unnoticed, despite the fact that RFA men (and women) have frequently given their lives to ensure the smooth operation of the Navy's ships.

Franco's Spain, the Second World War, Korea, Suez, Aden, Oman, Northern Ireland, Rhodesia, Bluff Cove, Kuwait, Iraq: the areas of our naval deployment have spanned the world, and in the present world climate there is no reason to think that our reach will contract. The naval history of this era has been written in blood, some of it belonging to the men and women of the RFA.

But who were the men who operated the ships that fuelled the Russian convoys and manhandled ammunition under a burning Pacific sun, during that second war which was to end all wars?

Just the same sort as carried out a pump-over, forty years later, while simultaneously refueling HMS *Plymouth*, as a force 10 gale and thirty-foot waves in the Southern Ocean tried to tear the guts out of their battered, rusty ships, and an Argentinian submarine played them a deadly game of hide-and-seek. And for those who don't remember, the ships were RFAs *Tidespring* and *Brambleleaf* and the place was 200 miles north of a tiny speck on the chart called South Georgia.

Chronicles of the Royal Navy are myriad, but the RFA's story still remains largely untold. Finding out about the ships isn't hard, but the story of the men who worked them still remains something of a mystery.

And it's that story that this book and its companion volume, *The Fourth Force*, sets out to tell.

Chapter 1

Supplying the Fleet ... Before the RFA

Prior to the development of reliable military aircraft, sea power, with its associated encouragement and protection of successful overseas trade, had historically been the key to a dominant position in the world order.

It was overwhelming naval superiority, supported by a system of shore bases, which allowed the Royal Navy's warships to protect Britain's vital trading routes and facilitated the expansion of British overseas possessions during the eighteenth and early nineteenth century. Control and successful exploitation of those colonies was also largely dependent upon sea power, although, ultimately, law and order in the areas concerned depended upon the presence of a well trained, professional standing army for the purposes of backing the civil administration. It is a clear indication of the reputation which her armed forces enjoyed that Great Britain was able to retain and financially exploit these colonial possessions, despite UK military personnel often being outnumbered by anything from a hundred to a thousand to one by the indigenous population. It was only with the appearance of Imperial Germany as a major European military, colonial and economic rival, in the nineteenth century and early twentieth century, that the Royal Navy's maritime superiority began to be questioned.

Two centuries before the British began their Imperial expansion, however, the foundations of what was to become the Royal Navy were laid by aggressive and adventurous Elizabethan sailors. The conflict with Spain, in both Europe and the New World, involved operations at far greater distances than was common in the earlier Tudor era, and brought new problems such as diseases caused by dietary deficiencies on long voyages. This was intimately related to the question of how to keep ships supplied with food and other staples far away from established shore facilities, when squadrons might be at sea for months or even years. Drake and Frobisher certainly took store ships with them when they raided Spain's American colonies, although they probably were not the first to make use of such vessels. These were just a heterogeneous collection of ordinary merchant ships scraped together as the needs of the fleet required and simply loaded with food, water and probably ammunition.[1]

In the centuries that followed, the Royal Navy established a more or less permanent presence in almost all the world's oceans. This was made possible by a network of bases gradually built up in the Mediterranean, North America, the Caribbean, and India, but regular voyages to and from these stations, and ever-longer patrols, placed greater emphasis on victualling. Even in European waters, the developing strategy of close blockade of enemy ports required longer stints of sea time, and a proper system

---

1 Sigwart (1969) supplies a comprehensive list, which indicates the diverse nature of these first, primitive auxiliaries.

to keep ships supplied and crews healthy. By the time of the Napoleonic Wars there was a well-practised organisation that chartered small merchant ships as victuallers and sent them out to meet the fleet – at times it could even supply some fresh provisions on a regular basis.

Despite improvements in both ships and armament in the intervening period, an Elizabethan seaman would probably have found life aboard ship very little changed in the two hundred or so years between Drake's trouncing of the Armada and the start of the Napoleonic wars. A seaman's food had altered very little because the 'technology' was not available to allow much change in his basic diet. Until the advent of canned food in the middle of the nineteenth century and refrigeration some years later, the means of preserving food on long voyages were relatively limited, being confined to drying, salting and pickling. Containers were either wooden casks or cloth bags.

Despite these limitations, the horror stories about life afloat in the Royal Navy during the Napoleonic wars are largely exaggeration and a moment's thought will show that they really can be nothing else. Sailing one of Nelson's 'wooden walls' was hard work. A seaman needed to be fit and strong and plainly he would not be either if his food was not both plentiful and of a reasonable quality. Contemporary on-board menus certainly reflect this. A Georgian seaman's rations consisted of a pound of bread or biscuit and a gallon of beer every day with a pound of salt pork on Sunday and Thursday, along with two pounds of beef issued on a Tuesday and Saturday. Half a pint of pease was issued four times a week and on the other days (Monday, Wednesday and Friday), they received a pint of oatmeal, two ounces of butter and ¼lb of cheese. It seems possible that these meatless or 'Banyan' days might have been alternated, so that by combining rations, two messes could concoct a good meal, even including a 'plum' duff, made with oatmeal and raisins, the latter either bought from the purser or issued in lieu of part of their beef ration. Anti-scorbutics, like sauerkraut, were also issued, although the usual anti-scurvy treatment was lemon or lime juice, usually mixed with the mens' rum ration, a mixture universally known as 'grog'.

This diet supplies an average daily intake of about 5000 calories, and although the rations sound unappetising, fresh meat and vegetables were also frequently issued. In addition, the lower deck had a number of ways of supplementing their food, particularly with fruit, which could be bought from the boats that invariably pulled alongside when any Royal Navy ship reached port or anchored off a friendly coast. Rice could be issued as an officially sanctioned substitute for bread, pease and cheese when a ship found itself on a foreign station, although it was not very popular.

Beer, perhaps surprisingly, was the navy's preferred drink during this period. It was not, however, quite the same product that is available today. Georgian beer was 'small' beer, which was only about 2 per cent alcohol (by comparison, modern beers are 4–5 per cent). Its main advantage over water was that, since it had been boiled during manufacture, it was reasonably sterile when it went into the cask and so would keep for some months without deterioration. Cask-stored water is unpleasant after a few weeks in a wooden container and over long sea voyages, the water casks would become a solid mass of green filaments before many months had passed, especially if the ship was serving in tropical waters.

Both officers and men were also entitled to a daily issue of spirits and water, half a pint per man per day, as well as a tobacco ration. Brandy, arrack or wine, both white and red, were all issued, depending upon where the ship was serving, although political pressure from an influential group of West Indian merchants ensured that by 1740 the usual issue was rum. Incidentally, grog, the Navy's name for the rum and water mixture that the sailors usually received, is attributed to Admiral Vernon, whose nickname of 'Old Grog' came from his habit of wearing a heavy silk cloak of a fabric known as 'grosgrain' (or 'grogram' to the lower deck). It was Vernon who introduced the issue of this mixture of rum and water, which in turn caused his nickname to be forever associated with the practice.

Once brought on board ship, it was the duty of the purser to organise the stowage of provisions so as to minimise wastage. His job was certainly no sinecure, because he was responsible for the quality of the provisions and any spoilt food had to be sent back to the victualling department and a claim, with a mountain of accompanying paperwork, made against his accounts. Moreover, any shortfall in those accounts was taken out of his pay! Interestingly enough, this natural wastage was the reason behind the system called the 'purser's pound', whereby a purser was allowed to issue food at a rate of fourteen ounces to the pound in order to take into account problems associated with spillage and loss in storage. Despite all of these disadvantages, a competent purser could make a good living, especially since he could supply small luxuries to the crew. Many even retired to become ship's chandlers.

Mealtimes on board a Georgian naval vessel had to be carefully organised, because a three-deck first rate might have a crew numbering over 800, more especially when one considers that a four-pound slab of salt beef had to be cooked for four or five hours to make it edible. Crews were organised into messes, usually of five or six men who worked together. Each man took a turn to be 'mess cook', probably for the week, and it was his job to collect that day's provisions, the captain allowing two periods a day, of between two to three hours each, for this. Food was collected in wooden mess kids, small, half tubs, with rope handles, usually made by the ship's cooper, who also had overall responsibility for all the casks.

Having obtained his mess's daily ration, the mess cook took it along to the galley where the meat was placed in a twine net marked with his mess's number and boiled for a couple of hours in a giant communal pot. If his mess wanted pudding that day, the mess cook mixed the flour, raisins and suet on the mess table before taking it in a tagged pudding bag to the galley, where it was also boiled. He whistled while doing this, because it is impossible to clandestinely eat raisins while whistling. Once cooked, the food was collected by the mess cook and brought along to whichever deck his mess was stationed, where he set out the mess table. This came complete with benches, the outer end of the table secured to the hull, while the other end was suspended from the deck above, either by ropes or rigid Y-shaped bars. These tables were arranged so that they could be stowed quickly when the ship was cleared for action.

Utensils were primitive, each man having an all-purpose knife, which he used for everything from cutting his food to killing the enemy. A wooden cup and a spoon for soup or duff completed his collection of utensils. He probably stowed both spoon and cup out of sight in his 'ditty' bag, such items being easily 'lost'. It appears that, apart from the watch on deck, the seamen ate together, although, of course, officers, midshipmen and warrant officers had separate messes.

Victualling: Production and distribution

Administrative responsibility for all naval supplies before 1965, both in the UK and abroad, was the responsibility of three separate and predominantly independent departments.

The Board of Ordnance

The Board of Ordnance could trace its ancestry back to the medieval beginnings of gunpowder artillery, but a formal Office of Ordnance was established by King Henry VIII in 1543 and renamed the Board of Ordnance in 1597. It was responsible for supplying guns, ammunition and related stores to both army and navy, and was independent of both, although reorganisation in the 1650s gave the navy short-lived control over the supply of its major weapons. The Board was abolished in 1855, having been blamed for many of the shortcomings brought to light by the Crimean war, and for a long period thereafter the army Ordnance Department was responsible for providing naval guns. This unsatisfactory situation was ameliorated by putting a member of the Board of Admiralty in charge of naval ordnance requirements and in October 1891 the Armament Supply Department (Naval) was established.

The Victualling Department

Another institution of ancient pedigree, in its modern form it can be dated to reforms carried out in 1683, when a board of salaried officers was set up. This organisation was responsible for the supply – both purchase and distribution – of all foodstuffs to the navy. It not only contracted for supplies, but also in time it became a manufacturer in its own right, running its own bakeries and breweries, for example. It was separate from the Navy Board (the navy's permanent bureaucracy, as opposed to the Admiralty, which tended to change with each government), but was subordinate to it, until the Navy Board itself was abolished in 1832 and its duties subsumed into the Admiralty. Ready-made clothing was added to the victuallers' remit in 1827 and in 1886 it also assumed responsibility for the examination of ship and store accounts.

The Naval Stores Department

This was a nineteenth-century development from a sub-department of the Navy Board, established as a sub-committee in 1796. Basically, this department supplied everything not available from the other two. This included clothing (until 1827), ship's equipment (rope, canvas, timber) and all the other essentials of shipboard life. From 1889, the senior civil servant in charge of this department was known as the Director of Stores.

Provisions were supplied to the Georgian navy by the Board of Victualling Commissioners, usually referred to as the Victualling Board. In its heyday this consisted of seven commissioners, with an establishment of clerks who did the day-to-day work of operating the victualling department. Early in the eighteenth century, much of the navy's food had been purchased from contractors, who supplied meat, beer or biscuit at a fixed price, but complaints about the quality of some of this food and its short weight meant that by 1793 (the start of the French Revolutionary and later Napoleonic wars) the victualling department had begun to prepare much of the navy's food on its own purpose-built premises. At first the organisation itself consisted of a network of breweries, bakeries, slaughterhouses and manufacturing yards where the food was produced, usually sited near one or other of the victualling yards. Later, all means of production was concentrated in the three big home yards at Deptford, Gosport (across the harbour from Portsmouth) and Plymouth. The hub of the system was the Royal Victualling Yard at Deptford, where most of the stores were delivered and tested before being shipped to the other victualling yards.

Food production was highly organised and on an industrial scale. Animals were bought and slaughtered, usually during the winter months, by the Board's butchers and meat was then cut into pieces, weighing about 4 pounds for beef and 2 pounds for pork, before being salted and packed in casks. Biscuit, made simply from flour, water and salt then stamped with a broad arrow before being baked, was sent out in plain linen bags. As long as these biscuits were kept dry, they remained perfectly edible. Once they were damp, however, weevils and the like quickly moved in. Considering that the usual place for food storage was the lower hold or even the bilge, meat and biscuits without maggots and weevils must have been the exception rather than the rule.

After production, the barrels of salted meat, bags of bread, casks of butter and dried pease that formed the seaman's staple diet were stored at the department's victualling yards, which then organised distribution. Usually located in or near the major dockyards, their efficient operation was the responsibility of an official known as the Agent Victualler. This individual organised the storage of all provisions, aided by the yard staff and several clerks. Manufacturing, when it was carried out by the Victualling Department, was not his responsibility, however. This was taken care of by tradesmen such as the master brewer, master baker and most importantly, the master cooper, who was responsible for manufacture of the casks used in food storage. All food was marked with a system of numbers and letters to show where these originated and when. There was a strict 'use by' system, salt meat and biscuit having to be issued within two years, while cheese and butter had a shelf life of only three months.

Besides the needs of the crew, wooden sailing ships also required a good deal of basic upkeep and supplies for this came to the vessel from the Naval Stores Department, or rather its outlets at dockyards such as Chatham, Deptford and Portsmouth. However, ordinance stores – such things as gunpowder, round shot, quick and slow match and even spare parts for gun carriages – were the exception, being supplied by the Board of Ordnance. Needless to say, special arrangements were made when handling tricky stuff such as gunpowder, and days when powder was being loaded were 'no fires, no lights', so only cold food could be served to crews of the ships involved.[2]

Even before the beginning of the Napoleonic wars, increasing colonial expansion was forcing the navy to take up an ever-more far-reaching role, and as a result of this there was a massively increased need for logistical support. In the strategic sense, this was supplied by a widespread system of shore bases, established at first in the Mediterranean (Gibraltar, Port Mahon, Malta), the West Indies and North America (Jamaica, Antigua, Halifax, Bermuda), later India (Bombay, Madras, Trincomalee), and eventually Aden, Singapore and Hong Kong. At the tactical level, however, the

2 Exhaustive information on victualling regulations is available at the pbenyon1.plus.com website shown in the reference section.

navy found that its warships were required to spend longer periods at sea, on blockade or patrol duties, when running out of essential victuals and stores and a resulting return to port for replenishment would severely handicap operational effectiveness. From this imperative there grew up a system of support ships, which were usually chartered merchant ships sailing between the shore bases and the fleet, instead of remaining permanently with the warships as Drake's store ships had usually done.

These early 'fleet auxiliaries', as the support craft came to be known, were, like their Tudor forerunners, a mixture of converted warships and merchantmen, usually chartered but in a few cases, Admiralty owned. Admiralty-owned vessels were operated by naval personnel, while the chartered vessels were simply ordinary merchant ships contracted to transport naval supplies instead of their usual cargo. During the American Revolutionary war supplying a large army on the other side of the Atlantic had produced a huge demand for transportation, and the Navy Board was charged with chartering both victuallers and troopships. At the same time, the Board of Ordnance contracted for shipping to move the army's arms and ammunition on an unprecedented scale, and the end result was a chaotic charter market in which the unregulated internal competition drove up prices and added friction to an already cumbersome process. Lessons were learned and in the next war in 1794 the Admiralty set up a Transport Board to administer a similar but global demand for shipping. This turned out to be so efficiently run that it was given additional responsibilities far outside its original remit. In 1796 it took over the care of prisoners of war from the overburdened Sick and Hurt Board, which itself was finally merged with the Transport Board in 1806. The transports were employed with great flexibility, and on distant stations were often diverted to other operations when their primary task had been completed. For this purpose the Transport Board periodically issued lists of which ships were operating where, for the benefit of the appropriate flag officers.

The Transport Board was abolished in 1817, only to reappear in 1862 as the Admiralty's Transport Department, which was established, according to the 1861 Select Committee, 'To carry out transport of every kind required by our Government to any part of our coast and to all our colonies and possessions, including India.' It was this department's responsibility to provide merchant shipping for all of the British fighting services, which it did until 1916 when it was transferred to the Ministry of Shipping.

During the Napoleonic wars it became standard practice to send a regular stream of victuallers out to fleets on station in order to maximise operational deployment. In the English Channel, cargoes often included live animals for slaughter and other fresh produce, whose value as anti-scorbutics was gradually accepted by the navy's administrators. Meetings were arranged at a network designated rendezvous, where the supply vessels would find the warships during a predetermined period. Apart from the modern convenience of arranging rendezvous by radio, this is more or less the way things are still done, with RFAs collecting supplies from shore bases and re-supplying the Fleet by both liquid and solid RAS, thus allowing the warships to remain permanently on station. However, in the age of sail replenishment was carried out at anchor rather than underway.

By the 1860s, the supply ships had become such a vital component of the logistics chain that an order in council was made, dated 9 July 1864, to the effect that the mercantile-crewed auxiliaries should fly a blue ensign defaced by the Admiralty Badge or Seal, to indicate that they were on Admiralty service.

Training of officers and seamen within the merchant service

Until the mid-nineteenth century, there was no formal training of masters and mates within the mercantile marine, and everything was learned at sea. A youngster simply joined a ship and worked his way up to employment as a mate by virtue of experience; the alternative was a simple form of indentured apprenticeship. The early forms of indenture or agreement were either with a specific master or more often, with the ship owner or company employing the young man. In both cases there was no formal examination and so it was up to the individual to prove his worth and obtain references. Later, the second method became the only method in use.

As the century progressed, it became increasingly obvious that this unregulated system could not meet levels of competence necessary within the rapidly developing shipping industry. The system was entirely dependent on an individual's intelligence and the ability of those aboard to provide instruction. However, with an age on entry of thirteen years or less, the prospective officer's formal education was far from complete and unlikely to be improved at sea, given the general academic level of his mentors. Development within the industry had clearly shown a need for increasing the academic standard of future masters and mates. Knowledge of practical seamanship and navigation while remaining critical to safe ship operations was plainly in itself no longer enough.

The beginning of the end for the old system came in 1848. In that year, James Murray placed before Parliament papers in which it was stated that the Merchant Service was greatly imperilled by the incompetence of British masters – a view supported by many in the industry, although by no means all. However, concern did exist among several of the more influential ship owners who, for obvious reasons, wished to see a uniform and tested method upon which to base, at least in part, an assessment of their masters' capabilities. This concern was also mirrored by the Royal Navy, simply because it relied heavily on trained merchant seamen to boost the competency and manning levels of the fleet in times of war.

The first half of the nineteenth century had seen unprecedented development in the maritime world. The advent of steam propulsion and iron hulls, which resulted in much larger ships, meant more cargo could be carried. And of course, the continued development of colonial and overseas trade meant that there was more cargo to transport. Though the old staples were still there, cargoes were becoming increasingly valuable and varied. In addition, a strong passenger trade had also developed with the expansion of the British Empire and the associated need to transport both civilian and military passengers overseas. These larger vessels, with bigger cargoes, meant more potential profit from each voyage, but conversely increased the financial cost of any ship lost. With this rapid increase in the size of ships and the introduction of machinery, vessels were becoming sophisticated and expensive to build. The cost of insurance of both ship and cargo grew in line with these developments and usually bore a direct relationship to the quality of a ship owner's crew. Insurers became increasingly concerned with the questionable levels of crew competence and the absence of a universal qualification by which they could assess the ability of a ship's officers.

Finally, an Act for improving the 'condition' (which presumably meant competence) of masters, mates and seamen was drawn up by the Board of Trade, under the direction of T H Farrer and subsequently became law in 1851. Although wide reaching in content, the salient feature of the Act was the establishment of Maritime Examination Boards in all major seaports throughout the United Kingdom. The Merchant Shipping Act was further amended and expanded, extending the powers of the Board of Trade (BoT) into all areas of business governing ships and seamen. Unfortunately, at this stage the Act excluded training and did not specify the length of apprenticeship or sea service before attendance at an examining board.

The first move towards formalising training resulted from the establishment of the Mercantile Service Association in the port of Liverpool and, shortly thereafter, similar bodies in London and other parts of the country. One of primary objectives was to establish schools for the training and education of boys and men for the Mercantile Marine Service. The setting up of school ships was not intended to bring about the demise of the old apprenticeship system or likewise prevent a boy 'signing on' and working his way up to AB and eventually a mate's or master's certificate. These were, in fact, intended to provide a level of academic and practical education that would enable the student to build on and, after a period of sea service, be more likely to obtain the newly introduced certificates of competency.

On 1 August 1859, the first Mercantile Marine School Ship, *Conway*, came into being. Moored in the Mersey off Rock Ferry, she was the first of the training ships to open, being closely followed three years later by her great rival, *Worcester*, in the Thames. Both were former naval ships of the line, which was reflected in the strict discipline and ethos of hard work applied on board. Principally intended to prepare boys for entry into the mercantile marine as apprentices (though they were usually titled cadets), these ships were the fore-runners of many similar establishments throughout the UK over the next one hundred years. Direct entry apprenticeships generally covered a period of four years, prior to taking the first Board of Trade examination. However, with the introduction of the first cadet training ship, it was agreed that a two- or three-year period in one of these vessels (even though they were static) would be recognised as equal to one year of actual sea service, thereby reducing an apprenticeship from the usual four-year term down to three. By the end of the century and following the Merchant Shipping Act 1894, specific areas of legislation came on to the statute books and established a minimum length of sea service before a candidate could be examined for any certificate of competency.

At this stage, there were not only concerns relating to the training of officers, but also that of seamen. The first recorded land-based training for boys going to sea was that provided by the Marine Society, established by Jonas Hanway in 1756, although these boys invariably entered the Royal Navy. The first Royal Navy-administered boy training establishment did not come into being for almost another one hundred years, while formalised training of boys entering the merchant marine as seamen was non-existent before 1865. With the arrival and fitting out of the former HMS *Indefatigable*, also in the Mersey, however, this situation was largely corrected and the pattern of pre-sea training was established until the present system of Merchant Service education was developed during the 1970s and the 1980s.

Science and tin cans

Along with the navy's advances in training and ship development, science was also improving its primitive techniques of food preservation. In France, just before Bonaparte's fall from power, a revolution of a totally different kind was taking place, and the man leading it was a self-taught confectioner from Paris named Nicholas Appert. He began his confectionery business in Paris in about 1780, but by 1795 had given up sweets and cakes to concentrate solely on food preservation. His method was simple. It consisted of placing good quality ingredients, such as vegetables, fruit, meat, soup and even milk, into glass containers, carefully heating these bottles for an appropriate length of time, which Appert had discovered by experiment, and then sealing them carefully. Unusually for an inventor, Appert was a shrewd businessman and he realised almost immediately that his 'preserves', while being acceptable to the ordinary man or woman in the street, had a far greater application with the military, especially the navy, whose rations were boring and unappetising at best.

Appert approached the French Navy, which tested his product. The sailors were enthusiastic, this testimonial from Admiral Allemand being fairly typical:

> I am so convinced, Sir, of the great advantages that would arise from the provision of these articles *for the use of the sick on board that* ... I should not hesitate to confirm my opinion, as much for the sake of the Government as for myself. (author's emphasis added)

Notice the emphasis on the use of preserved fruit and vegetables for the sick, possibly those down with scurvy. This remained a predominant feature of even the Royal Navy, until later developments in canning technology brought the price of tinned goods down to a level that made these available to everybody.

In Britain, the first food processors was the firm of Donkin, Hall & Gamble and it is significant that it was also the first to use tinned steel containers, because John Hall, one of the original partners, only appears to have gone in to the business in order to rid his Dartford ironworks of the excess quantities of tin plate it had inadvertently produced! Improvement in the canning process was rapid, with the invention of the autoclave steriliser in the 1850s and, slightly later, development of a simple, in-expensive method of can production. In fact, canning food of all types became so simple and reliable that the Royal Navy even opened its own cannery at Deptford, in 1871, although only after it became involved in a famous scandal about the quality of tinned food supplied by a number of commercial canners.

Preserved or canned meat was issued, along with preserved potatoes, on foreign stations, from about April 1847. Unfortunately, complaints about the quality of this canned meat began in the period 1848–51 and in 1852 an examination of samples found that the contents included what the report coyly termed 'improper substances' (the content of quite a number of the cans was actually green). Incidentally, it was a measure of official indifference to servicemen's diet that this examination had only been brought about when *The Times* reported that the smell in the neighbourhood surrounding the site where the meat was stored had become so overpowering that the local residents complained – and this was meat that was still in tins.

This appears to have been a temporary problem, however, associated with a set of inefficient contractors, because, even earlier, in April 1850, the Admiralty had found alternative suppliers for canned meat, from North and South America and Australia. Nevertheless, a considerable period was still to elapse before these new style foodstuffs became a regular addition to the serviceman's diet. It was not until June 1905, for example, that the Admiralty announced salt beef was to be phased out of the sailor's diet, although salt pork was to remain on the menu, one day in three, until February 1926. Only then was it replaced by fresh or frozen meats, with canned meat substituted when neither of the others was available. With improved refrigeration and cold room facilities aboard ship, a wide range of fresh meats could now be carried and this, along with the improved training of cooks, brought about the introduction of a much more varied and healthy diet to the navy's ships. Further improvements to Royal Navy victualling during this period also included the introduction of baking ovens as part of the equipment for Royal Navy warships, so as to supply the crews with both fresh bread and roast and baked meats.

The first trials of such an oven, which could produce baked meals for 300 men, took place aboard the depot ship *Hannibal* at Portsmouth in 1863, although as late as 1900, a committee set up to look in to the navy's diet concluded that it could not recommend that additional ovens and cooks should be provided in seagoing ships. By 1912, the situation had improved, with extra pay sanctioned for 'Bakery staffs of ships fitted with bakeries when employed in making bread for other ships not so fitted.' All of this seems to indicate that depot ships and the newer, heavier fleet units were probably fitted with bakeries as a matter of routine and were supplying bread to the smaller, older units not fitted with ovens, such as light cruisers, destroyers and submarines.

Alongside improved victualling, the other great driver of logistical change in the nineteenth century was the introduction of mechanical propulsion. Steam – generated from coal – began rapidly to replace wind as the navy's motive power, and led to the establishment of coaling facilities at existing shore bases and the addition of chartered colliers to the expanding auxiliary fleet. Inevitably, this led to an increased demand for shipping by the Naval Stores Department, with its vessels, of necessity, falling into two major categories – ships owned and operated by the Admiralty and so employed more or less full time as auxiliaries and a second, increasingly important, group of ships taken up on charter, employed as and when needed.

In order to identify the origins of particular ships, an Admiralty circular letter, dated 3 August 1905, directed that an auxiliary vessel manned by a mercantile crew and owned by the Admiralty should, in future be styled a 'Royal Fleet Auxiliary' (RFA). Ships on temporary transport charter to the Admiralty were to be designated 'Mercantile Fleet Auxiliaries' (MFAs), although these days they are more commonly referred to as 'Ships Taken Up From Trade' (STUFT).

Thus, the history of the RFA fleet dates from the issue of this letter.

RFA Letter 1905 – Letter marking the origin of the Royal Fleet Auxiliary

CIRCULAR LETTER No 9 T 3487   Admiralty sw
                        1905   3rd August 1905

My Lord Commissioners of the Admiralty have decided that the title 'HMS' shall in future be strictly confined to commissioned ships flying the White Ensign and shall never be applied to fleet auxiliaries which are manned by mercantile crews, whether they are owned by the Admiralty or taken up on Transport charter.

My Lords are pleased to direct that auxiliaries which belong to the Admiralty shall in future be styled as 'ROYAL FLEET AUXILIARIES' and that those which are taken up on Transport charter shall be styled 'MERCANTILE FLEET AUXILIARIES'.

The special character of any of these ships should be denoted after the name and whenever brevity is desired the initials RFA or MFA should be used. Thus the *Maine* should be styled RFA *Maine*, Hospital Ship, and the *Sirdar*, MFA *Sirdar*, Collier Transport.

By Command of their Lordships,

Evan Macgregor

All Commanders-in-Chief, Captains,
Commanders, Commanding Officers of HM Ships & Vessels.

Chapter 2

The Beginning: 1905–14

The story of the RFA from 1905 to the end of the Second World War is concerned, in the beginning at least, with the development of its system of logistics supply based upon the Royal Navy's enormous overseas bases. In those early years, it was predominantly a freighting service and it was only just prior to the Second World War, that real attention began, belatedly, to focus on techniques for delivering vital supplies, both in the form of fuel and dry stores, while at sea, due to concerns over the vulnerability of the navy's bases to aircraft attack.

It should have been clear from the beginning, especially in light of the US Navy's First World War experiences, that these duties would require a fleet of highly specialised, fast ships, specifically designed for replenishment duties. For reasons of both finance and policy, however, such a fleet would not even to begin to make an appearance until some time after the Second World War. Unfortunately for the servicemen and women concerned, British involvement in both the Atlantic and Pacific during the Second World War was to significantly reveal the shortcomings in this approach to the problem of fuelling and storing ships while maintaining them on station at sea.

In the beginning, however, it was legal problems with registration that were to most concern those involved in the operation of the embryo RFA fleet.

When the Admiralty tried to register an RFA as a merchant vessel under the Merchant Shipping Act 1894 for the first time, in this case the hospital ship *Maine*, it was found that it application could not be upheld.

Under the 1894 Act, 64/64ths of a ship had to be owned by a British subject or subjects for that vessel to be registered as British. Neither the Sovereign, whose property the vessel was deemed to be nor the Admiralty, in whose name it was to be registered, were eligible under the Act, so RFAs were registered as the property of The Lords Commissioners of the Admiralty with the managing owner listed as the Secretary of the Board of Admiralty.

Despite the difficulties encountered at the time, the Admiralty had never been under any legal obligation to register its government-owned auxiliaries under the 1894 Act. Failure to register would, however, have made status questionable and the resulting lack of any formal documentation could have made entry into foreign ports difficult.

In practical terms, registration as a British merchant ship also had distinct advantages. It meant an RFA could enter a port, collect a load of fuel or dry stores and sail again to replenish a warship, without any special documentation or time limits. This proved particularly useful in wartime when RFAs and MFAs or ships taken up from trade (STUFT, as later designated) could use foreign ports, without interference from local authorities, which would not have been the case if they had been unregistered merchant vessels or warships. The Admiralty also circumvented the problem of RFAs entering neutral ports to accept cargoes of fuel oil during the First

World War by transferring the management of some of its fleet to commercial companies. This legal device allowed RFAs to sail under the Red Ensign as oiler transports and so avoid potential complications with neutrality laws.

Admiralty-owned auxiliaries were designated RFAs from 1905 and were so described in Admiralty Transport Department papers from 1906, although it was 1913 before the term made its appearance in the *Navy List*. The Admiralty Blue Ensign was approved by the Admiralty and Board of Trade in 1908 for Admiralty-*owned* and operated RFAs (see *The Royal Fleet Auxiliary: A Century of Service*, Appendix C, for an interesting discussion of the history of the RFA's Blue Ensign).

However, this was not the end of complications with the registration issue. Registration as a British merchant ship brings with it a number of requirements, governing surveys, life saving equipment, and particularly operation, which appear to have made for difficulties when applied to the Admiralty's RFAs.

Fortunately, there was a loophole. Under Section 80 of the then recently introduced Merchant Shipping Act 1906, the Crown could make an order in council to introduce new regulations regarding the way in which government-owned ships could be operated while still registered as British merchant ships under the Merchant Shipping Acts.

After extremely complex and lengthy discussions by lawyers in both the Admiralty and Whitehall, such an administrative device was finally put in place in 1911, when Admiralty Order in Council for the Regulation of Naval Service No. 121 was approved. This now allowed the registration, as British merchant ships, under the Merchant Shipping Acts, of 'Government vessels in the service of the Admiralty not forming part of the Royal Navy'.

This is how RFAs were subsequently classified and operated, until their post-Falklands 'change of status', in 1989, to 'Government ships on non-commercial service'.

This did not, as has been sometimes maintained in the past, establish the RFA as a service. It simply clarified the nature of the *ships* then owned by the Admiralty and the ways in which these could be operated. Registration established the legal position within the framework of the Merchant Shipping Act. It implied nothing about the status of the crews.

These vessels could now carry out their logistics role as RFAs supplying the Royal Navy, while being managed, regulated and manned as British merchant ships, with ordinary, *non-specialist* Merchant Navy crews. They were at the same time made exempt from certain requirements specified in Board of Trade regulations. Despite these exemptions, RFAs, then and now, invariably conformed in full to all of the Board of Trade regulations that applied to the class of vessel to which they belonged. Well, usually.

In wartime, RFAs tend to operate in ways that suit the navy rather than the Board of Trade. During the Falklands war, for example, *Tidespring* went south with a swimming pool full of AS12 missiles, while *Sir Percivale* left her home port of Marchwood, so stuffed with men and equipment that, as her captain put it, 'The ship finally sailed from the jetty [at Marchwood] on Monday the 5th of April at 1820Z, 14 inches over-loaded and in possession of a quite lethal deck cargo.'

Despite this 'clarification' of their position, by the end of the First World War, the RFA fleet had become such a miscellaneous collection of vessels, some purpose built, some converted warships, with yet others on long-term charter from foreign owners or managed by commercial shipping companies, that there was still a lot of confusion about correct designations – confusion which, according to some sources, appears to have lasted until the Second World War. And, given the complications in which it found itself, why *did* the Admiralty change the status quo, when the system it had seemed to work perfectly well, despite the constraints placed on non-registered merchant ships?

During the period between 1905 and August 1914, the Admiralty bought or chartered several vessels that were registered and operated as RFAs, some of which subsequently underwent specialist conversion, in order to better fulfil their new role.

Petroleum joined this early flotilla at its inception, becoming the RFA's first tanker when she was purchased by the Admiralty in March 1905.

Petroleum was built by Swan, Hunter & Wigham Richardson Ltd, Wallsend, Newcastle, in 1903, for the Texas oil trade. Her owner was based in Liverpool and her builders had also retained a one-third interest in the vessel. After completion, however, she was not used until the Admiralty began to make enquiries about her, early in 1905.

Built with six holds for the carriage of petrol – the tankerman's nightmare – *Petroleum* had a total oil cargo capacity of about 6200 tons, with bunker capacity for both fuel oil and coal of 668 and 632 tons respectively. Her cargo holds extended right up to the hull plating, so despite being equipped with the requisite stiffening to bring her up to Lloyd's Register requirements, when carrying petrol, even a moderate collision could have resulted in a disastrous inferno.

Accommodation, at the time of purchase, was for a total crew of thirty-seven, of which twenty-five were firemen, seamen and boys. Cabins for the captain and mates were under the bridge amidships, with the engineer officers on the main deck aft. Crew quarters, situated in the fore part of the ship, were communal and equipped with ordinary mercantile bunks.

Her power plant was interesting, even a little unusual. Supplied by the North Eastern Marine Engineering Co Ltd, her main engine was a conventional triple-expansion steam engine, supplied by three main boilers and one auxiliary. According to the 1905 Admiralty survey, however, these boilers were arranged for burning *either* coal or oil fuel, although they were *not* of the more familiar 'dual fuel' type, oil fuel being burnt by a separate Rusden & Ecles steam spraying system. Again according to the survey, these boilers were intended to burn coal on the outward journey to Texas and oil fuel on the homeward, it being recorded that five days were required to make the necessary changes to the boiler and bunker fittings.

Fuel oil at that time was considerably cheaper than coal in the Texas refinery ports so, presumably, and this can only be conjecture, the owners felt that sufficient savings would be made using the cheaper fuel in each locality to justify the slow turn around time. Even in those days, however, shipyard costs must surely have prohibited the work being carried out there, so presumably, the fittings were designed so that the engine room personnel could make any changes necessary.

One further point of significance concerning her power plant is that she was relatively fast, with a top speed of 13 knots.

The Admiralty surveyor who inspected her seems to have been satisfied with her material condition, despite a lot of rust on both the hull and in her boilers. He also stated that the price her owners wanted was fair, although the Admiralty had a list of modifications to be made by the builders before delivery.

These specified several changes specifically to do with her replenishment role, including the supply of 600 feet (about 200 metres) of Admiralty pattern metallic hose, to be completed before purchase. One change was particularly interesting in this context, the addition of a 5-inch connecting pipe, with valve, in the pump room to enable the pumps to draw from the pipelines on deck *after* breaking connection with the receiving vessels. Of course, nowadays it is done the other way round, in that the RFA blows compressed air through the hose, thus emptying the residual oil into the warship's tanks. Given the detailed nature of this and her other modifications, it is clear that, even at this early stage, the way in which the Royal Navy's future replenishment operations would be organised was being very critically examined and appraised by *someone*.

However, nowhere in the list of modifications from the Admiralty is there any mention of changes to the type of fuel used to run the engines. Presumably, she entered service as a coal burner, retaining her facility for a quick change to oil. Incidentally, the navy certainly must have intended that she become an oil burner at some point because, last on the list of modifications, is the stipulation that the builders supply '... 5 spare burners (Rusden & Ecles) for the oil fuel installation'.

Later, in 1905, presumably after entering Admiralty service, she was involved in a collision. It could not have been anything to do with her oiling at sea experiments, because these did not start until the beginning of the following year.

The damage seems to have been significant, however, because she was returned to her builders for repair, with Lloyd's Register insisting that '... repairs to the vessel due to damage she sustained through collision be made under our survey and to our satisfaction'.

In August 1905, the Admiralty wrote to the classing committee of Lloyd's Register, stating that '... the vessel had been purchased by them and would be solely employed upon Naval Service in future, and requesting that her name be removed from the Register book'.

Lloyd's Register agreed to the removal, although this seems to raise a number of significant questions regarding her future operation. For example:

(1) Why was she removed from the register book?
(2) Was it because she was intended for oiling-at-sea experiments for which she could not be insured?
(3) If these experiments were so dangerous, how was she crewed?
(4) Did the Admiralty at least consider that removal from the register might be a way forward for all RFAs involved in replenishment duties? Following on from this, was someone, even at this early stage, considering a two-tier service, with a class of specialist fast fleet tankers in prospect (perhaps either the latterly cancelled *Olympia* class or the 5000-ton Fast Leaf class?).

This is, of course, what eventually happened in the early 1960s when the navy began to designate RFAs as either 'front line support' or 'freighting support'.
(see chapter four : " The Fourth Force": volume II).

Petroleum certainly had a Royal Navy master during this period, a Captain J R Williams RN, because the letter about the July 1905 survey is addressed to him, although the crew was definitely Merchant Navy, as evidenced by another letter in the

National Archive, addressed to the Admiral Superintendent, Gibraltar, appointing a Merchant Navy officer, Mr Norton Aplin, as third officer, replacing another Merchant Navy officer who was transferred to RFA *Maine*.

This certainly seems to suggest that the crew, at least, was Merchant Navy, from the beginning of Petroleum's service. So, how was that managed after the vessel was de-registered and, presumably, without the crew having the reassurance of a Lloyd's Register survey or inspection? This sort of trouble also occurred during the suggested de-registration of vessels after the Falklands War (see Chapter 10, *The Fourth Force*, by the same author) and there was a very significant amount of discussion between unions and management before a solution was reached. Why did the crew allow it so quietly in 1905?

Whatever their original reasons, by 1907 (after her replenishment trials), the Admiralty was happy for her to be re-entered into the Lloyd's Register book. It did, however, make it clear at the time that it would not be availing itself of any of Lloyd's Register's facilities in respect of survey and classification.

Further additions to the RFA fleet during 1905–14 included the hospital ship *Maine*, which was the very first vessel to be registered as an RFA and the first RFA-manned hospital ship of that name. *Kharki* also joined the fleet during this period, being purchased by the Admiralty in 1901. Built originally as a collier, she was subsequently converted to transport lubricating oil as well as being equipped for RAS. Two more RAS-capable RFAs, *Burma* and *Trefoil*, of the 2000-ton *Burma* class, joined the RFA fleet in 1911 and 1913 respectively.

On a smaller scale, the first 1000-ton *Attendant* class harbour tankers came into service during this period, as well as another collier, RFA *Mercedes*, which was to be used exhaustively between 1905 and 1912, in a vain attempt to develop a reliable technique for coaling-at-sea.

Maine was launched in 1887, as *Swansea*, by William Gray & Co, West Hartlepool. Originally intended as a cargo, passenger and cattle ship, by 1888 her name had been changed to *Maine*.

With the outbreak of the Boer war in 1899, a committee of American ladies in London, under the presidency of Lady Randolph Churchill (mother of Winston), organised social events to raise money for the *Maine* to be converted into a hospital ship. In November 1899, a fund-raising *café chantant* benefit, with tickets at one guinea each, was held at Claridges Hotel, London with the Prince of Wales and other royalty in attendance. In New York, other fund-raising events were under way, including a 'society tea' which was organised by Mrs Hugo de Bathe (better known as Lillie Langtry).

Maine was eventually converted at a cost of about $150,000, with much of this contributed by the American Ladies' Hospital Ship Society. Later, the *New York Times* printed the names of those who had contributed. In addition, donations were further acknowledged by the award of a medal. Usually in white metal, members of the American Ladies' committee received their medals in silver.

During the South African War, *Maine* served as a base hospital at Durban and, in addition, brought the injured from South Africa to the Royal Victoria Military Hospital at Netley, on Southampton Water. She did, however, remain an American vessel during this period, with US nurses encouraged to sign on. *Maine* also served on the China Station during the Boxer rebellion (1900–01).

Her Royal Navy career began on 25 June 1901, when the owner of *Maine*, Mr Bernard N Baker, chairman and owner of the Atlantic Transport Company, wrote to the First Lord of the Admiralty, the Earl of Selborne, offering his company's hospital ship *Maine* to the British government as a free gift. The offer was accepted with alacrity and reported both to the House of Lords on 1 July 1901 and at length in *The Times* on the following day. Having completed the necessary formalities, the US hospital ship *Maine* became the His Majesty's Hospital Ship (HMHS) *Maine*, and finally RFA *Maine* in 1905.

Maine was lost on 17 June 1914, when she ran aground in thick fog on the Isle of Mull, west Scotland, during a Fleet exercise. Although her patients and crew were safely rescued after taking to the ship's boats, *Maine* was abandoned.

The Admiralty announced on 21 June 1914 that, due to the extensive damage and the age of the vessel, she was declared a total loss. To preserve the memories of the ship, the new hospital ship *Mediator*, then currently fitting out, was to be completed as soon as possible and would be renamed *Maine*.

Another interesting vessel joined the Navy in 1912, with the purchase of the cargo steamer *Knight Companion*, which had been completed two years earlier. As the repair ship *Reliance*, she joined two other vessels, *Cyclops* and *Assistance*, both of which had been fitted out as floating workshop and distilling ships before introduction to the Royal Navy's fleet some years before – *Cyclops* in 1905 and *Assistance* in 1901.

Reliance was scheduled for major modifications that would make her a considerable improvement on the two earlier vessels. Her equipment was extensive and the Admiralty memo that detailed the navy's requirements runs to four closely typed pages.

A foundry, pattern shop, carpenter's and electrical workshops, light and heavy machine shops, coppersmith's shop, boiler shop, even a sail loft with an electrically operated sewing machine were included in the specification, together with a circular saw, which was required to have 50 feet (about 18 metres) clearance at each end. With this level of equipment, *Reliance* seemed well equipped to repair anything that might come her way.

Her crew numbers reflected this commitment to repair at sea. Combined deck, engine room and pursers departments numbered sixty officers and men, while the engineering/repair shop complement was 117 officers and artisans, this last presumably being skilled men who had served an apprenticeship.

From 1914 to the end of the First World War, she served in the Mediterranean, and was sold in 1919 to the Italian firm of Parodi & Accame, of Genoa, and renamed *Emanuele Accame*.

Service aboard

Royal Fleet Auxiliary crews were not exclusively Merchant Navy personnel during this pre-war period. Some of the officers, such as *Petroleum*'s master, had RN, RNR, RNVR and Merchant Marine Reserve (MMR) appointments.

Initially, crews were employed on 'yard craft' agreements. *Petroleum*'s crew had been sent to Gibraltar in 1905 while thus employed. Later, *Maine* and *Petroleum* both *appear* to have become understandable exceptions to this, at least from 1906, although the form of their agreements has not, as yet, come to light.

Difficulties certainly arose with those RFA crews that were on yard craft agreements, apparently because such agreements did not grant masters the disciplinary powers some of them deemed necessary. This is hardly surprising because a yard craft agreement means that the men aboard such a vessel are effectively dockyard employees. They usually even slept ashore, which perhaps explains a certain lack of discipline! The master of RFA *Kharki* actually wrote to the Admiralty in 1911, suggesting that his vessel be placed on some other form of agreement, which allowed him to fine the crew for breaches of discipline, because they were becoming uncontrollable!

Employment after the 1911 Order in Council (No. 121) seems to have usually been under normal Merchant Navy terms, with officers, petty officers and ratings signing Board of Trade articles of agreement of varying types (*eg* home trade, foreign going, etc.) for the duration of the voyage with the master, who himself was invariably under contract to the Admiralty.

Perhaps surprisingly, it was the Director of Transports, head of the Admiralty's Transport Department, who was responsible for appointing RFA masters and officers in this period, from 1907. This official also had responsibility for sailing orders, provision of crews and action with the Board of Trade and Lloyd's Register on matters such as classification. Clearly, management during this period was not simple, because the Director of Stores, head of the Department of Naval Stores, still appears to have been responsible for the management, finance and running of freighting tankers, fleet attendant tankers, colliers, repair ships, water tankers and salvage vessels, not to mention a few other miscellaneous craft.

Typical monthly rates of pay aboard *Petroleum* for a voyage beginning 7 February 1911 were: chief officer £12, third officer £7, boatswain £5 17s, carpenter £6 10s, able seaman £4 7s and ordinary seaman £2 10s.

The purser received £14, although why his wages should be more than the chief officer's is anyone's guess.

Engine-room personnel were better paid than the deck department, with the chief engineer receiving £21 a month, third engineer £11 (just £1 less than the chief officer), while a leading stoker took home £5 (13 shillings more than an AB).

The catering team were the worst paid. *Petroleum*'s first steward received £7, while the cook's wage was only £6 10s – poor pay for someone many consider the most important person aboard, not excluding the master himself. Anyone sailing any distance with a cook who does not know his business will very quickly understand why!

Crews were also much smaller than those found in modern RFAs, despite the fact that *Burma*, at least, was still involved in oiling at sea trials. *Petroleum*'s crew for that February voyage was just eight officers and thirty ratings including stokers, stewards and the cook, while *Burma* had a crew of just thirty upon completion, with only one second officer and one third officer. That is less than half of the crew of a modern RFA fast fleet tanker, such as *Wave Knight*, which has a complement of seventy-eight, including specialist navigating officers as well as weapons officers and ratings.

Crew list: RFA *Burma* upon completion 1911			
Captain	1	Chief engineer	1
Chief officer	1	Second engineer	1
Second officer	1	Third engineer	1
Third officer	1	Fourth engineer	1
Boatswain	1	Pumpman	1
W/T operator (PO)	1	Donkeyman	1
Seamen	8	Greaser	1
Stewards	2	Firemen	6
Cook	1		—
	—		13
	17		

Crew (total) 30 officers and ratings

Final transition: Coal to oil

Change within the Royal Navy is, plainly enough, invariably reflected by associated changes in the Royal Fleet Auxiliary and this has never been more marked than during the navy's move from coal to oil burning.

In many ways, this transition may have been more significant than the earlier transition from sail to steam, especially since it was almost immediately followed by Britain's headlong plunge into the First World War. Certainly, it was undoubtedly more abrupt, thanks mostly to a pocket dynamo by the name of Sir John Fisher, then First Sea Lord and known to every man on the lower deck as 'Jackie'.

His major contribution to the pre-First World War navy is usually considered to be HMS *Dreadnought*, but he also worked at a far more subtle level than his often acknowledged role in the introduction of both innovative ships and advancement of competent, younger men over the heads of more senior officers.

Caustic and opinionated, he was, perhaps surprisingly, quite ready to listen to, and often act upon, the views and advice of the capable, younger officers who, in forming his staff, had also earned his hard-won respect. Fisher began to demonstrate this modern, forward thinking approach of his, first, while in command of the Mediterranean Fleet then later, and perhaps most convincingly, soon after his appointment as First Sea Lord.

At that time, naval strategic thinking was based almost wholly around the blockade concept. Keep the enemy starved of supplies and then defeat him, if he ventured out of port, in a pitched battle using superior weight of ships and firepower.

Fisher saw immediately that the introduction of the torpedo and small, fast vessels, especially submarines, equipped to use such a weapon, changed all this. Battleships venturing near an enemy coast could immediately be attacked by these fast, heavily armed craft and put out of action, probably without inflicting any losses on the enemy. To counter such a threat, he introduced destroyers, originally called torpedo boat destroyers, to the navy and advocated their use as protection for the capital ships against the torpedo boat and submarine threat. Even the enormously powerful big gun battleships would be of little use, he claimed, almost before *Dreadnought*, first in that class and his own brainchild, had rolled off the slips. So clear was Fisher about the future of naval warfare in this respect, that, upon seeing a submarine at one Spithead Review, he said '... there goes the battleship of the future'.

His ideas about the nature of future naval engagements were also revolutionary. Although armour and large-calibre guns were desirable, to Fisher, speed was the most important consideration in battleship design, both for strategic combination and tactical deployment:

Speed was to be '... the first desideratum. It is the *weather gage* of the old days. You then fight when it suits you best. Some people don't want it for battleships but *they are wrong*, because both strategy and tactics demand speed'.

Having the fastest ships, as he often reiterated, allowed a commander to decide when, where and how to fight, which then also inevitably meant he could dictate the course of the battle. And that battle, according to Fisher, should be fought on Britain's frontiers, those frontiers being '... the coasts of the enemy and we ought to be there five minutes after war is declared!'

Tirpitz, who became Secretary of State for the Imperial Naval Office and so effectively Commander-in-Chief of the German Navy in 1897, did not share Fisher's advanced thinking. To Tirpitz, only one thing mattered. For Germany, a fleet larger in terms of capital ships than the Royal Navy. The British could then, somehow, be forced to attack the German battleships in their own waters and be easily annihilated. After all, the major fleet action was the Royal Navy's sole tactic, enshrined in policy since the days of Nelson?

With this end in view, Tirpitz persuaded Germany's Kaiser, the superficial and vacillating Wilhelm II, to introduce a series of naval laws, which set the broad limits for future naval expenditure and allowed Tirpitz to begin building battleships at a rate of three or four a year.

Upon completion of his Grand Fleet, Tirpitz intended initially to destroy the Royal Navy, before going on to dominate the world's oceans, thus allowing Germany to achieve political and economic dominance of Europe and, eventually, the world.

It must have seemed simple to the men in Berlin, but unfortunately for them, Admiralty staff had correctly interpreted their intentions almost as soon as their building programme had begun.

In 1902, after the visit of an Admiralty official to the naval shipyards of Kiel and Wilhelmshaven, where the new German battleships were building, an Admiralty confidential memorandum made its appearance. It was unequivocal in its conclusions about the formidable strength of the German Navy and it finished by stating 'Against England alone is such a weapon as the modern German Navy necessary; against England, unless all available evidence and all probability combine to mislead, that weapon is being prepared.'

The British, however, were not being told anything of which that their press and media had not made them well aware already. Germany was widely seen as both an economic and military threat. So much so that, by 1903, the German ambassador in London was forced to concede 'As long as I have known England, I have never observed here such bitterness towards another nation as at present exists towards us ...'

From these beginnings sprang what opposing politicians and, later, historians called 'the Great Naval Race' – an escalated capital ship building programme on the part of both Germany and Great Britain, to determine who would dominate the world's oceans.

By the eve of the First World War, Germany had failed, falling far short of her goal.

Against Jellicoe's Grand Fleet of twenty-one Dreadnoughts, eight powerful pre-Dreadnoughts and four battlecruisers, the Germans had only thirteen Dreadnoughts, eight pre-Dreadnoughts and three battlecruisers. Moreover, the British were armed with 13.5-inch and 12-inch guns against which the German 12-inch and 11-inch seemed puny. There was also another factor. The Royal Navy had a tradition of winning, whatever the odds, and her ships were manned by a very hard core of regulars steeped in that tradition, unlike the young conscripts who were serving out their three years in the German fleet.

Consequently, the German navy felt itself inferior in ships, men and morale and her fleet was to remain bottled up in Wilhelmshaven, until it ventured out briefly in 1916, under the command of Admiral Scheer. Jellicoe and Beatty caught the German Grand Fleet off Jutland and Scheer was forced to turn for home immediately, sacrificing his destroyers and battlecruisers to cover the retreat of the giant battleships. Only nightfall saved him and the Grand Fleet remained in port until the war's end, eventually being scuttled in Scapa Flow by their embittered crews, in 1919.

The German Navy had been beaten psychologically before it had a chance to perform and Fisher was instrumental in turning the Royal Navy into the lethal instrument Jellicoe and Beatty were to use later to such good effect in bringing this about.

How far Fisher had earlier been concerned in the development of the RFA's fuel replenishment and logistics role is impossible to say but there are certain indications which suggest that his involvement must have been pivotal.

Sir John Fisher was sworn in as First Sea Lord on Trafalgar Day, 21 October 1904, following breakfast with King Edward VII, at Buckingham Palace. His tenure was to last six years, until 1910, when he was forced from office, although his innovative policies were carried on to some extent by his successor, Sir Arthur Wilson, the gunnery expert.

Purchase of *Petroleum*, the first Admiralty oil tanker, was confirmed early in March 1905. Significantly, the letter confirming purchase also required *Petroleum* to be modified for what can only have been an experimental replenishment role, indicating that she was bought specifically for that purpose. Circular letter No. 9 T 3487 of August 1905, specifically introduced the term 'Royal Fleet Auxiliary' and, perhaps more importantly, distinguished between them and Mercantile Fleet Auxiliaries (MFAs). Fisher's involvement in these changes can only be speculative but certainly the timing of the introductions at least seems persuasive.

As First Sea Lord, Sir John must have been involved in all the initial stages of the decision to buy *Petroleum* and of her crewing arrangements, although the details of the transaction would have been left to Admiralty staff. He was, after all, the main driving force behind the introduction of turbine power and oil firing in warships and given his dynamic thinking in other departments, it is inconceivable that he had not given thought to supplying the fuel for his oil-fired battleships. It remains to be seen what advantage might have been accrued by distinguishing between RFAs and MFAs, but it is conceivable that this was done originally as a first step to introducing naval manning to the Admiralty owned auxiliaries and their use for front-line support.

Fisher's ideas on naval strategy also support this view of the oil supply question. It would, after all, be of little use arriving on the enemy's coast, as he put it, 'five minutes after war is declared' only to be subsequently obliged to steam away the moment fuel got low. He must have had some ideas about fuelling ships on station. And that probably explains the sudden rash of fuelling-at-sea trials and the modification for replenishment of the Admiralty-designed *Burma* class, which began construction in 1908.

Until the introduction of fuel oil, coaling its ships was probably the biggest headache the pre-war, peacetime navy faced. Since ships were now forced to put into designated shore bases to take on a load of coal, their radius of operations was significantly reduced, which meant more ships had to be deployed to make up the shortfall, using more coal, leading to even more ships being needed to transport the extra fuel. Anything up to a quarter of the fleet might be engaged in refuelling at any one time and this was obviously dead against all Fisher's ideas about speed and deployment. Plainly, such a situation could not be allowed to continue.

Coaling at sea was an obvious solution to the problem but that was not quite as simple as it may at first appear. Coaling a battleship, even in the predictable confines of a good anchorage, was a dirty, exhausting job. It involved most of the vessel's crew for five or six hours, although cooks, stewards and sick berth attendants were usually excused this duty. And, once the fuel was aboard, the crew then had to get the ship clean again.

Coaling began with the Admiralty collier being brought alongside the warship. Some of the warship's crew were transferred to the hold of the collier, where they began to fill the 2-cwt (about 100-kg) bags, one man shovelling the coal while his partner held the neck of the bag open. As they were filled, bags were initially stacked along the side of the hold before being attached to a hemp coaling strop, usually ten to twelve to a strop. These strops were then attached to a wire rope, referred to as a 'whip', which, in turn, was attached to a derrick, either the collier's or the warship's, depending upon which was most convenient. The bags were then swung up on to the deck of the warship, and were placed in wheel barrows or trolleys and transported to the chute, which led into the vessel's bunkers. Here they were emptied down the chute into the bunker and the empty bags returned to the collier for refilling. Rates of about 250 tons an hour were quite a normal expectation, but since an average warship, for example HMS *King Edward VII*, needed about 1200 tons at any one refuelling, the task could take anything up to six hours. Clearly, trying to carry out a similar operation between a collier and warship while at sea was going to be fraught with problems.

The first trial of a technique for coaling at sea was attempted by the Royal Navy, off the Azores, in 1890. Colliers were lashed alongside each of the ten warships involved in the trial, with thick fenders between the vessels to prevent damage. Coal was then transferred by derrick in the normal way, the warships taking on sufficient to return to Torbay, some 1800 miles, or six days steaming, away.

With the loss of their cargo, however, the colliers became lighter and with the consequent increase in pitching, several sustained minor damage. Sea conditions during the trial were very good, and it was clear to all involved, that, had the weather worsened even marginally, coaling would have been impossible.

The US Navy also undertook some coaling-at-sea trials, its first, between the collier USS *Marcellus* and the battleship USS *Massachusetts*, in 1899. The battleship towed the collier 100–150 metres astern at a speed of about six knots and transfer was made by means of a 'tramway' between the vessels. Later, in 1914, the US Navy tried another method using a device called a 'Spencer Miller' cableway. This trial was conducted between USS *South Carolina* and the collier USS *Cyclops*.

In this procedure, the collier was taken in tow and a cable secured between the two ships, and which supported a carriage containing two 800-lb bags of coal. This carriage was hauled from the collier to the warship, where the bags were subsequently landed on a platform in front of the forward 12-inch gun turret, before being carried to the bunkers.

Admittedly, the cableway worked reasonably well, the Americans finding it safe to use even in a moderate gale. Unfortunately, transfer rates were only about 20–25 tons per hour and since the warship was steaming during the entire operation and so consuming 3–4 tons of fuel an hour, effective transfer rates were only 16–20 tons an hour. This meant a battleship with a full load of about 1200 tons would need to be coaling continuously for 60 hours before she was refuelled, while steaming the whole time at 5 knots, making her a perfect target for any submarine or torpedo boat that came along. And if the vessel steamed continuously at only 10 knots, the whole procedure would have to be repeated 14 days later.

Admiralty trials of similar equipment were initially conducted, in 1906, on a Commander Metcalfe's apparatus, using the chartered collier *Torridge* and ships from the Channel Fleet. These trials proved inconclusive. Sir John Forsey concluded in a memo at present in the National Archive, that the Metcalfe apparatus should be rejected as more expensive and less efficient than its competitors.

After this initial setback, the navy began its final set of coaling at sea trials with RFA *Mercedes* in 1910, over eight years after the ship had been purchased by the Admiralty.

Originally, she had been designed for the Admiralty by Christie & Co. of Cardiff as a collier, carrying coal between New Zealand and China, to supply the requirements of the China Fleet. She was claimed to be the best collier of her day and, with her eight derricks and four Temperley Transporters, it was felt she should routinely be able to supply at least 300 tons an hour. She was also fitted with arc lights for coaling at night. It has been suggested that Admiralty trials were undertaken of a US-built Spencer Miller apparatus modified by the Temperly Transporter Company. No corroborative evidence has come to light in Admiralty records of such a trial, however, and, unfortunately, neither has any further information with regard to the *Mercedes* experimental coaling gear.

Unfortunately, her equipment (whatever it was) appears to have proved unsatisfactory, and after final, inconclusive trials had been conducted between *Mercedes* and HMS *Dominion*, sometime in 1912, the whole idea of coaling at sea was abandoned as unworkable. After the failure of these final 1912 replenishment trials, *Mercedes* was converted to carry lubricating oil in the tanks originally designed for sea water ballast, until she was sold in 1920.

Fortunately for the Royal Navy, the failure of the *Mercedes* replenishment trials become irrelevant, because the 1912 Royal Commission on Fuel and Engines, chaired by Admiral of the Fleet Lord Fisher, decided that 'Oil-firing over coal produces higher speed, increased radius of action, speedier and easier refuelling, reduction in stokehold personnel by 50% and quicker initial production of steam, saving in cost of construction.'

In the light of these recommendations, oil was gradually to replace coal as the Royal Navy's fuel of choice, although even as late as 1913, the five *Revenge* class battleships and about a dozen destroyers had been designed to use both fuels.

These dual-fuel ships were all equipped with steam reciprocating engines, arrangements having been made so that coal could be burnt in the normal way, with fuel oil sprayed into the furnace when this was required, in a way somewhat similar to a modern oil-burning steam ship.

The change to fuel oil had certainly been anticipated somewhere else, however, because, of course, from as early as January 1906, the navy had been conducting oiling-at-sea experiments with *Petroleum*. Although her replenishment-at-sea rig suffered from several disadvantages, most notably its tendency to break due to the high pumping pressures required, it was clear to many that an 'afloat replenishment' capability was what the navy needed. This anticipated change was hardly surprising, since Sir John Fisher had been known from as early as 1895 as 'The Oil Maniac', because of his championing of oil as the future fuel of the navy.

With the prospect of the navy's increasing dependence on fuel oil becoming a stark reality, especially after the appearance of the *Queen Elizabeth* class, two decisions were quickly taken, although when and by whom is not quite clear.

First, since the Navy needed a reliable source for its fuel oil, the Anglo-Persian Oil Co Ltd (later BP), was founded, with the first Lord of the Admiralty, Winston Churchill, heavily, although surreptitiously, involved in its formation.

The company commenced operations in Iran (then Persia), with the British government Anglo-Persian's major shareholder.

Large-scale production of oil products commenced in 1913, with Anglo-Persian's main customers the Royal Navy, HM Government, UK industry and the British Empire. From 1913 to the early 1950s, when the Persian oil crisis saw BP's Iranian assets nationalised, the Royal Navy was paying the princely sum of one pound *a ton* for crude oil.

Although refining and storage costs added substantially to this initial figure, the navy still had access to a supply of refined furnace fuel oil at significantly less than the world market price. This did not, however, stop them charging NATO and the US Navy the full international market price for fuel whenever ships from one of those navies refuelled at a British base.

Having established a reliable source of supply for crude oil, the Admiralty's next major headache was to get the refined fuel to where ships could use it. Refineries and storage facilities were accordingly built both in the UK and overseas and at about the same time the navy began to purchase and build its own fleet of tankers for transporting fuel from this diverse network of storage areas to its major bases. Small harbour tankers, such as the *Attendant* class vessels or lighters would subsequently refuel Royal Navy ships in harbour from these depots, where alongside berths were either not in use or unavailable to larger vessels.

Initially, it was intended that all RFA vessels would be managed by the Admiralty's Director of Stores, but organising the Directorate and the new RFA service that went with it took so long that many vessels were placed under commercial management for a considerable period. Nothing about RFA management was straightforward during this pre-war decade, however, and some vessels, particularly colliers, were the responsibility of the Director of Transports, with several other departments also sharing responsibility for Admiralty vessels.

By 1908, clearly influenced by what they must have seen as future needs, Admiralty planners had introduced the first RFA tanker construction programme, ostensibly after a recommendation by the then Director of Stores, Sir John Forsey. It is not generally known that Forsey's reasons for introducing *Burma* had nothing to do with an innovative approach to replenishment at sea. Rather, the reasons were economic.

He had originally planned to have Chatham Dockyard build four 500-ton barges to use for transporting oil to ports around the coast. By 1908, the position had changed sufficiently for him to decide to abandon that idea in favour of one ship of between 1000 and 2000 tons. What he wanted was a simple oil tanker. It was not until the Admiralty got their hands on the plans that the idea of making her RAS-capable occurred to anyone. And, all of this was happening, once again, while Sir John Fisher was First Sea Lord. In fact, all of the purpose-designed, RAS-capable classes appeared, at least in design terms, during his tenure at the Admiralty.

Burma, launched in 1911, was the initial result of the 1908 programme. Of only 2000-tons capacity, fairly small by present day standards (*Wave Knight*, for example, can carry about 5000 tonnes of DIESO, 3000 tonnes of aviation fuel, and water besides), she was equipped for refuelling at sea by the stirrup method and fuelling alongside (also known as 'rafting up'), that is, replenishing vessels in harbour or a sheltered anchorage. Significantly perhaps, given the difficulties inherent in the stirrup method, the RAS capacity of this class does not seem to have been extensively used.

Oiling-at-sea experiments, however, using bronze hoses, had begun sometime before both *Petroleum*'s and *Burma*'s appearance, in 1905, with the 1893-built tanker *Henri Rieth*. The only reference found, so far, to these trials is a mention in the report by C-in-C Atlantic Fleet, dated 31 March 1906, in which he refers to '300 ft of metallic hose which was originally purchased for trial in the SS "Henri Rieth" in connection with the supply of oil fuel to HM Ships when underway at sea ...'

No mention is made as to whether these trials were carried out and the first detailed report of the results of oiling-at-sea trials are those between *Petroleum* and the battleship HMS *Victorious*, submitted by the C-in-C Atlantic Fleet in the same report, dated 31 March 1906.

Petroleum was not only the Admiralty's first tanker, but also she appears to have been the first RFA with purpose-built modifications to enable her to oil a Royal Navy ship at sea.

She began trials of this technique late in March 1906, with a practice pump-over to HMS *Victorious*. Curiously, these trials were carried out with water not fuel oil, because *Victorious* was a coal burner. Presumably, the Admiralty used her to assess the sort of problems that might develop when oiling large warships. Destroyers were, for the most part, oil fuelled by this time and criteria and equipment requirements for oiling destroyers at sea were also claimed to have been agreed in a coaling-at-sea conference at the Admiralty on 5 December 1906.

A report on the *Petroleum/Victorious* trials records that these were carried out while *Petroleum* was being towed, using 6.5-inch (16.5-cm) wire hawser, with the vessels 90 fathoms (180 metres) apart.

Twenty-seven lengths of hose, each 20 feet long, were required to span the distance between the ships. These were coupled up beforehand, attached or 'seized' on to a 3-inch wire jackstay, with a 5.5-inch wire used as a travelling jackstay for the hose. Rope 'pendants' attached to roller shackles were used to secure the hose to this 5.5-inch wire and the hose was hauled along the wire by a separate 3.5-inch wire from the towing ship, the roller shackles being secured to the 5.5-inch wire as the hose was paid out. Clearly, this was an early form of the justly maligned 'stirrup' method and using it, the two ships managed to transfer 115 tons of *water* per hour.

The report concludes that this arrangement for oiling-at-sea should be satisfactory, at speeds of up to 12 knots, in fine weather at sea. This conclusion was reached despite the fact that passing the hoses, on their stirrup rig, between *Victorious* and *Petroleum* took 5 hours, although this did include a 1-hour break for meals, with a further 3 hours to recover the hoses back to the RFA! (By way of comparison, the crew of a modern RFA, such as *Wave Knight*, would usually expect to take about 15 minutes to get ready for a pump-over, and about 2–5 minutes after that to connect to the receiving ship. Similar time is needed to disconnect.)

Both steel and bronze hoses were used during these trials aboard *Petroleum* (although, her master actually refers to the latter as 'copper') and it was finally concluded that 'bronze' was best, although it appeared to be more affected by fuel oil than the steel type.

Despite the disadvantages of her equipment and stability problems, RFA *Burma* was also involved in some unsuccessful oiling-at-sea trials in 1911. Arrangements were similar to those of *Petroleum*, except that it had been decided that, when oiling a destroyer, *Burma* should do the towing, with positions reversed when refuelling a larger vessel, such as a battleship.

Trials began well. Test pumping carried out while she was tied up in Greenock dockyard showed she could pump a respectable 350 tons of water/hour through her pair of 5-inch (13-cm) hoses, which were 160 metres long. That was, of course, unless the high pumping pressure did not burst them, which it frequently did. And when she went to sea, as might be expected, the stirrup method proved, at best, clumsy and at worst, extremely dangerous, especially with any sort of sea running.

This was hardly surprising, given this description, and implied criticism, of the procedure used for securing the stirrups when hauling the hose outboard:

> It was found that when the hose was being hauled outboard, hardly time enough was allowed to detach the stirrup from the rail, pass it under the bracket, hook it on the towing wire and set the spring before it passed over the stern, and consequently several were not hooked on, making an increased length of unsupported hose. This is most inadvisable. In the reverse operation when hauling in the hose after oiling had been finished, difficulty was again experienced in getting the stirrups off in time, and consequently the hauling in had to be stopped occasionally.
>
> A man was subsequently placed outboard to detach the stirrups, and hauling in proceeded without a stop, but this is a dangerous proceeding and should not be allowed.

No wonder the old time RFA men advised anyone using this method to 'keep a bucket handy to collect all the spare thumbs'!

In the light of the thirty or so years that elapsed between *Petroleum*'s purchase, the later *Burma* experiments in 1911 and the Royal Navy's eventual development of a reliable fuelling at sea rig during 1941–3, it may be of interest to note some comments made at the time of *Petroleum*'s purchase, in 1905 (Sigwart, 1969):

... she will be used to follow the Atlantic Fleet, and the pumping arrangements are so designed that she can be towed *behind* a battleship and a *flexible hose* passed from the forecastle to the battleship through which fuel can be pumped in any ordinary weather *at sea*. (author's emphasis)

When in harbour, connections have been arranged so that oil can be pumped through the side when the vessel is lying alongside one of HM ships. In case of need, oil can also be pumped over the stern ...

... The purchase of SS *Petroleum* shows that the Navy have determined extensively to adopt fuel oil.

Clearly, this further confirms that the ship was bought with the sole end in view of developing reliable technology for refuelling at sea. Many in the Royal Navy were in favour of the idea, so why:

(1) Did the navy settle for 'rafting up' as its main refuelling procedure, without apparently making further, more serious attempts to develop *reliable* RAS technology? Cost might have been an issue but it cannot have been the whole story.

(2) Apparently ignore RAS developments in other countries, particularly the United States, with which scientific and technical relations were harmonious and which had been using rubber hoses hung, on a single wooden saddle or trough, for fuel replenishment since 1917?

(3) Specifically, ignore the development of synthetic rubber hose technology, which was to revolutionise replenishment-at-sea and which the navy had in place barely 12 months after the capture of the German auxiliary *Lothringen* in 1940? Or were they ignoring it?

Although extensive oiling-at-sea trials were still being carried out by the British, fuelling alongside continued to be the predominant technique in use by the Royal Navy until the beginning of the Second World War, despite the fact that the United States, Japan and most significantly, the German Navy, had quickly seen the advantages inherent in oiling-at-sea. This was to have considerable repercussions during the early stages of the Atlantic war, when, in 1939–40, the inability to refuel warships, particularly convoy escorts, had dire consequences.

Although it is not generally acknowledged either, the stirrup method was not the only method under consideration by the Admiralty during this period.

In December 1913, a Captain Fairfield approached the Admiralty with a revolutionary idea for oiling-at-sea, using a steel bound, leather hose, 130 fathoms (about 250 metres) long, which he claimed could be used in one piece. The towing hawser itself consisted of a number of flexible steel, wire ropes, running parallel with and attached to the hose, and 'of sufficient strength to take the whole of the towing forces'.

More wire ropes were bound around the hose to secure the towing wires and prevent the hose from bursting. The hose was to be secured to both the receiving and delivering ships by attaching the towing lines to sleeve pieces with strong collars on the inboard end which would, in turn, be attached to pedestals mounted on turntables. This would, the inventor felt, give sufficient freedom of movement to keep the collars and hoses in a straight line when the vessel yawed.

The Admiralty had several serious objections to Fairfield's invention, in that they could neither see how the hose was to be cleared of oil, nor how it was to be repaired or stored. Interestingly, the inventor's suggestion was that compressed air was used to clear the hose, while it could be stored on a large drum similar to that used aboard cable ships. As anyone who has served with the RFA will know quite well, compressed air is universally used to clear hoses and the newest astern liquid replenishment technology is a device called the Hudson reel, which consists of a rubber hose, on a large reel, which is streamed astern to the receiving ship, although admittedly ships nowadays are not towed but maintain position by station keeping, thus doing away with the need for Fairfield's admittedly over-complex towing arrangements.

Repairing Fairfield's device also was not so straightforward. The inventor suggested that the outer sheathing and wire reinforcement be cut, whereupon the hose could be repaired and the sheathing reinstated. What an interesting exercise *that* might have been, at night, with any sort of sea running.

Of course, nothing ever came of Fairfield's invention, the inventor being kindly informed that:

> ... the Admiralty felt the matter to be of considerable importance, and would welcome any practical proposals for facilitating oiling ships at sea and hoped that, after hearing this and discussing the matter with his friends, he would be able to write to the Admiralty in such a way as to permit steps being taken to test the value of the proposal.

Just what the Admiralty considered the necessary 'steps' to be, had been made very clear to the unfortunate captain early in the meeting when the minutes recorded: 'The possibility of making a definite trial, free of expense to the Admiralty, was discussed, but the inventor was not able to say that he could make a definite proposal.'

Perhaps Fairfield should have tried his luck with the Americans ... or the Germans.

By 1912, in one final, important, pre-war development, initial installations of Marconi wireless telegraphy (W/T) had begun to be made into RFA ships, along with generators that were intended both to run these sets and the proposed electric lighting systems, which were also to be installed in the selected vessels. Operators during this period were usually civilian telegraphists, employed by the Marconi Company.

Technological innovation in the early RFA had begun well but for reasons which are not quite clear, this early impetus was not maintained.

Abandonment of the fuelling at sea trials does appear to have coincided with Sir John Fisher's replacement as First Sea Lord. He may well have been the impetus behind this early drive to solve the problem of replenishment at sea and, with his influence gone, and less far-sighted individuals taking his place, further efforts were abandoned.

It can only be speculation but it seems at least reasonable to ask, given the distinction that was made between RFAs and MFAs, along with the extensive RAS modification of *Petroleum* before purchase, in what direction the new RFA fleet might have been taken?

Did Sir John intend to have a purpose-built, navy-manned replenishment fleet, of which *Petroleum* was the first member?

Did he then further intend that this should be separate from the freighting service, which would then make use of the Admiralty's MFAs?

And so should we be writing here ... Sir John Fisher, founder of the Royal Fleet Auxiliary service?

Whatever the reasons behind it, no Royal Navy ship would routinely refuel at sea until the Second World War and then the technology used would be largely developments of German or US equipment, despite the fact that many of the early replenishment trials had been conducted by the British.

Fortunately, this lack of a replenishment-at-sea capacity was not to prove too great a disadvantage during the First World War, because the Royal Navy, with the exception of the Battle of Coronel, was only to engage in major fleet actions against the Germans in the North Sea, where refuelling (or recoaling) could take place at one of the large UK bases. Despite still being predominantly an oil transport and freighting service after 1918, the First World War was also to bring in its wake an unprecedented expansion of both the RFA fleet and its role within the UK armed forces.

RFA Fleet January 1905–December 1914

Ship name	Type	In service	Left service	Comments
Maine (ex Swansea)	Hospital ship	1900	1914	Total loss after stranding.
Kharki	Oiler	1900	1931	Former collier converted for transport of lubricating oil.
Petroleum	Oiler	1905	1936	
Mercedes	Collier	1908	1920	
Aquarius (ex Hampstead)	Water tanker	1902	1920	Purchased as distilling ship 1902 and completed as a depot ship 6.1907. 8th destroyer force, Firth of Forth 1914–15, Mediterranean sub depot ship 1915. Sold 14.5.1920 to mercantile interests
Isla	Petrol carrier	1907	1921	
Reliance (ex Knight Companion)	Repair ship	1916	1919	
Burma	Oiler	1911	1935	Burma class
Trefoil	Oiler	1917	1935	Burma class
Turmoil	Oiler	1917	1935	Burma class
Mixol	Oiler	1916	1947	Burma class
Thermol	Oiler	1916	1946	Burma class
Attendant	Oiler	1914	1934	Attendant class
Carol	Oiler	1914	1935	Attendant class
Ferol	Oiler	1914	1920	Attendant class
Servitor	Oiler	1914	1932	Attendant class

Chapter 3

The First World War

Origins

Ostensibly, the initial cause of the First World War was the assassination at Sarajevo, in Bosnia, of the heir presumptive to the Austrian and Hungarian thrones, Archduke Francis (Franz) Ferdinand, by Serb nationalist Gavrilo Princep.

This led the Austro-Hungarian Empire to declare war on Serbia on 28 July 1914. Russia then partially mobilised against Austria, which prompted Germany to declare war on Russia. German troops then moved into Luxembourg, and Germany declared war on France the same day.

Germany now informed the Belgian government that it intended to attack France through Belgium. The Belgians refused to allow the passage of troops so the German army marched anyway. As a result of this infringement of Belgian neutrality, Britain declared war on Germany on 4 August 1914.

In just six days the world was set aflame for four horrific years.

Although the sequence of events that finally culminated in war occurred over a very short period, in reality, Europe had been on the edge of this sort of madness for decades.

Nineteenth-century Europe was permeated by a spirit of intense nationalism, with pride in national identity seen as a citizen's most essential virtue. Survival of the fittest had become the ruling doctrine, in terms of both individuals and countries. Away from the battlefield, this still placed the major powers in direct competition, vying for the biggest share of any established or potential markets for themselves.

Industrial revolution had taken place in Britain at the end of the eighteenth century, closely followed by France some years later and then Germany after 1870, vastly increasing the manufacturing potential of these countries. They had always been the major protagonists in European warfare and now the battlegrounds shifted to world trade. And the market they were most intent upon dividing was Africa.

Africa was a market ripe for a huge influx of Europe-made goods and during 1898–1914, the economic rivalry between Great Britain, France and Germany in this area came close to precipitating a major European war on several occasions, in places as far apart as Morocco, the Balkans and, later, Turkey.

Military, and particularly naval, expansion, together with unprecedented technological advances, exacerbated these colonial rivalries and to prevent isolation in the event of war, several countries also sought a nebulous safety in military treaties offering mutual protection. This led to a further increase in tension and the grouping of the major European powers into two hostile military alliances: the Triple Alliance of Germany, Austria-Hungary and Italy and the Triple Entente of Great Britain, France and Russia. Great Britain also entered into agreements with Japan to safeguard her

Far East possessions. It was British naval officers, in fact, who had, years before, trained many of the senior officers in the Japanese fleet (mainly composed of British-built ships), which defeated the Russians so resoundingly at the Battle of Tsushima in May 1905.

Europe was an armed camp just waiting for the spark from Sarajevo which set it aflame. Even if Franz Ferdinand had lived to a ripe, old age, it would probably have made no difference. War, sooner or later, was inevitable.

The Royal Fleet Auxiliary in the First World War

The coming of this, the first Great War of the twentieth century, saw the RFA begin an immediate expansion. With only thirteen vessels in service on the eve of war, in August 1914, the fleet had well over 160 by the end of 1918, including the hospital ship *Maine*. Many of these auxiliaries were also designed and built specifically for Admiralty service, such as the two 1000-ton classes, the 2000-ton class and the 5000-ton (Fast Leaf) class.

By way of comparison, the United States, which possessed one of the biggest auxiliary fleets of all the Allied countries, after Great Britain, had only four purpose-built USN-commissioned ships and nineteen chartered merchant tankers by the war's end (*Grey Steel and Black Oil*, p. 25).

Tankers, including vessels for the carriage of water, spirit and petrol, made up the bulk of this RFA fleet, with nearly one hundred in service during 1918.

Early additions included the *Attendant* and *Creosol* classes for local port and harbour duties as well as several vessels in the *Burma* and *Belgol* classes, fitted for RAS by the stirrup method and designed to operate off shore.

A number of 5000-ton twin-screw tankers of the Admiralty-designed *Trinol* class, later known as the Fast Leaf class, came into service in 1917. These were of special significance, being over 400 feet long, capable of 16 knots and so comparable in size and speed to vessels the Americans were using at the time to RAS their destroyers while underway.

Initially, the Fast Leafs were designed as Fleet attendant tankers, with all of the necessary equipment for oiling at sea. However, in December 1916, only four months after *Trinol*'s launch, it was decided to convert them into convoy escorts. All of the carefully tested oiling-at-sea fittings were removed, and appearances were altered to make each ship as dissimilar as possible and their specification altered to allow the addition of three 4.7-inch quick firing guns and two 12-pounders. There was even some speculation about depth charges and a bomb howitzer!

By January 1917, this had all changed again and they were now to be used as special service vessels (or 'Q' ships), thereby, as the Admiralty put it, '... combining the double function of overseas traders and patrol vessels' (source: National Archive).

Their main function was to be conveying oil from one or more of the American or Caribbean ports to the UK, although, eventually, it appears to have been decided that they would be used only to take in oil from Jamaica or possibly Bermuda. They would then be routed home via the Florida Strait, where they might be lucky enough to meet a submarine, although the Admiralty were very specific that they should not go looking for trouble!

By the end of January 1917, the situation changed again, when the Director of

Transports somehow found himself assuming responsibility for the, as yet, unfinished ships of the Fast Leaf class.

On his instructions, sent to the Captain Superintendent of Contract Built Ships, all six were to be transferred, upon completion, to Lane & Macandrew Ltd, London. This company would then register the vessels merchant ships and arrange for their operation as *privately* owned oiler transports. They were to be renamed, for example, RFA *Texol* becoming *Appleleaf*, *Bornol* becoming *Orangeleaf*. The last two sentences of this memo make interesting reading:

> ... but the original names should be used (in correspondence and otherwise) until the vessels are on the point of sailing. The new names should not be communicated to any one and *care should be taken to avoid connecting the former with the new names.* (author's emphasis)

Presumably, this last warning relates to trouble they may have been having with the United States over neutrality issues and what constituted private ownership. The Fast Leaf class was to continue under the management of Lane & Macandrew, as privately owned oilers, until after the war, a practice which also characterised the operation of a number of other classes as well as individual vessels, including the largest tanker then owned by the Admiralty, RFA *Olympia*.

Later renamed *Santa Margherita*, it was originally intended that four vessels of this type would be built, but, for reasons unknown (although expense, in terms of both original cost and operating expenses, might have been the issue again), the last three were cancelled.

Olympia, Admiralty-designed and originally laid down in 1913, utilised the two biggest diesel engines available at the time. These were eight-cylinder, single acting monsters capable of generating 2500 bhp, built by Vickers Ltd of Barrow, which was also responsible for building the ship itself. Over 450 feet long and with a massive displacement for the time of 13,450 tons, fully loaded, she was also unusual for having all-electric auxiliaries.

Although there appears to have been some discussion about using her as a diesel test-bed, upon completion in 1916 she was renamed *Santa Margherita* and immediately transferred to commercial management, under T Royden & Sons, until she was bought by Anglo-Saxon Petroleum Co Ltd in 1919 and renamed *Marinula*. She finished her career as an oil hulk in 1946, and was broken up at Newport in 1951.

Many of these Admiralty-designed tankers were built and commissioned in an amazingly short time. To quote just one example, *Elmol*, of the 1000-ton *Creosol* class of harbour tankers, was launched on 23 July and completed in just over a month, on 27 August. Even the *Trinol* or Fast Leaf class, big, complex ships by the standards of those days and subjected to changes in design and extensive modifications, only took six or seven months from launch to completion. By way of illustration, *Trinol*, the first of that class, was launched on 4 August 1916 and completed by 11 March 1917.

As well as deploying its purpose-built auxiliaries, a large, miscellaneous collection of freighting tankers were also chartered or requisitioned by the Admiralty, most of these being taken up during 1916–18. Some were operated under commercial management as Red Ensign oilers, although several others were Admiralty owned.

Of particular interest in this context are eighteen ships in what may usefully be termed the Lane & Macandrew Leaf group, to distinguish them from the *Trinol* or

Fast Leaf class. Some were given '-ol' suffixed names, although they were definitely not sisterships.

Shortly after launch, all were registered with their new Leaf names when taken over for management by Lane & Macandrew, in 1917. Admiralty documents also state that these vessels were not only to be managed by this company, but also ownership was to be transferred to Lane & Macandrew.

None of these ships appear in the *Navy List* for 1917, which includes details of RFAs and other Admiralty auxiliaries, indicating that they were not Admiralty registered, whatever their ownership. Sigwart (1969), however, suggests that the Director of Stores had some involvement in their operation and manning. Some certainly began life as cargo ships or even dummy battleships, being converted to freighting oilers by simply inserting cylindrical tanks into the holds.

Together with its oilers, the RFA fleet also included a number of more specialised vessels. *Bacchus*, the first in a long and distinguished line of dry store and water carriers of that name, submarine depot ships, which included *Aro*, the first of this type, accommodation ships, and one repair ship were part of the RFA fleet during this period along with several tugs, salvage vessels and lifting vessels. A collection of Port of London Authority hopper barges was even converted and used as oil carriers during 1916–17, when German submarine attacks were causing substantial losses of Allied merchant ships. Certain vessels that had been on special duties, such as the kite balloon ship HMS Manica, a number of 'Q' or special service ships, as well as dummy battleships such as *Ruthenia* were also later transferred to RFA service.

Perhaps most notably, several of the popular, long-serving War class were laid down in the last year of the war, with the first of these vessels, *War Bahadur*, being launched in 1918. A small number of this extremely prolific class was still operating in a freighting role with the RFA as late as 1958.

Operation, management and classification of Admiralty-employed auxiliaries

Administration of RFAs during this period was still not quite as clear cut as it was to later become, with vessels administered and managed under several different schemes. Matters were even further complicated because it appears no one department had sole responsibility for them. The Director of Naval Construction, the Director of Naval Equipment, the Director of Dockyards and Dockyard Works and the Director of Victualling all had certain responsibilities for RFAs.

The operation of auxiliary vessels generally falls roughly into two, mutually dependent areas of responsibility:

- *Deployments*, which covered where they were sent and what they did and was usually decided by the relevant Admiralty department or departments; and
- *Management and administration*, which consisted of engagement of crew, refits, safety issues, Lloyd's Register inspections and all of the other details that allow a merchant vessel to operate safely at sea.

Upon the establishment of the RFA in 1905, management became chiefly the responsibility of the Naval Stores Department under its Director of Stores. Several coasting vessels were operated by both the Victualling Department and the Armament Supply Department, while some colliers and hired transports were operated by the Admiralty Transport Department, headed by the Director of Transports, who also had other responsibilities. The latter department was subsequently incorporated into the Ministry of Shipping in 1917, becoming the core of this new organisation, with particular responsibility for meeting the shipping needs of the fighting services.

The Ministry of Shipping was a wartime department brought into being to ensure a proper distribution of the available merchant fleet. Merchant ships were in very short supply at the time and, apparently, certain government departments and, in particular, the Army and Air Force, were reluctant to accept the decisions of the Admiralty's Director of Transports regarding deployments, because they suspected the navy of prioritising its own requirements!

Despite this reorganisation, there were periods during the First World War when the management of many Admiralty-owned auxiliaries passed into the hands of commercial shipping companies. This frequently resulted in re-registration and/or renaming.

If a ship was owned by the Admiralty and managed on its behalf by the Department of Naval Stores or a commercial company, that vessel was classified as an RFA. This is what happened to the War class, between 1922 and 1938. These ships were operated by commercial companies during this period, but owned by the Admiralty and registered as such. They consequently appear in the *Navy List* as RFAs.

Another alternative was for a vessel to be chartered by the Admiralty and managed by the Department of Naval Stores. This was the case for the later Leaf classes, for example, which were re-registered under their Leaf names and operated on bareboat charter, from 1958. Such vessels were also RFAs and this is how they appear on the *Navy List*. Eventually, all Admiralty owned or bareboat chartered auxiliaries were operated in this way, right up to the present day, although management and administration is currently the responsibility of the RFA itself, ultimately in the person of the Commodore RFA.

Ships might also have been bought out of Admiralty funds and so owned by it, and placed under commercial management. This occurred specifically during the First World War and for a short time after, when some ships were managed by commercial companies and registered as privately owned merchant ships (oiler transports), although still, in reality, the property of the Admiralty, having been purchased out of the Navy Vote. These were operated under the Red Ensign, specifically so as to get around US neutrality legislation and allow them to bring their cargoes of oil back to the recently constructed oil tank farms at various ports in the UK.

This happened, as previously discussed, with all six *Trinol* class vessels, when these were transferred to the management of Lane & Macandrew in 1917, as well as that company's more miscellaneous Leaf group. It is debatable whether they should be classified as RFAs, because they had been bought out of the Navy Vote and so were Admiralty property or as MFAs, because of their registered ownership. Although no vessel in either group is listed on the First World War *Navy List*s as an auxiliary, here they are included as RFAs. Finally, ships may be chartered by the Admiralty but remain under their owner's commercial management. This happened with the Ships Taken Up From Trade (STUFT) during the Falklands war and several vessels from occupied countries during the Second World War. Such vessels are MFAs.

'Q' ships, special service ships and other specialised RFAs

Although RFA activities during the First World War were mostly confined to fuel and stores freighting, there were several ships in specialist roles that were still registered as, or later became, RFAs. One interesting departure from normal logistics operations was the use of some auxiliaries, chartered by, or transferred to, the navy, as special service ships or decoy vessels. The existence of these 'Q' ships, so called because their home port was Queenstown, in Ireland, was one of Britain's most closely guarded wartime secrets. It has also been suggested that the Q derives from 'query', this being derived from the secret nature of the vessels.

Heavily armed and manned by Royal Navy personnel, they were usually dispatched into areas of intense submarine activity. Their weapons were hidden and when a submarine surfaced and began to bombard the disguised merchant vessel with its deck gun, as it usually did to husband its ruinously expensive torpedoes, the Q ship's crew would rapidly uncover its own armament and engage the submarine. Some notable successes were achieved by these ships, which were all renamed with the designation HMS, so that they could be legitimately classed as warships. They were also obliged to hoist the White Ensign before opening fire, otherwise their actions were illegal.

The Q ships came in all shapes and sizes from schooners and fishing vessels to the 600-ton *Hyderbad*, the only decoy vessel purpose built for its role.

Armament, which usually consisted of one 4-inch (102-mm) and two 12-pounder guns, was hidden in a number of ways. Hinged bulwarks, dummy superstructures, deck cargoes, and even dummy boats were all used to conceal the ship's weapons. As time went on and the Germans become aware of their existence, the ships were forced to adopt even greater secrecy and more elaborate disguises.

Along with canvas additions to the superstructure and frequent name changes, many other techniques were developed to convince the U-boats that the Q ships were genuine. These included disguises for the crew such as men being made up as black merchant seamen or the captain's 'wife'. On one ship, the 'cook' was equipped with a stuffed parrot in a cage. A simulated abandon-ship routine was often put into operation whereby half the crew, nicknamed the 'panic party', would leave ship while the other half would remain hidden aboard to man the guns. When it became apparent, later in the war, that the decoys were likely to be torpedoed, their holds were filled with buoyant material, such as balsa wood or cork, to keep them afloat.

One particularly successful scheme was the trawler-submarine plan. The Q ship would leave port towing an old submarine that was submerged and connected to the decoy by telephone. When attacked, the decoy vessel would release the submarine, which, in turn, attacked the surfaced and relatively helpless enemy U-boat.

Estimates vary as to the effectiveness of Q ships. Some sources claim these sank roughly 30 per cent of the U-boats destroyed by surface forces, while others put the figure at less than 10 per cent. Successes were highest in the early part of the war when the number of decoy vessels was limited but, when numbers increased in later years, the Germans became aware of the operation and successes declined. It is claimed that that there were as many as 366 Q ships, although, once again, other sources put the figure at less than 200. Certainly, at least sixty-one were lost during the war, nearly all of the larger vessels being torpedoed without warning.

RFAs used during the First World War as Q ships

Argo
Store carrier (RFA): Built 1906, 1250 tons gross. Purchased 19.12.1917 for Q ship role; later in use as store carrier. Sold about 1939.

Carrigan Head
Built 1901, 4201 tons. Hired as a supply ship (RFA) 4.8.1914, commissioned as a decoy ship (Q4) 1.6.1916, escort ship 8.1917 to 2.1919 (also served as decoy ship *Suffolk Coast*).

Intaba
Built 1910, 4,808 tons gross. Hired as a store carrier (RFA) 5.8.1914–5.1.1918. Operated as Q2 6.1916–7.1917.

Lyons
Built 1885, 537 tons gross. Hired as a salvage vessel (RFA) 8.1914. Decoy ship 5.1915–11.1915. Returned 12.1915.

Tay and Tyne
Built 1909, 556 tons gross. Hired as a decoy ship 28.6 1917. Purchased 26.9.1917 and converted to store carrier (RFA), renamed *Industry* 1920. Sold 31.10.1924.

Westphalia
Built 1914, 1467 tons gross. Hired as a store carrier (RFA) 21.10.1914–6.1916 and as decoy ship 7.3.1917. Sunk 11.2.1918 by U-boat in the Irish Sea.

A number of ships later destined for RFA service were also taken over by the Admiralty, early in the war, for conversion to dummy warships.

Originally, it was Winston Churchill, as First Lord of the Admiralty, who suggested that the navy might use ordinary merchant ships to fool the enemy into thinking the Royal Navy had more warships than was actually the case. This had become necessary because although it had more modern Dreadnought battleships than the Germans, on paper, by October 1914, things had begun to go badly wrong for the British, especially at sea.

One of the Royal Navy's older Dreadnoughts, HMS *Audacious*, had been lost to a mine during battle practice in the North Atlantic in mid October, while several others, including HMS *Ajax*, *Orion* and Admiral Sir John Jellicoe's own flag ship, the super-Dreadnought *Iron Duke*, suffered engine defects.

Jellicoe could now only muster seventeen operational battleships, out of a total of twenty-one, against Germany's thirteen, while the German Grand Fleet had eighty-eight destroyers compared with the Royal Navy's forty-two. The Germans were also in control on land and fighting hard for the possession of Calais, while it also seemed likely that Turkey would enter the war in the Middle East on the side of the Germans.

In desperation, Churchill decided upon the construction of a dummy fleet. The First and Third Sea Lords received their written instructions from him on 21 October

1914. They were to select ten merchant vessels, then distribute them among a number of private shipyards, where wood and canvas was to be used to construct turrets, bridge works and all the other fittings necessary to make these vessel resemble battleships when viewed from either the air or through a periscope.

However, the Admiralty requisitioned fourteen ships including both freighters and passenger liners. The Belfast shipyard of Harland & Wolff Ltd was selected to do the work, which came as something of a surprise, considering the trouble that was flaring in Ulster over home rule.

The first vessels of what became known as the Special Service Squadron joined the Grand Fleet at Scapa Flow on 7 December 1914. Unfortunately, for vessels meant to masquerade as warships, they were not quite quick enough. True, one or two could make as much as 15 knots, but some of the older ships could barely make 9 knots, while *Perthshire* was struggling to make 7 knots!

Jellicoe decided that their speed, or rather lack of it, made them a liability and would not allow them to accompany the Fleet. Later, several of the squadron took part in the Dardanelles campaign, where the steamer *Merion* (dummy battleship HMS *Tiger*) was torpedoed. *Cevic* (dummy battleship HMS *Queen Mary*) was also used to patrol America's eastern seaboard, where her presence resulted in the internment of two German commerce raiders.

By the middle of 1915, however, no one had been able to think of any useful employment for the dummies and so the squadron was disbanded. All of the ships concerned were consequently converted for other duties, nine going on to serve in the RFA, either as tankers, store ships or, in one case, as a kite balloon ship.

Dummy battlecruisers that later became RFAs

Bayol
(ex dummy battlecruiser *Queen Mary*, renamed 1915; ex *Cevic*) Oiler (RFA): Built 1894, 8455 tons gross,, renamed *Bayleaf* 1919. Sold 1919, renamed *Pyrula*.

Patrician
Built 1901, 7470 tons gross. Hired as dummy battlecruiser HMS *Invincible* 30.11.1914. Purchased 1915, renamed *Teakol*. Oiler (RFA) 1915, renamed *Vineleaf* 1917. Sold 12.7.1919, renamed *British Vine*.

Dummy battleships that later became RFAs

Abadol
(ex dummy battleship *Iron Duke*, renamed 7.7.1915, ex *Montezuma*), oiler (RFA), 7345 tons gross, 485 ft x 59 ft, renamed *Oakleaf* 7.2.1917. Lost 25.7.1917.

City of Oxford
Built 1882, 7430 tons gross. Purchased as the dummy battleship *St Vincent* 20.10.1914; kite balloon ship 17.7.1915, sold 1920.

Mount Royal
7044 tons gross. Hired as dummy battleship *Marlborough* 10.1914, converted to oiler (RFA) 1915, renamed *Rangol*, purchased 10.7.1916, renamed *Mapleleaf* 7.11.1916. Sold 12.7.1919, renamed *British Maple*.

Montcalm
Built 1897, 5487 tons gross. Hired as dummy battleship *Audacious* 10.1914. Purchased 29.1.1916, converted to oiler (RFA) renamed *Crenella* 18.11.1916. Sold 22.10.1919 to Anglo-Saxon Petroleum Co Ltd.

Perthshire
Built 1893, 5865 tons gross. Purchased 28.10.1914 as dummy battleship *Vanguard*. Water carrier (RFA) 1915, oiler 1919, store carrier 1921, sold 26.2.1934, broken up in Italy.

Ruthenia
(ex *Lake Champlain*) built 1900, 11,850 tons gross. Purchased as a dummy battleship *King George V* 1.11.1914. Water carrier (RFA) 1915, oiler 1920. Oil hulk at Singapore from 26.3.1931, captured by the Japanese, renamed *Choran Maru*.

Tyrolia
Built 1899, 7535 tons. Hired as dummy battleship *Centurion* 8.1914, purchased 11.1914 and renamed *Saxol*, oiler (RFA) 9.6.1916, renamed *Aspenleaf* 10.1916. Sold 12.9.1919 to Anglo-Saxon Petroleum Co Ltd.

One of the most interesting and dangerous jobs during this period, involving several vessels that would later become RFAs, was their attachment to the Naval Balloon Section, serving as kite balloon ships (KBSs). Intended to act as naval gunnery observers, these balloon ships directed the fire of warships onto targets that were out of the larger vessel's visual range. Unfortunately, the enemy, in this case the Turkish army, soon realised what was going on and used all their efforts towards shooting down the kite balloon together with the unfortunate occupant of the basket!

The three vessels that would serve as RFAs were commissioned as KBSs in 1915 and so were designated warships. Kite balloon ships were used in the Dardenelles campaign and later in East Africa, although HMS *Manica*, the first, was returned to the UK, late in 1915.

Vessels used as kite balloon ships that later became RFAs

Canning
Built 1896, 5375 tons gross. Commissioned as KBS 29.6.1915, depot ship (Scapa Flow attached to Flying Squadron) 1917. Sold 12.2.1920.

City of Oxford
Built 1882, 7430 tons gross. Purchased as the dummy battleship *St Vincent* 20.10.1914, kite balloon ship 17.7.1915. Sold 1920.

Manica
Built 1900, 4120 tons gross. Hired as KBS 11.3.1915, later purchased. Served in home waters as KBS 1915–16, possibly as training vessel. Renamed *Huntball* 1917 and in service as Red Ensign collier servicing UK naval bases. Sold 1920.

Three more RFAs were also commissioned during the First World War as torpedo sub-depot ships, stationed at Rosyth, Cromarty and Scapa Flow between 1915 and 1918.

His Majesty's Ships *Aro*, *Sobo* and *Sokoto* were all purchased from Elder Dempster & Co Ltd, Liverpool. They do not appear to have been very extensively equipped for the job, because, although no contemporary record of their actual conversion still exists, there is a record of a memo from the Director of Dockyards and Dockyard Works about accommodation for the extra personnel.

This consisted of one engineer officer, one chargeman, seven fitters, one copper-smith and ten labourers that made up the workshop staff, personnel for the gyro house ashore, consisting of one chargeman, four fitters and eight labourers and the boom defence staff of two Lieutenants, one chief petty officer and twelve ratings. A surgeon or sick berth attendant was also provided for along with what the memo refers to as 'a proper proportion of domestics'.

This record shows that workshop personnel aboard one of these sub depot ships was only about twenty men whereas, by comparison, the Royal Navy's repair ship, *Reliance*, had a staff of well over one hundred to run her workshops. These submarine depot ships were not seagoing vessels, rather being stationed in their respective harbours with the submarines coming to them for refuelling and rearming and with a workshop staff of only twenty, even one submarine must have kept everyone quite busy.

The Admiralty only paid £55,000 for all three, so their material condition may have been less than perfect. In 1919–20, they were sold to new owners.

Before leaving the subject of logistic supply for submarines, it may be of interest to note that originally, it was planned to fit the *Belgol* class of 2000-ton oilers with two 26.5-kW generating sets, as the Admiralty memo puts it, '… the increased power to be available for re-charging the batteries of submarines, if required'.

The date on the memo is 6 April 1916, so there must have been others in the Admiralty whose experience had taught the coming importance of submarines, even after Sir John Fisher's departure.

RFAs used as submarine depot ships

Aro
Torpedo sub-depot ship at Rosyth 1915–18 (ex *Albertville*, purchased 10.1914) 3794 tons gross. Transport 14.8.1918. Sold to W R Davis & Co 1.1920.

Sobo
Torpedo sub-depot ship at Cromarty 1915–18, 4160 tons gross. Purchased 10.1914.
Sold to W R Davis & Co 12.2.1920.

Sokoto
Torpedo sub-depot ship at Scapa Flow 1915–18, 3870 tons gross. Purchased
10.1914. Sold 9.8.1919 to mercantile interests.

One of the most unusual uses ships were put to during the war was as accommodation vessels. No RFA was ever used in this role but several were associated with
the service during this period.

They were peculiar vessels in many respects, being used in a variety of situations
where on-shore accommodation was either not available or limited. Several, such as
HMS *Eaglet*, were elderly, wooden walled, sailing vessels, which, with masts removed,
were moored or anchored conveniently for the workers or service personnel who were
using them. Newer, steel ships, such as *Sunhill*, were also used.

Officers and crew members drafted to RFAs were among the personnel who used
HMS *Eagle*, which was based at Liverpool. By 1918, the name *Eagle* was required for an
early aircraft carrier and so the home for RFA crews was renamed HMS *Eaglet*.

Eagle/Eaglet was a former third rate ship of the line that had been built in 1804 and
was taken over as an RN drill ship in 1911 by the Royal Naval Volunteer Reserve. Upon
general mobilisation in 1914 most of the Reserve, instead of going to sea with the
Fleet, was drafted to the Royal Naval Division (RND), where they fought alongside the
army at Antwerp, Gallipoli and, from 1916, on the Western Front.

Originally, it was intended that the Royal Naval Division be formed into three
brigades, each of four battalions of 1000 men, a total of 12,000 naval and marine
personnel of various ranks and ratings.

At the time, it was stated that the 12,000 would be taken from '... the active service
and reserve officers and men *not immediately required* for service in the Fleet' (author's
emphasis).

However, heavy personnel commitments for the navy's warships began to arise
almost immediately and it became imperative to recall most, if not all, of the trained
men who made up the Royal Naval Division. Of course, this proved impossible
because, once they had them, the army were very reluctant to part with any of its
manpower. The result was a double dislocation of fighting personnel in that naval
ratings had to be retrained for military duties while the Admiralty were forced to enter
new men from shore and hurriedly train them for naval duties. This unfortunate
diversion of trained naval ratings into the RND was a mistake which was to become
increasingly important as the war went on.

This sort of error in the distribution of skilled personnel was not an isolated
incident. Admiralty planners had made another fundamental manning error, early in
the war, when they removed the majority of officers and men from all their harbour
establishments, replacing them with smaller numbers of Reserve personnel.
Unfortunately, harbour establishments included all the gunnery and torpedo schools

and this resulted in the cessation of all training in these disciplines for the duration of the war.

It soon became obvious, as if it had not been all along, that such weapons training was vital and had to carry on, but, by now, it could only be restarted on a much smaller scale. In most cases, a school's staff consisted of retired officers and pensioners although as the war progressed and the numbers of men to be trained increased, so did the schools' staffs. Somewhat belatedly, after the war, provision was made for retaining the training establishments at their peace-time complements.

RFAs used as repair ships or accommodation ships

Bacchus
Built by Hamilton & Co, 1915, purchased 1915 as store carrier and later converted to repair ship. Dimensions 295 ft x 44 ft x 12.5 ft, displacement about 3500 tons

Princetown
Built 1902, 6060 tons gross. German prize *Adalbert*, commissioned as repair ship 17.12.1914. Sold 23.12.1916. Sigwart (1969) claims that she also served as an accommodation ship for workmen employed by the Director of Dockyards.

Assistance (RN)
Built 1901, 9600 tons. Dimensions: 436 ft pp x 53 ft x 20 ft. Guns: 10 x 3-pdr. Machinery: Triple expansion. Boilers: Cylindrical. Fitted with Howden's forced draught. 4000 ihp, speed 12 knots. Coal 2180 tons. Fitted as floating workshop and distilling ship. Complement 283.

Cyclops (RN)
(ex *Indrabarah* 1905) Dimensions 460 ft pp x 55 ft x 21 ft. Guns 6 x 4-inch. Machinery triple expansion. 3500 ihp, speed 11.75 knots. Coal capacity 1595 tons. Fitted as floating workshop and distilling ship. Complement 294.

Reliance
(ex *Knight Companion*) Repair ship 9220 tons, 469.5 ft x 58 ft. Purchased 14.11.1912. Sold 17.12.1919.

Victorious II (RN)
Repair ship and Scapa Flow destroyer depot ship.

Scotstoun (RN)
Completed July 1916. Built by Yarrows, as repair ship for Insect and Fly slass gunboats. Dimensions: 132 ft pp 150 ft oa x 31 ft x 3.25 ft draught, 300 tons. speed 7.7 knots. Compound surface condensing engines, 200 ihp. Loco boiler. Oil: 20/36 tons. Registration as RFA uncertain

Sunhill (RN)
Launched 1895 by Laing, Sunderland, 837 tons. (Previously *General Havelock*, *Kennet*). Hired as an accommodation ship and based at Portsmouth harbour 23.9.1915–6.1920. Broken up 1928.

Victory II (RN)
Accommodation ship.

In wartime, salvage is an important consideration for any maritime force. Many of the salvage vessels in use with the navy were registered RFAs and along with these vessels, the RFA also operated another, more specialised class, the lifting vessels.

Lifting vessels were employed for the recovery of more or less complete vessels from shallow water. Two lifting vessels would approach the wreck at low tide, lower a strong cable attached to the lifting vessel's gantry, located on the bow, and attach this cable to some part of the wreck. The cable was then be tightened up and the lifting vessels settled down to wait for high tide.

As the tide rose so, of course, did the lifting vessels, which in turn raised the wreck from the bottom. The two lifting vessels then headed for shallow water, where the wreck eventually grounded. If it was still too deep for convenience, the procedure could be repeated until the wreck was completely accessible.

RFAs used during salvage and lifting vessels

Buffalo
Mooring vessel, 750 tons, 135 ft x 27.5 ft. Bow McLachlan 25.1.1916. Sunk 4.4.1941 on British mine off Singapore.

Bullfrog
Salvage vessel, 895 tons, 131 ft x 36 ft, purchased 1915, sold 2.1923 to Carriden Ship Breaking Co.

Fidget
Salvage vessel, 837 tons, 150 ft x 28.5 ft, purchased 1915, sold 8.1921 to J R Thomson.

Holdfast
Salvage vessel, 783 tons, 125 ft x 35 ft. Purchased 1915, sold 3.1923 Carriden Ship Breaking Co.

Mariner
Composite screw sloop, 970 tons, 167 ft x 32 ft, Devonport Dockyard 23.6.1884. Boom defence vessel 1903, salvage vessel 1917. Sold to Hughes Bolckow, Blyth, 1929, for breaking up.

Melita
(ex *Ringdove*). Composite screw sloop, 750 ihp, speed 11 knots, 970 tons, 167 ft x 32 ft, Malta Dockyard 20.3.1888. Boom defence vessel 5.1905, salvage vessel *Ringdove* 12.1915, sold Falmouth Docks Board 9.7.1920.

Racer
Composite screw gun vessel, 1100 ihp, speed 11 knots, 970 tons, 167 ft x 32 ft, Devonport Dockyard 6.8.1884. Sloop 1885, salvage vessel 1917. Sold to Hughes Bolckow, Blyth, 6.11.1928, for breaking up.

Reindeer
Composite screw sloop, 970 tons, 167 ft x 32 ft, Devonport Dockyard 14.11.1883. Boom defence vessel 1904, salvage vessel 1917. Re-engined 1918 by Fairfield. Sold 12.7.1924 to Halifax Shipyards as salvage vessel.

Thrush
Composite screw sloop (previously HMS *Thrush*) Launched 22.6.1889 by Scotts, Greenock. Bought for RFA service 1916, foundered off County Antrim 11.4.1917.

Defensively equipped merchant ships (DEMS)

In addition to the navy's Q ships, many ordinary merchant vessels, including several RFAs, in service during the war were fitted with weapons. Usual equipment was a 4- or 6-inch gun, for which the vessel's deck had to be especially stiffened. Darken-ship equipment, magazines and ready-use lockers were also fitted, although the ships were not allowed large quantities of ammunition. The usual issue was between forty and ninety rounds and since the Royal Navy expect to be able to fire six rounds per minute, this meant the RFAs could sustain fire, at that rate, for between 7 and 15 minutes.

In reality, this was not quite as disastrous as it appears, since the merchant ship's main antagonist was the submarine, which usually surfaced to attack its victim with its deck gun, thus reserving its expensive torpedoes for a more important target. Submarines were not armoured, so a single round through the hull or conning tower was often sufficient to force the U-boat's surrender. Guns aboard DEMS were operated either by specially trained Merchant Navy gun crews or Royal Navy personnel.

Mines were also a major problem during this conflict and many of the UK's merchant vessels were fitted with paravane bow protection gear as well as guns.

Service afloat

As might be expected, crewing arrangements during the First World War were quite different from those in place during the previous decade, with the oilers operated in two quite separate ways.

Admiralty-owned oilers that had been transferred to commercial management to be operated under the Red Ensign, were crewed by Merchant Navy personnel who signed standard Board of Trade articles. The rest of the fleet continued to sail under the RFA's own Blue Ensign.

Senior officers (masters, chief officers) in RFAs flying the Blue Ensign were all appointed to the Royal Naval Reserve (RNR), while much of the rest of the crew, including some junior officers, were appointed to the Mercantile Marine Reserve (MMR). As such they all were subject to Royal Navy discipline and were obliged to sign a form T.124X (for commissioned vessels), or some form of that document, to that effect.

Royal Fleet Auxiliary captains and chief engineers on RFAs were appointed to the rank of lieutenant RNR or engineer lieutenant RNR with chief officers and second engineers ranked as sub-lieutenant RNR or engineer sub-lieutenant RNR. Writers became RNR paymasters. In addition, some crew members were Royal Navy ratings, for example, gunners and some signallers, while most telegraphists were RNVR or RNR ratings. Officers are all listed in the 1917 *Navy List* under RNR rank.

This re-rating system frequently resulted in discord because some merchant seamen aboard a number of RFAs were employed by the Transport Department, on separate transport agreements (usually some form of T124). In particular, this meant that men recruited into the regular services (either navy or army) could find themselves serving in a ship with others nominally junior to them, and of less service, who were receiving higher rates of pay, simply because the latter had been recruited under one of these agreements.

The MMR seaman served not only on RFAs but also on naval warships and through the whole of the war the records of the Commonwealth War Graves Commission show that 1699 were killed. During the war, the RFA lost at least twelve officers of RNR rank and forty-nine MMR ratings.

The effects of serving under naval discipline were keenly felt in some quarters of the RFA. Crew records show that between 27 May 1916 and 3 October 1919, while subject to naval discipline, over 130 crew members (both officers and ratings) were registered as having deserted. A further sixteen were shown as being 'absent without leave', while six were noted as having 'failed to return to their ship'. The ships with the worst record were *Fortol* and *Petroleum*, both having recorded nearly twenty crew members as deserted. A few records show that when arrested the deserter faced imprisonment.

Court martial offences, apart from desertion, were mainly concerned with drunkenness, with a total of more than forty courts martial (thirty-nine officers and five ratings) convened between May 1916 and October 1919. There were, however, several cases brought of a quite different type. These included the master of *Barkol*, found guilty of stranding his ship, two hapless RFA ratings who were charged with sodomy (homosexual activities being a criminal offence in those days) and a switchboard operator, aboard *Reliance*, found guilty of sleeping on watch.

Punishments ranged from 'dismissed the service (although this was extremely rare) to a period of detention in prison or for lesser offences, in cells or naval detention quarters (NDQ). Court martial records show that eight RFA crew members were sentenced to prison in the period covered, while twenty-five received sentences in cells or NDQs, for matters other than desertion. Only ratings appear to have received prison sentences for their offences, officers being generally reprimanded and/or dismissed their ship.

Despite being subject to naval discipline, employment conditions for Merchant

Navy personnel aboard RFAs actually saw some improvement during this period with an Order in Council in 1914, which approved the provision of pensions, grants and allowances for officers, ratings and dependants of those injured or disabled while serving aboard auxiliaries.

Pay and bonuses also received a boost, in the same year, when the Admiralty agreed to pay the men serving on its auxiliaries a war bonus, 15 per cent for masters, officers and engineers and £1 a month for the rest of the crew. Further, perhaps more significant, improvements came in 1917, with the wartime introduction of the National Maritime Board.

This government-controlled organisation was set up to organise wage negotiations in the shipping industry, after a series of seamens' strikes in 1917 had threatened the smooth operation of the war effort. So successful were its activities, that it was reorganised as a permanent body in 1919. Later, unfortunately, it was to become embroiled in the controversies associated with the Joint Control Policy.

Introduced by the National Union of Seamen and the employer's Shipping Federation, this policy aimed to ensure seafarers could only gain employment if in possession of a form endorsed by both organisations. It was alleged that the policy was widely used to force 'agitators, communists and undesirables' out of employment in the industry, although how far this was true is difficult to say.

The First World War

The war on land

Military operations began in 1914 on three fronts; the Western (Franco-Belgian), the Eastern (Russian) and the Southern (Serbian). When Turkey allied herself with the Germans, entering the war in November 1914, Great Britain also became embroiled with the Turks in Mesopotamia and the Dardanelles.

Initially, the Germans had planned to crush France quickly in the Western theatre while the Austro-Hungarian army, reinforced by a small section of the German forces, would delay the Russians in the east. German success was based around the Schlieffen plan, named after the Count von Schlieffen, who had been German chief of staff between 1891 and 1907. His plan called for powerful German forces to sweep through Belgium, outflank the French, turn behind its army, before surrounding and crushing it.

During autumn 1914, things seemed to be going Germany's way. Moving swiftly across the frontier, they pushed the Belgians back to Antwerp before, in turn, defeating the French at Charleroi and the British Expeditionary Force at Mons. The Allies retreated to the River Marne but the Germans fought their way across and the fall of Paris seemed so inevitable that the French government moved to Bordeaux.

The Germans, however, had overreached themselves and the French turned their right flank, pushing them back to the River Aisne.

After three major battles, Aisne, the Somme and the first battle of Arras, the French and Germans were at stalemate. The German advance to the French Channel ports was blocked when the Belgians flooded a region of the River Yser and British extended the Allied line to Ypres, in the south-west corner of Belgium. In early October, the Germans tried to break through the British lines in Belgium, but were checked in a series of engagements known collectively as the Battle of Flanders. The Allies attacked in turn in December 1914, along the entire front from Nieuport in the west to Verdun in the east, but without making any significant gains.

The Battle of Flanders concluded the war of movement on the Western Front and the fighting now settled down to a period of trench warfare which lasted until nearly the end of the war in 1918. Each side laid siege to the other's trench system, which consisted of a series of parallel lines of interconnecting trenches, protected by barbed wire. Troops lived in the indescribable squalor of these muddy fortifications, the monotony and bad food only varied by periodic bouts of disease and occasional attempts to break through the enemy's lines, which met with an unvarying lack of success.

Even the major offensives such as Verdun, Ypres and the Somme, which lasted from July to November 1916 and cost 1.5 million lives, did not advance the front any significant distance. It was not until the entry of the United States in 1917 and the use of tanks during the Hundred Day Offensive that the Germans were driven back, although the Royal Navy's blockade, which had shut off all imports and resulted in increasingly severe food rationing for both civilians and the military, was also instrumental in the deterioration of the army's morale.

Finally, after a desperate rearguard action by a starving and increasingly mutinous German army, Kaiser Wilhelm II abdicated and on 9 December, the Weimar Republic was declared.

Gallipoli and the Dardanelles

While the Allied and German armies were playing out their bloody stalemate on the Western Front, the Russians, who had initially been successfully occupied in the East, began to come under increasing pressure, when the Turks, after declaring war on 29 October 1914, launched an invasion of the Russian Caucasuses.

Although the hard-pressed Russian army pushed back the Turks, Turkish pressure compelled the Russians to demand that the British launch a diversionary attack on Turkey.

Consequently, in February 1915, British naval forces, commanded by General Sir Ian Hamilton, began a bombardment of Turkey's Dardanelles forts, aided, from April 1915, by the RNAS's newly arrived kite balloon section, or rather the only vessel it then had in service, HMS *Manica*.

The initial bombardment of the Dardanelles forts had shown that the Turks had concealed guns very cleverly and both aeroplanes and seaplanes having proved ineffective as artillery spotters, the navy demanded observation balloons.

Spherical balloons had proved positively dangerous in an observation role and so the men of the RNAS's newly established kite balloon section were concentrating all their efforts and training, as might be expected, on kite balloons. These looked rather like an elongated sausage with stabilising fins and the British had none.

Fortunately, the French did. An officer with a winning smile, who also spoke French, was packed off to Paris with orders to 'borrow' the necessary equipment. Shortly afterwards, he returned, having not only borrowed a balloon but also a winch with all its cable. He also appears to have spoken highly, if incoherently, of French generosity and hospitality!

However, the KBS's problems were only just beginning. According to the book, balloon ascents required a large, unrestricted open space, something in short supply on the Gallipoli peninsula, where all of the open space was in the hands of the enemy.

Lesser men would have despaired. Not the Royal Navy. It decided to take its open space with it in the form of a specially adapted ship.

In just seventeen days, it had found its ship, an old manure filled tramp named *Manica*. Having emptied out the manure, fitted a long sloping deck between forecastle and waist, along with a dynamo, hydrogen compressor, wireless hut, crew quarters and collected the necessary personnel and stores, it sailed for Gallipoli.

Manica and her kite balloon were an instant success. Arriving on 16 April 1915, by 12 May she had directed the fire of several British warships onto numerous targets, including a 7000-ton Turkish transport, which was sunk by just three rounds from one of HMS *Queen Elizabeth*'s big guns.

Unfortunately, *Manica*'s success was not reflected in the rest of the campaign.

The navy's initial bombardments, which had been designed to force a passage through the Dardanelles to Constantinople, without the intervention of ground troops, failed spectacularly, culminating in the loss of three British warships to mines on 18 March 1915.

In the light of this failure, the Secretary of State for War, Lord Kitchener, appointed General Sir Ian Hamilton to head a 70,000-strong Mediterranean Expeditionary Force, composed of British, Canadian and Indian troops together with the Australian and New Zealand Army Corps (ANZAC) and a division of the French Foreign Legion. A division of the Royal Naval Battalion was also part of the force. Its mission was simple. All that it was required to do was seize the Gallipoli peninsula and clear the way for the Royal Navy to capture the Turkish capital, Constantinople (now Istanbul).

The assault was to be two pronged. British troops of the 29th division were to land at Cape Helles, before pushing inland and capturing Achi Baba, while the the ANZACs, under Lt General Birdwood, would land further north and capture the Sair Bair heights. HMS *Ark Royal*, then equipped with Sopwith seaplanes, and *Manica* were sent in support of the Australians and New Zealanders.

The combined assault was launched on 25 April 1915, but hostile terrain and a ferocious Turkish defence stopped the advance and the campaign quickly degenerated into the hopeless deadlock of trench warfare, now all too familiar to most of the soldiers. Incidentally, it was during this campaign the ANZACs first earned their nickname, 'Diggers', when their assault on the Sari Bair Heights failed and they were forced back on to the beach at Ari Burnu, and had to quickly 'dig in'.

Hanging on grimly to the high ground, the Turkish forces kept up a constant rain of shell fire on the Allied troops, who were finding it extremely difficult to dig trenches that would protect them from this bombardment. And it was not long before disease, in particular dysentery, caused by the extreme heat and unsanitary conditions, began to exact a greater toll than the Turkish gunfire.

The Allies made repeated attempts to break through the Turkish lines without achieving any notable success and in October 1915, Sir Charles Monro relieved the unsuccessful Hamilton of command. Monro's first recommendation was to evacuate and this the force speedily did in December 1915, leaving behind 36,000 Commonwealth, 10,000 French and about 86,000 Turks who had lost their lives during those bloody months of 1915.

Naval involvement

British and Commonwealth naval forces had three clear-cut objectives, whatever theatre they were involved in;

Protection of the friendly coastlines, especially the UK, protection and safe transport of troops to theatres of water and logistics supply once they were established and protection of trade routes and merchant ships while on passage.

The North Sea, Atlantic and English Channel

The North Sea was the main theatre for surface action during the war. With several of its major bases, such as Scapa Flow nearby, the Royal Navy could concentrate its Grand Fleet so as to keep merchant shipping out of the Baltic and the German North Sea ports, while maintaining a close watch on the German High Seas Fleet. Although close blockade was impractical and dangerous, given the German's extensive fleet of submarines and torpedo boats, the relative positions of the two countries meant that German merchant shipping could only approach its home ports via a fixed number of routes, all of which the Royal Navy could patrol efficiently enough to prevent all but a trickle of ships getting through.

Although oiling-at-sea experiments still continued, mostly between RFA oilers and destroyers, the RFA's main job was to freight oil and other essential stores, such as fuel and ammunition, to Scapa Flow, Rosyth and other important Royal Navy bases in the UK and abroad. *Creosol*, *Vitol* and *Innistrahull* were all sunk during the war.

At sea in August 1914, German naval operations began with a bad miscalculation.

Anticipating that the British would take a considerable period to organise, despite concerns expressed by the army, the German navy was caught by surprise when the Royal Navy managed to transport the main bulk of the British Expeditionary Force to France in just nine days, between 12 and 21 August. Submarines and destroyers, patrolling the area of the Heligoland Bight, protected the crossing by keeping the German fleet in port, while the British Grand Fleet remained in the centre of the North Sea, ready if it was needed.

These patrols were soon to yield an unexpected bonus. Early in the war, German destroyers had been assigned to make regular daily patrols in the area of the Heligoland Bight. Intent on limiting this type of activity, two British naval officers, Commodores Tyrwhitt and Keyes, persuaded the Admiralty to authorise an attack on the destroyers as they returned to their base.

The attack was a marked success. Tyrwhitt and Keyes' combined force of destroyers and submarines, supported by six light cruisers and Vice Admiral Beatty's five battlecruisers, sunk a destroyer, two torpedo boats and three light cruisers, as well as damaging a number of other vessels. On the British side, one of the supporting light cruiser flotillas, commanded by Commodore W Goodenough was badly damaged. German casualties were 712 killed, 149 wounded and 336 captured while British losses were comparatively light with thirty-five killed and fifty-five wounded.

Although it was a major victory for the Royal Navy, its most far-reaching effect was psychological, in that the Kaiser himself, upon hearing of the raid, ordered the German fleet to remain in port and avoid any contact with superior forces. Unfortunately, this did not reduce the commitment in ships the Royal Navy were still obliged to ensure the German fleet did not go to sea but its effect on the morale and efficiency of the German crews must have been devastating.

Despite this initial success, the war at sea was not all to go Britain's way, however.

In December 1914, under orders from his superior, Admiral von Friedrich, Admiral Franz von Hipper led his ships down the east coast and shelled the towns of Scarborough, Whitby and Hartlepool, killing 108 civilians and wounding 525.

British public and political opinion was outraged, particularly since Hipper's force escaped completely unscathed. Buoyed by this success, Hipper decide to try another sortie, this time against the British fishing fleet while it was working off the Dogger Bank, in January 1915.

This time, however, he was caught. His radio messages were intercepted and decoded and Beatty trapped him, sinking the armoured cruiser *Blücher* and causing heavy damage to *Seylditz*. Total German losses were 954 men killed, eighty wounded and 189 captured, while British casualties amounted to fifteen killed and thirty-two wounded, despite heavy damage to both Beatty's flagship, HMS *Lion*, and a destroyer.

Although this was claimed as a British victory, it was clear that there were still problems with the Royal Navy's capital ships, particularly with regard to the potentially disastrous effects of a shell hitting a gun turret and the resulting ammunition fires. British fire control had also been poor. Apart from the one-sided action against the *Blücher*, the British only made seven heavy-calibre hits as opposed to twenty-two by the Germans during this action. Later, the Battle of Jutland, fought in the summer of the following year, would starkly reveal these weaknesses in British technology.

By summer 1916, it was clear to the German government that something must be done to break the British stranglehold on their North Sea ports.

Unfortunately for the German navy, by now the British had twenty-eight Dreadnought class battleships to Germany's sixteen. As well as this existing numerical superiority, the British blockade was causing the Germans to fall well behind in production of all war materials, especially battleships. Clearly, in any sort of major fleet action, the Germans would be outnumbered, without any chance of victory. So, senior staff in the German navy devised a plan to lure part of the British Grand Fleet into a trap where it might be destroyed, thus reducing the Royal Navy's numerical superiority.

Once again the Admiralty intercepted German radio traffic on 28 May, which made it clear that the Germans were planning a big offensive. Jellicoe left Scapa Flow on the 30th, followed the next day by Beatty from the Firth of Forth, who was leading a force of six battlecruisers and four battleships.

Beatty encountered Hipper's fast scouting group of five battlecruisers on the afternoon of 31 May and pursued these, until the German High Seas Fleet commanded by Admiral von Scheer, appeared, Beatty losing two battleships in the process.

With the appearance of the German's main force, Beatty turned his battlecruisers through 180 degrees. With the four super Dreadnoughts of Sir Hugh Evan Thomas's 5th Battle Squadron acting as his rearguard, he then retreated, eventually drawing the Germans into action against Jellicoe's battleships.

After much manoeuvring, during which the British inflicted heavy damage on a number of German warships, Scheer retreated with his Dreadnoughts, ordering Hipper's four remaining battle cruisers and his destroyers to attack the enemy, thereby covering his retreat. Hipper's lightly armoured battlecruisers sustained major damage from the accurate fire of the British Dreadnoughts, which also succeeded in sinking a German destroyer. Further losses were sustained on both sides in the inconclusive night action that followed but poor communications and delays in informing Jellicoe of German radio messages which the Admiralty had intercepted meant that, when the British C-in-C finally learnt the German fleet's correct position at 04:15 on 1 June, Scheer was well on his way home and too far away to catch.

Jutland is reputed to be the largest naval battle in history, involving a total of 250 ships from both sides, as well as being the last major fleet action fought between steel warships. British casualties totalled over 6000 killed, 510 wounded and 177 captured, while the Germans lost 2551 killed, with 507 wounded. British ships made up of three battlecruisers, three armoured cruisers and eight destroyers, totalling 113,300 tons, were lost, while German losses were one pre-dreadnought, five light cruisers, six destroyers and a submarine – a total of 62,300 tons.

Despite the fact that British losses were far heavier than those of the Germans and the way in which the shortcomings of British warship design emerged, Jutland was undoubtedly a British strategic victory.

In the wake of the damage to which the German ships had been subjected, the Kaiser once again ordered that there be no further fleet-to-fleet contact. The German High Seas Fleet was to remain in harbour for the duration of the war, although the British still felt it to be enough of a potential threat to require a concentration of battleships in the North Sea.

The final word is perhaps best left to a German Naval expert, Captain Persius, who wrote, in November 1918, only days after the Armistice: 'Our fleet losses were severe. On 1 June 1916, it was clear to every thinking person that this battle must, and would be, the last one.'

Although major fleet actions were strictly confined to the North Sea during the First World War, the Atlantic saw a different type of action, which in many ways was just as significant.

Finding that its U-boats were of limited effectiveness against British warships, the German navy quickly found them to be much more useful against the British merchant fleet, which the UK was entirely dependent upon for most of its resources.

Before the war, submarines had been regarded as morally dubious weapons and had been made the subject of a number of international agreements. Under the terms of these agreements, submarines were supposed to surface and give the crew time to abandon ship before attacking any vessel, either with torpedoes or gunfire. Of course, any procedure of this sort sacrificed the U-boats greatest weapon, surprise, as well as making it extremely vulnerable to attack while on the surface. Not surprisingly, in February 1915, even before the battle of Jutland, the German navy abandoned these international constraints and began a campaign of unrestricted submarine warfare. However, in September of the same year it temporarily called an end to this policy, after the sinking of *Lusitania* had inflamed US public opinion and caused rapid deterioration in German–American relations. They had only sunk 750,000 tons of Allied shipping and their fleet of sixteen long-range submarines had proven too small for effectiveness.

After Jutland and with the German U-boat building programme gathering pace, Germany once again returned to unrestricted submarine warfare, in summer 1916, sinking over 250,000 tons of shipping in just a few weeks. Once again, German–American tension increased, especially after the sinking of the steamer *Sussex* and the loss of a number of American lives, and as a result this second campaign was also halted.

Early in 1917, however, the campaign of unrestricted submarine warfare was reintroduced, following immediately after the appointment of generals Ludendorff and Hindenburg to the German High Command.

During 1916, the German army had received a terrible battering from Allied forces at Verdun and the Somme. Unable to see a way of breaking the bloody stalemate on land, Germany's leaders decided upon one last desperate throw of the dice. They would institute another campaign of unrestricted submarine warfare, gambling that the U-boats would starve Britain into surrender before US intervention decided the matter on the battlefronts.

In the end, it was a close run thing. Beginning their campaign at the end of 1916, before the end of the year German U-boats were sinking about a third of a million tons of sllied shipping a month. In April 1917, U-boats had accounted for 400,000 tons of shipping in just the first half of that month. By now, the United States had entered the war, but Britain was down to only six weeks' reserves of food.

The Royal Navy had begun to fight back, however. Employing hydrophone listening apparatus, mines, depth charges, Q ships and several other devices, it had some success against the raiders but the major advance came when the decision was made to operate merchant ships as part of a convoy system. Shipping losses now began to decline for the first time, although they were still worryingly high for some months; losses in September 1917, for example, were over 300,000 tons. But by this time, the crisis was over. The United States had entered the war and now the Allies' final victory was inevitable.

An interesting consequence of US involvement in the Atlantic convoy war was its need to develop a reliable method for refuelling at sea. Given the distances involved in its operations in the Pacific (and the US government's growing fear of the Japanese), its need to develop refuelling technology was far more pressing than that experienced by the Royal Navy. This was reflected, in turn, by the speed at which a reliable RAS procedure was developed in the pre-war period by the US Navy.

A few years prior to their entry into the war, in 1913, the US Navy commissioned two tankers, specifically designed for naval service, which it designated 'fuel ships' or 'oil carriers' (the term 'oiler' came into use later).

Named *Kanawha* and *Maumee*, the first was powered by two triple-expansion reciprocating steam engines, a power plant twice the size of that usually installed in a commercial vessel of the same size. Rated at 5200 shaft horsepower (shp), this was expected to give her a cruising speed 14 knots, necessary to allow her to keep up with the fleet while fuelling. *Maumee*, however, was a radical departure for the Americans, in that she was to be equipped with diesel engines.

Since the US Navy had very little practical experience of building diesel engines, it was decided, in 1913, to send a promising young officer, one Chester W Nimitz (later to command the Pacific Fleet after Pearl Harbor), to Germany to gain the relevant expertise. Nimitz returned with the necessary plans in autumn 1913, and the engines were duly built and installed, entirely by the New York Navy Yard.

Commissioned on 23 October 1916 under the command of Lt Cdr H C Dinger, *Maumee* began life with a naval crew of forty-five and Nimitz as the executive officer and chief engineer.

Initially, she was involved in supplying fuel and water to US Navy ships during fleet exercises in the Caribbean. At the time, such operations were always carried out in protected waters, with the auxiliary moored to the ship she was supplying. Having used this period to train their crew to a reasonable degree of proficiency with the ship's specialised fuelling gear, her officers then began to discuss the possibility of refuelling destroyers at sea.

Having done some extensive initial research on the fuel systems of the warships involved, when the United States entered the war on 6 April 1916, *Maumee*'s crew was ready.

Submarine activity was having a devastating effect on the British merchant fleet, so the Secretary of the Navy immediately ordered a division of destroyers across the Atlantic to support the convoys. Unfortunately, these destroyers did not have enough fuel endurance to reach a British port, so *Maumee* was dispatched to a position mid-ocean to refuel them en-route.

Maumee's procedure for refuelling consisted of towing the destroyer alongside so that the fuel lines could be secured between the vessels, in what was a forerunner of the modern 'abeam' method. The destroyer to be refuelled was secured to *Maumee* by a 10-inch towing hawser and two 6-inch breast ropes and with all secure, fuel was pumped across through two 3-inch rubber hoses. One end of each hose was attached to the regular fuelling connection aboard the auxiliary, while the other end passed to the destroyer and was simply inserted into the open manhole of that vessel's fuel bunker. In order to keep them clear of the sea, the hoses were supported by a wooden hose carrier, or saddle, suspended from one of *Maunee*'s cargo booms. Clearly, this rig shared many characteristics with those in use today, and it proved just as successful.

Her first customers were the ships of the 5th Destroyer Division, all 750-tonners with a limited fuel capacity. In a moderate sea and with *Maumee* rolling between 10 and 20 degrees, she still managed to refuel all six destroyers in a little over 10 hours, transferring 20,000 gallons (just under 90 tons) of fuel to each vessel at the respectable rate of 32,000 gallons (approximately 140 tons) an hour. Despite the inexperience of the crews, time from approach to disconnection after fuelling was complete averaged just 75 minutes. Significantly, *Maumee*'s captain even suggested that it would be practical to dispense with the towing lines, allowing the auxiliary to maintain a steady course while the receiving ship adjusted its speed and course to remain abreast of the oiler.

By 5 July 1917, *Maumee* had more than proven the effectiveness of oiling at sea, having refuelled a total of thirty-four destroyers on their way to Europe. The US Navy was to continue its attempts to develop a reliable method for refuelling at sea, through the 1920s, driven by the fear that its next war would be in the Pacific against the powerful Japanese fleet.

Mediterranean, Pacific, Far East and the South Atlantic

Apart from the abortive invasion of the Dardanelles, Royal Navy activity in the Mediterranean was confined to blockade duty around the major ports of what was then the Ottoman Empire. Freighting duties presumably took the RFA to major bases like Gibraltar, Malta and Cyprus, but records of these activities are, as yet, unavailable.

Farther afield, Vice-Admiral Graf von Spee found himself, at the outbreak of war, in command of Germany's East Asia Squadron, consisting of two armoured cruisers and three light cruisers. All were modern ships with officers hand-picked by Tirpitz himself. This force was based at the German concession of Tsingtao, although von Spee quickly abandoned his base when Japan entered the war on the side of the Allies.

Early in October, an intercepted radio message informed the British that von Spee planned to attack the vital trading routes along the west coast of South America and the West Indies Squadron, commanded by Rear-Admiral Sir Christopher Cradock was sent to stop him. Cradock had only two elderly armoured cruisers, one modern light cruiser, HMS *Glasgow*, and an armed merchant cruiser, all manned by relatively inexperienced crews to pit against Spee's vastly superior force.

The two forces engaged late on 1 November 1914, off the port of Coronel . The guns of the modern German ships outranged the smaller, casemate mounted guns on the elderly British ships and both the British armoured cruisers were sunk, although

HMS *Glasgow*, the modern light cruiser and the armed merchant cruiser *Otranto* managed to escape.

However, the ships of Spee's squadron had used up about half of their ammunition reserves and were short of coal. A captured British freighter solved the fuel problem but, instead of sailing for home, Spee proposed a raid on the Falkland Islands to increase stocks.

Unfortunately for the German squadron, the British were waiting. On 8 December after a running fight south of the Falklands, which lasted most of the day, four out of Spee's five warships had been sunk, only the light cruiser *Dresden* escaping the battle.

Spee's defeat brought to an end commerce raiding by ships of the German navy, although Germany did manage to put several armed merchant ships into service as commerce raiders until the end of the war.

North Russia: The Archangel River Expedition

In March 1917, the Russian Tsar, Nicholas II, abdicated and a provisional, democratic Russian government was formed under Alexander Kerensky.

Kerensky's government decided to continue the fight against the Germans on the Eastern Front. In response to the Tsar's abdication, the United States declared war on Germany and began sending military aid to the Russians. Unfortunately, the Russian June offensive was crushed and faced with mutinies and desertions in the army, the democratic government collapsed, to be replaced by Lenin's Soviet Bolsheviks in October 1917.

Five months later, the Bolsheviks signed a treaty with the Germans, ending the war on the Eastern Front and leaving the Germans free to reinforce their faltering Western Front.

Strategic considerations, in particular fears that the Germans might succeed in capturing Murmansk, Archangel and the important Murmansk–Petrograd railway, led the Allies to decide to 'intervene' in northern Russia. The reasons for this operation were threefold; they needed to prevent American war material, stockpiled in Archangel, from falling into German or Bolshevik hands, the Czech Legion had to be rescued, stranded as it was on the Trans-Siberian Railway and the Allied leaders also hoped to re-establish an Eastern front manned by the Czech Legion and anti-Bolshevik Russian citizens, thus relieving pressure in the west.

A combined force of Royal Navy ships, Royal Air Force bombers and seaplanes together with British, US, Commonwealth and some Continental troops were sent into the White Sea and had some initial success, occupying the city of Archangel itself on 2 August 1918. Allied forces were forced to halt in their advance 100 miles south of Archangel, however, and soon after, following ineffective actions along the Vaga and northern Dvina rivers, the Allies began a slow withdrawal in September 1918.

Several RFAs were deployed with the Royal Navy on this expedition, although these do not appear to have had an easy time of it.

One account, now in the archives of the University of Sunderland, describes what must been an extremely unpleasant trip by an unknown Royal Navy ship, in company with RFAs *Bacchus* and *Cyclops* and the Russian Navy's ice breaker *Svyatagor*.

They left Murmansk at noon on a Saturday. The contributor, whose name is unknown, gives no date, but given the later report of the state of the ice, it must have been later in the campaign, since records show Archangel is icebound from about November to March.

Things went well, the convoy maintaining an average speed of 12 knots until about 9am on Sunday, putting them about 250 miles from Murmansk, probably in the mouth of the White Sea, near Ponoj, when they began to encounter pack ice. By 9:30, the ice was 7 feet (approximately 2 metres) thick and *Bacchus* could proceed no further. *Svyatagor*, then the most powerful ice breaker in the world, tried to break the ice around *Bacchus*, but soon all the ships were stuck fast, 180 miles from Archangel, 20 miles from the nearest land and the ice now estimated to be 12-feet thick.

Archangel was radioed for assistance and two Russian icebreakers were sighted at 8pm although it was 2am, another six hours before the Russian ships reached the stranded convoy.

At 10:30 the next morning, Monday, they tried again to move the ships, but could not make any headway. The icebreakers, with their specially strengthened hulls, could force a passage, but, in the 10 degrees below zero temperatures, it would close again almost immediately. During the day, the convoy progressed as little as 3 miles in 4 hours. With nightfall and the associated fall in temperature, they managed another 6 miles.

Inside, the ships were wet through, huge amounts of condensation forming on the steel plates from the action of the cold outside and the hot steam pipes inside. Moisture dropped onto the faces of the sleeping men all night, although no sleep was usually possible because of the terrific bumps the ships were receiving when they ran into a larger than normal piece of ice than.

Gradually, however, as the convoy struggled south the ice began to thin, and by the following Saturday, a week after leaving Murmansk, they were able to maintain a steady 10 knots, which allowed them to reach Archangel, having been trapped in the surrounding ice field for 6 days.

In the Baltic, the Royal Navy's Baltic Squadron hemmed in the Bolshevik's Baltic Fleet in its naval base at Kronstadt, St Petersburg and destroyed many of its ships, although British losses in the minefields were also significant.

By April 1919, the Americans had fought their last major battle of the expedition and they and everyone else were on their way home, 5 months after the European phase of the war had finished with the November Armistice.

Ships deployed during Archangel River Expedition (September 1918–April 1919)

Bacchus – store ship
Aro – torpedo sub-depot ship
Cyclops – repair ship

British naval involvement in war was crucial to the final Allied victory.

Land forces had reached a bloody stalemate, especially on the Western Front, and it was only the Royal Navy's ruthlessly efficient blockade of Germany's North Sea ports and the consequent starvation of her population, both military and civilian, which resulted in her eventual defeat.

Responsible for the transport of vital war supplies, the 130 ships of the RFA fleet had also played a crucial role, but financial constraints in the bitterly hard years of the 1920s and the 1930s would see numbers reduced until less than half the ships remained, and none of which would have equipment that was reliable enough to allow them to undertake a routine replenishment at sea role, which was to prove terrifyingly significant in the years of the Second World War.

RFA fleet 1917–18

Ship name	Type	In service	Left service	Comments
Anchorite	Mooring vessel	1916	1918	ex *Progress* 1916; renamed *Hermit* 1944
Appleleaf	Tanker	1917	1946	Fast Leaf class
Aquarius	Depot ship	1907	1920	ex *Hampstead*
Argo	Store carrier	1917	1921	
Ashleaf	Tanker	1916	1917	
Aspenleaf	Tanker	1916	1919	
Attendant	Tanker	1914	1935	*Attendant* class
Bacchus	Store carrier	1915	1936	
Barkol	Tanker	1917	1920	
Battersol	Tanker	1916	1920	
Bayleaf	Tanker	1916	1919	
Beechleaf	Tanker	1917	1919	
Belgol	Tanker	1917	1953	*Belgol* class
Birchleaf	Tanker	1916	1919	
Birchol	Tanker	1917	1939	*Creosol* class
Bison	Store/ armament carrier	1914	1918	
Blackol	Tanker	1916	1920	
Blackstone	Oil carrier	1915	1921	Sold 1921 to M S Hilton
Boxleaf	Tanker	1916	1919	
Boxol	Tanker	1917	1947	*Creosol* class
Brambleleaf	Tanker	1917	1942	Fast Leaf class
Briarleaf	Tanker	1916	1919	
British Beacon	Tanker	1918	1948	Purchased by Admiralty and under British Tanker Co Ltd management until 1936, when transferred to DoS and renamed *Olcades*
British Lantern	Tanker	1918	1946	Purchased by Admiralty and under British Tanker Co Ltd management until 1936, when transferred to DoS and renamed *Oligarch*
British Light	Tanker	1918	1947	Purchased by Admiralty and under British Tanker Co Ltd management until 1936, when transferred to DoS and renamed *Olwen*

British Star	Tanker	1918	1946	Purchased by Admiralty and under British Tanker Co Ltd management until 1936, when transferred to DoS and renamed *Olynthus*
Buffalo	Lifting vessel	1916	1920	
Bullfrog	Salvage vessel	1915	1923	Sold 1921 for breaking up
Burma	Tanker	1911	1935	*Burma* class
Canning	Depot ship	1917	1920	Commissioned as kite balloon ship 1915; sold 1920
Carol	Tanker	1914	1935	*Attendant* class
Celerol	Tanker	1917	1958	*Belgol* class
Cherryleaf	Tanker	1917	1947	Fast Leaf class
City of Oxford	Depot ship	1916	1920	Commissioned as dummy battleship HMS *St Vincent* 1914, converted to kite balloon shop 1915
Crenella	Tanker/ store ship	1916	1919	ex *Montcalm*; commissioned as dummy battleship HMS *Audacious* 1914; renamed *Crenella* 1916; sold 1919
Creosol	Tanker	1916	1918	*Creosol* class
Cyclops	Repair ship	1905	1919	ex *Indrabarah*
Dapper	Salvage ship	1915	1923	
Delphinula	Tanker	1915	1946	ex *Bayu Maru*
Distol	Tanker	1916	1947	*Creosol* class
Dockleaf	Tanker	1917	1919	
Dredgol	Tanker	1918	1935	Built as dredger
Ebonol	Tanker	1917	1942	*Creosol* class
Elderol	Tanker	1917	1959	*Creosol* class
Elmleaf	Tanker	1917	1919	
Elmol	Tanker	1917	1959	*Creosol* class
Fernleaf	Tanker	1917	1920	
Ferol	Tanker	1915	1920	*Attendant* class
Fidget	Salvage vessel	1915	1921	Sold 1921 to J R Thomson
Fortol	Tanker	1917	1958	*Belgol* class
Francol	Tanker	1917	1942	*Belgol* class
Greenol	Tanker	1916	1920	
Hickorol	Tanker	1918	1948	*Creosol* class
Holdfast	Salvage vessel	1915	1923	Sold 1923 for breaking up
Hollyleaf	Tanker	1917	1919	
Hughli	Salvage vessel	1915	1919	Wrecked off Nieuport
Hungerford	Stores/ distilling vessel	1915	1917	ex *Lauterfels* (German)
Industry	Store ship	1914	1918	ex Q ship *Tay and Tyne*
Innisfree	Water carrier	1915	1920	
Innisinver	Water carrier	1915	1920	
Innisjura	Water carrier	1915	1920	
Innishannon	Water carrier	1915	1921	

Innisulva	Water carrier	1915	1920	
Innistrahull	Water carrier	1915	1916	Wrecked
Isla	Tanker/ spirit carrier	1907	1921	Admiralty's first spirit carrier
Kharkhi	Tanker	1907	1931	
Kimmerol	Tanker	1916	1949	*Creosol* class
Kurumba	Tanker	1916	1919	Built to Admiralty order for Royal Australian Navy; used for a time by RFA until sold to Australian government.
Larchol	Tanker	1917	1959	*Creosol* class
Laurelleaf	Tanker	1916	1919	
Limeleaf	Tanker	1916	1919	
Limol	Tanker	1917	1959	*Creosol* class
Limpet	Mooring vessel	1915	1922	Sold 1922
Lucia	Depot ship	1915	1916	ex *Spreewald* (German)
Maine	Hospital ship	1905	1914	
Manica	Store ship	1915	1917	Originally kite balloon ship. Renamed *Huntball* 1917
Mapleleaf	Tanker	1916	1919	
Mariner	Salvage vessel	1917	1929	
Melita	Salvage vessel	1915	1920	ex *Ringdove*
Mercedes	Collier	1905	1920	
Messenger	Mooring vessel	1916	1919	
Mixol	Tanker	1916	1948	*Burma* class
Mollusc	Mooring vessel	1916	1919	
Montenol	Tanker	1917	1942	*Belgol* class
Nigeria	Store ship	1916	1919	
Oakleaf	Tanker	1915	1917	
Orangeleaf	Tanker	1916	1947	Fast Leaf class
Palmleaf	Tanker	1916	1917	
Palmol	Tanker	1916	1920	*Creosol* class
Pearleaf	Tanker	1916	1946	
Perthshire	Stores ship	1915	1935	Originally dummy battleship HMS *Vanguard*
Petrella	Spirit carrier	1918	1946	
Petrobus	Spirit carrier	1917	1959	
Petroleum	Tanker	1905	1936	
Philol	Tanker	1916	1956	*Creosol* class
Plumleaf	Tanker	1916	1942	Fast Leaf class
Polavon	Distilling ship	1915	1917	ex *Gutenfels* (German)
Polgowan	Fleet messenger/ collier	1915	1916	ex *Macedonia* (German)

Polmont	Water tanker	1915	1916	ex *Karpat* (Austro-Hungarian)
Polshannon	Tanker	1915	1919	ex *Birkenfels* (German)
Prestol	Tanker	1917	1958	*Belgol* class
Princetown	Repair ship	1916	1917	ex *Prinz Adalbert* (German)
Purfol	Tanker	1916	1920	ex *PLA Hopper Barge No 6*
Racer	Salvage vessel	1917	1928	
Rapidol	Tanker	1917	1948	*Belgol* class
Reindeer	Salvage vessel	1917	1924	
Reliance	Repair ship	1916	1919	ex *Knight Companion*, commissioned under White Ensign 1913
Roseleaf	Tanker	1916	1920	
Ruthenia	Tanker	1915	1949	
Santa Margherita	Tanker	1916	1920	
Scotol	Tanker	1916	1949	*Creosol* class
Serbol	Tanker	1916	1958	*Belgol* class
Servitor	Tanker	1915	1922	*Attendant* class
Silverol	Tanker	1916	1920	ex *PLA Hopper Barge No 8*
Slavol	Tanker	1917	1942	*Belgol* class
Sobo	Torpedo sub-depot ship	1915	1920	
Sokoto	Torpedo sub-depot ship	1915	1919	
Sprucol	Tanker	1917	1920	*Creosol* class
Steadfast	Mooring vessel	1916	1922	ex *Ohio* 1916
Sunhill	Accommodation vessel	1915	1920	Not an RFA but included here because RFA personnel were her exclusive occupants for long periods
Teakol	Tanker	1917	1920	*Creosol* class
Thermol	Tanker	1916	1947	*Burma* class
Thrush	Salvage vessel	1915	1917	Wrecked off Northern Ireland
Trefoil	Tanker	1913	1935	*Burma* class
Trinculo	Mooring vessel	1916	1922	Sold 1922, renamed *Yantlet*
Turmoil	Tanker	1917	1935	*Burma* class
Victorious	Repair ship	1916	1923	
Vineleaf	Tanker	1916	1919	
Viscol	Tanker	1916	1947	*Creosol* class
Vitol	Tanker	1917	1918	*Belgol* class
Volunteer	Mooring vessel	1916	1921	Renamed *Volens* 1918
Waterwitch	Dispatch vessel	1915	1923	ex *Resit Pasa* (Turkish)
Wave	Dispatch vessel	1914	1921	

Note: Included here is the Lane & Macandrew Ltd managed Leaf group under the later Leaf names.

Chapter 4

Cargo Tramps, Freighting Tankers and Franco's Spain (1918–39)

Despite the vast wartime increase in the number of Admiralty-owned merchant vessels, when the Armistice came, it found the Admiralty, through its Naval Stores Department, responsible for the management of very few of its own auxiliaries.

Although Fleet attendant tankers on port and harbour duties were run by the Admiralty's coaling officers, the Shipping Controller was still registered owner of another twenty-eight freighting tankers that had been purchased out of the Navy Vote and so were Crown property. Further complications arose because many naval auxiliaries were actually under commercial management. To take just one example, the Fast Leaf or *Trinol* class, described in the previous chapter, had been built for Admiralty service under one name, then registered as privately owned vessels under another so as to be operated by one of the designated management companies as 'Red Ensign' oilers. Registered ownership of the Lane & MacAndrew Leaf group was also transferred to that company during the First World War, with the Admiralty then actually chartering back its own tankers so they could operate as Red Ensign oilers!

Clearly, a remedy to this situation was urgently needed and so, during the 1920s and the 1930s, many older vessels were sold or exchanged and ownership of its auxiliaries returned to the Admiralty. In particular, before its dissolution, the Ministry of Shipping purchased fifteen new vessels, the Z tankers or War class, in exchange for sixteen vessels considered less suitable for RFA operations, which that ministry subsequently sold. Over eighty vessels were lost from the fleet between the end of the war and 1923, many of these specialist vessels designed for repair, salvage and depot work, significantly decreasing the navy's technical support network.

There were several good reasons for control of its oil-carrying fleet to be returned to the Admiralty after the First World War, principally because continuing operations with the management companies as 'middlemen' was seen as expensive, inefficient and unnecessary. The Admiralty had its own facilities for docking, refit and repair of its auxiliaries, could supply stores, particularly victualling stores, more cheaply and would also be able to keep a closer eye on recruitment. This last point was considered important since it was sometimes necessary to place tankers under Fleet orders and the navy wanted officers familiar with naval operations, particularly signalling and discipline, in charge of their oilers, preferably permanently employed by the Admiralty and holding RNR commissions. Despite these sound financial and operational considerations, transfer of the Admiralty's vessels did not proceed quickly.

Ownership of the vessels began to be returned to Admiralty in 1921, just before the dissolution of the Ministry of Shipping. Changes to management, however, could not be arranged quite so conveniently.

The Director of Stores officially took over management of all RFAs from the

Ministry of Shipping in October 1921 but, in practice, because of a lack of the necessary infrastructure within this department, many vessels were to remain under commercial control for considerable periods. In particular, a number of the War class were with their management companies until just before the Second World War. *War Krishna*, for example, remained under commercial control until December 1937.

The Director was now, however, wholly responsible for the RFA fleet, his duties no longer split with the Director of Transport. He and his department were concerned with the management, financial administration and all other requirements entailed in running Admiralty vessels employed in transporting naval stores or attached to the Fleet Fuelling Services, once these vessels had finally left commercial management. These duties included, among other things, manning, victualling, docking, refits and surveys. In addition, the director now also assumed responsibility for those Admiralty-owned freighting tankers still under commercial management as well as the Fleet supply ship net work in the Mediterranean. Quite what his responsibilities were with regard to the commercially managed vessels, however, is not quite clear.

Reflecting the increasingly technical nature of his job, a technical adviser was appointed to his staff in 1920, followed a year later, in 1921, by a technical assistant. Later, these posts became marine superintendent and engineer superintendent respectively. Curiously, the first technical adviser was Commander W Gregory RNR, while the engineering role fell to a civilian, Mr J Brown. No record remains of why it was felt necessary to appoint non-RFA personnel to these posts.

Although registered under the 1911 order in council and thus exempt from certain provisions of the Merchant Shipping Acts, RFAs were still effectively merchant ships, manned by British merchant seamen. Skilled manpower was at a premium in the Merchant Service during this period and the Admiralty, by observing the main requirements of their vessel's merchant ship classification, could still recruit high quality personnel within this contracting labour force.

The RFAs were consequently equipped to comply with normal Board of Trade regulations for lifeboats, safety and life-saving equipment. Some had also begun to be fitted with wireless telegraphy (W/T) installations in the pre-war period, invariably Marconi's standard 1.5 kW outfit, which was common to most merchant ships at that time. Later, equipment was upgraded in line with recommendation from the 1932 Madrid International Radio Conference, vessels over 1000 tons being equipped with Marconi 2 kW installations.

Post-war, civilian W/T operators began to replace the naval telegraphists aboard RFAs, although the situation was initially confused, with *Olna*, for example, having RN W/T equipment operated by a civilian. Prior to the Second World War, W/T installations were always supplied on a hire and maintenance basis by Marconi International Radio Co Ltd and usually operated by Admiralty employees, although, in many vessels under commercial management, Marconi supplied operators as well.

Reflecting their commercial origins and crewing arrangements, between the wars, Admiralty auxiliaries were regularly employed on charter. Several worked for firms such as Anglo-Iranian Petroleum Co Ltd (later BP) and Anglo-Saxon Petroleum Co Ltd (later Shell) for long periods, and even when on Royal Navy business, freighting tankers often used their spare cargo space to carry government stores to a number of Royal Navy dockyards, such as Malta and Bermuda.

Financial stringency also forced the Admiralty to place some of its vessels in reserve.

In the case of the Fast Leaf class, however, laid up during 1922–6, this proved to be no saving. Deterioration of steel structural work necessitated spending more money to return them to operational status than would probably have been the case if the ships had remained in service, even if operated at a loss. In 1926, five of the six Fast Leafs were chartered to Anglo-Saxon Petroleum until 1930, when they returned to Admiralty service. *Brambleleaf* was the exception, entering service with the Mediterranean Fleet in 1925 and remaining there throughout the war until sold for scrap in 1947.

Between 1921 and 1932, despite occasionally operating vessels at freight rates that did not cover their operating costs, revenue from chartering exceeded £1.25 million.

Few new vessels were introduced to the RFA fleet in this early period between the wars, the largest single group being the War class of standard design freighting tankers. Another class of tanker began service in 1920 when the first four vessels in the 10,000-ton Ol-class, *Olcades*, *Olynthus*, *Oligarch* and *Olwen*, were transferred to Admiralty ownership. The other two Class members, *Olna* and *Oleander*, joined the fleet two years later, in 1922 and the new RFA-manned hospital ship *Maine* also came into service, a year before that, in 1921.

War Bahadur, the first of the War class of freighting tankers, was launched in 1918, with those vessels in the same class that became RFAs following in 1919 and 1920.

They were all originally A and B class wartime standard dry cargo ships, modified as freighting tankers by the insertion of oil tanks in their cargo holds, then designated Z class and capable of carrying some 7400 tons of oil cargo in that form. Despite having coal bunkers capable of accepting 1393 tons of that fuel, all tankers of this class were oil burners, equipped with single screw, and triple expansion steam engines. Fuel consumption was about 22 tons a day, at 67 revolutions per minute, which gave a speed of 10 knots when fully loaded and 11 knots empty. This class had oil bunkers for 700 tons, giving them a range of approximately 7600 nautical miles without refuelling.

As well as their oil tanks, the Z class also had two dry cargo holds, one forward and the other aft, which were sometimes used for carrying naval stores. Easy to steer, with stable, sea-kindly hulls, many were long serving ships with a proven record of reliability, although their ballasting instructions make it clear that, while at sea, not more than one pair of main tanks should not be left 'slack' (*ie* empty) at any time, so perhaps there were some concerns about the class's design and inherent stability. They were never fitted with any type of RAS equipment.

Several of these tankers were employed on charter and their reliability is clearly demonstrated when one considers the record of *War Mehtar*, thought by many who sailed in her to be one of the best in the class.

In 1926, she was chartered for two years to the Anglo-Persian Oil Co Ltd. During that period she carried twenty-five charter cargoes, covering a distance of 133,616 miles at an average speed of about 9.5 knots. For most voyages she appears to have been fully loaded. Sadly, her luck ran out on 20 December 1941, when she was torpedoed off Harwich by a group of German E-boats.

Despite their proven reliability, the War class do not appear to have been very robust ships. Sigwart (1969) mentions that they were not sufficiently strong to stand hard driving and this is reflected in an unfortunate accident, involving HMS Renown and *War Bahadur*, at Penang in 1922.

During the south-west monsoon, the harbour at Penang sometimes experiences big ground swells. *War Bahadur* was refuelling *Renown* and with the change of tide and increasing lightness of the oiler as she emptied her tanks into the warship, she began to roll excessively and damaged her side against the warship's pontoon, which had been put in place to prevent damage to the warship's own plating.

Although her captain reported that the Singapore dockyard made good progress with the repair, in the end, nine frames had to be taken out for straightening and twelve plates removed from the hull. According to the master, the initial construction of lightweight Isherwood framing was insufficient for the job for which she was intended and extensive transverse framing should also have been included in her hull design. This story and the extensive damage caused in what might really be seen as a normal operation is not quite so surprising when consideration is given to the vessel's initial design.

War Bahadur was in the first group of War class tankers, fitted with five cargo tanks. Previous to this incident. they were found to be subject to a good deal of rivet leakage, so the nine vessels in the later group, built in and after 1920, had seven cargo tanks and extra bulkheads. Despite these modifications, apparently they still leaked!

This was not the only complaint levelled at the War class.

Cold storage provision was found to be quite insufficient when operating in the extremes of temperature experienced in the Persian Gulf, a frequent destination for these tankers. In the light of this, Davies & Newman Ltd, which managed *War Krishna* in 1922, asked the Admiralty if a cooling chamber could be built aboard this vessel.

Around the same time, the Director of Stores received a similar complaint from Hunting & Son Ltd, which managed *War Sepoy*, *War Sirdar* and *War Mehtar*, about the conditions that its crews were also experiencing aboard these vessels. A number of modifications were suggested by the Director of Stores, including fans, bigger ventilators, a bigger sanitary tank for the rating's WC (apparently the old WC invariably overflowed when in use) and a new cooling chamber. This chamber was to be state of the art, its insulation being of granulated cork, with a floor lined in lead sheeting.

Devonport dockyard hurriedly complied and *War Krishna* forthwith left for Rio, with all her modifications fully operational. Unfortunately for the crew, there appears to have been a rather significant design flaw in the ship's cooling chamber.

Cooling chambers in those days were not refrigerated. Temperature was maintained by packing ice in the chamber and around the stored food and, sadly, granulated cork and lead appear to have lacked something in the way of insulating properties.

Initially, when the ship left port on 14 August, this chamber and the nearby vegetable store contained a total of 4 tons of ice. Even so, with the external temperature a fairly mild 80° F, the cooling chamber was still at 50° F, about 10° C above freezing. Fifteen days later, the ice was gone and the temperature matched that of the exterior of the chamber. Nobody aboard was worried about that, however, because according to the master's report, the meat and most of the vegetables had all become unfit for consumption barely 7 days out of port. One hind quarter of beef which had been hung in the chamber was, in fact, found to be covered with about half an inch of white fungus!

Unfortunately, no record exists of the resulting correspondence in the aftermath of this voyage nor of any subsequent modifications the Director of Stores may have suggested. Although, it is not hard to guess what the crew must have thought!

Many War class ships remained in service throughout the Second World War, both in the UK and on foreign stations. *War Brahmin*, the last in service, was only finally scrapped in 1960, having been in the RFA fleet for 40 years.

Operation of the 10,000-ton early British class tankers serves as a good example of how many RFA tankers were managed between the wars.

Bought by the Admiralty in 1918, the first four ships in this class (*British Beacon, British Lantern, British Light* and *British Star*), were built as conventional tankers, designed for commercial operation. All four were managed by the British Tanker Co Ltd (BTC) from their launch, in 1918, until they were taken over by the Director of Stores, in 1936, although they appear on the *Navy List* as RFAs under their 'British'-prefixed names, as early as 1922. During this early period of BTC management, they were mainly employed on commercial charter and upon transfer to the Admiralty, undertook largely similar work, filling oil tanks at the navy's extensive network of dockyards and bases.

Olna and *Oleander* were unlike the four preceding members of this class in that they were both constructed at naval dockyards, although Sigwart (1969) says that they were similar in design to the *British Isles* class of commercial tanker.

Unfortunately, post-war financial constraints played a major part in their design and construction and they were largely built of equipment and fittings left over from obsolete warships and which had been stored in the dockyard. As a consequence, their performance was unsatisfactory, to say the least, with correspondingly high maintenance bills. *Oleander* can hardly have been helped, either, by a main engine bed plate which was found to be cracked just after completion and remained so throughout her service life!

Understandably, amongst old time RFA men, both ships had a poor reputation and it is said that *OLNA* stood for Old Lots of Naval Arisings, although Olna Firth in the Shetlands seems a kinder, not to say more likely, origin for her name!

Both vessels were managed by Davies & Newman Ltd from their launch, *Olna* in 1921 and *Oleander* in 1922, although Sigwart (1969) states that they were RFA manned while with this company. Presumably, this meant that the crew's wage bill was paid by the Admiralty, through the Director of Stores, with all other aspects of management the responsibility of Davies & Newman Ltd. The advantages of such an arrangement to either party is difficult to envisage, although he claimed that it held for a number of other commercially managed, Admiralty owned, freighting tankers during this period.

Management of both vessels was transferred to the DoS in 1936 and all six of the class subsequently saw service during the Second World War.

Although the RFA's role during the inter-war years was predominantly as an oil freighting service, it also operated a number of store or fleet supply ships. As well as older vessels, such as *Perthshire*, which was reconditioned as a fleet stores ship at Malta in 1925, two new store ships, *Reliant* and *Bacchus* were also accepted into the fleet before the Second World War.

Built as *London Importer* for the Furness, Withy & Co Ltd, London, *Reliant* entered service in 1933. Her conversion to a fleet supply ship for naval and victualling stores was begun by fitting out the shelter 'tweendeck with store racks, bins, containers and electric lights. She was also equipped with a large inflammable store which was provided with a steel hatch cover and overhead flooding pipes and sprinklers as well as the necessary racking, designed to hold the inflammable material, presumably petrol, in drums. With a total cargo capacity of 11,000 tons, *Reliant* carried twice that of the elderly *Perthshire*, whose duties she soon took over. Accommodation was sufficient for a mercantile crew of 143, including the sixty Maltese labourers that were sometimes carried. Next to the RFA crew quarters amidships, there were even six spare cabins for the occasional passenger.

Curiously, she was yet another of those merchant ships originally designed to run on either coal or oil. She was certainly never intended to use coal while on naval service, because part of the coal storage facilities was fitted out as the naval stores office during her conversion. Most of her service life was with the Mediterranean and Far East fleets, until 1948, when she was sold out of service, being finally scrapped in 1962.

Bacchus began service with the RFA fleet as a store carrier in 1936. In October 1939, she was fitted with a water distilling plant and thereafter saw service at Scapa Flow and in the Clyde until 1941, when she was converted to a naval stores issuing ship.

With her conversion complete, she was sent to the East Indies station in 1942, before later joining the Pacific Fleet Train. Reconverted to a stores carrier at Hong Kong in 1946, from that time until her sale in 1962, she manned by Seychellois ratings and flew the Seychelles ensign instead of the RFA Jack on her forward mast.

Early in her RFA career, *Bacchus* replaced the older RFA of the same name on what came to be known as the 'Overseas Freighting Service' run. Organised by the Director of Stores, *Bacchus* was employed on this five-week voyage between Chatham, Gibraltar and Malta, carrying naval stores and the occasional passenger.

With the increasing sophistication of warships and their improved crew conditions, in the wake of the Second World War, a second regular freighting run was organised between the UK, Ceylon, Singapore and Hong Kong. *Bacchus* and *Fort Constantine* undertook this schedule, usually managing four trips each year, while the pre-war service to Malta and Gibraltar was continued with two other Fort class vessels, *Fort Dunvegan* and *Fort Beauharnois*, operating a regular schedule of ten trips.

Later, in 1962, the sea freighting service was enhanced by the addition of two sister ships, yet another *Bacchus* and *Hebe*. Designed specifically for Admiralty sea-freighting duties, most of their bulk stores were carried in containers. These containers were developed for the Admiralty, in 1947, by the Superintending Naval Stores officer at Chatham Naval Dockyard, a Mr Montgomery. Known originally as Chatham containers, this soon became shortened to CHACON .

A CHACON was basically a wooden crate measuring just over 2 m x 2 m x 1.5 m. It contained a shelved, four-wheeled trolley, these shelves being loaded with the required stores, in boxes or trays, by one or other of the UK Naval Store Depots. Trolleys were then returned to their crates and sealed. Prepared in this way, CHACONs could be safely handled by forklift trucks, cranes or derricks and greatly facilitated the movement of stores both between ships and on to the quayside. Later, refrigerated containers were also introduced to RFA store ships.

RFA fleet losses 1919–23

Ship name	Type	In service	Left service
Anchorite	Mooring vessel	1916	1918
Aquarius	Depot ship	1907	1920
Argo	Store carrier	1917	1921
Ashleaf	Tanker	1916	1917
Aspenleaf	Tanker	1916	1919
Barkol	Tanker	1917	1920
Battersol	Tanker	1916	1920
Bayleaf (1)	Tanker	1916	1919
Beechleaf	Tanker	1917	1919
Birchleaf	Tanker	1916	1919
Bison	Store/armament carrier	1914	1918
Blackol	Tanker	1916	1920
Blackstone	Oil carrier	1915	1920
Boxleaf	Tanker	1916	1919
Briarleaf	Tanker	1916	1919
Buffalo	Lifting vessel	1916	1920
Bullfrog	Salvage vessel	1915	1923
Canning	Depot ship	1917	1920
City of Oxford	Depot ship	1916	1920
Crenella	Tanker/store ship	1916	1920
Creosol	Tanker	1916	1918
Cyclops	Repair ship	1905	1919
Dapper	Salvage vessel	1915	1923
Dockleaf	Tanker	1917	1919
Elmleaf	Tanker	1917	1919
Fernleaf	Tanker	1917	1920
Ferol	Tanker	1915	1920
Fidget	Salvage vessel	1915	1921
Greenol	Tanker	1916	1920
Holdfast	Salvage vessel	1915	1923
Hollyleaf	Tanker	1917	1919
Hughli	Salvage vessel	1915	1919
Hungerford	Stores/ distilling vessel	1915	1917
Industry (1)	Store ship	1914	1918
Innisfree	Water carrier	1915	1920
Innisinver	Water carrier	1915	1920
Innisjura	Water carrier	1915	1920
Innishannon	Water carrier	1915	1920
Innisulva	Water carrier	1915	1920
Innistrahull	Water carrier	1916	1916
Isla	Tanker/spirit carrier	1907	1921
Kimmerol	Tanker	1916	1949
Kurumba	Tanker	1916	1919

Laurelleaf	Tanker	1916	1919
Limeleaf	Tanker	1916	1919
Limpet	Mooring vessel	1915	1922
Lucia	Depot ship	1915	1916
Maine (1)	Hospital ship	1905	1914
Manica	Store ship	1915	1917
Mapleleaf	Tanker	1916	1919
Melita	Salvage vessel	1915	1920
Mercedes	Collier	1905	1920
Messenger	Mooring vessel	1916	1919
Mollusc	Mooring vessel	1916	1919
Nigeria	Store ship	1916	1919
Oakleaf	Tanker	1915	1917
Orangeleaf (1)	Tanker	1916	1947
Palmleaf	Tanker	1916	1917
Palmol	Tanker	1916	1920
Polavon	Distilling ship	1915	1917
Polgowan	Fleet messenger/collier	1915	1916
Polmont	Water tanker	1915	1916
Polshannon	Tanker	1915	1919
Princetown	Repair ship	1916	1917
Purfol	Tanker	1916	1920
Reliance	Repair ship	1916	1919
Roseleaf	Tanker	1916	1920
Santa Margherita	Tanker	1916	1920
Servitor	Tanker	1915	1922
Silverol	Tanker	1916	1920
Sobo	Torpedo sub-depot ship	1915	1920
Sokoto	Torpedo sub-depot ship	1915	1919
Sprucol	Tanker	1917	1920
Steadfast	Mooring vessel	1917	1922
Sunhill	Accommodation vessel	1915	1920
Teakol	Tanker	1917	1920
Thrush	Salvage vessel	1915	1917
Trinculo	Mooring vessel	1915	1922
Victorious	Repair ship	1916	1923
Vineleaf	Tanker	1916	1919
Vitol	Tanker	1917	1918
Volunteer	Mooring vessel	1914	1921
Waterwitch	Dispatch vessel	1915	1923
Wave	Dispatch vessel	1914	1921

Life aboard

Employment conditions in the RFA after the First World War soon reverted to their original peacetime status. As in the pre-war period, these were similar to the

Merchant Navy, with officers and ratings employed on the usual fixed-term contracts, otherwise known as Board of Trade articles of agreement or simply articles, of between six months to three years. All officers were required to be in possession of the appropriate Board of Trade ticket, for the rank they expected to hold. Ratings were now engaged from the Joint Supply Organisation of the National Maritime Board, later known more simply as the Merchant Navy Pool, usually for a single voyage, also under articles to the master. Conditions of service were invariably those laid down by the National Maritime Board (NMB) and were in line with those originally introduced by the Ministry of Shipping. Victualling was usually of a higher standard than required by the NMB, in the hope of attracting the best officers and men to crew the Admiralty's auxiliaries.

After its wartime success, the NMB had been reorganised as a permanent body in 1919. Consisting of representatives of the shipowners and a number of other societies and unions, it quickly set about establishing national wage rates for all grades of seaman, the first time such rates had ever been enforced. The board was also responsible for setting minimum rates of leave and overtime as well as fixing conditions of employment for all British merchant seamen. Due to the subsequent contraction of the British Merchant Navy, the board was run down and ceased operations in 1990. Its role in RFA operations had also become much reduced because, by then, well over 90 per cent of the service's personnel had company service contracts (CSCs), the conditions of which were determined by the MoD and the Treasury.

From 1918, all merchant seamen serving in British merchant ships were required to be registered on the central index registers of the Registrar General of Shipping and Seamen. (These registers form a good starting point for anyone interested in tracing RFA or Merchant Navy personnel.) Registers may be found at the Customs House of each port of registry or, and this is more likely, they may now have been transferred to the local record office.

Not surprisingly, the UK was not the only source for RFA recruitment. Freighting tankers employed in the Far East, for example, were often crewed by Chinese ratings, such measures having been found to be both more convenient and economical than employing Europeans. One well known, later example of this practise occurred with the Round Table class ships, which were exclusively manned by Hong Kong Chinese ratings from their first introduction in 1963 until 1989, when *Sir Lancelot* paid off as the last RFA crewed by ratings of this nationality.

Originally, Hong Kong Chinese seamen were employed in the British Merchant Navy through a system operated by the boarding house keepers, or compradores. These men found ships for their seamen and supported them while they were ashore, in return for a proportion of each man's wages. Many shipping companies employed their own compradore, although this never seems to have been an Admiralty practice.

Local personnel were also recruited for fleet attendant tankers, when they were based on the Mediterranean, Cape, East Indies and China stations. The RFA crews in this and later periods included Indian, Maltese, Sri Lankan and Seychelloise, among others. There is even a record of a whole crew of one of the Wave class tankers exclusively composed of Shetland islanders!

It was, in fact, not uncommon for whole crews to be composed of a single national group in this way, because it alleviated potential problems with diet, religion and other factors. Among such crews, rates of pay and victualling allowances were usually fixed in line with local conditions. It may also be of interest to note here that in December 1931, Sir Bolton Eyres-Monsell, then First Lord of the Admiralty, reported that in ships of the Royal Fleet Auxiliary, there were 554 coloured seamen. This figure included 382 Chinese, 139 Lascars (Indian nationals) and thirty-three West Indians. For reasons best known to him, he felt constrained to add that: 'All were in ships based on foreign stations, which rarely, if ever, visited the UK, except for repairs.'

Employment records for this period are so incomplete that it is difficult to say what sort of proportion of the total RFA workforce these 554 represent.

It was also during the 1920s that Merchant Navy uniforms finally became standardised, with the order in council of 13 December 1921, authorising the introduction of distinctive gold lace and colours to indicate an officer's specialisation. Deck officers wore plain gold badges, engineers purple, while electrical officers wore pale green. White became the colour for the purser's department and perhaps appropriately, ship's surgeons wore red. It still remains unclear when the RFA adopted the diamond that now differentiates them from both Royal and Merchant navies.

Although they now had a new uniform, little seems to have been done during these inter-war years to address the far more important problem of retaining a core of high-quality personnel. Company service contracts, which would have gone some way to address this problem, were not available for officers until 1936 and it was 1947 before petty officers who had served a full year aboard an RFA were eligible for permanent employment.

Perhaps inevitably, this led to a peculiar attitude, especially on the part of the navy, whereby RFAs were looked on as somehow not quite reliable, an attitude which had not been entirely lost among some older Royal Navy officers by as late as the 1960s, even though, by then, the RFA was almost universally acknowledged to be the most professional, efficient service of its kind afloat. Strangely enough, this did not seem to apply to social contacts. One ex-RFA officer, writing about his service in 1931, recorded that provided an RFA officer's face and behaviour fitted, many naval officers were prepared to be friendly and welcome them on board their ships. A number of RFA officers serving during later periods have also assured me that they often received a cordial welcome when visiting Royal Navy warships as well. Since the Falklands war, of course, RFA and navy personnel have regularly been given the opportunity of changing places and serving aboard each other's ships. I understand, though, that the RFA officers have sometimes been surprised at the sparseness of naval accommodation!

The Admiralty's short-sighted approach to the retention of quality personnel was unfortunate because competent men were needed now more than ever, with the several new classes of ships that were being taken into the fleet and their increasing operational complexity. The RFA personnel manning the tankers and later store ships received none of the specialist training that is so much a characteristic of today's service. In fairness, however, such training was probably considered unnecessary since the service's pre-war duties still consisted mainly of freighting fuel and dry stores to the numerous land bases responsible for supplying the warships of the various fleets, along with harbour and station duties.

This preponderance of shore refuelling points also probably explains the Royal Navy's lack of interest in developing a reliable system for replenishing fuel at sea.

The incredible diversity of bases operated by the Royal Navy during this period may

come as something of a surprise, especially to those of us who are more used to the
financial limitations that determine the current level of naval operations. Without going
into great and exhausting detail, it is probably accurate to say that, in any ocean where
they regularly operated during the 1920s and the 1930s, no British warship was ever
more than seven days steaming from a readily available source of fuel oil. And since that
was the case, clearly, replenishment-at-sea did not hold the same attractions for the
Royal Navy as it did for the US Navy, the main area of operations for which was the
Pacific, and which, with both its size and lack of refuelling facilities, posed vastly different
problems in terms of both solid and liquid replenishment. So it is perhaps not surprising
that it would be the United States, along with Germany and Japan, that led the way in
developing reliable systems for refuelling at sea in the years between the wars.

British dockyards and naval bases pre-1945

An HM dockyard is here defined as an establishment in which dry dock facilities
exist. A HM naval base was one where there was no dry dock although all the other
services were available to a greater or lesser extent.

UK dockyards pre-1900

Devonport	Fuel oil probably available prior to 1916
Portsmouth	Fuel oil probably available prior to 1916
Pembroke	Fuel oil probably available prior to 1916
Chatham	Fuel oil probably available prior to 1916
Rosyth	Fuel oil probably available prior to 1916
Scapa Flow	Fuel oil probably available prior to 1916
Sheerness	Probably joint with Chatham

Cobh (Queenstown) Ireland – fuel status unknown
(may originally have been known as Haulbowline)

UK naval bases

Portland	Fuel oil probably available prior to 1916
Londonderry	Established for service during the Second World War

UK oil fuel depots

Invergordon	Possibly in operation by 1920s
Loch Ewe	Established for service during the Second World War
Campbeltown	Established for service during the Second World War

Overseas dockyards, all pre-1900

Halifax NS (RCN by WWI)	Fuel oil probably available
Esquimalt BC (RCN by WWI)	Fuel oil probably available
Ireland Isl. Bermuda	Fuel oil probably available
Gibraltar	Fuel oil probably available
Valletta (Malta)	Fuel oil probably available
Alexandria (Egypt)	Fuel oil probably available
Bombay (RN/RIM)	Fuel oil probably available
Simonstownown, South Africa	Fuel oil probably available
Sydney, Australia (RAN by 1914)	Fuel oil probably available
Auckland NZ (probably RNZN by 1914)	Fuel oil probably available
Singapore	Post-1920

Overseas naval bases

Madras (RN/RIM)	Oil stocks held here from September 1914
Trincomalee, Ceylon	Came to prominence after fall of Singapore, although was in use earlier. Tanks were also located at China Bay in 1941.
Hong Kong (Victoria Is) at Kowloon	RN dry dock facilities also existed on the mainland
Freetown (Sierra Leone)	Established for service during the Second World War
Trinidad	Established for service during the Second World War
Aden	Established for service during the Second World War
Bahrain	Established for service during the Second World War

Overseas oil fuel depots

Kilindini, Kenya (Mombasa)	Status not known
Stanley, Falkland Is	Established about 1916

Allied naval bases were also available to the Royal Navy during the First World War: *eg* Dakar, West Africa (France) was a particularly good strategic location.
Allied and friendly commercial sources also made fuel available at numerous ports throughout the world, but these were also highly concentrated in the main areas of maritime operations.

Fuel was clearly always available within relatively short steaming distances, during the First World War and up to about 1936, the start of the Spanish Civil War. German and Italian involvement in both the Atlantic and Mediterranean after 1939 was to cause serious changes, for the worse, to the fuel supply situation.

Replenishment-at-sea between the wars

Despite Germany's surrender in autumn 1918, international relations, even between the Allies, were still marred by distrust and instability.

In an attempt to defuse the naval situation, Britain, the United States and Japan met in Washington for the 1921–2 Arms Limitation Conference. As a result of their deliberations, these three countries, then the world's major maritime powers, agreed to limit the size of their navies and the warships they would produce in future.

The United States found little reassurance in these treaties, however. Japan had taken over all of Germany's possessions in the central Pacific and was now seen as a major threat to the United States and its most likely opponent in the event of another major war. American naval thinking, had therefore switched from Atlantic problems to the vastly different theatre of the Pacific and the immense distances that would be involved in logistics supply, basically fuel, food and ammunition, in the event of a war with Japan. Fleet distributions reflected US commitment to this idea when, soon after the Washington Conference, elements of both Atlantic and Pacific fleets were merged into a single US fleet and moved to the West Coast.

During this inter-war period, the US Joint Army-Navy Board developed a series of war plans. They were called the 'colour plans' because colour codes were assigned to each nation; the code for Japan was War Plan Orange.

By summer 1924, the basic strategy for Orange had been agreed. In the event of war with Japan, the US fleet would be mobilised as quickly as possible and sent to the western Pacific. Hawaii was to be the centre of mobilisation, although many considered that the main battles would be further west and involve fighting to hold on to US possessions in this western Pacific region, such as Guam and the Philippine Islands. Given that fleet dispositions in this situation would involve distances of over 8000 miles, refuelling at sea, for the smaller fleet units at least, would be essential.

Planners on the Joint Board did not fool themselves about the logistic requirements of the battle fleet they were proposing and they envisaged a supply 'train' of at least 200 ships, half of which would need to be tankers. And, of course, that was where the US Navy's problems really began.

No peace-time navy could even begin to afford the cost of such an auxiliary force, so the planners solved this problem by maintaining that the shortfall in auxiliary ships would be met by chartering ordinary merchant tonnage. Except, no cargo ship or tanker in the whole of the US merchant fleet was up to the job.

Wartime experiences and its post-war fleet problems had shown senior US naval officers exactly what characteristics its auxiliary tankers required.

Primarily, they should have crews equipped and trained for oiling at sea, using both abeam and astern rigs. Such crews should also participate as part of the regular naval exercises. Auxiliary tankers should have a service speed of at least 15 knots (later increased to 16 knots and finally to 18–19 knots), have an oil cargo capacity of at least, 10,000 tons, a fuel endurance of 6000 miles (again later increased to 10,000 miles) and be armed with 5-inch or 6-inch guns.

Unfortunately, what the US Navy actually had, as late as 1933, were six, twenty-year old oilers of the *Kanawha* class, none of which had even been designed for speeds in excess of 14 knots. It was highly unlikely that these ageing relics could even make 14 knots, let alone cruise at that speed. And it was no good looking to the merchant marine for a solution, either, because even the newest tankers were only being designed for top speeds of 13–14 knots.

Early in the 1930s, however, this lack of fast merchant men had been foreseen by the Orange planners and they had formulated a plan that allowed tanker companies to build and operate fast tankers with government aid.

In essence, their plan was simple.

Tanker companies would build ships capable of the 16–18 knots the navy wanted, at the same time incorporating the other features, such as fuel endurance, deck stiffening, extra crew quarters, that a naval auxiliary would require, such requirements being referred to as 'national defence features'.

These ships would be either be built to plans and specifications supplied by the Joint Board for the Standardisation of Merchant Vessels or a design agreed by that body. In peacetime, they would be operated as normal freighting tankers and any differential in both building and operating costs would be met by the government, in the form of a subsidy to the tanker company. In wartime, they would be requisitioned and converted to high speed naval auxiliaries.

It was this high service speed which caused the problem.

Briefly, a tanker with a beam of 68 feet and a length of about 490 feet, would need an engine developing just under 4500 shp to have a service speed of 13 knots. To achieve a service speed of 15 knots, however, required some 7000 shp, and for just 1.5

knots extra speed, *ie* a service speed of 16.5 knots, an engine producing over 12,000 shp would be needed!

This proved an impossible compromise so in February 1937, the US government's General Board offered another way out. Merchant ships suitable for conversion to naval auxiliary vessels would now form two groups:

(1) Those acceptable to the navy in time of war; and
(2) A special class of fast fleet auxiliary that would be needed to accompany the fleet in time of war.

By now, however, the US Navy had also realised that what it really needed was a fast fleet tanker of its own.

In January 1938, after much behind the scenes manoeuvring, an agreement was signed between the United States Maritime Commission and Standard Oil of New Jersey for the construction of twelve commercial high-speed tankers that were to include several national defence features required by the navy. These features would be paid for by the government.

Two weeks after the building contracts for these twelve tankers were signed, Admiral William Leahy, Chief of Naval Operations, wrote to the Maritime Commission, telling it that the Navy Department wanted to acquire the first of these tankers immediately upon completion, for conversion to a fleet oiler.

By now, however, with the spur of increasing European tension, the US government had realised the inadequacy of its previous naval building programme and decided to act. Both Houses of Congress rapidly agreed a $1 billion naval expansion bill, which came to be known as the Second Vinson Act.

With the passing into law of this act, in early May, the navy found its size was to be increased by 20 per cent, with appropriations made available for forty-six warships, twenty-six auxiliaries of various types and 950 aircraft. This total included provision for five modern fleet oilers, which the navy decided to obtain by acquiring four more of Standard Oil's tankers then under construction, thus saving a full year of building time. Standard Oil was perfectly agreeable but legal complications arose and the matter was finally referred to the President.

Roosevelt endorsed the transfer without hesitation and *Cimarron*, the first of these national defence features (NDF) tankers, was launched on 7 January. Having completed her acceptance trials and preliminary conversion, she was commissioned into the US Fleet on 20 March 1939. She was immediately dispatched to Houston, there to load fuel oil for Pearl Harbor.

With a top speed, fully loaded, of over 19 knots, a length of 553 feet and a beam of 75 feet, she was the fastest and among the largest tankers in the world at that time.

Almost immediately, the navy acquired two more Standard Oil tankers, *Neosho*, commissioned on 8 August 1939, and *Platte*, commissioned on 1 December. United States Navy auxiliaries since the First World War have been manned by US Navy personnel and are ships commissioned into service with the USN.

Both *Cimarron* and *Neosho* were only minimally equipped for fleet oiling duties prior to commissioning because of the need to use both to transport oil to the rapidly expanding naval base at Pearl Harbor. Unlike her sisters, however, *Platte* was extensively altered after commissioning for her fleet replenishment role.

Modifications included; increased crew quarters (facilities were improved from sufficient for sixty-nine officers and men to eventually make room for over 300), RAS, towing, signalling, navigation and naval radio equipment, storage and delivery arrangements for FFO, diesel fuel, petrol and lubricating oil, improved office and storeroom space and more boats and boat handling facilities. No armament was installed aboard *Platte* although the question certainly appears to have been considered.

Cimarron did thirteen trips to Pearl Harbor, freighting fuel oil, before she was taken in to the Philadelphia Navy Yard for her first refit in September 1940. She stayed six months, finally emerging as a fully equipped fleet oiler. Not only had she undergone all of the modifications incorporated earlier into *Platte*, she was extensively armed as well .

Main armament consisted of four 5-inch/38 calibre anti-aircraft guns, two positioned forward on the forecastle and the remaining two on the after deck house, with the ammunition handling rooms directly below the guns. These AA guns and her searchlights were linked to a computerised Mark 37 fire-control system, at that time the most advanced of its type available anywhere. Secondary armament consisted of eight 0.50 cal. machine guns placed in pairs on both sides of the pilot house and on top of the after deck house.

Only *Cimarron*, *Platte* and the later *Salamonie* were equipped in this fashion, the other naval tankers being armed with four 3-inch guns and a single 5-inch. Later, in 1942, the 0.50 cal. machine guns were replaced with the immensely more effective 20-mm single and 40-mm twin Oerlikon. By December 1944, the standard armament ft for US Navy oilers was one 5/38 dual-purpose gun, four 3/50 AA guns, four 40-mm AA guns, and eight 20-mm AA guns.

Meanwhile, the plan to build commercial tankers with national defence features that could supply the fleet at speeds up to 16.5 knots was proceeding well. On 9 February 1940, Socony-Vacuum Oil Company agreed to build six NDF tankers for the Maritime Commission, all capable of the navy's required service speed of 16.5 knots. The Maritime Commission would pay the extra cost of any national defence features, such as bigger engines and boilers, with Socony meeting the increased operating costs. Only two of these ships had been completed when Japan attacked Pearl Harbor on 7 December 1941 and they and their sisters were immediately taken over by the navy.

These first two ships were commissioned as the USS Kennebec (AO-36) and *Merrimack* (AO-37) on 4 February 1942, with three of her sisters, *Winooski* (AO-38), *Kanakee* (AO-39) and *Lackawanna* (AO-40) acquired immediately they were completed and commissioned soon after. In August 1942, the last of the six, *Neosho* (AO-48) was commissioned.

By the end of 1942, the US Navy had acquired twenty-three NDF tankers from a number of American oil companies. All were brand new, capable of at least 16.5 knots and were being rapidly converted for abeam oiling at sea and armed for their role as fleet oilers, which would make them a perfect addition to the US Navy's Pacific Fleet Train during their Pacific war and final assault on Japan.

Characteristics of USN *Cimarron* class, RN Wave class, *Olna* and *Northmark*

Specifications	*Cimarron* class	*Wave* class	*Olna*	*Nothmark*
Length overall	553 ft	492.4–493.8 ft	583.4 ft	550 ft
Breadth	75 ft	64.1–64.3 ft	70.2 ft	72.5 ft
Deadweight tons	18,300	11,900	17,520	22,000
Cargo capacity	150,000 barrels	9680 tons	14,600 tons	12,000 tons
Trial speed/ horsepower	19.5 kts/16,900 shp	13–15 kts/6800 bhp	19 kts/13,000 shp	21 kts/22,000 shp
Armament	1 x 5-in LA/HA gun, 4 x 3-in AA guns, 4 x 40-mm Bofors, 8 x 20-mm Oerlikon	1 x 4-in LA/HA, 4 x 20-mm Oerlikons, 2 x machine guns	1 x 4-in LA/HA, 4 x single 40-mm Bofors, 8 x 20-mm Oerlikon	3 x 6-in guns, AA guns and smaller calibre machine guns

Note: Trials speed of 17.9–18.2 knots was attained by *Wave Ruler* for a short period. None of the other vessels in this class appeared to match this.

British refuelling at sea trials during this period reflected none of the urgency shown by the Americans.

Oil supplies to the UK mainland itself were reasonably well addressed when in 1925, the UK government set up a sub-committee of the Committee of Imperial Defence (CID), called the Oil Fuel Board (or Oil Board).

This organisation had responsibility for examining problems relating to control and allocation of oil supplies, which included military and commercial tanker requirements. Thought must have been given to the European situation some years before the outbreak of war because, in 1934, the Oil Board was asked to prepare oil supply plans for a European war, with a target date of January 1941. Later the next year, it set up a sub-committee of its own, called the Tanker Tonnage Committee, specifically organised to assess the military requirement for tankers and exercise control over the use of both British and neutral vessels. Both the Director of Stores and the Director of Sea Transport were involved with the business of this committee on behalf of the Admiralty. In consequence of the work of these various committees, both the UK's wartime oil requirements and the strength of the tanker fleet needed to meet these requirements had been calculated to a nicety, well before the start of the Second World War. Unfortunately, such calculation seems to have taken little account of the effectiveness of German U-boats.

Practical plans for refuelling at sea so as to allow the Royal Navy to operate away from its hugely vulnerable supply bases, were, unfortunately, not so well advanced.

An initial trial was conducted after the First World War, in 1923, between two RFAs, *Prestol*, which towed *Carol*. Details of the operation are sketchy and it is not even clear in what direction oil transfer took place. Three years later, a new system was tried, which involved towing the receiving ship with a hawser passed through the fuel hose. As might be guessed this technique, known as the 'ose hawser' method had a number of disadvantages and was quickly discarded, in favour of the older 'stirrup astern' refuelling system.

Real progress in refuelling at sea began in 1937, when trials began with what was called the 'trough' method. This was a quite revolutionary departure from previous techniques in that it was carried out with vessels steaming abeam of each other, in the way the US Navy had been refuelling destroyers since 1917 using five rubber hoses.

These trials and the later adoption of a buoyant rubber hose, in 1942, paved the way for the adoption of refuelling at sea as the navy's preferred method of replenishment and greatly simplified later operations with the US Navy in the Pacific.

Fleet organisation and deployments

The fleets that made up the Royal Navy during the 1920s and the 1930s were far more autonomous in all operations than in the post-war period, especially in terms of the role RFA vessels undertook.

The RFAs attached to both the Mediterranean and Far East fleets were usually controlled operationally by the flag officer in command. Management also seems to have been partly organised by the naval personnel concerned, rather than the office of the Director of Stores. Refits, repairs and other routine work was carried out locally, as in the case of *War Bahadur* at Singapore, although expenditure still appear to have been cleared with London before any work was carried out.

Freighting oil and dry stores was not the only thing that occupied RFA vessels during this period, however. The RFA *Racer*, an elderly Admiralty salvage vessel, spent the summers between 1919 and 1924 on a treasure hunt!

Under cover of darkness on 24 January 1917, the 17,000-ton White Star liner *Laurentic*, converted in 1915 to an armed merchant cruiser, had slipped out of Lough Swilly, on Ireland's west coast, heading for Halifax, Nova Scotia. In her second class baggage room was 43 tons of gold, destined for the United States, as part payment for food and war materials.

She had just reached the entrance to the lough when a tremendous explosion rocked the vessel. *Laurentic* had hit a mine and the crew swiftly abandoned ship, not however, before releasing three of their shipmates who had been incarcerated in the ship's cells.

Ten minutes after the last man had leapt overboard, she hit the bed of the Atlantic, 132 feet (40 metres) down.

Fortunately, some years before, the Admiralty had established a Royal Navy salvage section, equipped with several specialist salvage craft. Of the four vessels in use during the First World War, *Ranger* and *Ringdove* both appear to have been commissioned vessels, while *Racer* and *Thrush*, the other two salvage craft, were RFAs. At least they appear on all the published lists as such, although there must have been a number of specialists in her crew, including the master. Diving operations in general, and salvage work in particular, requires highly trained, very experienced personnel, most especially in the period under discussion, before the invention of the demand valve and with operations carried out by hard hat divers using the first of the newly devised decompression tables.

Commander G C C Damant RN, in command of the section and this expedition, faced several other problems, apart from the extreme depth.

Laurentic was not only deep, but also she was exposed to the full run of Atlantic weather, from both north and west. Fortunately for Damant and his team, the easiest access to the gold was via the entry port, which, because the ship lay on her side was only in about 60 feet (less than 20 metres) of water.

It was not all good news, though. Lough Swilly experienced an almost continual and wholly unpredictable surface swell, which meant the salvage vessel had to moored at all four corners to maintain it in position above the wreck. Surface drag on a diving vessel in those days, of course, had to be almost wholly eliminated because any movement was instantly relayed to the hose that connected the diver to his air supply, supplied by a cumbersome, deck mounted pump. Air hose was remarkably fragile and easily cut, so a stable surface platform was vitally important. Fortunately, undersea conditions were more settled and, once the surface vessel was secured, work could begin.

Having located the ship's entry port, the divers blasted off its twin steel doors with primitive gun cotton charges. Unfortunately, the charges pushed the doors into the ship and they had to be subsequently pulled out and then slung and hoisted to the surface.

The team's problems had only just begun, however. Behind the entry port there were tons of smashed furniture and waterlogged stores that had to be cleared, revealing an iron gate which also had to be blown clear before the divers had clear access to the baggage room's steel door. They cut through this with a sledge hammer and cold chisel revealing the gold in boxes, 1 foot square and 5 inches deep. However, each box weighed in the region of 140 lbs (64 kg). Despite this, by the following morning, the team had four of the boxes out of the wreck and on the deck of the salvage vessel.

Then their luck turned.

They had previously had their share of problems with the weather, mid-winter gales and snow squalls in particular ensuring that only short intervals could be spent over the wreck. Just after their discovery of the boxes, however, there was a particularly vicious period of bad weather and when it had cleared, there were signs that something had gone very badly wrong. Chairs, tables, smashed wooden panelling, in fact, everything that could float, was leaving *Laurentic*, and coming to the surface. One dive was enough to confirm Damant's worst fears.

That last storm had ripped the liner in half, collapsing her decks and moving her significantly. The entry port the team had been using was now on the sea bed and the collapsing decks had blocked all access to the baggage room. Refusing to accept defeat, Damant's men forced a passage with explosives, shoring the corridor as they went, until, once again, they reached the baggage room. Here, more disappointment waited. Where the baggage room had been was only a gaping hole. The remaining 40 tons of gold had filtered through the wreckage and become scattered over the sea bed.

Still undeterred, the team cut away over 2000 tons of steel before exposing sufficient of the sea bed to start recovery of the bullion. This could only be done by feeling through the freezing, razor-sharp sand with bare hands, rubbing away skin and fingernails and leaving the hands raw and bloody after a day's work.

By the end of 1917, when the weather had deteriorated too much to allow operations to continue, Damant's team had salvaged just over 5 tons of gold, 542 bars in all.

The team returned to the site in 1919, in *Racer*, and carried on operations, weather permitting, until 1924, by which time 3186 out of the original 3211 ingots had been recovered. In the face of mounting costs, the Admiralty decided to abandon the remaining twenty-five elusive ingots. *Racer*'s crew received a salvage award of one eighth of 1 per cent of the total recovered, which worked out to about £100 per man, valued at some £3000 today. In addition, King George V approved the award of nine OBEs to the crew and divers of the little salvage sloop, for meritorious services. *Racer* was sold in 1928.

Not all of the RFA's activities were so financially rewarding, although they could be equally dangerous. A year before, during 1927, *War Diwan* was involved in a rescue, for which several members of her crew received the bronze medal for gallantry in saving life at sea.

While on a voyage from Seville to St John's during March 1926, the schooner *Cecil John* encountered a succession of gales, which, combined with the resulting heavy seas, tore her rudder from its fixings. Her hull was also badly breached, causing a number of major leaks, although the crew could keep her afloat by continual pumping.

Just as darkness set in on 22 March, her flares were seen by *War Diwan*. With the schooner sinking under them, her crew launched their own boat, but it was smashed to pieces by the heavy seas both vessels were still experiencing.

War Diwan's master immediately launched his vessel's own lifeboat, manned by his second officer, Lester Newman, and some of the crew. This time, the RFA men got their boat alongside the schooner and took off the master and her five crew members. Each member of the lifeboat's crew was awarded a bronze medal.

Storms are a feature of life at sea and RFA men see more than their fair share, although the crew of *War Bahadur* might be forgiven for thinking their experience was somewhat unique, when an Atlantic storm tore off the top of their ship!

The old War class was on her way back to the UK, in January 1938, when she encountered heavy squalls and mountainous seas, forcing her to heave to. The storm began to worsen early on Friday afternoon and during the next twenty four hours, she received a tremendous battering. Finally, one wave, described by her master as '... a huge black wall, higher than the foremast ...' struck the bridge, carrying away the upper and lower parts, which included the master's cabin and the wireless office.

Along with the destruction of the bridge, derricks were twisted, the funnel holed, its stays snapped and the No 3 lifeboat lost. Hatch covers and storerooms were also smashed to matchwood by hundreds of tons of water which deluged the decks.

In a desperate attempt to keep her afloat, around 1000 tons of oil was jettisoned from her No 3 tank. This lightened and stabilised the ship, allowing her to ride more easily but she was still sinking into the trough of every wave and becoming increasingly unmanageable.

After firing distress rockets, communications were finally established with the merchant vessel *San Quirino*, which, in turn sent out an SOS, to which HMS *Wolverine* responded.

In the best RFA tradition, her master, Captain Rees, and his men refused to abandon their ship. Despite the appalling conditions, they managed to get her underway, steering from the reserve steering position in the top after end of the engine room. With *Wolverine* in company, she made Plymouth, three days later, under her own steam.

All of the crew survived the ordeal but the ship was not so lucky. She was never repaired and remained in Devonport as the dockyard fuelling hulk, before being scrapped in 1947.

The 1930s: Europe in turmoil

In the increasingly unstable global situation of the 1930s, the Royal Navy began to recognise the effective role that aircraft would play in wartime and the consequent vulnerability of its enormous and long established naval bases. In the light of this, the Admiralty convened a Supply Ships Committee, in 1936, to consider what auxiliaries might be needed to supply the navy under wartime conditions. It role was to:

'... consider the numbers and types of auxiliary vessels (except oilers, colliers and hospital ships) required for maintaining supplies to the fleet in certain emergencies and the arrangements for manning and fitting out the vessels required, taking into consideration the possibility of certain bases not being available and others having to be improvised, and to make recommendation.'

Formed on 5 November 1936, the committee included representatives from the Director of Stores, Victualling, Armament Supply and Plans departments, as well as members of the military. One of the committee's hypothetical 'certain emergencies' was the loss of both Hong Kong and Singapore, but the Admiralty assured its members that 'Singapore would always be available'! Some of their recommendations would later materially affect the development and deployment of the British Pacific Fleet Train in this region.

Recommendations from the committee saw an increase in numbers of store ships, particularly armament carriers, modernisation of existing shore bases and fuelling depots and, most important in the long term, serious attempts to develop a reliable rig for oiling-at-sea, although the financial climate at the time still imposed considerable limitations. Alongside these suggested improvements, the then Director of Stores, Sir William Gick was also instrumental in introducing both the Ranger and Dale classes of modern tanker, the first of the latter being launched in 1937, while the Ranger class, the first class of vessels purpose designed for the Navy since 1917, came into service some four years later, in 1941.

And in the view of many observers, these ships would soon be needed, as war clouds had been gathering over Europe for a considerable period, with the rise of Hitler's National Socialism in Germany during 1933 and Mussolini's fascists in Italy two years later.

War flared up first in Spain on 18 July 1936, when Franco's fascist Falange movement, calling themselves Nationalists but led, in the main, by disenchanted army officers, started a revolt against the elected republican government. Italy and Germany quickly began sending both arms and men to help the Nationalists, who also included most of the army. By the end of 1936, Franco's forces, having systematically beaten the poorly equipped republican army in almost every battle, were in control of half the country including the key industrial areas of Basque and Catalonia. Madrid was besieged and the war settled down to a battle for the capital while Franco set about cleaning out the remaining pockets of government resistance.

The British had not bothered themselves over-much with Spain's troubles, although there are stories among older RFA men that several RFAs were involved in covertly supplying the republicans, one or more of these vessels even reportedly being boarded by fascist naval forces. If true, such activities are difficult to reconcile with the British government's vociferously declared policy of non-intervention in Spain during this period. What ever else was going on, RFA *Maine* was certainly deployed, however, offering hospital support, while based on Malta, until 1938.

Despite neutrality rules, Spanish waters were not especially safe for British shipping. *War Bahadur* actually had five shells dropped within one thousand yards of her, while towing a water lighter through the Strait of Gibraltar. The crew of the old War class ship quickly hoisted a large White Ensign and sounded her siren, whereupon the firing instantly ceased.

After a number of similar incidents, several involving fascist submarines attacking merchant ships supplying the government forces, however, international naval patrols were established under the terms of the Nyon Agreement to enforce maritime law and prevent acts of piracy, with ships operating under its protection displaying two coloured vertical stripes amidships. Several RFA tankers were assigned to station duties to replenish the British contingent serving in this area and so were painted with these markings: *Cherryleaf* while at Barcelona, *Brambleleaf* at Oran, *Plumleaf* at Gibraltar and *Montenol*, taken out of reserve for this assignment, at La Rochelle. *Bacchus* was similarly protected, during on her normal overseas freighting run.

By early 1939, Spain was effectively in Franco's hands, while Austria had already been invaded and Czechoslovakia annexed by Germany.

In the UK, during the same period, there were several improvements and innovations in maritime affairs including the formation of the Merchant Navy Training Board (MNTB) and the adoption of a standard colour scheme (including funnel markings) for RFAs (see Appendix 2).

Founded by the Chamber of Shipping in 1937, the MNTB was, and indeed still is, the major centre of expertise on all aspects of careers, qualifications and education within the shipping industry. Although the RFA is responsible for its own training programmes, basic qualifications for both officers and men are the same as similar individuals in the Merchant Navy undertake, although currently RFA personnel take several, more specialised courses before going to sea. Even in the twenty-first century, many RFA officers and crew members are still recruited from the Merchant Navy.

Clearly, however, during this pre-Second World War period, the RFA as an organised service still had no real existence.

Apart from the new Dale class, what the Admiralty had was several commercially built tankers and store ships, most without extensive modifications. All of these ships were used to transport fuel and dry stores to the navy's massive overseas bases and fuel depots, which, with the advent of the Luftwaffe, were looking increasingly vulnerable. When the Admiralty-owned ships were not transporting naval stores, these were chartered out, like run-of-the-mill merchant ships. Many were over 20 years old and they were all slow, especially when compared to a modern warship or even a submarine.

Although, by 1938, all RFA vessels were managed by the Director of Stores, they were still crewed by ordinary Merchant Navy officers and petty officers on a variety of contracts, with ratings usually only employed for a single voyage. Little wonder then that what amounted to Admiralty policy had resulted in almost no progress being made in developing a system for replenishment-at-sea, while many fuelling-at-sea trials had ended inconclusively. So inconclusively, in fact, that a committee set up that same year to discuss the subject of fuelling at sea by HM ships decided that only destroyers need be equipped for this operation and that '... operations undertaken by these ships (*ie* all other warships) will not usually preclude them from oiling at a sheltered base ...'!

Perhaps even more mystifying is that this had occurred while the Americans were producing fast fleet tankers capable of replenishing a destroyer or aircraft carrier at sea, while steaming at over 19 knots.

So when, on 1 September 1939, Hitler's troops invaded Poland and two days later, Britain, France, Australia and New Zealand declared war on Germany, the Royal Navy was still largely dependent on harbour refuelling and replenishment and without a reliable method in prospect for refuelling at sea.

Furthermore, much its essential supplies, like fuel, ammunition and food were being transported across vast stretches of hostile ocean in what was, for the most part, a miscellaneous collection of slow, unarmed and highly vulnerable commercial tankers and merchant ships, operated by Merchant Navy personnel, without any specialist training or knowledge of what would be required of them, during what was to become the most logistically complex war ever fought at sea.

RFA Fleet 1936

Name	Type	Begun service	Left service	Class
Appleleaf	Tanker	1917	1946	Trinol
Bacchus	Store ship	1936	1962	
Belgol	Tanker	1917	1958	Belgol
Birchol	Harbour tanker	1917	1939	Creosol
Boxol	Harbour tanker	1917	1948	Cresol
Brambleleaf	Tanker	1917	1946	Trinol
Celerol	Tanker	1917	1958	Belgol
Cherryleaf	Tanker	1917	1946	Trinol
Delphinula	Tanker	1915	1946	
Distol	Harbour tanker	1916	1947	Creosol
Ebonol	Harbour tanker	1917	1942	Creosol
Elderol	Harbour tanker	1917	1959	Creosol
Elmol	Harbour tanker	1917	1959	Creosol
Fortol	Tanker	1917	1958	Belgol
Francol	Tanker	1917	1942	Belgol
Hickorol	Harbour tanker	1918	1948	Creosol
Kimmerol	Harbour tanker	1916	1947	Creosol
Larchol	Harbour tanker	1917	1958	Creosol
Limol	Harbour tanker	1917	1959	Creosol
Maine	Hospital ship	1921	1947	
Mixol	Tanker	1916	1948	Burma
Montenol	Tanker	1917	1942	Belgol
Nora	Coastal stores	1932	1939	
Olcades (British Beacon)	Tanker	1919	1952	Ol
Oleander	Tanker	1917	1940	Ol
Oligarch (British Lantern)	Tanker	1919	1946	Ol
Olna	Tanker	1921	1941	Ol
Olwen (British Light)	Tanker	1919	1946	Ol
Olynthus (British Star)	Tanker	1919	1947	Ol
Orangeleaf	Tanker	1917	1947	Trinol
Pearleaf	Tanker	1917	1946	Trinol
Petrella	Spirit carrier	1918	1946	Pet
Petrobus	Spirit carrier	1918	1959	Pet
Petroleum	Tanker	1905	1937	
Petronel	Spirit carrier	1918	1945	Pet
Philol	Harbour tanker	1916	1949	Creosol
Plumleaf	Tanker	1917	1942	Trinol
Prestol	Tanker	1917	1958	Belgol
Rapidol	Tanker	1917	1948	Belgol
Red Dragon	Fuel hulk	1918	1946	
Reliant	Stores ship	1933	1948	
Ruthenia	Fuel hulk	1914	1949	
Scotol	Harbour tanker	1916	1947	Creosol

Serbol	Tanker	1918	1958	*Belgol*
Slavol	Tanker	1917	1942	
Thermol	Tanker	1916	1947	*Burma*
Viscol	Tanker	1916	1947	*Creosol*
War Afridi	Tanker	1921	1958	War
War Bahadur	Tanker	1921	1946	War
War Bharata	Tanker	1921	1947	War
War Brahmin	Tanker	1921	1959	War
War Diwan	Tanker	1921	1944	War
War Hindoo	Tanker	1921	1958	War
War Krishna	Tanker	1921	1947	War
War Mehtar	Tanker	1920	1941	War
War Nawab	Tanker	1921	1946	War
War Nizam	Tanker	1921	1946	War
War Pathan	Tanker	1921	1947	War
War Pindari	Tanker	1921	1947	War
War Sepoy	Tanker	1919	1940	War
War Sirdar	Tanker	1920	1942	War
War Sudra	Tanker	1920	1948	War

In 1936, the RFA fleet was certainly beginning to show its age. With a strength of sixty-two vessels, its newest tankers were the War and Ol classes, most of which were over fifteen years old. Apart from the twenty-year-old 15-knot Fast Leaf class, they were all slow (10–11 knots) and few had any replenishment at sea capacity.

Lighters, tugs and other vessels on yard and harbour craft agreements have been omitted from this list. Details of these vessels can be found in the relevant copy of the *Navy List*, 'List of Store Ships and Royal Fleet Auxiliaries'.

Chapter 5

The Second World War:
The Atlantic and North Sea

Composition of the RFA fleet at the start of the Second World War all too clearly reflected its predominantly freighting support role, supplying the navy's enormous and highly vulnerable supply bases that had been its logistic mainstay since the First World War. Numbering more than seventy vessels in 1939, it consisted of several classes of tankers, most equipped for oiling alongside, although some had the experimental trough or the earlier unreliable stirrup rigs for oiling at sea, both types employing fragile Admiralty metal hoses. As well as its tanker fleet, the RFA also had two well equipped, reasonably modern store ships, *Reliant* and *Bacchus*. Although neither was fitted for replenishment at sea, *Bacchus*, the more recent addition of the two, did often carry armament stores.

Operation of RFA vessels during the Second World War remained the responsibility of the Director of Stores, who organised pay, crew appointments and stores as before. Tanker requirements for all of the services, including Admiralty chartered vessels, however, was organised by a new Tanker Tonnage Allocation Committee, which replaced the old Tanker Tonnage Committee in 1940. Any extra merchant ship tonnage which the navy needed also had to be agreed with the newly recreated Ministry of Shipping, in much the same way as occurred in the First World War. Later, in 1941, this ministry was merged with the Ministry of Transport, to become the Ministry of War Transport (MoWT). Not only did the MoWT organise the deployment of merchant ships and their distribution to convoys, but also it was responsible for designing and building several classes of wartime tankers.

Modernisation and a change in role for the RFA were also imminent, however, with the appearance of more specialised and better equipped auxiliaries. In particular, during this early period of the war, three Landing Ships Gantry (LSGs), based on the new Dale class, and specifically designed for amphibious operations, were taken into the fleet, as well as the 3000-ton Ranger class of tankers

Initially, the Dales were designed as freighting tankers, the navy having only two pre-war classes in use.

The first, of six vessels all built in 1937, was based on the British Tanker Company (BTC) type 'three twelves' design, so called because they displaced 12,000 tons and could do 12 knots on approximately 12 tons of fuel a day. Bought by the Admiralty from BTC while building, they were equipped with diesel engines, which performed slightly less well than their BTC equivalents, giving a service speed of only 11.5 knots. Bunker capacity was 880 tons and with a consumption of 12 tons per day at 11.5 knots, this gives an immense endurance of over 20,000 nautical miles

In 1939, the Admiralty bought two more tankers, of the Shell Oil 12,000-ton type, in order to evaluate their performance against their BTC vessels. *Cairndale* and

Cedardale came to be known as the second Dale class. Performance was similar to the first class, with a service speed of approximately 11.5 knots, although they were only bunkered for 750 tons of diesel. Both classes saw much service and proved to be robust, reliable ships. Several vessels in both classes were fitted with various types of defensive armament.

The third and largest group of ten vessels, which included the LSGs *Derwentdale*, *Dewdale* and *Ennerdale*, were war construction MoWT standard tankers, most of them built and acquired in 1941.

Seven of these MoWT vessels, including *Derwentdale* and *Dewdale*, were fitted with diesel engines. The three remaining ships, which included *Ennerdale*, were steam powered, their engines never proving particularly reliable, and often subject to inexplicable and inconvenient breakdowns between refits.

Amphibious warfare had come to the forefront of the General Staff's thinking, particularly in the Mediterranean theatre and in order to facilitate this sort of operation, *Derwentdale*, *Dewdale* and *Ennerdale* were converted, while still under construction, into Landing Ships Gantry (LSG). These ships were designed to carry fourteen landing craft – Mechanised Mk 1 (LCM(1)) – as well as several military transport vehicles. For moving and launching the LCMs, each LSG was fitted with two 32-ton gantries, one forward and one aft of the central bridge, each gantry being capable of a vertical lift of 32 feet.

Dewdale was a good representative of the class. Built and engined by Harland & Wolff Ltd in 1941, she was of 8398 tons gross, and was powered by a Harland & Wolff/Burmeister & Wain diesel.

Unlike the tanker versions, her forehold and Nos 8 and 9 tanks were fitted with 'tween decks modified to accommodate 150 extra naval and military personnel. Extra accommodation was also built on the bridge and boat deck aft, for the personnel handling the military vehicles. These LSGs were well armed, too, having one 4.7-inch quick-firing gun, three 2-pounder pompoms, six 20-mm Oerlikons as well as a number of 0.303 Bren guns.

Unfortunately, in their haste to redesign the Dales as LSGs, one of the planners forgot that landing craft also need crews and no provision was initially made for their accommodation. All three ships were subsequently modified, however, apparently before entering service.

Initially, the Admiralty and MoWT rather optimistically agreed that, because of a shortage of tanker tonnage, the LSGs should undertake a dual role, remaining available as tankers when not freighting landing craft. For this reason, they were also allowed to remain RFAs. Such a perfect compromise, unfortunately, never materialised because amphibious operations became so numerous that they were in constant use with the army for amphibious assaults. This necessitated the RFA personnel who were still operating the vessels learning the complexities of amphibious warfare more or less as they went along and also operating in ways for which they had never signed on. It says much about the attitude of the RFA men involved that they just seem to have got on with the job, regardless of the conditions and dangers they were experiencing.

One of *Dewdale*'s naval party, who was with her from her launch, had some enlightening information about some aspects of her construction. He was a member of an LCM crew and he certainly seemed to have no problems with the landing craft crew accommodation. This was subsequently modified again in 1943 and a workshop for the LCMs also added, when she returned to the UK after receiving bomb damage during the closing stages of Operation 'Torch':

RFA Dewdale arrived at Inverary at the northern end of Loch Fyne in July 1941, brand new from Cammell Laird's yard at Birkenhead. Of the then standard Admiralty oiler design of the 12,000-ton dwt, she had been modified to carry 14 LCM Mk1 landing craft, each weighing about 20 tons empty. These craft rested on steel troughs running fore and aft, three abreast in the fore and after well decks.

Two gantry structures, before and abaft the amidships bridge structure were used to hoist the craft in and out the ship. A folding extension on each side of each gantry, when lowered outboard, allowed the travelling crane to traverse outboard immediately before the landing craft to be hoisted. Two steel beams, from each of which two shackles hung, were lowered until the shackles dropped over a lug in each corner of the craft's deck, then with shackle pins secured the craft was hoisted, traversed inboard and lowered on to any of the three troughs that were vacant.

A hawser from a winch, via a snatch block then hauled the LCM either aft, for the after well deck or for'ard in the case of the forward well deck. Six LCMs in 2 rows of three abreast were carried for'ard and eight aft, as the aftermost position on the starboard side was obstructed by a large diameter oil pipe leading up on to the poop deck, which was used for re-fuelling aft. The last craft to be hoisted, of course would be those berthed under the gantry, in the outboard positions, which did not need to be hauled for'ard or aft. Each gantry had one crane, which meant that two craft could be lowered or hoisted at one time, but not from both sides of the same gantry at once.

The addition of all this top hamper meant that Dewdale's carrying capacity was reduced to about 7500 tons. Two other RFA's were similarly converted, Derwentdale, diesel driven like Dewdale and the steam engined Ennerdale, which arrived at Inverary from the Tyne at the same time as Dewdale, also fresh from the builder's yard.

As a stoker fresh from training in petrol and diesel engines at Hayling Island (HMS Northney), and at Inverary (HMS Quebec), I was one of the landing craft crews drafted to the two ships. Each LCM had a crew of three – coxswain, seaman and stoker, so with motor mechanics, wiremen, a seaman PO and three officers (RNVR Lieutenant, Sub-Lieutenant and Engineer Lieutenant), the landing craft party alone came to over 50 persons, add to this the DEMS party, for the 4-inch gun aft (that on Dewdale, by the way was built at Kure Dockyard, Japan in 1915) and various Army personnel for tanks, scout cars, etc, carried and it will be seen as a considerable addition to the ship's normal Merchant Navy compliment. However, accommodation seemed adequate at all times and we had a spacious mess deck on the lower level of the bridge structure, port side.

We ferried the 14 LCMs allotted to Dewdale out to the ship and commenced a long series of exercises, hoisting, lowering, beaching, ferrying stores and so forth, before sailing to Gourock and from there, at the beginning of August, to Scapa Flow for a very big exercise. The convoy that left the Clyde early on a Friday morning comprised about 20 Combined Operations ships of which I can recall Karanja, Keren, Royal Ulsterman, Royal Scotsman, Queen Emma and Princess Beatrix, all flying the white ensign and Winchester Castle, Ormonde, Narkunda, Batory, Clan Macdonald, Macharda and Silverstreak all flying the red ensign with the two RFAs Dewdale and Ennerdale. Incidentally when we returned to the Clyde after the exercise, we were hailed by the examination vessel at the Clyde boom;

'Ahoy there Dewdale, are you white ensign or red ensign?' to which the Master replied, 'We are blue ensign'.

As to the exercise itself, it was rather a shambles, but I believe that many lessons were learnt and quickly applied – Operation Torch in North Africa was only 15 months away.

Lowering landing craft in a 'strong blow' at 0200hrs in Scapa Flow and searching for ships to embark troops, then seeking the right beaches on which to land was quite an experience. One afternoon, whilst at anchor in the Flow, a destroyer came astern of us and with just enough way on her to stem the tide, a line was passed across, followed by a re-fuelling hose of the usual bronze spiral pattern. I might say here that these refueling operations were, of course nothing to do with us of the landing craft party, being handled entirely by the RFA crew, but we naturally took a great deal of interest. The destroyer was painted in a 'Western approaches' colour scheme of white and two shades of green and I believe she was one of the 'E' class – Echo or Eclipse possibly. The refuelling was coupled up inboard to the outer end of the pipe previously mentioned that passed up on to the poop, from the pumping complex on the well deck, beneath the landing craft troughs.

We sailed from Scapa Flow on a Friday afternoon, arriving back at the Clyde anchorage, near the mouth of Loch Long early on the Sunday morning. About 3 weeks later, on a Friday afternoon (September 5 or 12) we sailed through the boom and spent the afternoon and early evening sailing up and down the Firth of Clyde, engaged for the first time in refuelling another vessel while under way. The recipient vessel was a sloop, identity unknown, but either one of the fleet minesweeper sloops, such as Seagull, Harrier or Hussar or one of the larger escort sloops of the Fleetwood class. Refuelling was carried out both alongside and with the 'receiver' trailing astern of Dewdale.

That night, instead of returning inside the boom (which stretched from the Loch lighthouse to a point just south of Dunoon), we anchored in Rothesay Bay; we turned in and awoke on Saturday morning to find ourselves at sea, with the Antrim coast to port and the Atlantic Ocean ahead of us. We were in a convoy, which took three weeks to reach Freetown, Sierra Leone. The sailing was so sudden that amongst other things we had no canteen stores aboard and a shortage of razor blades resulted in nearly all of the LCM party getting 'permission to grow'. A varied collection of beards resulted. We found Ennerdale in the convoy with us, though how she got there, I don't know. During the voyage Dewdale twice refuelled HMS Wellington, one of our escorting sloops. This ship is now moored alongside the Thames Embankment as the HQ ship of the Honourable Company of Master Mariners. Replenishment took place with the ships steaming abreast on both occasions, but the second time, well down in the South Atlantic, the bow line between the two ships parted, the bows swung away from each other and the strain came upon the fuelling hose, which being spirally wound bronze strip, just pulled out and released black bunker oil everywhere.

Once arrived in Freetown, Dewdale and Ennerdale became what the Americans would call 'station oilers', being used to replenish the escorts of all convoys that put in there, from the beginning of October 1941, to the end of January 1942, dozens of corvettes, trawlers, destroyers, at least one armed yacht and other assorted craft refuelled from these two ships.

One destroyer that I clearly recall was HMS Stanley, ex USS McCalla – reduced from a 'four stacker' to a two funnels and with a British vee-fronted bridge structure. She was alongside Dewdale more than once, before being lost in the South Atlantic on December 1941. The biggest ship we topped up was the cruiser HMS Devonshire, the next biggest being HMS Sirius (I think it was Sirius – definitely one of the Dido class). In these two cases, of course, the Dewdale had to 'up anchor' and move alongside the receiver. The biggest job that fell to the landing craft crews was to act as 'Liberty boats' for HMS Prince of Wales, which put into Freetown on her way out to Singapore, and her end. About five LCMs were used and I well remember being told to 'lay-off' whilst they lowered pea-stick fenders before we brought our 20-ton LCM alongside her 14 inch armour belt! Shore leave in Freetown was only from 1400 hrs to 1745 hrs for all British personnel, but some three hours was quite enough for most purposes, including getting 'paralytic'!

Another ship I recall alongside us was HMS Engadine, a Clan liner, converted as an aircraft transport, which arrived with a convoy one Sunday morning, early in January 1942. She had encountered severe weather and several Fairey Swordfish aircraft carried in her well decks were badly battered. Here I might say our LCMs once positioned on the troughs were secured to the ships deck by chains, tightened by bottle screws and I cannot recall a single case of them shifting at sea.

In the interval between leaving Scapa Flow and sailing for Freetown we had carried out more exercises in the Forth of Clyde and had embarked a battery of the Royal Horse Artillery, who accompanied us to West Africa. Their equipment included a small tank – type unknown, but weighing only about 8 tons, a scout car and about four mobile 40mm Bofors guns. As there was no tractor for these guns, they had to be manhandled up the ramp of the LCM. Each piece of equipment was allotted to one LCM and securely lashed down. They remained thus all the time, except for one interlude. Some time in December Dewdale and Ennerdale sailed through the boom at Freetown to take part in exercises on Lumley beach south of Freetown harbour entrance, in the Atlantic surf. Also taking part in this were the two pioneer tank landing ships Bachaquero and Misoa, both converted from shallow draft 'Maracaibo' tankers and both flying the white ensign. Princess Beatrix, Queen Emma, Royal Ulsterman and Royal Scotsman also took part I think but I missed all this, as I was on HM Hospital Ship Oxfordshire having an operation for a hernia. Dewdale and Ennerdale were themselves topped-up from time to time by a series of mainly Mercantile tankers, but I can remember one of the Slavol type RFAs, distinctive with its high fronted bridge structure, alongside us once.

On going alongside HMS Devonshire, Dewdale sustained damage to the port side, for'ard folding gantry extension, which could no longer be lowered. Rumours of going to Cape Town, Durban and elsewhere flew about and there was also a distinct 'buzz' about the impending Madagascar operation, but on a Monday evening late in January, Dewdale left Freetown, accompanied only by an armed trawler. Until we were through the boom, none of us knew which way the ship would turn South to South Africa, or North and possibly home! It turned out to be 'right hand down a bit' and we headed northwards. As HMS Stanley and HMS Dunedin had both been sunk in the vicinity of Freetown within the previous two months, we didn't think much of a single escort, but the following Sunday morning we sailed into Gibraltar harbour and tied up at the detached mole there, after a very pleasant voyage

More speculation now, as rumours abounded. In the harbour at Gib was Dewdale's sister Denbydale, not converted to a landing craft carrier, but with her back broken by Italian limpet mines, attached whilst she was alongside the detached mole where we now lay.

The troopship Llangibby Castle, her stem blown off, was undergoing repairs in dry-dock, but she was floated out uncompleted for Dewdale to enter, bottom scraping and painting followed, but no repairs were carried out to the damaged gantry, as we had in the fore-peak a large number of packing cases labelled S.N.O. HMS Stag, Port Said, which had remained untouched since we left the Clyde, we all thought that our destination might be eastward, through the Med, but on a Sunday morning two weeks after arriving, we sailed from Gib with a homeward bound convoy.

Eventually sailing through the Clyde boom once more to our familiar anchorage. This would be early March 1942. We had to unload all Naval stores, which were ferried to Greenock and the LCMs were tied up in the James Watt dock, before we were sent on leave from HMS Sandhurst, which served as a destroyer depot ship there.

On returning from 10 days leave, we naval ratings learned that our three officers, the Chief and PO motor mechanics, plus some seamen stokers from RFA Ennerdale who had returned from Freetown with us on board Dewdale, had been recalled from leave after five days and were sailing in a convoy that night from the Clyde, to join RFA Derwentdale at Durban, bound for Madagascar!

In fact, on reporting on board HMS Daffodil (ex LNER Train Ferry No 3, converted to carry about 13 LCMs, which were launched down the stern ramp), three of us were detailed off to take an LCM and proceed to Albert Dock, Greenock to pick up 'urgent stores for HMS Illustrious', which lay near Daffodil at the Tail o the Bank, and which was sailing with the convoy that night. The 'urgent stores' turned out to be about 20 parcels of tombola books, which were duly delivered to the big aircraft carrier; this was 23 March 1942.

That ended my association with Dewdale and the RFA; I have often wondered why we were sent out to Freetown that winter, the general explanation was to get away from bombing at home, had Dewdale not damaged her gantry as she did, I might have got as far as Madagascar myself!

Although the Ranger class ships were also tankers, any structural similarity to the Dales stopped there.

Of 3313 tons gross and designed as a replacement for the 2000-ton *Belgol* class, *Black Ranger*, the first to be launched by Harland & Wolff, Belfast, was also powered by a 6-cylinder Harland & Wolff/Burmeister & Wain diesel engine. Her bunkers held some 300 tons of fuel, with a daily consumption of 14 tons, at a speed of 14 knots or 350 nautical miles a day. This gives her a respectable radius of action of some 7000 nautical miles and, being fitted with the same engine as several of the much larger Dale class, they were, according to Sigwart (1968) '... quite exceptionally manoeuvrable ...', although finally equipped with only a single screw, instead of the twin screw arrangement that had originally been discussed.

Cargo consisted of 2600 tons FFO, 550 tons of diesel fuel and 90 tons of petrol, most dangerous of all tanker cargoes. Reflecting this danger, her petrol tanks were surrounded by water ballast tanks, while the deck above the petrol tanks was covered in 2-inch steel armour.

Her sister ships were similar in all respects, except *Gold Ranger*, *Grey Ranger* and *Green Ranger*, termed by some authorities the G class, had Doxford diesel engines and slightly different accommodation. Originally fitted for astern replenishment by stirrup rig, these were among the first RFAs to be modified to allow operation of the new rubber hose, both abeam and astern. All of the Rangers were also later fitted with 42-foot derricks, port and starboard, so that they could dispense fuel and water by the new trough method.

With an eye to increasing the classes overall adapability, Sigwart (1969) says that their forecastles were also designed and strengthened to carry a 30-foot, 9-ton RAF refuelling barge for flying boats. The original 1939 plan, however, shows this craft stowed on the deck next to the forecastle. No Ranger ever carried the refuelling barge, although experiments were carried out with *Green Ranger*, during her service as a white oil carrier, with a 30-foot cabin cruiser adapted for towing a refuelling hose to a waiting flying boat. This craft was further modified to allow it to transport drums of lubricating oil as well.

Rangers were among the best armed and protected of all the wartime RFAs, with armoured petrol tanks and 4-inch plastic armour around the bridge, although originally it had been intended to fit protection only for the cargo. At some point before building began, those arrangements were changed and, as a class, the Rangers were the first RFAs to be fitted with this type of bridge protection. Armament varied from ship to ship, but included 4-inch L/A and 12-pounder HA/LA guns, 40-mm Bofors, 20-mm Oerlikons and Lewis guns. *Blue Ranger* was the only member of the class fitted with a Hispano 20-mm Mk 1 cannon, in her forward gun position. The combined magazine and shell room was two decks below the aft 4-inch L/A gun platform, which was mounted above the deck, and, surprisingly, there appears to be no hoist between them, at least not on the only plan available for the class as originally built.

Overall conformation was also unusual, reflecting the designer's preoccupation with wartime service. When originally completed, Rangers had the foremast on the port bow and a dummy plate funnel forward, with the wheelhouse offset to port. The real funnel, which was very short, was also on the port quarter and there were a number of canvas 'deckhouses'. All these modifications were provided for camouflage and it was said to have helped *Brown Ranger* at least, on her maiden voyage to Gibraltar, because she saw the tracks of several torpedoes, probably aimed at her, but which hit and sunk a City liner just astern of her. Quite how her peculiar conformation acted as camouflage and a U-boat-'confuser', is, however, somewhat difficult to envisage.

Initial sea trials of *Black Ranger* were successful, the ship recording a top speed of 14 knots at 109 rpm, although this was slightly below her full power, set at 116.5 rpm. Her turning circle was good – 700-feet diameter to starboard, even better to port at a bare 600 feet and she could complete both in about 4.5 minutes. A pretty good ship. Unfortunately, when *Blue Ranger* underwent her trials and the crew came to fire the 12-pounder HA/LA gun, things did not go quite as expected. On firing the fourth round, the shock wave shattered a 0.25-inch plate glass window in the aft end of the chart room, 24 feet away. Despite this slight problem, all the armament, including this gun was described as '... in perfect working order ...'!

Something similar happened aboard *Bishopdale*, on the way to Darwin, in 1943. Deck stiffening and provision for weapons was something of an afterthought on these Dale class oilers, as this passage makes all too clear. One of her crew takes up the story:

> ... The same day it was decided to fire the four inch gun which was mounted above our (the engineer's) accommodation. Off-duty engineers were to be part of the gun crew. The exercise went off alight but what a mess was left!
>
> All our hand basins came off the walls of our cabins, shower water pipes came

loose, the second Engineer happened to be in the stairway coming up from the lower deck and the shock of the vibration sent him backwards down the stairs – very painful. It was unanimously decided that the gun would never be used again!

A number of other specialised classes were also introduced during the war, including both the Fresh and Spa classes of water carrier. Later additions included several of the Wave class of turbine-engined fleet oiler and several the long serving, early Fort class store ships. Many chartered merchant ships were also in Admiralty service during this period, but as none are shown in either the *Navy List* as RFAs, they should properly be regarded as Mercantile Fleet Auxiliaries or MFAs.

Life aboard

During World War II, in contrast to the previous conflict, few RFA officers held RNR or RNVR commissions. In the 1941 *Navy List*, only eight RFAs were commanded by masters who were retired naval officers or held an RNR commission. These ships were *Bishopdale, Olna, Orangeleaf, Rapidol, War Krishna, War Nawab, War Sirdar* and *War Sudra.*

For some inexplicable reason, *Darkdale* had a Lieutenant (E) as her chief engineer, although her master was RFA. It is hard to know if this was a deliberate policy or just a coincidence, the RNR commissions these masters held being unconnected with their RFA employment. By 1942, eight RFAs were still under the command of retired or reserve naval officers, although they were not all the same ships as the previous year. These ships were *Berta, Bishopdale, Cedardale, Empire Salvage, Rapidol, War Bharata, War Krishna* and *War Nawab.*

Employment conditions were similar to those in the pre-war ships, with articles signed between the master and officers and crew for every voyage. These were invariably NMB-agreed MoWT articles and entitled RFA crews to rates of pay, NMB-agreed seafarer's war risk money and VE and VJ allowance, in exactly the same way as officers and crew in commercial ships. Admiralty contracts were more specific about the times and ways in which RFA officers could be relieved, however.

With the introduction of the Essential Work (Merchant Navy) Order 1941, conditions for the crew, at least, were very significantly improved, because it was this order that created the Merchant Navy Reserve Pool. This should not be confused with the Merchant Navy Pool, which was a much earlier organisation also known as the Joint Supply Organisation of the NMB.

Creation of the Merchant Navy Reserve Pool was designed to ensure that there were always seamen available to man merchant navy vessels and in order to encourage this, for the first time the government paid merchant sailors to remain in the pool while ashore. Permanent employment meant responsibilities, however. All those who had served at sea in the last five years were now required to register with the Registrar General of Shipping and Seamen, which marked the start of a new Central Register for Seamen that lasted until 1972, although the Reserve Pool itself was disbanded in 1946.

Defensively equipped merchant ships (DEMS)

Royal Fleet Auxiliaries had been equipped with a variety of weapons during the First World War, but, in the build up to the second conflict, special efforts were made to ensure adequate protection for these vessels.

A number of provisions were made for fitting weapons to RFAs serving in areas considered dangerous, such as the China Station, during a policy review in 1934. Weapons were generally to be 4-inch, 4.7-inch, 3-inch or 12-pounder guns. Ammunition could not, however, be carried unless authorised by a C-in-C and magazine and shell stowage was not large – forty to eighty rounds for the 4-inch and 3-inch guns and about one hundred rounds for the 12-pounders. Anti-mine equipment (paravanes) was also fitted to some newer vessels.

In order to further address the problem of arming merchant ships in general, not just RFA ships, the Admiralty set up the Shipping Defence Advisory Committee (SDAC) in 1936. Chaired by the Deputy Chief of Naval Staff, it also included representatives from interested bodies in the shipping industry. At its first meeting, addressed by no less a person than the First Sea Lord, it was agreed to set up sub-committees, all reporting back to the main body and each concerned with some aspect of merchant ship defence. These committees dealt with areas such as communications, anti-mine equipment, defensive armament, convoy requirements and training. They were also responsible for organising equipment tests, including further paravane trials, conducted this time by *Olna* and *Oleander*.

Reliant was involved in trials of a similar type of paravane equipment in 1937. Her crew achieved good times during these trials, lowering the DNC boom in about 13 minutes, while the ship was moving at 5 knots, and recovering it in an even better time of 9 minutes, while at the same speed. Manoeuvring exercises were also carried out safely, the ship staying well within the designated 'swept' area without difficulty, even when towing the paravane with the DNC boom lowered. Towing trials also appear to have been successful, although the master did report that, upon recovery, the tail casting of the port paravane was cracked.

During October of the same year, in a slightly more ominous turn of events, it was also suggested that provision be made aboard *Reliant* for decontamination in case of gas attack. Arrangements were not overly complex, consisting of the utilisation of an existing bathroom as a decontamination (D/C) station, with provision of a steam supply to the bath for decontaminating clothing and metal grids to weigh the clothing down during this process. Presumably such precautions were against gas delivered in the form of bombs, because it is difficult to envisage any other form of gas attack that could be mounted at sea. Just how effective these may have been remains to be seen, although, perhaps fortunately, there is no record of an attack of this sort being made on *Reliant*, or any other RFA.

By August 1939, the SDAC had been largely superseded by the Admiralty's Defensively Equipped Merchant Ship (DEMS) organisation, which was reformed as a section of its Trade Division. With war imminent, the head of this section took over responsibility for arming merchant ships and assigning and training both service and Merchant Navy personnel.

It is often claimed that the Second World War caught the British by surprise and it has to be admitted that armament and aircraft production, for example, was not as full a state of readiness as would have been desirable. The Royal Navy, however, was not quite so unprepared. By the end of 1938 and prior to the formation of the DEMS organisation, the Director of Naval Construction (DNC) had plans in place for adapting over 350 British merchant ships to receive weapons. This included deck stiffening and ammunition stowage.

Initially, RFA ships were equipped with a 4-inch low-angle (LA) gun and a 3-inch high-angle (HA) gun, but, by 1943, armament aboard RFAs had increased and become more standardised. In general, they were fitted with a 4-inch LA or HA/LA gun, a 12-pounder HA/LA or 3-inch LA gun, between four and six 20-mm Oerlikon for anti-aircraft defence, two 0.50 cal single Colt machine guns and a variety of anti-mine equipment. Occasionally, larger RFAs might have more anti-aircraft guns and some were fitted with depth charge chutes, smoke making apparatus, torpedo nets, ASDIC (later americanised to SONAR) and radar. In addition, many RFAs were demagnetised or degaussed, often designated simply DG, as a further defence against magnetic mines.

To augment the RFA's 'on the job' approach to gunnery, from 1939, RFA officers were sent for DEMS training, on what was termed Merchant Navy defence courses. Crew members were expected to attend these courses as well, which were run by the Royal Navy at major ports, including London, Liverpool and Southampton. Two specialist courses were also available at these centres for Merchant Navy crew members; an eleven-day Merchant Seaman Gunner (MSG) course and a shorter course, of four days for Mercantile Machine Gunner (MMG). Certificates of proficiency were awarded for both and qualified men also received a gunnery allowance of 6d (2½p) as MSG and 3d a day as MMG. Most importantly, training on anti-aircraft weapons was also provided and this was to have fundamental significance when British merchant ships, RFAs included, saw action with the British Pacific Fleet Train.

Gun crews aboard RFAs were initially meant to consist of a trained naval rating as gunlayer or 'captain of the gun' in each RFA or Merchant Navy ship with embarked DEMS personnel. These gunlayers would then be assisted by trained Merchant Navy crew men, qualified as MSG. Unfortunately, the demand for trained personnel was significantly under estimated by the DEMS organisation and there were shortages until training caught up with demand. DEMS gunners intended for service aboard merchant vessels entered the Royal Navy in the normal way, first undergoing the normal ten weeks of basic recruit training. This was followed by an intensive four-week gunnery course, after which they would be assigned to a merchant ship. They signed articles like the rest of the crew and were responsible for care and maintenance of all defensive equipment, weapons drills and training. They could be rostered as lookouts and as sentries while in port but could only be employed on normal ship duties in an emergency. Ship owners were responsible for DEMS accommodation, food and pay, for which they were reimbursed by the Admiralty.

As well as their gun crews, larger ships carried an armament officer who was responsible for all defensive operations, including weapon maintenance, although sometimes an RNVR officer might be appointed as well, designated DEMS gunnery officer. Duties were similar for both officers and there does seem to have been significant overlap in many areas.

Armed merchant ships quickly proved themselves a very effective addition to convoy defence. By VE day, over 9500 Allied merchant ships had been equipped with weapons and during August 1942 to April 1943, with some 120 recorded contacts with U-boats, seventy-nine of the merchant ships involved managed to escape. During the whole of the war, the anti-aircraft guns on merchant ships were credited with destroying or badly damaging over 300 aircraft.

Armament aboard RFAs in 1938		
Ship class	Armament	Ammunition stowage
Dale	One 4-in LA gun, one 3-in HA gun	48 rounds 4-in, 40 rounds 3-in
Ol	One 4-in LA gun, one 3-in HA gun	48 rounds 4-in, 40 rounds 3-in
Leaf	One 4-in LA gun, one 3-in HA gun	As considered necessary
War	Some had one 4-in or one 12-pdr gun	40 rounds 4-in, 100 rounds 12-pdr
2000-ton	One 4-in LA gun, one 3-in HA gun	As necessary
Reliant, Bacchus	One 4-in LA gun, one 3-in HA gun	As necessary
Coastal store carriers (Robert Middleton, Robert Dundas)	One HA/LA gun or one 12-pdr	As necessary

Q ships

The Q ships had proved a successful addition to Royal Navy strength during the First World War, which was probably what prompted their attempted reintroduction at the beginning of the Second World War. Unfortunately, times and conditions had changed significantly and Q or 'special service freighters' were to prove remarkably unsuccessful during this later war.

With war imminent, a Q ship committee was set up in July 1939 to discuss the question of the operation and armament. Little action appears to have been subsequently taken until the invasion of Poland and Britain's declaration of war but then things began to move quickly. Churchill recalled Vice-Admiral Gordon Campbell out of retirement and gave him authority to requisition a number of merchant vessels as Q ships. Campbell had won a VC and a DSO while serving on First World War Q ships and he had also been a member of the 1939 committee, so the Prime Minister's choice was a good one.

Unfortunately, Campbell found himself beset with difficulties almost from the start. Merchant ship tonnage was in extremely short supply in this early phase of the war and the situation was to become much worse as time went on. The Ministry of Shipping and its successor, the MoWT, were reluctant to allow Campbell the use of any modern ships and he was finally forced to settle for nine antiquated coal burners, which were totally unsuited for the work they would be called upon to do.

These ships were divided into two groups. Six would be used for oceanic operations while the remaining three, HMS *Beauly*, *Orchy* and *PC 74* undertook only coastal voyages. All nine ships were extensively refitted at one of several naval dockyards, their equipment including Mk 2 7-inch and 12-pounder guns as well as Lewis machine guns, depth charges, 21-inch torpedo tubes and, in some cases, even ASDIC. The last Royal Navy Q ship, which was not part of this first group, was the 2456-ton French merchant ship *Le Rhin*, commissioned as HMS *Fidelity* (D 57). She was converted in September 1940, to carry a torpedo defence net, four 4-inch (10-cm) guns, four torpedo tubes, two OS2U Kingfisher float planes, and a motor torpedo boat, *MTB 105*. Two British freighters, *City of Dieppe* and *City of Tokyo* were also fitted out to act as store ships and munitions carriers, supplying ammunition and torpedoes to the oceanic vessels. HMS names were used at sea, the ships reverting to their RFA designations while in harbour.

It was originally intended that these special service freighters should be stationed at the rear of the convoys they accompanied so as to keep an initial listening watch and then give warning of an attack. After the submarine attack, the Q ship was meant to obtain a contact and then direct the escorts to the attacking U-boat, unless the freighter's master felt he could carry out an attack himself. It was also considered, perhaps more reasonably in the light of First World War U-boat attack patterns, that the Q ship might be stationed some way behind the convoy as though she were a straggler. Here, it was felt, they could engage any enemy submarine that might be tempted to surface, intent upon sinking the apparently defenceless merchant ship with gunfire.

Unfortunately, these Q ships operated in the North Atlantic and, later, in Indian Ocean, without engaging a single submarine. U-boat commanders had learned the lessons of the First World War and reticent to engage in surface duels with merchant ships. Instead, they used surface launched torpedoes and succeeded in sinking two of the six ocean-going vessels, all of which were too slow and antiquated, both for the job they had to do and the long ocean voyages they were expected to undertake. The overcrowding necessitated by their increased complements did not help matters, either.

By the beginning of 1941, the Admiralty had realised their mistake and on 2 March 1941, sent a signal ordering the Q ships to cease operations. Four of the remaining vessels continued the war as armed merchant cruisers but they were as singularly unsuccessful in this type of operation as they had been previously. By October 1941, all had returned to commercial service, with the exception of *Fidelity*, which was sunk by *U 435* on 30 December 1942, during the battle to defend Convoy ON-154.

Q ships were also used briefly by the US Navy during the period just after Pearl Harbor, known as 'Operation Drumbeat'.

Early 1942 caught the American coastal shipping community largely unprepared for war. Ships were on passage showing normal navigation lights and following the usual coastal routes, which were marked by lit navigation buoys, while ashore there was no blackout.

Between New York and Cape Race, in those early weeks the U-boats decimated US coastal shipping. In response, the US Navy fitted out a number of Q ships, and deployed them both independently along the coast and as part of the coastal convoys. No American Q ship ever reported even sighting a submarine and by May 1942, coastal air and sea patrols had rendered the eastern seaboard too dangerous for continued U-boat activity. The Q ships continued in service until near the end of the war, when the remaining four were removed from the *Naval Vessel Register*.

British Q ships

Commissioned as	Served as (RFA)	Eventual fate
HMS *Botlea*	*Lambridge*, then as armed merchant cruiser	Scuttled 1945 with poison gas shells
HMS *Cape Howe*	*Prunella*	Sunk 21 June 1940
HMS *Cape Sable*	*Cyprus*, then as armed merchant cruiser	Returned to normal freighting
HMS *City of Durban*	*Brutus*, then as armed merchant cruiser	Returned to normal freighting
HMS *King Gruffydd*	*Maunder*, then as armed merchant cruiser	Torpedoed and sunk 17 March 1943, while on normal convoy duty
HMS *Willamette Valley*	*Edgehill*	Sunk 29 June 1940
HMS *Beauly*	*Looe*	Returned to normal freighting
HMS *Orchy*	*Antoine*	Returned to normal freighting
HMS *PC 74*	*Chatsgrove*	Returned to normal freighting

Special store ships	Served as (RFA)	Eventual fate
City of Dieppe	*City of Dieppe*	Returned to normal freighting
City of Tokio	*City of Tokyo*	Returned to normal freighting

US Q ships

Original name	Served as	Comments
Wave (Boston beam trawler)	USS *Captor* (PYC 40)	Returned to normal duties
Evelyn	USS *Asterion* (AK 100)	Returned to normal freighting
Carolyn	USS *Atik* (AK 101)	Sunk on first mission, 26 March 1942
Gulf Dawn (tanker)	USS *Big Horn*	Returned to normal freighting
Irene Myrtle (schooner)	USS *Irene Forsythe* (IX 93)	Returned to normal freighting

Convoys on which British Q ships sailed

Ship name	Convoy	Route	Departure date
City of Tokio	OB21	Liverpool (coastwise)	17 October 1939
Lambridge	HX69	Halifax–Liverpool	28 August 1940
City of Dieppe	HX193	Halifax–Liverpool	7 June 1942
City of Dieppe	HX194	Halifax–Liverpool	14 June 1942
City of Dieppe	OS39	Liverpool–Freetown	30 August 1942
City of Dieppe	KMS17	Liverpool–Algiers	18 June 1943

The Atlantic

Convoy operations and escort oilers

By far the greater part of the navy's duties during the war in both the Atlantic and northern Russia consisted of acting as convoy escorts. They defended the seemingly endless stream of ships crossing the North Atlantic from US ports, ferrying material coastwise around Britain or on the round trip north to the north Russia ports.

The Atlantic war began disastrously for the Royal Navy. Both the aircraft carrier *Courageous* and the battleship *Royal Oak* were sunk in autumn 1939, the battleship actually being torpedoed by the *U 47* in the supposedly impregnable anchorage of Scapa Flow. In September of the same year, German submarines also sunk twenty-six British merchant ships, without warning, despite having signed a convention to the effect that 'persons embarked on merchant ships must be safeguarded before these ships are sunk'.

Maintaining the supply of food and materials into Britain was of the foremost importance, however, so in the light of these losses and drawing on expertise gained in the previous war, the British sailed their slower ships in convoys; large formations of anything up to sixty ships, protected by anti-submarine warship escorts. Faster ships, capable of more than 15 knots, were allowed to sail alone but by the end of 1939, German submarines had sunk over one hundred ships sailing independently with the loss of only four of those sailing in convoy.

Despite these precautions, initial merchant ships losses, even in convoy, were still heavy because a lack of fast, long-range escorts meant that the navy could only maintain convoy escorts into the North Atlantic for about one hundred miles west of Ireland. After that, vessels scattered and it was, literally, every ship for itself.

By June 1940, the area covered had only been extended by about 500 miles. This was more than counterbalanced by the availability of French and Norwegian submarine bases after Dunkirk and the occupation of France, together with the increased range of the new German U-boats. Unlike the previous war, during the Second World War, U-boats tended to attack merchant ships while on the surface, which meant that the only British detection system, ASDIC (later SONAR), could not find them. Moreover, as soon as he had enough submarines, Dönitz organised his appallingly effective 'wolf pack' system. In essence, this was simple. A U-boat, finding a convoy, radioed its position, and all the available submarines then converged on it. With nightfall, they attacked. And they kept on attacking, and sinking ships, until their torpedoes were gone.

These combined factors meant that, in April 1941, U-boats and Focke-Wulf 200 long-range bombers sank over one hundred Allied ships, mostly British, a record for any month of the war. And to make matters worse, in June of that year, the terrible Russian convoys also began. Despite everything the navy and RAF could do, Britain was starving to death and, although the United States entered the war in December 1941, the Battle of the Atlantic remained at a critical stage.

Events might still have turned either way, especially as, to begin with, the United States had convoy escort problems of its own.

Chapter 6

The Atlantic: Turning the Tide

The United States had been supplying Britain with food and armaments since the fall of Dunkirk, first on a 'cash-and-carry' basis, which rapidly depleted UK dollar reserves, and then on the more advantageous 'lend-lease'. Concrete help in the Atlantic war, however, began clandestinely, early in 1941. Senior officers from Britain and the United States met in Washington during January to discuss the form of their joint strategy, if and when the United States became involved in the European war. Out of these discussions emerged an Anglo-US accord called the ABC-1 Staff Agreement, which, among other things, assigned to America the role of protecting Atlantic shipping.

Within a month, a US Commander-in-Chief, Atlantic Fleet, had been appointed and by March, a support force of twenty-seven destroyers and four squadrons of twelve Catalina flying boats were training for escort work. Roosevelt established America as Greenland's protector in April after signing an agreement with the Danish government-in-exile to that effect and two months later, in June, he sent the First Brigade of the US Marine Corps to relieve the British garrison of Iceland. American ships and aircraft began Atlantic escort duty, between Iceland and the United States, in July 1941 and US Navy ships were assigned to full time convoy escort duty soon after Hitler declared war on the US in December 1941. At that point, Dönitz began his attacks on America's largely defenceless coastal convoys, which then also became in desperate need of warship protection.

The US Navy had been preparing for its Pacific war since 1920, by including refuelling operations in all their exercises and designing their post-First World War destroyers with a cruising range of 5500 nautical miles, at 15 knots, running straight in fair weather.

Unfortunately, their fuel consumption calculations proved sadly overoptimistic, it being impossible to take into account the fuel demands of a destroyer on escort duty. This sometimes required steaming at an average of 20 knots, with long periods at 30 knots, putting up fuel consumption and reducing the escort's range accordingly, often to less than 4000 nautical miles. The US Navy was thus forced to operate their purpose-built oilers as part of many of the convoys which their destroyers escorted, making them unavailable for duty with their own USN Pacific Fleet Train.

To make matters worse, British experience and ship losses had made it clear that air cover for convoys was essential. With this in mind, the US Navy began a program of converting a number of their fast merchant ships to aircraft carriers. Lack of merchant tonnage meant that four of the US Navy's *Cimarron* class fast fleet oilers were included in this programme, along with a number of the 500-feet long, 16,000-ton freighting tankers designated C3, which reduced their oiler complement still further. The four *Cimarron* class vessels proved a lucky choice, however, because not only did their twin-screw design give them better mobility than the C3s, but they were also able to act as convoy escort oilers so their refuelling capacity was not lost after all.

Escort deployments changed after the Atlantic convoy conference of March 1943, with the British and Canadian navies assuming complete responsibility for the North Atlantic, from that date.

As the need for escort refuelling became vital, RFAs were frequently deployed as escort oilers on these Atlantic convoys. Both trough and stirrup methods were used, although while these techniques employed the Admiralty 5-inch metal hose, it was far from a routine procedure. Introduction of the rubber hose, in 1943, simplified matters tremendously and made full escort cover possible, since the crossing from Halifax or the American ports could not be done without refuelling the warships.

Admiralty tankers equipped for RAS were in very short supply, however, and with convoys sometimes sailing at a rate of ten or twelve a week, navy oilers could not be found for all of them. Consequently, the majority of tankers used for refuelling the Atlantic escorts were not RFAs. They were what came to be known as 'convoy escort oilers' and most were simply new, large, fast tankers modified for refuelling by deploying a 5-inch hose over the stern to the receiving warship.

Development of the convoy escort oiler began in 1941, when an RFA oiler, equipped for fuelling abeam, was stationed at Sierra Leone and used to refuel convoys leaving Freetown. Buoyant 5-inch (13-cm) rubber hose began to be produced during the spring of 1942, as a result of trials aboard the captured German oiler *Lothringen*. After further successful trials of British manufactured hose aboard *Eaglesdale*, commercial tankers began to be fitted for fuelling astern using this hose. Eventually, this was to become the standard method, although early fears of a rubber shortage meant that canvas hoses often had to be substituted for the superior rubber type.

Although trials of several different refuelling rigs were made, these escort oilers were initially equipped with one of two types of astern refuelling gear; platform, stirrup rail and buoyant hose or 'emergency outfit'. This emergency outfit consisted of deck mounted wooden or steel rollers supporting a bouyant hose, which was attached to a hawser and then streamed through a roller fairlead. Necessary ancillary equipment, pipework, valves, with sometimes an additional pump, was also included in the installation. The 'outfit' proved so easy to install and use that it soon became the standard type of oiling at sea rig fitted to convoy escort oilers. 'Blondin' rigs were also considered, according, to Admiralty documents, but never extensively used.

Provision of these convoy escort oilers was initially the responsibility of the Director of Stores. Unfortunately, because of the number of departments involved, organisation of oiling at sea facilities in Atlantic convoys became so confused and inadequate that, in February 1943, it was decided to place overall responsibility with the Director of Trade Division (DTD) of the Admiralty. The DTD began by organising the appointment of escort oiler supervising officers or EOSOs at every major port where convoys were assembled. Although officially staff officers attached to the flag officer in charge of convoys (FOIC), these officers were actually responsible to DTD for oiling at sea operations. They were usually naval officers, lieutenant-commander or commander in rank, although EOSO (Glasgow) was an RFA master.

There then began what can only be described as a running fight between DTD and the Ministry of War Transport (MoWT) for the UK's available tankers.

The DTD wanted either; at least fifty escort oilers permanently assigned to that duty and removed from freighting duties completely or eighty fully equipped oilers that could also be used by MoWT for freighting. This would allow what the Navy regarded as the minimum of two escort oilers for each convoy to be reached. Tankers were always in short supply throughout the war, however, which meant that DTD could only order the necessary oiling at sea gear to be installed during a scheduled refit. As well as the problem of equipping escort oilers, the MoWT's responsibilities for ensuring sufficient UK oil reserves often forced it to prioritise fuel requirements over a convoy's need for an escort oiler, adding to the navy's problems.

Trade Division's answer to this situation was simple. RFA masters and officers had previously been appointed as technical officers by the DoS and, with help from some of these individuals, the DTD began installing outfits into as many tankers as they could get their hands on. In the beginning, most of the escort oilers had emergency rigs, which in some cases consisted simply of a few lengths of canvas hose, laid over the stern rail. By August 1943, thirty-nine ships had been fitted, although there was a continual drain on the DTD's resources as equipped escort oilers and more importantly, their trained crews, were removed from the escort oiler force by the MoWT, which assigned them to other duties. Polite letters exchanged between senior members of the Admiralty and the head of the MoWT resulted in the suggestion by the latter that the Admiralty was overestimating their escort oiler requirement and that perhaps the Americans could be persuaded to supply a few more tankers? The MoWT never yielded from its position that all chartered tankers were Red Ensign vessels and so must remain at its sole disposal. Nor, according to Admiralty papers, were they particularly receptive to the navy's contention that escort oilers were doing a vital service for every ship in the convoys they accompanied.

By the end of the war, 144 ships had been fitted with RAS gear, including eight Liberty ships. Ninety-one were available for the Atlantic, although the DTD acknowledged that at least thirty of these were of 'very partial efficiency'. Despite these very significant problems, the MoWT was still requisitioning oilers without more than a cursory acknowledgement of escort requirements.

Bad feeling between the two departments appears to have run high, with little regard for each other's problems. A flavour of this comes through in a paragraph from the Admiralty's final report on *Oiling at Sea in Trade Convoys* (PRO:ADM 116/4982), '... by plugging away at new fittings, we managed to make good the losses caused by MoWT withdrawals, and to build up a net working strength which did the work, although on the slightest of margins'.

As well as their convoy replenishment operations, RFA vessels were sometimes deployed in both Atlantic and coastal convoys on normal freighting runs. Those on coastal trips were frequently forced to endure the fire-storm in the infamous 'Hell fire Corner' off Dover and a number were lost there and in the Atlantic.

In a peculiar twist of fate, *War Sepoy* was sunk in 1940, while in Dover Harbour. An air raid on 19 July damaged the old tanker so badly that she could not be moved and during a subsequent air raid, on the 25th, she sustained further damage, causing her to burn out and break in two. Subsequently, she was filled with concrete and used to block the western harbour entrance. Three other War class ships were also sunk during the Second World War: *War Mehtar*, torpedoed off Great Yarmouth in December 1941, *War Diwan*, mined in the Scheldt estuary in December 1944 and *War Sirdar*, sunk, while under Japanese control, by a US Navy submarine.

Aldersdale, *Oligarch* and several of the Ranger class also accompanied twenty-three of the seventy-eight Russian (or Arctic) convoys. This included the infamous convoy

PQ17, in which twenty-four of the thirty-four merchant ships in the group, including *Aldersdale*, were sunk.

Convoy PQ17 left Hvalfjord, Iceland on 27 June 1942, bound for Archangel. Shortly after leaving the Denmark Strait and heading into open sea, the convoy was spotted and shadowed by *U 456*. *Grey Ranger* had previously been damaged by collision with an iceberg and it was decided that she should maintain a fuelling position north-east of Jan Mayen Island while *Aldersdale* took over her refuelling duties.

She began operations at 0605 on 1 July, refuelling a succession of British and US warships until 2300, with supply rates between 72 tons and 130 tons per hour for the Royal Navy ships and 213 tons per hour to the Americans. She commenced fuelling again on 3 July at 1450, continuing until 0625 on the following morning, refuelling at least seventeen ships during those two periods (more may actually have been refuelled but the Admiralty record is unclear on this point).

On the evening of the 4th, the convoy was ordered to scatter due to reports of heavy enemy activity. *Aldersdale*'s master gave the time of this communication as 1800, in the form of a signal from the commodore's ship. She appears to have spent the night alone, before establishing 'sign 1' communication with one of the escorts, HMS *Salamander*, at about 1430 on the 5th.

Forty minutes later, at 1510, four aircraft were seen approaching from astern. Two attacked from that direction and, despite the ship's gun crews opening fire with all her armament that would bear, one aircraft managed to drop three bombs that exploded right under the ship. This completely disabled the main engines and caused extensive damage to the engine room, boiler room and after pump room.

With *Aldersdale* making water fast into the engine room, the entire crew abandoned ship, using three of her lifeboats and being quickly picked up by *Salamander*, which was standing by. Almost immediately, the master, chief officer, chief engineer and several volunteers reboarded her to see if she could be towed. Unfortunately, she was too badly damaged and the master's party returned to *Salamander*, which attempted unsuccessfully to sink the tanker with gunfire and depth charges. She was still afloat two days later, on 7 July, when she was torpedoed and sunk by the German *U 457*. Her master, chief engineer and chief officer received the DSC for their actions and her bo'sun and one of the pumpmen received the DSM.

Gray Ranger was also lost on an Arctic convoy, in September 1942. Barely a year old, she was fitted with new and experimental oiling-at-sea equipment, including the first successful design of self-tensioning winch, which made her loss even more unfortunate.

Gray Ranger left Iceland as part of convoy QP14, acting as escort oiler. She had reached Arctic waters, just south of Jan Mayen Island, when she was torpedoed by *U 435* at about 0630. Her engine was completely wrecked and since any effort to tow her by her accompanying sister ships would have been extremely dangerous, due to presence of enemy submarines, she was abandoned and sunk by naval gunfire. Her crew was picked up by accompanying vessels in the convoy. Casualties were three officers, including the radio officer, and three crewmen killed, one officer injured. The rest of the crew, including the master, chief engineer and her DEMS crew were landed safely.

Not all convoys were as disastrous as PQ17. However, ships on these Arctic trips all endured atrocious weather, freezing seas and continual threats from surface vessels, submarine and aircraft during their voyages from Iceland, and later Loch Ewe, to the Soviet ports of Archangel and Murmansk. Adding to the enemy's activities, the cold was so intense that even touching a metal surface with an ungloved hand would result in the skin being literally ripped from the fingers.

Novels and films of the time notwithstanding, it should not be thought that only British and US merchant ships sailed on the Atlantic and Russian convoys.

Chartered merchant ships, even those equipped for escort oiling or in Admiralty service, came from a variety of sources during war. An especially large proportion was from Scandinavian countries, including Norway, which made 74 per cent of her ocean-going merchant fleet available to the Allies.

Norway was overrun and occupied early in spring 1940. Within weeks, the Norwegian government had requisitioned all Norwegian merchant vessels outside of home waters and turned their operation over to the newly formed Norwegian Shipping and Trade Mission (Nortraship), which had been set up in London. Run by the Norwegian minister of shipping, Oivind Lorentzen, Nortraship chartered vessels to British and US government departments, which included the Admiralty, as well as private tanker companies.

Ownership of all Norwegian vessels during this period remained with their original owners. Neither the *Navy List* for 1941 or 1942 show any Norwegian ship listed as an Admiralty auxiliary nor does Lloyd's Register book show any Norwegian ship registered to the Admiralty as owner. RFAs for the same period show the 'Admiralty' as registered owner in Lloyd's Register book and they are listed as auxiliaries in the *Navy List*.

Norwegian merchant ships in Admiralty service were employed as MFAs, exactly within the meaning of Ewan MacGregor's 1905 letter, chartered when the navy needed extra tanker tonnage. This also applies to the other foreign ships chartered for Admiralty service, such as the Danish motor tanker *Aase Mærsk*, which served as an armed escort oiler with the Pacific Fleet Train, although she was also an MFA. One notable exception is the small Dutch tanker *Ingeborg*, which was taken over, registered and manned by the Admiralty in 1940. Significantly, she does appear in the *Navy List* as an RFA.

By the end of 1943, Atlantic convoy duty was beginning to become almost a matter of routine. More than that, the Royal Navy was on the offensive. Development of a radar set small enough to be carried by boat or aircraft and the capture of an 'Enigma' decoding machine had turned the tide decisively in Britain's favour.

Capture of Enigma gave the Admiralty detailed knowledge of the U-boat dispositions as soon as the submarines' crews themselves had it. This enabled the bigger, faster, better armed escorts and small aircraft carriers that were coming into service, to destroy the U-boats 'wolf-packs' before they could launch an attack. Unlike in 1941, an attack on a U-boat in 1943 almost certainly meant a destroyed U-boat and the Royal Navy, characteristically, took full and ruthless advantage of their superior knowledge and equipment.

Admiral Dönitz, the submariner's commander, made the entire extent of the problem clear to his Fuhrer in May, 1943: '... what is decisive is that enemy aircraft are equipped with a new location device which enables them to detect and attack submarines on the surface in any weather conditions ... much the largest number of submarines are being sunk by aircraft'.

Of course. it is quite clear now that Dönitz was totally unaware that the British had captured an Enigma decoding machine and were also reading his messages, as well as spotting his U-boats with their radar.

In May, German submarine losses rose from about 13 per cent of those at sea to slightly over 30 per cent, a sure sign of the effectiveness of the British response. By September 1943, the German submarines had lost the offensive in the Atlantic war and were never able to dominate that theatre again.

The U-boats sunk 2828 Allied merchant ships and 145 warships by the end of the war and, in return, the Allied navies destroyed 785 U-boats out of a fleet of 1162. Over 32,000 allied merchant seamen died at sea during the war, all of them volunteers, out of a total 145,000, an overall casualty rate higher than any of the armed services. And able seamen did all this for £9 per month and half a crown per day danger money.

Their sacrifice is commemorated at a number of memorials in the UK and abroad, in particular, the Tower Hill Memorial, London (known also as the Merchant Navy Memorial).

Second World War Atlantic and Arctic convoys involving RFAs

Convoys during WW2 were all given an identification code. This consisted of a two letter prefix, occasionally three, and a number. In some cases there would be a letter suffix to the number; eg PQ14, WVP 21 and JW51A.

Convoys listed here are identified simply by their identification codes and only those with more than two convoys in a series are included. Numbers in brackets indicate number of convoys in this series, accompanied by RFAs. (EO) indicates ship was escort oiler.

Atlantic convoys

CU: New York–Liverpool, 1944–5 (5)
Wave Monarch, Wave Emperor

HX: New York/Halifax–Liverpool/Dover, 1939–44 (20)
Abbeydale, Aldersdale, Arndale, Cairndale, Darkdale, Delphinula, Denbydale, Echodale, Empire Salvage, Oleander, Oligarch, Olwen, Olynthus, Orangeleaf, Scottish American

OA: River Thames–northern UK ports, 1940 (5)
Abbeydale, Delphinula, Prestol, Robert Dundas

OB/ON: Liverpool–various ports, 1939–45 (27)
Abbeydale, Aldersdale, Amdale, Bishopdale, British Lady (EO), *Cairndale, Cedardale, Darkdale, Delphinula, Denbydale, Derwentdale, Echodale, Oleander, Oligarch*

RFAs also formed part of Welsh, Irish and American coastal convoys

Russian convoys
PQ/JW: Iceland–Russia (Archangel/Murmansk), 1941–5) (13)
Aldersdale (EO), *Black Ranger* (EO), *Blue Ranger* (EO), *Gray Ranger* (EO), *Oligarch*

QP/RA: Russia–Iceland, 1941–5 (8)
Black Ranger (EO), *Blue Ranger* (EO), *Gray Ranger* (EO), *Oligarch*

RU: Iceland (Reykjavik)–Loch Ewe, 1942–4 (6)
Belgol, *Blue Ranger* (EO), *Fortol*, *Freshlake*, *Rapidol*, *War Bharata*

Surface warfare and the German 'super battleships'

German U-boats and 'wolf pack tactics' were the navy's main problem during convoy voyages, but adding to these dangers were the German surface raiders. Fast, heavily armed battleships, heavy cruisers and pocket battleships, potentially, they presented a continual threat to allied shipping.

Convinced that his ships could never match the Royal Navy on the surface, Grand Admiral Erich Raeder, C-in-C of the German navy had, early in the war, advocated destroying Britain's merchant fleet. This would break the fragile lifeline of her overseas trade, and condemn the country to slow starvation. In line with this global strategy, Raeder had also suggested operations against the Suez Canal and in the Red Sea, because of its effect on supplies to the UK from her colonies.

Raeder was convinced that surface sea power, in particular big battleships, allied to Dönitz's U-boats, was the way to win the naval war. Fatally, he seems to have completely ignored the contribution aircraft could and did make in the battle and based all his plans on the development of bigger, faster and better armed capital ships.

As a first step in implementing these plans, as well as U-boats, the German shipyards began to turn out battleships such as *Tirpitz* and *Bismarck*, and the battlecruisers *Scharnhorst* and *Gneisenau*. In line with his policy of concentrating on the Atlantic convoys, however, Raeder also introduced the concept of the pocket battleship, such as *Graf Spee*, lightly protected but heavily armed and capable of high speeds, whose presence, it was hoped, would force the British to try and protect the vital convoys with their own battleships, thus depriving other theatres of these big, powerful ships.

Things did not work out quite as Raeder planned, although the British were forced to detach a number of capital ships to deal with this surface threat. These were often accompanied by RFA ships, although during most of these operations, the larger battleships could not be refuelled at sea.

The first of Germany's 'super warships' to be attacked was the *Graf Spee*, which had slipped out of the Baltic and into the Atlantic just before war was declared. Subsequently, she attacked nine unprepared British merchant ships before being intercepted by the British South Atlantic squadron on 13 December, 1939. Support for her operations was provided by the supply tanker *Altmark*, among the first of this type of vessel to be equipped for oiling at sea.

Caught off the River Plate by a cruiser force consisting of HMS *Exeter*, *Ajax* and RNZS

Achilles, *Graf Spee* tried to make a fight of it. *Exeter*'s 8-inch guns easily penetrated her light armour, however, and an early hit went through two decks before exploding, wrecking her boiler room and fuel separating system. The desalination unit was also destroyed, making it impossible to run her engines without major repairs.

In view of the heavy damage already sustained, *Graf Spee* sought refuge in Montevideo harbour to refit. Facilities were denied her by Uruguay, however, and she was forced to leave under the neutrality rules without making repairs. In order to save his crew from destruction against what he thought were impossible odds, her captain, Hans Langsdorff, scuttled *Graf Spee* outside the harbour entrance. Three days later, Langsdorff shot himself.

Olynthus had accompanied the British group and during the battle, it is said that a signal was sent to her from the C-in-C, which read '... if Graf Spee comes your way, let her through ...'.

After the battle, the old RFA set about refuelling the warships. *Ajax* began replenishing in the shelter of San Borombon Bay, on 15 December. Unfortunately, she was only able to take on 200 tons of fuel before the hawsers holding the two ships together parted in the severe weather. *Achilles* was luckier, managing to complete her refuelling on the night of the 16th off Rouen Bank, while *Ajax* and *Cumberland*, which had joined the group after the battle, kept watch.

Destruction of the *Graf Spee* seemed to make Raeder more determined than ever to win the surface war. He quickly ordered the mobilisation of several more of his super ships, sending the sister ships, *Scharnhorst* and *Gneisenau* into the Atlantic on a commerce raid. They made a formidable combination but, on finding that they were loose, the British reinforced many of their convoys with a single, slow, but well armed battleship. Although many of these ships were First World War veterans, the tactic worked. The Germans refused to engage the old battleships, leaving them in search of easier targets. *Scharnhorst* and *Gneisenau* sank only twenty-one merchant ships before running for Brest, where they arrived on 22 March 1941. Even here, although able to repair and refuel, the ships were still subjected to continual air attacks by the Royal Air Force.

Raeder was not about to give up, though, and early in 1941, he evolved another plan. This time it involved the 42,000-ton *Bismarck*, then the world's largest warship, leading a battle group through the Atlantic. *Bismarck* and *Prinz Eugen* would join *Scharnhorst*, *Gneisenau* and *Tirpitz*. Then together, this massive battle group would devastate the North Atlantic convoy routes. Unfortunately for Raeder's plans, *Scharnhorst* and *Gneisenau* could not leave Brest because of mechanical problems and *Tirpitz* had not yet completed her sea trials.

Bismarck, in company with the heavy cruiser *Prinz Eugen*, left Gotenhafen (Gdynia) on the morning of 19 May 1941. After slipping down the Baltic and through the Kattegat, they put into Bergen to refuel. For reasons unknown, only *Prinz Eugen* filled her tanks and subsequently both ships put to sea, accompanied by a destroyer screen.

Aerial reconnaissance by the Fleet Air Arm found the two German warships gone from Bergen on 22 May. With this news, the Home Fleet was finally able to leave harbour, having been forced to wait for a definite sighting because they were unable to refuel their battleships at sea.

Bismark and *Prinz Eugen* were detected in the Denmark Strait on evening of 23 May by the heavy cruisers, HMS *Suffolk* and *Norfolk*, which shadowed the German vessels, until two of their own heavy units, *Prince of Wales* and *Hood* intercepted them on the morning of 24 May. Fire was exchanged and *Hood* was hit amidships by a shell from *Bismark's* fifth salvo, which penetrated her thin deck and exploded in one of her magazines, causing her to break in half and sink within minutes; 1415 crewmen, including the group leader, Admiral Holland, went down with the ship, leaving only three survivors.

Bismark, however, had also been hit. Most seriously, one of her fuel tanks had been damaged, allowing sea water to enter and contaminate the contents. With all her armament still operational, although forced to slow her speed to 20 knots to conserve fuel, she headed for St Nazaire. Here, Admiral Lutjens, who was aboard the giant ship and in command of the German battle group, was confident she could be quickly repaired. *Prinz Eugen* was ordered to proceed on the mission alone.

The Royal Navy had other ideas. Every unit that could be spared was set to hunting the *Bismarck* and during the evening of 24 May, she was attacked and damaged by Swordfish torpedo bombers from HMS *Victorious*. This attack caused her forward boiler room to flood, bringing down her bow and forcing Lutjens to reduce her speed still further, to 16 knots.

Despite almost escaping her pursuers by a three-quarter turn to the east, on 26 May, she was located again by a Catalina from Coastal Command 209 Squadron. With her position known, Force H was diverted from Gibraltar to engage her. Force H consisted of the aircraft carrier HMS *Ark Royal*, the battleship *Renown* and the cruiser *Sheffield*. They should also have been accompanied by the oiler *Cairndale*, but unfortunately she was torpedoed and sunk, on 30 May, when trying to join them, with the loss of two officers and two ratings killed and four ratings injured.

Ark Royal launched her Swordfish at about 19:25 on the 26th. Unfortunately, her pilots mistook HMS *Sheffield* for *Bismarck* and attacked, using torpedoes equipped with magnetic detonators. This proved beneficial to the British as none of the torpedoes exploded. Returning swiftly to the carrier, the aircraft were re-armed with torpedoes equipped with contact detonators before setting out again. In almost complete darkness, the Swordfish found their quarry and attacked. As a result, a single torpedo hit jammed *Bismarck's* rudder and steering gear, rendering her virtually unmanoeuvrable.

Forced to steam in a gigantic circle and under almost constant torpedo attack during the night from a flotilla of destroyers led by Captain Philip Vian, dawn found *Bismarck* confronted by the battleships HMS *Rodney* and *King George V*. By this time, the capital ships on both sides were seriously short of fuel, with the position more serious for the British since they could not refuel their battleships at sea. *Bismarck's* crew refused to admit defeat, however, and the giant ship opened fire. With her rudder disabled and speed down to 7 knots, she had little chance. After thirty minutes of pounding from the guns of the Royal Navy, her own weapons fell silent and she slowly began to sink.

Although *Bismarck's* upperworks and armament were all but destroyed, her ensign still flew. Hull and engines also remained reasonably sound, so Lindemann, her captain, ordered her scuttled in order to prevent the ship's capture. Only about 115 survived from her 2200-man crew. One of those survivors, incidentally, was a black and white patched cat who was picked up from a plank by HMS *Cossack*. Named Oscar by the crew, he survived the sinking of both *Cossack* and later, *Ark Royal*, eventually ending his days in a seaman's home in Belfast, where he died in 1955.

After the sinking of *Bismarck*, *Scharnhorst* and *Gneisenau* remained in Brest, along with *Prinz Eugen* which had arrived there after leaving *Bismarck*, until February 1942. In that month, with his warships still subject to the continual attentions of the RAF, Hitler ordered them moved back to their home bases. Under cover of night they escaped from harbour and, in a breathtakingly daring move, steamed up the English Channel and home to Germany, beating off attacks from the RAF, Royal Navy and the coastal artillery as they went.

During this voyage, *Gneisenau* struck a mine off the Dutch coast and was later badly damaged by bombs while in dry dock, making her unable to put to sea again.

Scharnhorst remained in harbour until December 1943, when she ventured out again on a convoy raid, this time accompanied by a destroyer screen. She had barely begun operations before being sunk by the British Home fleet, in a spectacularly successful night action off Norway, known later as the Battle of North Cape.

Tirpitz fared no better. She was attacked by midget submarines and immobilised for seven months in September 1943, without ever leaving harbour. Eventually repaired, she was attacked again, this time by the Fleet Air Arm, which once again rendered her useless. Support for the aircraft carriers during this operation ('Tungsten') was provided by *Black Ranger* and *Blue Ranger*. Moved to Tromsø, repairs were still in progress when *Tirpitz* was finally sunk by the RAF. *Prinz Eugen*, the last of the super warships, survived the war, but was never again used in the Atlantic theatre.

Destruction of the last of Germany's super battleships and decimation of her U-boat forces, now left the way open for increased convoy operations. Vast quantities of men and munitions began to pour into Britain, ready for Operation 'Overlord', the Allies' long-awaited attack on Hitler's 'Fortress Europe'.

Chapter 7

The Second World War: The Mediterranean

Until Dunkirk and the occupation of their country, the French had concentrated their fleet in the Mediterranean, under an agreement made with their British allies. Britain also had an important fleet in this area, one of her largest collections of warships, stationed there to keep open vital supply routes to her major colonies via the Suez Canal. These ships gave the Allies control of most of the coast and all of the sea lanes.

Main potential opposition to the British and French in the Mediterranean was the Italian navy, although the Italian government avoided any form of confrontation until the fall of France was assured in summer 1940.

An accelerated programme of naval shipbuilding had been begun by the Italian fascist dictator, Benito Mussolini, soon after he took office, with the clearly stated intention of establishing Italian control of the Mediterranean. Generally well designed, the Italian capital ships suffered from a lack of radar and, in some cases, poor deck armour, although guns, rangefinder systems and fire control were generally excellent. They also lacked a fleet air arm, which meant any air support had to be provided by the land-based Regia Aeronautica. This was to prove significant later, at Taranto, when the Italians could make no effective response to the British use of carrier-based aircraft against their capital ships. German naval involvement in the Mediterranean was limited to U-boat attacks, principally on British, and later, US convoys.

With the British evacuation from Dunkirk barely complete and the French army in disarray, Italy declared war on Britain on 10 June 1940. Malta was attacked the next day by Italian bombers and when France surrendered on the 24th, Britain found herself alone.

Faced by a Vichy French regime of doubtful loyalty and still in possession of the French navy's Mediterranean-based capital ships, the British ordered Vichy to 'place those ships out of German reach'. When this peculiarly worded ultimatum was ignored, Cunningham's Force H bombarded the major part of the French fleet, then in the harbour of Mers-el-Kebir in Algeria, and destroyed it. This allowed the Royal Navy to give their full attention to the Italian navy.

British naval action in the Mediterranean began in earnest when aircraft of the Royal Navy's Fleet Air Arm successfully attacked the Italian fleet in the port of Taranto on 11 November 1940. Flying from HMS *Illustrious*, then part of Force H, the Fairy Swordfish torpedo bombers badly damaged two Italian battleships and sank a third. Not only did this attack put half the Italian fleet out of action for several months, it also forced it to use harbours farther north on the mainland. Italian warships were now safely out of range of aircraft from the Royal Navy's carriers, but it also limited their ability to attack the vital Malta-bound convoys. Four months later, off Cape Matapan, ships of the British and Australian navies achieved another crushing victory, when, in March 1941, they attacked a major Italian naval group. Three Italian heavy cruisers and four destroyers were sunk and the battleship *Vittorio Veneto* badly damaged, while British losses were one torpedo plane, with some light damage to the warships.

Unfortunately, these successes did not continue. Although the British had quickly defeated the Italian army in North Africa, Wavell and O'Connor, the generals in charge, were forced to halt their successful advance, which easily might have pushed the Italians completely out of the country, in January 1941. Instead, Wavell was ordered to stay where he was. Even more disastrously, he was instructed to dispatch nearly 60,000 men, a major proportion of his available force, to reinforce Greece, despite the dangerous proximity of the Afrika Korps, now commanded by Erwin Rommel.

Three weeks later, Greece had fallen and the British were being driven out of Crete by the German's first, and only, major airborne assault. German air superiority also caused the loss of nine Royal Navy ships and damage to a number of others during these operations.

With Greece and Crete occupied, Hitler turned his attention to the invasion of Russia, a decision that would eventually turn out to be his biggest mistake. He had already sent Field Marshal Erwin Rommel to take care of the British in North Africa.

Rommel arrived in North Africa in February 1941 and almost immediately launched an attack on the British. By the end of March, his Afrika Korps and its Italian allies were driving the outnumbered British and Australians across Egypt towards the Suez Canal. They stopped him at Sollum, in April, leaving the Australian 9th Division besieged in Tobruk until December, when General Auchinleck, who had relieved the badly under-supplied Wavell, launched a counterattack. Rommel was pushed back towards Tripoli but refused to stay there. In January 1942, he began to advance again. This time, his forces reached and occupied a line extending from Al Gazala, on the coast, inland to Bir Hacheim, still some miles west of Tobruk, which stayed in Allied hands. Here Rommel found his army stalled for want of supplies until May 1942.

It stalled because the Royal Navy were sinking his supply ships at will, having beaten the Italian Fleet so badly at Taranto and Matapan that it refused to fight the British again. Equally important, Malta was still available to the British as a submarine and bomber base from which to attack Rommel's convoys.

Malta was Britain's only naval base in the central Mediterranean, protecting the highly vulnerable route between Gibraltar and Alexandria. It was Malta and the aircraft and naval vessels based there which gave the Royal Navy control of coastal North Africa, protecting in turn her Persian oil supplies, the Suez Canal and trade routes to India and the Far East. Malta had to be supplied and defended and that meant convoys, even while Britain was engaged in the desperate struggle for North Africa.

Convoy operations to both Malta and Alexandria during 1940, with only the Italian navy to contend with, were relatively successful. The Italian ships had no air cover and the Royal Navy forced a passage for the merchant ships in their care with relatively little trouble.

This pattern shifted, however, early in 1941. By then, Rommel's Afrika Korps was beginning operations in Libya and a huge Luftwaffe contingent moved to Sicily, from where it began to mount successful attacks on Malta. Despite these attacks, in the second half of 1941, bombers based on the island sank 60 per cent of Axis shipping routed to North Africa, leaving Rommel stranded, first outside Tobruk, then later, on the line between El Gazala and Bir Hacheim for those vital months from January to May 1942.

Rommel himself returned to Berlin in January 1942, to plead with Hitler for an attack on Malta, which would destroy the island's capacity to sink his supply ships. Hitler responded by reinforcing the Luftwaffe's Sicilian contingent and during the early months of 1942, intense air raids on Malta-bound convoys caused the island's supplies to reach a perilously low level. Lack of aircraft meant the island could no longer function as an effective offensive base, leaving Axis supply convoys largely untroubled. Several submarines and destroyers had also been sunk in the harbour and it was only the arrival of supply ships from Operation 'Pedestal', especially the fuel carried by the badly damaged British tanker *Ohio*, which prevented Malta's surrender in August. 1942, however, was to prove the turning point in both North Africa and the Mediterranean.

Although sufficient supplies had reached Rommel's forces by May 1942 for him to drive the Allies back to El Alamein, supply problems and the strategic situation forced him to halt there. He never managed to advance any further.

By mid-August, supplies from 'Pedestal' and aircraft flown in from Royal Navy carriers had given Malta a fresh impetus. On 23 October, Montgomery's 8th Army began to cut its way out of El Alamein and by 3 November, Rommel, who was by then a sick man, was retreating across the Western Desert. With siege conditions lifted after the German retreat and resupply once again possible, British forces based on Malta intensified raids on Rommel's supply lines and transport ships. The Afrika Korps could not regroup until it had been driven back into Tunisia and even here, attacks from the Malta-based ships and aircraft reduced supplies to a trickle.

Allied forces landed in French North Africa as part of Operation 'Torch' on 8 November 1942, to reinforce the 8th Army and on the 11th, the Vichy French naval commander, Admiral Darlan, surrendered. Despite setbacks caused by the weather and enemy reinforcements, by the end of May 1943, the last German soldier had left North Africa and the Allies were ready to invade Italy.

Royal Fleet Auxiliary vessels had frequently accompanied convoys between the UK and Gibraltar, on both freighting duties and in their increasingly important role as escort oilers. In addition, several served as Gibraltar harbour oilers. *Brown Ranger*, for example, refuelled the escorts for Malta convoys designated Operations 'Substance' (July 1941) and 'Halberd' (September 1941), while assigned to this station.

These operations were all conducted in the same way. *Brown Ranger* left Gibraltar with a destroyer escort, frequently only a single warship, refuelled the escorts, then returned to anchor in Gibraltar harbour. Later, during Operation 'Harpoon' (June 1942), however, *Brown Ranger* was detached with an escort (designated Force Y) and sent to rendezvous with the warships while the convoy was on passage. This meeting took place on 13 June 1942, and despite delays caused by the oiler being 25 miles off her rendezvous, *Brown Ranger* still refuelled eleven destroyers, her crew working far into the night to accomplish this. Force Y then remained on station for six days, in an area extensively patrolled by enemy submarines, ready to fuel the returning escorts, because no fuel was available in Malta. Even the navy could not believe her good luck in not being sunk, one naval officer remarking '... That the oiler Brown Ranger was allowed to cruise for some six days or more, unmolested across the enemy submarine areas, appears to be the fault of the enemy ...'.

Dingledale and *Brown Ranger* were also involved in refuelling the warships taking part in Operation 'Pedestal' (August 1942), which was most important and famous of all the Malta convoys. This replenishment followed a similar pattern to those carried out previously. Designated Force R, the two fleet oilers left harbour with a tug and an escort of corvettes. Rendezvous with the convoy took place at 0645 on 11 August and by 2030 the RFAs had successfully refuelled three cruisers and twenty-six destroyers. Force R remained cruising in the Western basin until it was certain no more of the escorting destroyers would require fuel, then returned to Gibraltar, arriving on the 16th.

Although no RFA vessel is recorded as having sailed on a Malta convoy, several Admiralty vessels were badly damaged or sunk while on service in the Mediterranean

Losses began with *Olna*, never considered a particularly good ship by the RFA men who manned her, having been constructed from left over spare parts during the financially difficult years of the early 1920s.

In May 1941, *Olna* was in Suda Bay, Crete, when the Germans began their initial bombing raids to soften up the island's garrison. Set on fire during one of these attacks, the crew managed to beach her but could not control the flames and she was abandoned and subsequently burnt out. Her officers were sent back to the UK, while the Chinese crew were repatriated to Singapore. The burnt out wreck fell into German hands upon the occupation in May 1941, although they did nothing with her and she was still there at the end of the war, fit only for scrap.

Italian frogmen used two man midget submarines (or 'manned torpedoes') to play an active part against Allied shipping during the war, operating either from conventional submarines or, later, from the specially converted mother ship *Olterra*. Interned early in the war in Algeciras, this vessel was secretly converted into a base ship during the early part of July 1942. These modifications included an underwater door cut in her hull, to allow the midget submarines to enter and return without detection. Italian frogmen conducted several operations from her and it was only with the downfall of Mussolini that she was towed into Gibraltar and her secret discovered.

In an earlier operation, during September 1941, the Italian submarine *Scire*, having collected eight crewmen for her embarked manned torpedoes from Cadiz, had slipped quietly through the strait, coming to rest just outside Gibraltar's harbour mouth. With full darkness, the submarine's commander disembarked his human cargo and the three midget submarines entered the harbour. Once inside, they fixed their torpedoes to the nearest merchant ships, set the timing devices and then swam back to Spain, arriving safely some hours later. All three charges exploded successfully, sinking or badly damaging their victims. One of these was *Denbydale*, which was lying alongside the mole and had her back broken.

She did not sink, however, coming to rest upright in the shallow water, and was used throughout the rest of the war as a fuelling and accommodation hulk. According to one observer, by the 1950s the ship had acquired mahogany railings, vintage furniture and a piano, achieving something of the status of an RFA club – a 'sort of home from home'.

Her engine was removed later in the war and shipped home in pieces to be used to re-engine her sister ship, the LSG *Derwentdale*. *Denbydale* remained in Gibraltar until 1957, when she was towed to Blyth and scrapped.

Plumleaf had relieved *Dredgol* as oiler on the Mediterranean Station in 1931, even exchanging crews with her at the same time. During the pre-war period the Mediterranean Fleet was usually stationed in Malta and *Plumleaf* was there, presumably as station oiler, when she was hit by bombs, on 26 March 1942, during an air raid on Malta harbour. Breaking free from her moorings, her stern went aground but the ship remained upright, only to receive further damage in another air raid on 4 April.

This time the old *Trinol* class RFA sank up to the level of her deck, in about 45 feet (15 metres) of water. All of the crew was evacuated safely, but when she was refloated in August 1947, she was found to be only fit for scrap. Unlike *Plumleaf*, *Cherryleaf* is also listed as Malta's station oiler during 1931–45 and she survived undamaged, to be sold for scrap in 1946.

In a bizarre twist of fate, *Slavol* was sunk on the same day, 26 March 1942. While on passage from Alexandria to Tobruk with a cargo of fuel oil, she was torpedoed by *U 205*, north-east of Sollum. This time, sadly, the crew were not so lucky as the men aboard *Plumleaf*. Thirty-one of the forty-nine-man Lascar crew were killed, together with five officers, including the radio officer. One officer was seriously injured.

Brambleleaf was also torpedoed on this Alexandria to Tobruk run, off Mersa Alun, on 10 June 1942. While on passage with Convoy AT49, she was hit between number 1 boiler room and the engine room. The entire engine room watch of thirteen men were killed instantly and fire broke out in her summer tanks. Although it was quickly extinguished, she was clearly badly damaged. Wounded and non-essential crew having been removed by destroyer, the remaining crew remained aboard, with a corvette standing by in case the situation worsened.

Daylight found her with a 28-degrees list and awash from the engine room aft. To make matters worse, she was soon spotted by the Luftwaffe. Despite repeated air attacks, however, she showed no signs of sinking and a party from a naval salvage vessel shored up bulkheads and hull before she was safely towed to Alexandria. She spent the rest of the war here, after repair, as an oil hulk. Despite later sinking by the stern in September 1944, after refloating she continued to give good service, until sold for scrap in 1947. There was a profitable, if unexpected, end to the story for her crew because, in a sudden burst of generosity, the MoWT actually made them a salvage award for her recovery! No record is available of how much it was, though.

Over a year was to pass before the next RFA vessel was lost, when *Oligarch* was torpedoed in the eastern Mediterranean. Although damaged, she was kept afloat and proceeded to Tobruk, under her own power, where she was used in harbour to fuel destroyers. After some minor repairs she was taken to Alexandria, in convoy UGS13, where she spent the rest of the war as a fuel hulk. Soon after the war, in 1946, she was steamed to Suez, loaded with obsolete ammunition and scuttled in the Red Sea.

Last of the RFA fleet damaged in the Mediterranean was *Abbeydale*, which was torpedoed on 27 June 1944 by *U 73*, 80 miles west of Algiers. Almost broken in two by the explosion, her empty cargo tanks kept her afloat and she was later rejoined by the staff of Taranto dockyard and returned to service.

Attack from mine, submarines and warships were not the only dangers Allied ships, including RFAs, faced in the Mediterranean. During the early part of the war, German agents were active in ports in the UK and overseas, making sabotage a real problem for those given the job of preventing it.

Ships mysteriously sinking days out from a foreign port, cargo fires and unexplained explosions in dock all added up to an efficient network of saboteurs, intent upon destroying or, at least, disabling Britain's merchant fleet. It had to be stopped and quickly. And the man the British government found for the job was biophysicist Lord Rothschild.

Spanish ports seemed to have the highest proportion of sabotaged vessels, with Gibraltar, in particular, bearing the brunt of the attacks. Charges in use by the saboteurs caused only minor damage and sailing delays, convincing the secret service that they must be small. However, given the success of the German agents, it was only a matter of time before they tried something larger, with a corresponding increase in damage and disruption to the merchant fleet, as well as the whole system of supply.

Torpedo nets and other security measures appeared to rule out an external source for the explosions, such as midget submarines, but how the bombs were getting on to the ships still remained a mystery. Clearly, some sort of spy or sabotage ring must be responsible and Rothschild quickly put together an organisation composed of Scotland Yard men and scientists to find out how it was done. The London policemen moved to the Rock and began assiduously re-examining every scrap of information that had already been obtained before their arrival. It was not all desk work, either. They visited ships, docks and war factories, mingling with the workers on and off duty. Finally, all that patient work was rewarded.

The Yard men discovered that German agents were bringing their bombs on board ship disguised as everyday objects. They might be in a suit case under a layer of clothing, or a lunchbox beneath real food or most ingeniously, in a thermos flask containing a quantity of liquid, which allowed it to withstand a superficial examination. This sort of saboteur was quickly eradicated when regulations were introduced making anyone carrying any sort of object prove that it did not contain an explosive device.

This dealt with the bombs carried aboard by agents, but the Germans were also using another trick. Agents would steal a crate of oranges or onions, fill the crate with high explosive and a detonating device, then replace the top layer of produce. The case was then returned to its original position to be loaded aboard by the dockyard workers. German agents used a variation of this technique when they tried to smuggle a bomb in a crate of eggs aboard HMS *Ark Royal*, while she was in Gibraltar harbour. Fortunately, the smuggler was stopped by a vigilant Spanish customs officer and the crate exploded, killing the saboteur and the unlucky officer, while the pair removed the crate to the nearby customs shed.

Not content with simply smuggling time bombs aboard ships, the German secret service also invented a way of attaching bombs to a vessel's hull below the waterline. Using specially designed underwater suits and oxygen rebreathing apparatus, agents would swim over from the Spanish mainland, fix their bombs and return the same way, undetected by the British. Once the use of these techniques had been established, however, the Royal Navy introduced specially trained squads of divers that patrolled the ships, dealing summarily with any saboteurs they might meet. Barbed wire aprons were also set about the ships hulls and, in addition, showers of small 5lb depth charges were thrown from fast patrol boats patrolling the harbours. So effective were these measures that German sabotage in Gibraltar soon all but ceased. Rothschild went on to direct anti-sabotage operations in Britain and Europe, being decorated for his work, after the war, by both the British and US governments.

The collier *Mercedes*; she was involved in the Admiralty's unsuccessful coaling-at-sea trials.

Mercedes coaling the River class destroyer HMS *Kennet*.

Petroleum, the first Admiralty tanker to test an RAS(L) rig.

First World War RFA officer (Mr A Ballantyne) in working uniform (*Left*).

Ballantyne in full dress uniform; note the sub-lieutenant RNR rank badge on the sleeve of his jacket (*Right*).

Thermol, 1911, one of the 2000-ton *Burma* class.

Appleleaf, one of the *Trinol* or Fast Leaf class, shown in 1933.

Prestol, 1917, of the second 2000-ton class.

Delphinula, acquired by the Admiralty in 1918; seen here in 1933.

Palmol, an early 1000-ton harbour tanker painted in dazzle camouflage, 1918.

Petronel, a 500-ton spirit carrier, alongside HMS *Repulse*, 1918.

War Diwan in 1936. Built at the end of the First World War, this class was an important element of the inter-war RFA.

War Bahadur, showing damage to bridge sustained during storm at sea in January 1938.

Oleander, 1922, an inter-war freighting tanker.

Broomdale, one of the Dale class of freighting tankers that came into service just before the Second World War.

Bacchus, 1936, an early store ship.

Robert Dundas, 1938, one of two coastal store carriers in this class.

Inter-war trials: the heavy cruiser HMS *Suffolk* refuelling the destroyer HMS *Verity* by stirrup method. Stirrups on rollers carry the hose suspended below the towline.

Stirrup rail and platform. This design was never used at sea because the hose was continually snagged by the rail supports.

Wartime fuelling astern using buoyant hose to supply a destroyer.

A destroyer refuelling astern. Here the warship has taken position, with the hose in a 'bight', to ease the strain on the refuelling rig.

Early wooden roller used aboard some convoy escort oilers (*Top*).

Hose connector aboard an oiler (*Above*).

A later arrangement for oiling at sea aboard convoy escort oilers, with the buoyant rubber hose laid on metal rollers (*Right*).

An early experimental method of depth charge transfer. Charges were attached to an oil drum by 30 feet of rope and then tipped over the side. The receiving warship then grappled the drum and pulled the charges aboard. Later methods were less hazardous.

Brown Ranger. This vessel spent part of the Second World War refuelling Malta-bound convoys.

Fort Dunvegan, one of a class of store ships based on war-standard hulls that served the RFA for many years after 1945 (*Top*).

Oakol, one of the second 1000-ton class of harbour tankers. Crews of these vessels were usually employed on harbour or yard craft agreements (*Above*).

Spalake, 1946, one of the Spa class of water tankers (*Below*).

In the immediate post-war years, the captured German naval support ship *Nordmark* was operated by the Royal Navy as HMS *Bulawayo* and used for extensive trials of underway replenishment systems. These photographs are from the reports on the experiments.

Three-trough refuelling rig suspended from heavy duty derrick (*Top*).

Early design of trough (*Above*).

Prototype quick-release hose fitting trialled aboard HMS *Bulawayo* (*Right*).

Replenishment operations are sometimes made difficult by the heavy seas generated by ships in close proximity to one-another, one of the important lessons of these trials.

Jackstay transfer, possibly lubricating oil.

Wave Sovereign, before the fitting of abeam replenishment equipment.

Wave Premier, simultaneously refuelling the destroyer HMAS *Bataan* and the aircraft carrier HMS *Glory*.

Mediterranean convoys accompanied by RFAs

HG: Gibraltar–UK, 1939–42 (14)
Abbeydale, Aldersdale, Arndale, Bedenham, Bishopdale, Cedardale, Dewdale,
Oleander, Perthshire, Serbol, Thermol, War Afridi, War Bharata, War Krishna

KS/SL: Mediterranean (slow)–Freetown (Sierra Leone)–UK, 1942–4 (15)

Convoys are listed jointly since these convoys frequently rendezvoused and
travelled together

Abbeydale, Celerol, Derwentdale, Dewdale, Dingledale, Echodale, Ennerdale, Scottish
American

KMS/OS: Mediterranean–Freetown, 1941–5 (32)

KMF and KMS convoys in October and November 1942 carried troops and
landing craft for the initial landings of Operation 'Torch'

Abbeydale, Bacchus, Belgol, Brown Ranger, Celerol, Derwentdale, Dewdale,
Dingledale, Dinsdale, Distol, Eaglesdale, Echodale, Empire Salvage, Ennerdale, Green
Ranger, Kimmerol, Montenol, Orangeleaf, Pearleaf, Prestol, Scottish American, Serbol,
Rapidol, War Krishna

Amphibious operations

The RFA ships were involved in many of the Allied amphibious operations during the
Second World War, with both the purpose-built LSGs and several oilers deployed in
the Mediterranean and later, the Pacific.

The LSGs were originally MoWT Dale class tankers, modified to carry fourteen
LCM Mk1 landing craft, each of about 20 tons unladen. The landing craft cargo of a
single 16-ton tank or vehicles was put aboard before it was embarked at the LSG's
port of departure and remained there during the voyage to the landing area. On
passage, these craft and their contents rested on steel troughs running fore and aft,
three abreast in the fore and after well decks, secured with chains and bottle screws.
Two gantry structures, one in front and one behind the amidships bridge structure
were used to hoist the craft in and out the ship. On each side of the gantries there was
a folding extension, which when moved inboard, allowed the travelling crane to
traverse inboard immediately before the landing craft to be hoisted. Two steel beams,
from each of which two shackles hung, were then lowered until the shackles dropped
over a lug in each corner of the craft's deck. With the shackle pins secured the craft was
hoisted, traversed out board and lowered on to the surface of the sea. The next landing
craft was then winched forward into the position for launching.

Once the LCM was afloat, the landing craft crew, usually coxwain, seaman and a
stoker, embarked. The vehicle crew joined them and the LCM then left the landing
ship's side and headed for the target beach.

With the landing operations finished, re-embarking the LCMs was fundamentally a reversal of the procedure for lowering. They were lifted from the sea by means of the travelling cranes and then lowered on to the rollers in any of the three troughs which were vacant. A hawser from a winch, via a snatch block, then hauled the LCM either aft, to a position on the after well deck or forward to the forward well deck. Six LCMs in two rows of three abreast were carried forward and eight aft, as the aftermost position on the starboard side was obstructed by a large diameter oil pipe leading up on to the poop deck, which was used for stern refuelling. The last two craft to be hoisted, of course, would be those berthed under the gantries, in the outboard positions, which did not need to be hauled forward or aft. Each gantry had one crane, which meant that two craft could be lowered or hoisted at one time, but not from both sides of the same gantry at once.

Plainly, immense difficulties would be encountered during either of these operation in any but the easiest of sea conditions, unlike the modern LPD(A)s, now in service with the RFA, which can launch a landing craft out of their stern dock, in winds up to force 5.

Operation 'Torch', launched in November 1942, was the Allies' first major amphibious assault on the coast of North Africa. Timed to coincide with the 8th Army's offensive from El Alamein, it consisted of three separate operations.

The first invasion group, termed the western group, was to be put ashore near the French Atlantic coast port of Casablanca. Consisting wholly of US troops, they were also commanded by an American, Rear-Admiral H K Hewitt. Once the troops had landed command would be the responsibility of the army, under General George Patton.

Designated Task Force 34, the US ships left Norfolk, Virginia, 3400 miles from their target, on 23 October. They were joined by a five-carrier air group on the 28th, which provided anti-submarine protection for the 107 ships of the convoy. On 7 November, the fleet split into three groups. The largest headed for Fedala, a beach just outside Casablanca, while the second element headed south for Safi, a tiny phosphate port 150 miles farther south along the Atlantic coast. Third and last objective assigned to the northern group was the airfield at Port Lyautey, which had the only heavy duty concrete runways in Morocco. By the 11th, the French in Casablanca had surrendered and turned all their port facilities over to the Americans. Safi fell easily on the 8th, followed by the airfield on the 10th, although only after hard fighting. Casablanca was now available as an entry port for massive reinforcement of men and material from America.

Meanwhile, further east in the Mediterranean, British and US forces of the Central and Eastern task forces were in the process of capturing Oran and Algiers, the capital of French Algeria.

Sailing from the Clyde and Scapa Flow, the 105 ships of the Central Task Force, commander Commodore T H Troubridge RN and the ninety-three ships of the Eastern Task Force, commanded by Vice Admiral H M Burrough RN, headed first for Gibraltar. Ignored by the Germans, who thought the force too small to attempt a landing, and with the only U-boat group in the vicinity of the strait drawn off in pursuit of an unfortunate Sierra Leone-bound convoy, the three huge troop and supply convoys, KMS1, KMS2 and KMF1, slipped through unscathed. Refuelling went smoothly and by daylight on 7 November, the Central and Eastern task forces, together with the assault convoys and covering warships of Gibraltar-based Force H, were on their way again. *Brown Ranger* and *Dingledale* were part of Force R, the fuelling support group accompanying Force H.

Oran was the target for the Central Task Force, which arrived off the coast at 1600 on 7 November. Split into seven waves, the ships approached the three assault beaches and began landing troops with little incident, although a sand bar on the central landing beach to the west of Oran did cause the loss of a number of landing craft and vehicles. *Dingledale* was part of the assault force whose troops and equipment landed at Arzew, the most easterly of the landing beaches, designated beach Z. This group was also accompanied by *Abbeydale*, as group oiler, which had left the Clyde with Convoy KMS2.

Despite the failure of a frontal assault on the harbour defences by two former cutters, *Walney* and *Hartland*, on the night of the 8th, by 1200 on 10 November, the city was in US hands.

Victory came even quicker in Algiers. Despite initial confusion during the landings, the combined British and US force landed almost without opposition, *Ennerdale* being present, although she could not land tanks due to a defect in her LCM gear. An American Ranger team captured the important airfield of Maison Blanche, near Algiers at around 0630. By 0900, RAF fighters from Gibraltar had refuelled there and were patrolling the landing beaches flanking Algiers.

In the harbour, two British destroyers, loaded with American Rangers, had tried to smash their way through the boom under cover of darkness, while the landings were going on outside the city. Unfortunately, they missed the channel and after coming under heavy fire only one, the elderly HMS *Broke*, managed to break through the boom. She berthed and disembarked her troops, who soon came under heavy small arms fire, before all were killed or captured. This proved to be another pointless waste of lives, because the French commander surrendered the city intact to the Americans later that morning. *Dewdale* arrived in Algiers harbour on the 9th, in order to refuel the destroyers and other vessels which composed the escort force. *Nasprite* was also present as a petrol carrier, with *Viscol* in service as a harbour oiler.

With Algiers in Allied hands, the next objective was to capture Tunis and the strategically essential French naval base at Bizerta as quickly as possible.

Unfortunately, desert roads would not allow the British and US armies now in coastal North Africa to move quickly overland from Algiers to Tunis without outdistancing their logistic support elements. Supply from the sea was the only way a quick advance could be achieved and this meant using the ports at Bougie and Bone.

Bougie was captured on the 11th, with the nearby airfield at Djidjelli falling into Allied hands the same day. Unfortunately, sea conditions prevented petrol from being landed and moved to the airfield, so air cover over Bougie was not in place until two days later, a fact the Germans and Italians fully exploited.

For reasons not readily apparent, *Dewdale* does not seem to have been used as a landing ship during this North African operation. Once again, she was pressed into use as an oiler, arriving Bougie harbour at 0600 on 11 November to begin refuelling duties.

Some time between 1000 and 1100 that day, thirty Junkers (Ju) 88s attacked the harbour, their principal targets being *Dewdale* and the Dutch troop transport *Marnix Van Sint Aldegonde*. Most of the planes were kept high by anti-aircraft fire, but, as the

London Gazette records: '... it was the gunnery efficiency of *Dewdale* and *Marnix* which undoubtedly saved these ships ...'.

Later the same day, at 1240, the harbour was again attacked, this time by six torpedo bombers. *Dewdale* opened fire and claimed to have got one of them, while the rest dropped their torpedoes at long range and left but not before a second bomber had been shot down by a Spitfire patrol from Algiers. *Dewdale* returned to Algiers that night, in convoy with two military transports and five other merchant ships, only to be hit a few days later in a port forward cargo tank during a night raid. Her luck seems to have been out, because she damaged again on the 20th, by a bomb dropped on a nearby jetty. She remained in Algiers until after the Normandy Invasion, finally proceeding to the UK on 15 October 1944. Later, she and *Ennerdale* both saw action together in the Allied re-occupation of Greece.

With North Africa in Allied hands, by May 1943 the invasion of Italy was seen by many on the General Staff as the next job.

And the way to Italy led through Sicily. The Sicily invasion, Operation 'Husky', began on 10 July 1943. Landings were made at several key sites, with Landing Ship Tank (LST) and Landing Craft Tank (LCT) in use for the first time. Facing the 180,000 strong invasion force were Italian and German troops with a combined strength of 400,000 men. This could easily have been more, except the British engineered a brilliant deception, arranging for the body of what seemed to be a British Royal Marines major to be washed ashore in Spain with papers on the body showing that the Allied invasion was to be in Sardinia, not Sicily. Hitler took the bait, moving troops out of Sicily for duty in Sardinia, with the result that Eisenhower and Montgomery's men were able to move quickly through the island.

Barely a month after the first Allied troops had waded ashore, Axis forces began an organised evacuation, on 11 August. The evacuation was well planned and executed, US troops reaching Messina on the 17th, only hours after the last German had departed.

Cedardale and *Pearleaf* both served as part of Force R, the group providing fuelling support for the destroyers of Force H. *Derwentdale* and *Ennerdale* were included in the assault groups that reached the beachheads in the first wave on 10 July, while *Nasprite*, then carrying petrol, was also in action on the beachheads in that first wave.

With Sicily safely in Allied hands, Mussolini's opponents organised a *coup d'etat*, deposing the Italian dictator and setting up a new government under Marshal Pietro Badoglio. A 'short military armistice' was signed with this new regime on 3 September and the Italy became aligned with the Allies. In response, Hitler reinforced the German troops already in Italy with the 1st SS Panzer Division and sank a number of ships of the Italian fleet as they tried to escape to Malta. He also had Mussolini rescued and placed at the head of a puppet government in northern Italy.

The man Hitler chose for the defence of the Italian mainland was General Albert Kesselring. Kesselring had had a good look at the Italian terrain over which the battles would be fought and arrived at the comforting conclusion that it would be an easy task to defend it. His Allied opponents agreed with him and later events were to prove both sides correct.

Montgomery's 8th Army crossed from Sicily to Calabria on 3 September 1943. His troops met little resistance, except from the single regiment of German troops that had the unenviable task of covering 17 miles of that coastline. Six days later, the British

1st Airborne Division landed by sea at Taranto, also without meeting significant opposition. On the same day, 165,000 troops of the Allied 5th Army, commanded by General Mark Clark, came ashore at Salerno (Operation 'Avalanche').

Unfortunately, six divisions of German troops were waiting at Salerno. Clark and his men encountered stiff resistance, before precise air strikes by the RAF, on the 14th, reduced the effectiveness of the German counterattacks, allowing the Americans to maintain their beachhead.

Derwentdale sailed from Bizerta on 7 September in assault convoy FSS2, reaching the Salerno beachhead with the Southern Attack Force on the 9th. While anchored, she was dive-bombed nineteen times, fortunately without being hit. Finally, however, her luck ran out when, at 1215 on the 15th, seven Stukas (Ju 87) came screaming out of the sun, clearly intent upon *Derwentdale* as the intended target. Five missed but the other two hit the deck above the engine room on the port side, tearing through the steel plates and exploding within the engine room. With his ship rapidly filling with water, her master ordered the anchor cable slipped and the crew managed to beach the tanker. *Derwentdale* was still sinking by the stern, however, and in order to keep her afloat, the crew pumped oil from the after tanks, the ship's pumps being operated by steam supplied from the tug *Hengist*. This raised the stern and hard work kept her afloat until 1730, when *Hengist* began towing the ship to Malta. Her engine was wrecked but after being towed back to the UK, it was replaced by those from *Denbydale*, which had been sunk in Gibraltar harbour by Italian frogmen. She did not come back into service until 1946, when, with her gantries removed, she returned to normal freighting duties.

Even after consolidation of the Salerno beachhead, the Allied advance was slow. Although Naples was quickly captured, falling into Allied hands in October 1943, the Allies were still only seventy miles from Salerno four months later, in January 1944, having collided with the German defensive lines. Stalled by bad weather and the enemy, the Allies suffered over 40,000 dead and wounded, with an additional 50,000 men sick – a total far exceeding the German casualties. Eisenhower and Montgomery had left the Italian front in December, being needed to plan the Normandy invasion, and the US general, Wilson, was appointed Supreme Commander of the Italian theatre in place of 'Ike'.

On 22 January 1944, he launched Operation 'Shingle', the unsuccessful landings at Anzio, which again remained stalled on the beach until Free French and Polish troops took Monte Cassino by storm, breaking the German 'Gustav' line, and allowing the Americans to break out of Anzio and march into Rome, on 4 June 1944, just before the Normandy invasions began.

Pressure was now being brought to bear on Hitler's troops from both France and Italy. Earlier in the war, Churchill had repeatedly referred to the southern Mediterranean as Hitler's 'soft underbelly' and this was to prove shockingly true. With the Russians also advancing from the east, the Fuhrer's days were numbered, especially with things now going well for the Allies in the Pacific.

Chapter 8

The Pacific and Indian Oceans

War in the Pacific began with the Japanese attack on Pearl Harbor.

Economic growth and development during the 1920s and the 1930s had led the Japanese government to believe that the country's best chance of international success was to establish a pan-Pacific empire. To achieve this, just like the old colonial empires of Britain and France, it needed its essential raw materials and potential customers under its own administrative control. Japan's first step towards achieving this desirable position was to invade China, in an attempt to secure that country's enormous potential wealth, together with an assured market for Japanese manufactured goods.

By 1940, with France and the Netherlands occupied and Britain fighting for her life, European colonial possessions in Asia looked vulnerable to Japanese occupation. From newly occupied China, the Japanese could easily move westward, occupying Burma, Malaya, French Indo-China (now Vietnam) and the Dutch East Indies (now Indonesia), giving them a strong base for their new empire.

In Japan's way, however, was the United States, still occupying the Philippines and many of the strategically important Pacific islands. Despite having declared the Philippines republic independent, the United States had retained control of its army, with the formidable General Douglas MacArthur in command. Japan tried desperately to persuade the Americans to allow their southward expansionist policies, but to no avail. Tensions in the region further escalated, when Roosevelt, six months after the fall of France and with a view to relieving Japanese pressure on China, imposed a ban on the sale of raw materials to Japan. This included oil and scrap iron and with almost no mineral or fuel reserves of its own, the Japanese soon felt the US embargo begin to bite.

In spring 1941, with her industries desperately short of oil, Japan opened negotiations with Washington, asking the United States to both lift their ban and stop sending aid to China. While these negotiations were still in progress, however, the Japanese moved fresh troops into Indo-China, securing that country's extensive agricultural resources. They also seized the harbour at Camranh Bay, which was ideally situated for an invasion of Malaya. Britain and the United States responded by freezing all Japanese assets under their control.

Japanese–US negotiations in Washington now became embittered and acrimonious and were not helped by the resignation of the moderate Japanese prime minister and the appointment in his place of the militarist General Hideki Tojo. Tojo's government immediately sent the United States an ultimatum, demanding it agrees to meet all of Japan's demands by 29 November 1941. Relations between the two countries did not improve and at 1128 on 7 December, Tokyo instructed Admiral Nomura, their Washington representative, to inform the Americans that negotiations were at an end. Acting on instructions from Japan's supreme naval commander, Admiral Yamamoto, at 0700 the same day, aircraft from six Japanese carriers attacked the US naval base at Pearl Harbor.

The Japanese carriers had not broken radio silence since leaving Japan on 26 November, thus giving the Americans no means of locating them. Inexperienced radar operators and initial uncertainty over the origin of the approaching aircraft also added to the confusion. Attacking in two waves, the first from the north in three sections and the second from the east, the Japanese achieved almost total surprise. They destroyed 349 aircraft, damaged or sank eighteen warships and killed 3700 service personnel and civilians. All achieved for the loss of fifty-five officers and ratings and twenty-nine aircraft, out of a total strike force of 353.

On the same day, Japanese forces attacked Hong Kong, Malaya and three US-held islands in the Pacific – Midway, Wake and Guam. The United States immediately declared war on Japan and Hitler made another disastrous mistake.

He, in turn, declared war on the United States.

It seems strange to contemplate, over sixty years after the event, but, during the early part of this century, the main preoccupation of American strategists was the problems of a two-ocean war and, specifically, just how dangerous and difficult it would be for America to fight one.

George Ball, who later became a senior presidential adviser, wrote:

> ... if Hitler had not made this decision and if he had simply done nothing, there would have been an enormous sentiment in the United States ... that the Pacific war now was our war and the European war was for the Europeans and we should concentrate all our efforts on the Japanese ....

It was, in fact, only the 'special relationship', which had grown up out of the mutual respect between Churchill and Roosevelt that resulted in Britain receiving any help at all from the United States before December 1941. And there were plenty in Washington, including the Chief of Naval Operations, Admiral Ernest King, who wanted nothing to do with the British. Later, King would even oppose Operation 'Torch', on the grounds that it was postponing his navy's more important Pacific offensives.

The Japanese swept east and west at frightening speed, capturing Guam on 10 December and Wake on the 23rd. On the day that their ground troops captured Guam, Japanese torpedo bombers, flying from air bases in Indo-China sank the Royal Navy's Force Z, consisting of the new battleship HMS *Prince of Wales* and the battlecruiser HMS *Repulse*.

Hong Kong fell, after a spirited defence, on Christmas day 1941, and by the middle of February, Rangoon, capital of Burma, and Singapore, Britain's biggest naval base in the Far East, were in Japanese hands. Japan now had control of the Malacca Strait, the main sea route between the Indian and Pacific oceans. And they were not slow to take advantage of this situation, quickly dispatching a force of five carriers, commanded by Admiral Nagumo, the officer who led the attack on Pearl Harbor, against British naval and air bases in Ceylon (now Sri Lanka). Although the Royal Navy, commanded by Admiral A B Cunningham, lost two cruisers and the aircraft carrier HMS *Hermes* during the series of actions that followed, it did make the Japanese realise that they had reached the limit of their carrier endurance. It also seems likely that the Royal Navy and RAF had inflicted more damage on what was Japan's irreplaceable, elite, striking force than intelligence reports at the time had revealed.

Japanese carriers never learned to replenish at sea from a chain of supply ships in the way the Americans did, later in the Pacific war. Nor were they able to replace their major fleet units and aircraft as quickly as the United States, despite their highly efficient industrial base.

Victory, perhaps, did not seem quite the certainty that Japan's politicians and senior officers had predicted. How this psychological defeat back would affect the later battles is impossible to say, but it certainly cannot have helped.

On land, however, the Japanese army experienced no such setbacks and its rapid advance continued. It captured the Dutch East Indies and even extended its sway northwards, into the Bering Sea. Bataan fell, on 8 April 1942, and its surrender was marked by the inhuman treatment and subsequent death of nearly 50,000 American and Filipino prisoners of war. The Philippines was finally captured on 6 May.

At least one group of RFA men also suffered brutal ill-treatment as prisoners of the Japanese, when *Francol* was sunk south of Java on 3 March 1942. Eight of her crew survived, to be made prisoners of war by the Japanese. Stories of Japanese cruelty to European POWs are very common, but one quote from a Lt Ota Tai, who was responsible for the administration of the camp where *Francol*'s crew was held, illustrates the attitude of the Japanese officer class.

It was made to the senior British officer of a POW camp, about two miles north of Macassar, Celebes, during the internment there of crews from a number of Allied ships, including *Francol*.

This officer, Lt Cdr G T Cooper RN, had asked about the Geneva Convention, which provoked Lt Tai to reply, '... don't talk to me of International Law. There is no such thing.'

During the period of their imprisonment, during 1942–5, officers and men in this camp received minimum rations, little clothing and almost no medical supplies. Much of the prisoner's food was stolen by the guards and, in consequence, the rations they received were barely adequate to maintain life. It has been suggested that this was a deliberate policy on the part of the Japanese government, which wanted maximum work from its prisoners, while incurring as little expense as possible. The diet of a prisoner in the camp during 1942 was:

Breakfast – 4 oz dry bread, ½ cup of coffee.
Dinner – 6 oz rice with greens and a little meat (less than 1oz) or a duck egg.
Supper – 8oz bread and one duck egg.

In 1943, this ration was reduced still further:

Breakfast – 6oz rice porridge, ½ oz sugar, ½ cup of coffee.
Dinner – 6 oz rice with greens.
Supper – 6oz rice with thin vegetable stew.

Lieutenant Commander Cooper states that these rations gave each man a total weight of food of 1½–2 pounds of food a day, during a period when most, if not all the prisoners were involved in heavy manual work, although a simple calculation shows the actual figure to be just over one pound, at 18 ounces. Certainly, the lack of vitamins, protein and fat was far more serious than even a simple calculation of weight would indicate and this lead to a widespread incidence of diseases associated with malnutrition.

In addition to poor rations, prisoners were subjected to consistently brutal treatment by the guards, in particular, by the warrant officer responsible for 'discipline', 3rd Class Petty Officer Yoshida. Between March 1942 and the Japanese surrender in 1945, over 180 men died from malnutrition, disease and physical abuse.

It is difficult to understand a mentality that allows and even relishes the daily barbarities practised on Allied POWs during their internment under the Japanese. Perhaps at least the motivation behind such actions does become clearer when one realises that similar treatment was also meted out to Japanese civilians, although no circumstances can possibly justify it.

Full details of the treatment of British servicemen by the Japanese are available at the website cited in the reference section of this book.

Two months after *Francol*'s sinking, in May 1942, the Allies finally began to hit back.

In one of the first amphibious landings of the war, Operation 'Ironclad', 13,000 British troops took control of the Vichy French occupied island of Madagascar. This island had assumed an importance out of all proportion to its size because Allied leaders thought its ports might be used by Japanese submarines to attack their highly vulnerable convoys. Japan had submarines with an immense range, in excess of 10,000 miles, so from Madagascar these could have menaced not just Pacific but even the Mediterranean convoy routes.

After extensive reconnaissance by the South African Air Force, Operation 'Ironclad' began with the 13th Assault Flotilla leaving the UK on the night of 23 March 1942. This group consisted of the LSG *Derwentdale* and four other merchant vessels carrying Landing Craft, Assault (LCA)s.

These ships initially joined an outward bound convoy for Durban, South Africa. Upon arrival, they rendezvoused with several other merchant ships and the Royal Navy warships that were to serve as their protective screen – HMS *Ramillies*, the carriers HMS *Illustrious* and *Indomitable*, two cruisers and a number of destroyers, corvettes and minesweepers. This assault group, accompanied by the oiler *Easdale*, left Durban on 25 April, bound for Madagascar.

First objective was the huge landlocked harbour of Diego Suarez and the port of Antisirane. Guided by lights that had been previously placed by reconnaissance groups, the unarmed merchant vessels, including *Derwentdale*, approached the shore on the night of 5 May, before releasing their landing craft, containing troops from the 5th Infantry Division, 29th Infantry Brigade and 5 Commando.

Conditions were calm with no moon and as planned, the landing craft moved towards the beaches of both Courrier Bay and Ambararata Bay, west of the objective. They landed, moved quickly overland and, following fierce fighting, Diego Suarez surrendered on the 7th, although not before significant Vichy forces had escaped to the south.

British forces were attacked three weeks later, on 29 May 1942, by midget submarines launched from the Japanese submarines *I-10*, *I-16* and *I-20*. One of these two-man submarines entered the harbour at Diego Suarez and managed to fire both its torpedoes, even though it was under depth charge attack from a pair of corvettes at the time. One torpedo seriously damaged *Ramillies*, while the other sank the oil tanker *British Loyalty*. The tanker was refloated shortly afterwards, but *Ramillies* was forced to return first to Durban, then to Plymouth before it could be properly repaired.

During summer 1942, two brigades of the 5th Infantry Division left the island and were replaced by troops from East Africa and Rhodesia as well as the South African 7th

Motorised Brigade. Landings were made later in the year, on 10 September at Majunga (Operation 'Stream') and on the 18th at Tamatave (Operation 'Jane'), both groups supported by *Easdale*, which accompanied the assault convoys as oiler. By the end of September, the capital, Tananarive, and the nearby town of Ambalavao had been captured without difficulty and with a final landing at Tulear on the 30th, the Allied commanders felt Madagascar was secure. Sporadic fighting continued, however, until 5 November, when the French commander, General Armand Annet, surrendered. Madagascar was used subsequently as a military base and received its independence from France in 1958.

Occupation of the Philippine Islands, on 6 May 1942, marked the end of the Japanese military advance. Their next objective was to extend their frontiers into the Coral Sea, thus threatening Australian communications with the United States. But they overreached themselves, in the process discovering their fundamental mistake at Pearl Harbor. They had sunk the US Navy's battleships but missed the far more important carriers, which had been absent.

Japanese forces forced a landing at Tulagi, in the Solomons Islands, on 3 and 4 May, although several of supporting warships were sunk by aircraft from the carrier USS *Yorktown*. The carriers *Lexington* and *Yorktown* then intercepted what was to have been Japan's second thrust, at Port Moresby.

In what came to be called the Battle of the Coral Sea, on 7 May 1942, US aircraft, commanded by Rear-Admiral Frank Fletcher, first sank the Japanese escort carrier *Shoho*. Japanese aircraft hit back, sinking a US destroyer and damaging one of the vitally important fleet oilers. Next day, the 8th, although hindered by bad weather, the Americans finally found the Japanese fleet carrier *Shokaku*, damaging it so badly that it was forced to return to Japan for repairs. *Lexington* was also hit, but still managed to steam away from the action. Unfortunately, she was so badly damaged by an internal explosion an hour later that she had to be sunk, although her aircraft and crew were all safely evacuated. *Yorktown* was also damaged but, more importantly, the Japanese carriers lost a significant number of aircraft, rendering them useless for the Battle of Midway, which was barely a month away. With its air cover gone, the invasion fleet aimed at Port Moresby was now forced to turn back, although the Japanese clearly intended to try again. Incidentally, the Battle of the Coral Sea was the first naval engagement in which neither side's ships sighted or fired directly upon the other. In a taste of the future, the whole battle was fought and decided in the air

Beaten in the Battle of the Coral Sea, Yamamoto turned his attention to Midway and it was there, on 4 June 1942, that the Americans scored their most resounding victory yet. Under the command of Admiral Chester Nimitz, aircraft from *Yorktown*, *Enterprise* and *Hornet*, sank all four Japanese carriers sent against them, for the loss of the already badly damaged *Yorktown* and a large number of aircraft. They were helped immeasurably in this battle by the absence of two major Japanese fleet carriers, *Shokaku* and *Zuikaku*, one damaged and the other suffering a depleted aircraft complement. This ensured parity in aircraft, although not carriers, and contributed significantly to the US victory.

Another factor that helped the US Navy to victory at Midway was Nimitz's courage in taking unconventional solutions to the problems facing him. *Yorktown*, after being hard hit in the Coral Sea, had returned to Pearl Harbor, where it had been estimated that she would have to go back to the United States for several months of repairs. That was no good to Nimitz, who would then have had only two serviceable carriers to oppose the Japanese fleet.

Her elevators were intact and her flight deck was repairable, however, and by working round the clock for three days, the shipyard at Pearl Harbor had *Yorktown* put back together and ready for sea. She was only good enough for a couple of weeks of operation, but that was all Nimitz needed. Several squadrons of aircraft were transferred from USS *Saratoga* and she sailed with repairs still going on even while she headed towards the Japanese fleet.

With the destruction of several major fleet units during The Battle of Midway, Japan's headlong advance across the Pacific was brought to a standstill.

Now, it was the turn of the Americans.

Although the Japanese had been stopped at Midway, this did not mark the end of their attempts to advance across the Pacific. They were still well established on the Solomons, with a strong base at Tulagi. They were also firmly entrenched in Papua New Guinea, on the easterly side of the Owen Stanley Mountains, which separated them from the Australian side of the range and the Australian base at Port Moresby. From their base in New Guinea, the Japanese now began preparations for an overland assault against Moresby. Port Moresby is only 300 miles from the northernmost tip of Australia and, with this potential threat in mind, the Allied commanders decided that the Japanese must be driven out of both the Solomons chain and New Guinea.

The Solomons campaign began on 7 August 1942, with assaults on Guadalcanal and Tulagi. In the months and years that followed the Americans fought a number of costly amphibious campaigns across the Pacific, which included the recapture of Manus and Leyte. By September 1944, the Solomon Islands, New Guinea and the Philippines were back in US hands and the Battle of Leyte Gulf, in October 1944, had all but eliminated the Japanese fleet as an offensive force.

Increasing numbers of British warships had begun to arrive at Ceylon at about the same time, allowing the Royal Navy to put pressure on the Japanese from another direction.

Over 50 per cent of Japan's fuel came from two oil refineries in the Palembang area of Sumatra. More importantly, these produced over three quarters of her aviation spirit, vital to the carrier-borne aircraft of her strike forces. In a series of operations between November 1944 and January 1945, a force of British carriers and warships under the command of Admiral Philip Vian, successfully attacked these refineries, destroying much of their infrastructure. Vian's force was refuelled at sea by *Echodale*, *Empire Salvage*, *Arndale* and one of the new Wave class, *Wave King*. Although, the warships completed refuelling, bad weather meant several of the oilers were damaged by contact with the escorting destroyers. In addition, the speed of fuel transfer was badly affected by the new buoyant hose parting at the joints. This was just a foretaste of conditions that would be experienced later with the British Pacific Fleet.

On mainland Asia, the Japanese were also being pushed out of Burma, helped by a naval force which recaptured Rangoon on 2 May 1945. This force, part of Operation 'Dracula', was accompanied by *Easedale*, *Brown Ranger* and *Olwen*.

With Japanese forces in retreat everywhere, early in spring 1945, the Americans were now poised to attack their first two major targets on Japanese soil, Iwo Jima and Okinawa.

In Washington and London, however, with the end of the war in sight, political considerations had begun to acquire a new importance.

Until late in 1944, the United States had conducted its naval and amphibious operations in the Pacific alone, while, in the process, liberating British territories and extending its influence in the region. In Whitehall, this began to give rise to concerns about both the loss of British prestige in an area of significant commercial importance and the corresponding US gains. It was therefore seen as imperative, both in political and military terms, to restore a British presence in the region and to deploy British military assets directly against Japan. The UK government and Churchill in particular, was determined that British territories, such as Hong Kong, should be recaptured by British forces. At the same time, those forces should be seen to be aiding the Americans and not just restoring the old colonial order in the area. In order to do that, they needed to form a British Pacific Fleet to join the US Pacific Fleet and show Americans that Britain was willing to commit her forces to their war.

So that is what they set about doing.

Chapter 9

The British Pacific Fleet Train

Politics had inaugurated the British Pacific Fleet and politics, along with contemplation of postwar British–US relations, also ensured it had to be more than a token force. John Winant, US Ambassador in London during this period, saw the situation clearly. He wrote:

> ... If we allow the British to limit their active participation to recapture areas which are to their selfish interests alone and not participate in smashing the war machine of Japan, if British soldiers don't cross the Atlantic for our Pacific ports, and if we shuck the British air force in order to prove our own dominance in the air, we will create in the United States a hatred for Great Britain that will make for schisms in the post war years that will defeat everything that men have died for in this war ...

Churchill offered the services of the Royal Navy in the assault on Japan during the 'OCTAGON', the second Quebec conference, in September 1944. He promised that the fleet would not only be powerful and well balanced but would also have a Fleet Train of 'ample proportions' that would ensure it was self-sustaining. Roosevelt accepted, against the advice of Admiral King, his Chief of Naval Operations.

King, insensitive or ignorant of the prevailing political currents, was against any British involvement for what he thought were a number of good and sufficient reasons. He made it perfectly clear to all concerned that the United States needed no help to easily finish the war in the Pacific alone, besides being very concerned about British logistic supply. A noted Washington Anglophobe, King was also against any operations that would assist the British in regaining their pre-war colonial holdings in the Pacific region.

Admiral Sir Bruce Fraser was appointed commander of the new British Pacific Fleet, the largest Britain had ever assembled, and he was determined that the Royal Navy would be a major part of any Pacific operation, King's views notwithstanding. His force was not going to be relegated to what he termed a 'back area', as the Australians felt they had been. In order to achieve this, he saw clearly that he would have integrate his command as closely as possible with the Americans. As a start in that direction, he ordered the British to adopt the US Navy's signal books and Admiral Nimitz obliged by sending both the books and a liaison team to every British warship. However, in the best traditions of both services, Anglo-US naval cooperation went further still.

At the Quebec conference, Admiral King had insisted that the British must be self supporting, down to the last nut, bolt and gallon of petrol, which meant that they would require their own fleet train. This was a collection of ships that would be concerned with moving supplies to wherever the British fleet was operating and supply them at sea, along lines that had already been well established by the US Navy. To many US officers, this rule seemed both pointless and unworkable so they simply ignored Admiral King. In fact, later, when the fleet was operational, US officers bluntly told Rear Admiral Douglas Fisher, commander of the British Fleet Train, that he could have anything and everything, '... that could be given without Admiral King's knowledge ...'.

There was an amusing incidence of this soon after the fleet left Sydney. One of the carriers was short of three Avenger aircraft and Fraser signalled Admiral Nimitz asking if they could have three when they got to Manus, as there were hundreds there. Nimitz replied that he was very sorry, but he could not. Fraser then asked his American liaison officer, what might be the problem? The officer thought about it for a while and then explained that the signal had gone through Washington so, of course, Admiral Nimitz was obliged to reply as he did. He assured Fraser that he thought it would be alright when they got there. Admiral Fraser remembered:

> ... I went up at about that time to have a look at Manus and I said to the American admiral in charge of the place, 'Look, do you think we could possibly borrow three Avengers from you?' And he said, 'Well, actually we don't issue them in less than six at a time. If you've got a bottle of whisky, you can have a dozen!' And he made me out a signal for them on the spot!

Despite unstinting US assistance, the Royal Navy still had big problems to overcome.

British warships were designed for service close to home and their refuelling arrangements, usually conducted over the stern of the oiler, were still primitive compared to those in use by the US Navy. Nor did they have any reliable system for re-supplying warships at sea with food or ammunition. Composition of the British Pacific Fleet Train would have to take all these factors into account.

By the early 1930s, British plans for resupplying its ships in the Pacific had centred around the presence of an intermediate base that would allow the Royal Navy to operate over the sort of distances it was accustomed to in the Atlantic and Medi-terranean. Aircraft development soon meant such a base was too vulnerable to air attack, so the Admiralty looked round for other options, which included replenish-ment at sea.

This finally resulted in the formation of a Supply Ships Committee in 1936 (see also Chapter 4). Its role was 'to consider the numbers and types of auxiliary vessels required for maintaining supplies to the Fleet in 'certain emergencies ... etc'.

This Committee was responsible for a number of logistic supply initiatives but their specific recommendations for support units needed by a Far East Fleet were thirteen store issuing/carrying ships, twenty to thirty armament store issuing ships (ASIS), one armament maintenanace ship, one mine depot ship, one torpedo repair ship, fourteen mine carriers, one naval stores issuing ship (NSIS) (with spare water distilling capa-city), two victualling stores issuing ships (VSIS), one large frozen meat carrying ship, and four store-carrying merchant ships of the 'China coaster' type.

This amounted to between fifty-eight and sixty-eight ships. All vessels should have maximum range of 4000 miles (US Navy specifications some years earlier had been at least 10,000 miles for fleet oilers; this committee, unfortunately, was not responsible for oilers, hospital ships or colliers). The committee further recommended that half of these vessels should be taken up for conversion before a war began, with the rest requisitioned as soon after it had started as possible. War time would quickly show that this was a case of 'far too little, far too late'! This sort of approach, incidentally, persisted into the post-war era, when it was suggested that what eventually became the

Admiralty's new Tide class oilers could also be used as chartered tankers, thereby increasing government revenue! A few ships of the requisite type and tonnage were actually converted by the Admiralty in 1939 and 1940, but by then Britain's losses of warships and merchant vessels was so catastrophic that the government was concerned more with survival than hypothetical logistics supply to a non-existent British Pacific Fleet. Anyway, ships in the necessary numbers were simply not available.

By April 1942, after Nagato's raid had all but pushed them out of the Indian Ocean, Britain's Eastern Fleet was forced to base itself at Kilindini, in East Africa, over 2500 miles from Ceylon. It was also 4000 miles from Singapore, the UK's most important Far East base, which was now in Japanese hands. Clearly, operations against Japan, over such distances, would be impossible for the British warships with their limited replenishment equipment and lack of supply ships. A year later, in May 1943, with these limitations in mind, Admiral Somerville (C-in-C Eastern Fleet), suggested a plan that involved establishing Eastern Fleet bases in recaptured enemy territory. His ideas were rejected but further discussion at this meeting evolved the concept of a 'Mobile Fleet Base Organisation', to allow for logistic support in areas away from established bases. In other words, an organised system for replenishment at sea.

Planning for this embryo fleet train, along much the same lines as the American model, proceeded through summer 1943 and by September, when all the relevant departments had submitted their requirements, it had reached an estimated size of seventy-four ships. The Admiralty approached the Ministry of War Transport (MoWT) with a request for this number of ships in September, 1943 and as might be expected, given the history between the two departments, that heralded the beginning of a long series of inter-departmental wrangles.

After a series of meetings between UK and US representatives, tentative deployment of a British naval force in the Pacific and the required number of auxiliaries had now been agreed upon. This culminated in a Washington meeting during January 1944, where both sides also agreed that the US Navy would share its excess facilities afloat and ashore in forward areas. In addition, the US Navy would maintain harbour defences, minimum port facilities and carry out emergency repairs to British warships damaged in battle. They would also make airfields under their control available to aircraft fom the British fleet, when carriers were at anchorages nearby. Despite their use of the phrase 'excess facilities' and the splendid picture that conjured up in British minds, US Navy representatives made it very clear that the Royal Navy would be solely responsible for its own naval, victualling, armament and aircraft stores.

One of the results of these Anglo-US meetings was that Admiralty estimates for a Pacific Fleet Train had increased, by April 1944, to 134 ships in total, ninety-four for the Pacific, with the rest operating in the Indian Ocean. The MoWT was appalled and suggested that perhaps the navy should supply its requirements out of tonnage it had already been allocated. In fairness, the MoWT did have immense problems ensuring the UK's food and raw material supplies. Fulfilling the navy's demands for a Pacific Fleet Train must have seemed like a nightmare, especially given the losses, in ships and experienced seamen, which Britain's Merchant Navy had suffered since 1939.

Churchill now took a hand. Late in April 1944, he ordered that the size of the Pacific Fleet itself would have to be determined by the size of the Fleet Train that could be made available, not vice versa. In turn, the size of the train would be determined by the number of merchant ships that Britain could spare, after its yearly import target of twenty-four million tons had been met.

Unfortunately, problems of merchant ship tonnage was actually out of MoWT control, because of an agreement reached earlier in the war with the US government. In order to maximise shipbuilding effort, it had been decided that UK shipyards would largely build warships, while the United States and Canada would take care of merchant ship requirements. That arrangement finally turned out to be to the Allies' advantage, because US and Canadian yards built ships in numbers for the BPF Train, which UK yards would have found impossible to match.

Gradually, a few ships intended for the train began to be made available for conversions, but the whole concept of the Pacific fleet and its supporting train had begun to be gripped by an increasing sense of inertia, only partly dispelled by the second Quebec conference. At least now a self-supporting British fleet had been promised to the Americans, in support of their Pacific operations, and Churchill's undertaking would have to be honoured. Admiralty planners made a whole new set of calculations and put a revised ship requirement to the MoWT in October 1944 – the so-called 'October Bid'. The Minister waited until 20 January 1945 before replying that '... he could not make shipping allocations of this sort'.

Things had, however, become a good deal easier by early February, with major improvements in the shipping situation. In consequence, Admiral Fraser reported that the BPF would have a strength of 100,000 men by July 1945, with 80,000–90,000 of them in the forward area. First elements of the Fleet Train were assembled in December 1944, because it had taken Admiralty planners that long to confirm just how the British Pacific Fleet was to be deployed and resupplied. Despite this delay, ships of the train were in Sydney, Australia, by January 1945 and operating with the fleet in March, an incredible achievement in just four months. With so little time to spare, the Fleet Train had to be formed from the vessels available and sent out as soon as they could put to sea, regardless of condition. These ships really were literally requisitioned from just about anywhere and this was reflected in the composition of the force and the poor state of some of its components. In particular, the lack of modern, large, fast oilers equipped for RAS would be critical and seriously limit the operating capabilities of the British Fleet. As the then Director of Stores pointed out, with perhaps more grasp of the realities than some:

> ... It is impossible to escape the obvious conclusion so forcefully brought before us that, even in time of war, the resources of the British Empire were incapable of providing the ships, bases and facillities necessary to maintain adequately the Pacific Fleet, operating as it was under exceptional circumstances, at great distances from the main force ....

The train eventually included merchant seamen and naval personnel from Europe, Asia and the Commonwealth, as well as the occupied countries. Although the problems of administration and deployment were enormous, by VJ (Victory in Japan) day, Task Force 112 (TF112), which comprised the Fleet Train and its escorting force, consisted of 125 ships, manned by 26,200 officers and men. In its final days, the train even boasted an amenities ship, *Menestheus*, in which the equipment included a brewery capable of producing 1800 gallons of beer per day! Despite this enormous concentration of ships, only US help had allowed the Royal Navy to play the worthwhile part it finally did in the Pacific.

Perhaps the most difficult problem facing officers trying to make the BPF operational was the size of the ocean they were fighting over. Distances which tankers and supply ships would have to cover were immense and quite out of the experience of most British naval officers. Admiral Fraser later explained it succinctly: '... distances involved are similar to those of a fleet based in Alexandria, with advanced anchorages at Gibraltar and the Azores, attacking the North American coast between Labrador and Nova Scotia ...'.

Two thousand miles from its main base, according to US trials, was about the limit at which the Fleet Train could reasonably expect to operate. This meant that Sydney, the BPF's main base and over 4000 miles from Japan, was too far from the target areas to use for routine replenishment.

Logistics supply was accordingly arranged in a series of steps. Sydney would serve as the main base, where the fleet would initially fuel and store, because of its extensive dockyard and repair facillities. A forward base would be established, somewhere between Sydney and Okinawa, the first US objective, where refuelling and minor repairs could be carried out. Ships too badly damaged for repair here would return to Sydney, from where replacements would also be supplied. Between the forward base and the target areas, there would be several designated operating areas where the warships returned to replenish from the waiting tankers and store ships, usually at two or three day intervals. Operating areas were simply squares of ocean in which tankers and store ships could wait, far enough from the enemy to be safe from airstrikes.

Manus, an island in the Admiralty group and about 200 miles north of Papua New Guinea, was selected for the BPF forward base. It was well suited for this purpose, the Americans having recaptured the island in May 1944 and quickly turned it into a major military facility. It had floating docks for battleship and destroyer repair, an airstrip, a 1500-bed hospital, fresh, filtered water and 150 miles of roads. There was even a 7000-seat open-air cinema! British officers of the BPF established their own camp, with the unstinting support of the USN officers at Manus, which eventually had harbour, communications and recreational facillities to rival the Americans. This is hardly surprising, because much of the equipment the Royal Navy ended up with came to them from their US Navy colleagues!

In order to ensure smooth operation of the Fleet Train, its administrative framework had begun to be organised long before any of its ships reached Sydney.

In spring 1944, Rear Admiral Charles Daniel, later Vice Admiral, Administration, BPF, arrived in Australia to begin negotiations with the Canberra government over the organisation of the fleet's logistics requirements. Admiral Daniel had earlier led the British team that negotiated US supply arrangements during the Washington meeting of January 1944, so had considerable experience of this type of negotiation.

He found labour disputes in the docks, supply difficulties and complexities of all kinds awaiting him, which made his job an organisational nightmare. It was later said of his appointment, by the Royal Navy's Official Historian, Captain S W Roskill, that '... if unspectacular compared to the command of a fighting squadron, (it) was certainly one of the most arduous allocated to a British flag officer during the entire war ...'.

As late as October 1944, when Rear Admiral D B Fisher was appointed Rear Admiral Fleet Train (RAFT), many of these difficulties were still unresolved. Such problems only added to Fisher's reponsibilities, which were far reaching enough already. They included not only logistics supply but also operations as diverse as mail delivery and the repair of both warships and his own fleet of merchant vessels.

After several months of arduous and frustrating planning, Admiral Fisher left the UK in December, arriving in Sydney on 7 January 1945 and taking command of the Fleet Train officially on the 29th. Vice Admiral Sir Bernard Rawlings, who had been placed in seagoing command of the BPF, duly presented him with a large green flag and a guard's whistle!

Admiral Fisher hoisted his flag (not the green one!) in the headquarters ship, HMS *Lothian* and on 24 February and he and his staff left Sydney for Manus, arriving on 2 March. *Lothian* was poorly designed as tropical accommodation as well as being very overcrowded, which resulted in Fisher and his staff spending several uncomfortable months. Fortunately, they were able to transfer to a new headquarters ship, the liner *Montclare*, in late May.

The main British fleet arrived at Manus on 7 March 1945 and its Fleet Train was kept busy refuelling and replenishing ships prior to Operation 'Iceberg', the Allied invasion of Okinawa.

Rawlings' ships left Manus on 18 March 1945, for the initial assault on Okinawa. Now designated Task Force 57 and under the command of US Admiral Spruance, the British were assigned the south-western flank of the combined fleet. Its first two logistic support groups, Task Unit 112/2/1 and Task Unit 112/2/5, which included the oilers *Cedardale*, *San Adolfo* and *San Ambrosio*, had sailed a day earlier, the 17th, so as to be in position to replenish the the warships. Task Force 112, made up of the remainder of the Fleet Train, left on the 19 for Leyte, from where it would operate. Arriving on the 26, it began by topping up its oilers from US Navy tankers, before commencing logistic supply to the BPF. *Brown Ranger* served at Leyte as a water tanker, later also serving with the forces which recaptured Hong Kong and Shanghai.

Aerial reinforcement of Okinawa's well-established garrison was easily carried out either directly from Japan or as a series of island 'jumps' from Formosa via the Amami Gunto and Sakishima Gunto island groups. It was the job of the British Fleet to prevent aircraft from Sakishima attacking the main US assault force.

The BPF arrived at Ulithi early on the morning of 20 March and began refuelling operations from the US installations there. It left Ulithi three days later and, by the 25th, had contacted its two task units to begin refuelling again. Despite problems due to high winds and some hose failure, fuelling was eventually completed, although several destroyers were forced to 'top up' from the escort carrier HMS *Striker*, which was accompanying the oilers. By the 26th, aircraft from the BPF were assaulting air bases in the target area. This operation continued until 20 April in the face of unceasing Kamikazi attacks by the Japanese. After a period of refitting, British forces returned to the seas around Okinawa from 4 to 25 May, when the Japanese finally abandoned the island.

British replenishment operations were carried out in designated operating areas every two or three days, the Fleet Train organised into three or four task units for this purpose. A typical task unit, such as T U 112/2/1, consisted of three tankers, an escort carrier and escort vessels. In the early stages, there was considerable shortage of stores issuing ships, so the tankers carried and issued food, ammunition and naval and air stores as well as transporting wounded.

Underway replenishment programmes followed by the task units were very complex.

When a task force had finished its two day strike at the target, it would withdraw to a convenient operating area (OA), usually making an arranged rendezvous with its refuelling group at dawn. Choice of a particular area usually depended on the weather, since the fleet and its train were now operating during the typhoon season. Prior to the rendezvous, support vessels from the task unit deployed to a prearranged plan, with its escorts also adopting an agreed screening pattern. The task force approached from the rear, slowed to the speed of the logistics group and individual ships took position for replenishment. Both escort groups then took up screening positions and refuelling could begin.

The RFA tankers usually arrived for service with the Fleet Train fitted for both astern and abeam replenishment, although Dale class RFAs were soon found to be too slow to refuel large ships abeam. Astern replenishment by bouyant hose was initially the preferred method for big ships, while destroyers and light cruisers usually refuelled abeam. This led to difficulties later, during periods of rough weather, when large British warships found it impossible to refuel from US tankers, which were only equipped for abeam replenishment. Both US Navy tankers and RFAs could replenish abeam on either side, although the design of some chartered tankers prevented these operating in this way and during the later stages of the Pacific war, the Fleet Train also found it expedient to go some way towards standardising both its equipment and operations to the US pattern. Commercial tankers and the RFA oliers had similar refuelling equipment and achieved comparable transfer rates – 150–175 tons/hour with a single hose, 300–400 tons/hour with a two-hose rig. Double hoses were used both abeam and astern, simultaneously although the big fleet carriers invariably used three hoses, the third carrying aviation spirit, which was usually the main requirement these vessels had when refueling. Tanker crews became so expert that they could refuel three ships at a time, a warship on either side and an aircraft carrier astern, as long as their pumping system could bear the strain.

While refuelling operations were going on, fresh aircraft would be flown from the escort carriers to the larger fleet carriers. Food and ammunition was transferred by 'whip and inhaul', because supply ships equipped for resupply at sea were in short supply with the Royal Navy during 'Iceberg'. With the battleships and carriers restored, it was the turn of the escorts and when all was complete, the task force returned to its target area. Empty support group vessels went back to one of the forward bases to resupply, which took each task unit 12–14 days. Some of the tankers could, however, remain in the OA because of the practice of 'topping up' between half empty tankers, thus allowing one full or nearly full oiler to remain on station while the vessel which had pumped over returned to base.

Two or three days later, the whole tedious, difficult, dangerous proceedure had to be endured again.

Absence of purpose-built supply ships and equipment failure, together with the low speed, small capacity and unreliability of many BPF oilers, meant replenishment could often take two days or more. American logistics groups, with their purpose built tankers and supply ships, manned by large crews of US Navy ratings, could, understandably, carry out similar operations far more quickly. What was seen as poor performance often led to open criticism by the crews of US Navy and even Royal Navy warships, which many in the Fleet Train felt to be unwarranted.

Presumably, with such comments in mind, a Royal Navy officer, writing a report on 'Oiling and Requisitioning at Sea', was moved to remark:

> It is quite clear that very few of the officers in the US Service Force are Seamen and indeed this is the opinion of those in the Force who are. Time and again things are done or left undone which would be unpardonable in the Royal Navy.
>
> It is also clear that the US ships are grossly overmanned. I doubt whether 10% of the officers and men in the Service have ever done a 'day's work' and certainly not day after day. I am convinced we can achieve the same results and better with half the numbers of men.
>
> I arrived in the US Pacific Fleet Service Force with a slight tendency to an inferiority complex. They have so much that we haven't got – particularly on the material plane. I am, however, leaving their Service Force convinced we are better seamen and that we can do all that they can do and better than they can do it.
>
> (*Author's note*: During this period, USN tankers had complements ranging from 260 to 350, including weapons ratings. The RFA's modern Wave class does much the same job with a total crew of 78.)

This oiling report (PRO: ADM199/1756) also had something to say about manning of the Royal Navy's auxilliaries. This passage from later in the same report:

> No mention has been made again of what is bound to be a controversial subject, namely – the manning of the RFAs by Royal Navy personnel – but it is considered that this is a most important recommendation. The fact that all USN Train ships are manned by USN personnel greatly strengthens the argument in favour of this recommendation.

It is difficult to be certain, but this report seems to show that it was their Fleet Train experiences that marked a hardening of the Royal Navy's preoccupation with naval manning for its auxilliaries. A preoccupation one might add which, justified or not, for some Royal Navy (and RFA) officers has lasted until the present day.

Fuel capacities and equipment of some Pacific Fleet Train tankers

Ship	Furnace fuel oil (tons)	Diesel fuel (tons)	Aviation spirit	Refuel astern	Refuel abeam
Arndale	11,400	–	500	1 hose	1 hose, either side
Dingledale	11,000	–	950	1 hose	1 hose, either side
Cedardale	11,000	–	950	1 hose	1 hose, either side
Brown Ranger	2500	500	900	1 hose	1 hose, either side
Green Ranger	2500	500	900	1 hose	1 hose, either side
Wave King	10,400	2420	980	1 hose	1 hose, either side
Wave Monarch	10,400	2420	980	1 hose	1 hose, either side
San Adolfo	9580	1400	–	1 hose	1 hose, either side

San Ambrosio	7450	1000	1900	1 hose	Not known
Aase Mærsk	9600	–	–	2 hoses	Not suitable
San Amado	7500	1000	1980	Not known	Not known

Note: Details for *San Amado* are recorded as: 'expected to be as *San Adolfo*'. The more modern Wave class ships were significantly better able to supply all of a task force's requirements, since they carried all fuel grades. Ranger class RFAs had much smaller FFO capacity and so were probably less useful for replenishment, although these did carry diesel fuel, which the bigger Dales could not.

Task forces were usually relieved after three weeks in a particular target area, when they returned to their forward bases, to replenish and rest their crews. In practice, however, staff shortages meant that the crews usually spent their time in Leyte or Manus loading supplies, instead of resting. Fleet Train crews were overworked, too, especially the men on tankers, and this manifested itself in unrest and dissatisfaction, often because of the different articles and terms of service in force.

In the escort carriers, for example, there was resentment because, although general service (*ie* naval) ratings and civilians signed under the MoWT T.124X agreement, were carrying out exactly the same duties, the civilians were receiving better rates of pay and terms of service. In other ships, trade union rules were enforced, under which men only worked according to their articles. On one occasion, this affected the RFA, when seven men from *Brown Ranger* refused to operate the ship's derrick, claiming such work was not within the terms of their articles. Although they were removed under armed guard, a naval court ruled that they were within their rights and released them, whereupon they returned to duty. By the end of the war, so many merchant seamen had been replaced by naval ratings, because of their refusal to work, that Admiral Fisher observed '... with the addition of a few officers and another few hundred ratings, the Fleet Train would have been fully White Ensign.'

It was significant, in light of post-war initiatives involving the RFA and the preceeding report, that he added that this would have been desirable from the start.

Okinawa was occupied by US amphibious forces on 21 June, the British fleet carriers having once again withstood kamikaze attacks by the Japanese airforce which would have sunk or disabled the more lightly armoured US carriers. Having seen the effect of the Japanese kamikaze on carriers from both forces, HMS *Indefatigable*'s US liason officer was moved to heartfelt comment: '... when a kamikazi hits a US carrier, it means six months of repair at Pearl. When a kamikaze hits a Limey carrier, it's just a case of "Sweepers, man your brooms".'

With the fall of Okinawa, most of the BPF ships and its train returned to Sydney for a well earned rest, although some were also assigned to Operation 'Inmate', the US strike at Truk .

A month and a half later, on 19 July 1945, the British and US fleets reassembled to attack the Japanese mainland. Admiral W F Halsey was now in command and with this change the BPF was redesignated Task Force 37. Increased distance from its main base presented further problems to the Fleet Train, problems so great that one RN Liason officer aboard USS *Shangri La*, admitted that if the war had not finished when it did '...

TF 37 ... would have been unable to continue operations because of lack of logistic support ...'

Aircraft from British carriers began the task forces operations by attacking airfields and railways at Honshu, the biggest of the Japanese home islands, on 17 July 1945, after the Americans were forced to cancel their own attack due to bad weather.

Relations between the British and US commanders had been unfailingly cordial up until now, with Admiral Halsey unreservedly helpful in supplying fuel and other necessities. Unfortunately, on 18 July, relations were soured by his largely political decision to exclude the British carriers from the aerial assault on Kure, an attack Admiral Vian, in command of the BPF carriers, felt was pointless anyway. Later, American historians were to agree with Vian.

Halsey justified himself in his autobiography, writing:

> ... it was imperative that we forestalled a possible postwar claim by Britain that that she had delivered even a part of the final blow which demolished the Japanese Fleet. I hated to admit a political factor into a military equation – my respect for Bert Rawlings and his fine men made me hate it doubly – but Mick (Rear Admiral Robert Carney) forced me to see ... an exclusively American attack was in ... American interests.

The British Pacific Fleet fought to the very end of the Pacific campaign, suffering some of its heaviest losses on 9 August, the day before Japan's surrender, when it attacked mainland airfields and several of Japan's remaining destroyers.

British forces performed creditably in the Pacific, despite immense logistics problems, although these difficulties certainly justified Admiral King's early reservations. Admiral Spruance acknowledged the part played by the Royal Navy, when the British Fleet left Okinawa for Australia. His signal read: 'I would express to you, to your officers and to your men, after 2 months operating as the Fifth Fleet Task Force, my appreciation of your fine work and cooperative spirit.'

And as one American historian, N E Sarantakes, wrote, many years later: 'When the British departed Okinawa on May 25th, they and their American allies could take pride in the operational work of the Task Force and the harmony in which the coalition partners had functioned.'

Which seems a fitting epitath for the men and ships of what came to be known as Britain's 'Forgotten Fleet'.

RFAs deployed as part of British Pacific Fleet Train

Oilers
Bishopdale, Cedardale, Eaglesdale, Brown Ranger, Green Ranger, Olna, Rapidol, Serbol, Wave Emperor, Wave Governor, Wave King, Wave Monarch

Store ships
Bacchus, Fort Constantine, Fort Dunvegan

Ships in the British Fleet Train (excluding RFAs)
HMSs *Adamant* (submarine depot ship), *Aorangi* (accommodation ship), *Artifex,*

Assistance (repair ships), *Berry Head* (repair ship), *Bonaventure* (submarine depot ship), *Deer Sound, Diligence, Dullisk Cove* (repair ships), *Empire Crest* (water carrier), *Fernmore* (boom carrier), *Flamborough Head* (repair ship), *Fort Colville* (aircraft store ship), *Langley* (aircraft store ship; later RFA), *Guardian* (netlayer), *King Salvor* (salvage ship; later RFA), *Lancashire* (accommodation ship), *Leonian* (boom carrier), *Maidstone* (submarine depot ship), *Montclare* (destroyer depot ship), *Resource* (repair ship), *Salvestor, Salvictor* (salvage ships), *Shillay* (danlayer),*Springdale* (repair ship), *Stagpool* (distilling ship), *Trodday* (danlayer), *Tyne* (destroyer depot ship), *Vacport* (water carrier), HMNZS *Kelantan* (repair ship); hospital ships: *Maunganui, Empire Clyde, Gerusalemme, Oxfordshire, Tjitalengka, Vasna.*

Oilers
Aase Mærsk, Carelia, Darst Creek, Golden Meadow, Iere, Loma Nova, San Adolfo, San Amado, San Ambrosio, Seven Sisters.

Store ships
Bosporus, City of Dieppe, Corinda, Darvel, Edna, Fort Alabama, Fort Edmonton, Fort Providence, Fort Wrangell, Gudrun Mærsk, Hermelin, Heron, Hickory Burn, Hickory Dale, Hickory Glen, Hickory Stream, Jaarstroom, Kheti, Kistna, Kola, Marudu, Pacheco, Prince de Liege, Princess Maria Pia, Prome, Robert Mærsk, San Andres, Slesvig, Thyra S.

Chapter 10

Final Days:
Europe, the Pacific and Armistice

Montgomery and Eisenhower had returned to Britain after the successful Sicilian campaign and, with these two in command, planning for Operation 'Overlord', the invasion of mainland Europe, entered a new phase. Originally, it had been intended that a simultaneous first day landing would be made by three divisions. Eisenhower, appointed Supreme Commander of 'Overlord' and Montgomery, his field commander, quickly decided that the attack would need at least five divisions to ensure that the troops in the initial landings would not be driven out of their bridgeheads by German reinforcements, which would certainly outnumber them.

Preparations were extensive and meticulous. Although it was impossible to keep the Germans from knowing that invasion was imminent, they were only able to obtain detailed photographic reconnaissance of restricted areas in southern Kent. Adding to this lack of air reconnaissance, Allied intelligence made sure that Rommel and Von Runstedt, in command of the German forces concentrated on the Channel coast, received plenty of conflicting and misleading information. Lacking vital intelligence, the German generals could not decide where the invasion might be expected. Their strategy was further disrupted by the systematic Allied bombing of French roads and railways, making rapid troop movements impossible. French resistance workers enthusiastically added their own contribution to this destruction and the resulting chaos.

With planning for the invasion well advanced, analysis of information obtained from reconnaissance of the landing beaches showed that the Germans had erected a complex and effective system of underwater obstacles. These were covered and therefore undetectable at high tide. If landing craft went into such a beach with the tide high, most of them would be caught by the obstacles and sunk. Waiting until low tide would not serve either, because then, although the obstacles could be seen and destroyed with demolition charges, troops would be exposed to heavy fire while they tried to move over long, exposed stretches of sand. The Dieppe raid, in 1942, had made it clear how disastrous such a landing could be and neither Eisenhower nor Montgomery were about to allow a repeat of this. So it was agreed that the first attacks would be carried out by tanks. For this sort of amphibious assault to succeed, however, they needed a special kind of tank. One that could swim!

Fortunately, there was an officer in the British army who had foreseen just such a situation. He was also Montgomery's brother-in-law, Major-General Percy (Hobo) Hobart, then in charge of the 79th (Experimental) Armoured Division, Royal Engineers. Hobart had devised or collected a number of specialised vehicles based on Churchill and Sherman tank chassis, which could dismantle beach defences without exposing troops to enemy fire. Known as 'Hobart's Funnies', his collection included the 'crocodile' a Churchill tank with the machine gun replaced with a flame thrower; the 'AVRE' (Armoured Vehicle, Royal Engineers), a Churchill whose main gun was now a Petard Spigot mortar, firing a 40-pound, HE filled projectile that looked like a flying dustbin when fired and had the effect of reducing pill boxes and road blocks to rubble; 'crab' tanks, Shermans modified to carry a mine 'flail', a weighted cylinder of rotating chains that exploded mines in the path of tanks; and the Sherman DD (Duplex Drive) amphibious tank, designed to be launched from LCTs at some distance from the beach and surprise the enemy, which would not be expecting their waterborne attackers. Montgomery offered half of 79th Division's 7000 vehicles to the Americans, but they remained unconvinced of the 'Funnies' effectiveness and reliability, refusing all but the Sherman DDs.

With planning complete, the Normandy landings (D-Day), first stage in the Allied invasion of Western Europe (Operation 'Overlord'), were scheduled for the summer of 1944, in the bay of the river Seine.

By June, everything was ready.

Late in May, Royal Navy motor torpedo boats (MTBs) began the initial preparations, laying a series of minefields, located so as to keep the German navy out of the invasion area. Allied minesweepers then cut a 10-mile wide swathe through the German's own Channel minefields, allowing ships of the invading forces clear, relatively safe access to the French coast.

With troops aboard ship and everything ready for the cross-Channel dash, bad weather struck and the invasion, originally intended for 5 June, had to be delayed. Fortunately, the Channel weather stabilised, with its customary summer quirkiness, and, by the morning of the 6th, airborne troops had, after initial difficulties, secured what would be the flanks of the invading forces. An intensive naval bombardment followed against the five designated landing beaches on the southern shore of the bay of the Seine – Utah, Omaha, Gold, Juno and Sword. The first two were the responsibility of the American 1st United States Army, leaving the other three to the British and Canadians of the British 2nd Army. With the naval shelling finished, amphibious tanks began driving ashore against the enemy landing obstacles, followed by a stream of men and equipment.

With the assistance of Hobart's 'Funnies', landings went to plan on the three British and Canadian beaches, a beachhead nearly six miles deep soon being firmly established at a cost of 3500 British and 1000 Canadian casualites. The Americans, without significant numbers of the 'Funnies', had a harder fight on 'Omaha'. Eventually, they forced their way off the beach against heavy resistance and established a smaller beachhead, 1.5 miles deep and about 8 miles long, incurring over 6000 casualties in the process. Utah, the second American beach, was relatively lightly defended and forces put ashore there quickly got off the sand and had made contact with one of their parachute divisions by the afternoon.

Amphibious operations early in the war, like the disastrous Dieppe raid, had shown that a secure harbour was essential for this sort of attack to achieve success. So when logistics supply began, which it did almost immediately the troops had landed, priority was given to the erection of two enormous, prefabricated harbours or 'Mulberrys'. Codenamed Mulberry A and B, the first off Omaha and the second off Gold, at Arromanches, they were constructed around two breakwaters, built up on a number of obsolete ships scuttled off the beaches for that purpose. Initially termed

'Gooseberries', similar breakwaters were also used off the other three beaches, although without further modification. Omaha's Mulberry was destroyed in a storm on 19 June but the Arromanches harbour functioned well for 10 months, landing 2.5 million men, 500,000 vehicles and 4 million tons of supplies for the invading forces. In addition to these static supply points, there was also a requirement for a huge mobile, refuelling operation.

An RFA Master, Captain E E Sigwart, was appointed to the staff of the Allied Naval Commander on the Beachhead, as Staff Officer (Fuel), where he assisted with the planning of this operation. What follows is based on his account (Sigwart 1969).

Fuelling during Operation 'Neptune' (the assault phase of 'Overlord') consisted mainly of supply to the 1000 or more landing craft that were operating a constant shuttle service of men and equipment from the landing ships to the beaches. During the planning phase of the operation it was assumed that the major refuelling requirement would be these 'ferry' landing craft, with depot ships, troop transports and bombarding warships requiring less attention from the refuelling organisation. This proved to be the case, but the utmost flexibility had to be maintained by the refuelling vessels, because unexpected calls were often made upon them.

Two RFAs were present during 'Neptune'; the tanker *Rapidol* and the coastal store ship *Robert Dundas*. Initially, *Rapidol* was intended to refuel the bombarding warships, but was quickly found to be of too deep draught and had to be replaced by the Maracaibo type Shell tanker *Juliana*. Although these conventional RFAs operated off the beaches, fuelling the landing craft was the responsibility of ten 'supply and repair' flotillas. Six were assigned to the British and Canadian beaches, Sword, Gold and Juno, while the remaining four operated off Omaha and Utah.

Each flotilla consisted of ten ordinary, dumb (unpowered), 'swim headed', flat bottomed Thames barges, 85feet long with a beam of 23 feet and a draught of 4.5 feet, temporarily fitted with engines that gave them a top speed of about 4.5 knots. Armed with twin Lewis guns and manned by naval ratings, these barges were of several types. For replenishment duties, each flotilla had six Landing Barge Oilers (LBO), and two Landing Barge Water (LBW), both types fitted with a 40-ton, 9000-gallon tank, served by two hand pumps and hoses. The LBOs each carried a different grade of petrol or diesel oil, with a large placard prominently displayed and stating the type of fuel aboard. Service on the fuelling barges was apparently very unpopular, both because the crews regarded them as nothing more than a giant floating bomb and because smoking was strictly forbidden at all times. In addition to its LBOs and LBWs, each flotilla also had a Landing Barge Emergency Repair (LBE) and a Landing Barge Kitchen (LBK). These LBKs were simply a large ship's galley, occupying the whole of the barge's hold and in continual operation, cooking and serving meals for both the barge crews and other members of the ferry parties. Equipped with oil fired ranges and even automated potato peelers, they carried enough provisions to feed around 900 men for a week and, with a normal crew of twenty-three, could supply 1600 hot and 800 cold meals daily. Their menu even included freshly baked bread!

Each flotilla also had three fuelling trawlers, which were former minesweepers, fitted with similar tanks and pumps to the LBOs. They were not much use for refuelling landing craft, their relatively deep draught preventing them from approaching the beach, so they were mainly used as tugs when the flotillas were required to change position. According to Sigwart (1969), the ultra-technical US Navy regarded these barge flotillas with initial scepticism, but having once seen them in operation, their attitude quickly changed and they even demanded extra barges, although none were actually available.

The LBOs and LBWs were replenished from coastal tankers, running a continual shuttle service from southern UK ports and operating to an extremely tight schedule. By D plus 90, early in September, Allied troops had captured several major ports and the refuelling operations were transferred to these locations.

Cherbourg was captured on 27 June and after seven and a half weeks of intense and bloody fighting through Normandy, on 26 July, the Americans broke through at the eastern end of the opposing defensive perimeter, the Germans having mistakenly concentrated their main strength in the west. Southern France was invaded on 15 August, in Operation 'Dragoon', which was supported by several RFAs carrying both fuel and equipment. Paris fell on the 24th and by 9 February 1945, British and Canadian troops, after many setbacks and mistakes, had reached the Rhine. Just over two months later, on 30 April, with the Russian army already in Berlin, Hitler committed suicide and the war in Europe was over.

In Italy, after taking Rome in June 1944, Allied troops advanced to a line defended by the Germans in the mountains north of Florence, where they were forced to stay during the winter of 1944–5. Attacks were renewed in April 1945 and by the end of the month, the German army in Italy was beaten.

With Iwo Jima and Okinawa in Allied hands by June 1945, British and American forces in the Pacific had begun air strikes on the Japanese mainland. Instead of then landing troops, Truman, the newly elected US President, Churchill and Chiang Kai-shek, China"s leader, called on Japan to surrender or face "prompt and utter destruction". Subsequent events are too well documented to need reiteration here. America"s first atomic bomb was dropped on Hiroshima on 6 August 1945, with a second on Nagasaki three days later. Japan surrendered the following morning, 10 August, and all fighting soon ceased.

The Second World War was over and the Allies had won. It now only remained to see who would win the peace.

RFA fleet 1939–45

Name	Type	Begun service	Left service	Class	Comments
Abbeydale	Tanker	1937	1960	Dale	Torpedoed 27 June 1941
Airsprite	Spirit carrier	1943	1965	Sprite	
Aldersdale	Tanker	1937	1942	Dale	Sunk 5 July 1942
Appleleaf	Tanker	1917	1946	Trinol	Scrapped 1946
Arndale	Tanker	1937	1960		Okinawa invasion with British Pacific Fleet Train
Bacchus	Store ship	1936	1962		Store ship with British Pacific Fleet Train
Belgol	Tanker	1917	1958	Belgol	
Berta	Tanker	1939	1945		
Birchol	Harbour tanker	1917	1939	Creosol	Lost by stranding 29 November 1939
Bishopdale	Tanker	1937	1970	Dale	Served in Pacific. Attacked by kamikaze bomber at Leyte
Black Ranger	Tanker	1941	1973	Ranger	
Blue Ranger	Tanker	1941	1972	Ranger	
Boardale	Tanker	1937	1940	Dale	Struck reef and sunk, Assund Fjord 30 April 1940
Boxol	Harbour tanker	1917	1948	Creosol	
Brambleleaf	Tanker	1917	1946	Trinol	Torpedoed 9 June 1942; kept afloat and towed to Alexandria, where in service as fuelling hulk.
British Lady	Tanker	1939		1945	Owned by Admiralty, but managed and manned by former owners. Not in Navy List as RFA.
Broomdale	Tanker	1937	1959	Dale	Bombed 16 May 1940. One casualty, ship undamaged.
Brown Ranger	Tanker	1941	1974	Ranger	
Cairndale	Tanker	1939	1941	Dale	Torpedoed west of Straits of Gibraltar; 30th May 1941. Four crew lost
Cedardale	Tanker	1939	1960	Dale	At Okinawa invasion
Celerol	Tanker	1917	1958	Belgol	
Cherryleaf	Tanker	1917	1946	Trinol	At Malta 1931–45, as station oiler
Danmark	Fuel hulk	1942	1946		
Darkdale	Tanker	1940	1941	Dale	Torpedoed off St Helena

Delphinula	Tanker	1915	1946		
Demeter	Stores hulk	1942	1946		
Denbydale	Tanker	1940	1955	Dale	
Derwentdale	LSG	1941	1957	Dale	
Dewdale	LSG	1941	1959	Dale	
Dingledale	Tanker	1942	1959	Dale	
Dinsdale	Tanker	1941	1941	Dale	Torpedoed on maiden voyage
Distol	Harbour tanker	1916	1947	*Creosol*	
Eaglesdale	Tanker	1942	1959	Dale	
Easedale	Tanker	1942	1959	Dale	
Ebonol	Harbour tanker	1917	1942	*Creosol*	On China station until 1941; scuttled to avoid capture by Japanese.
Echodale	Tanker	1941	1961	Dale	
Elderol	Harbour tanker	1917	1959	*Creosol*	Sunk by gunfire from Japanese fleet 1942
Elmol	Harbour tanker	1917	1959	*Creosol*	
Empire Salvage	Tanker	1941	1946		
Ennerdale	Tanker	1941	1958	Dale	
Freshbrook	Water tanker	1941	1946	Fresh	
Freshburn	Water tanker	1944	1946	Fresh	
Freshener	Water tanker	1942	1946	Fresh	
Freshet	Water tanker	1940	1946	Fresh	
Freshford	Water tanker	1944	1946	Fresh	
Freshlake	Water tanker	1942	1946	Fresh	
Freshmere	Water tanker	1943	1946	Fresh	
Freshpond	Water tanker	1945	1945	Fresh	
Freshpool	Water tanker	1943	1946	Fresh	
Freshtarn	Water tanker	1944	1946	Fresh	
Freshwater	Water tanker	1940	1946	Fresh	
Freshwell	Water tanker	1943	1946	Fresh	

Fortol	Tanker	1917	1958	*Belgol*	
Francol	Tanker	1917	1942	*Belgol*	
Gold Ranger	Tanker	1941	1973	Ranger	
Gray Ranger	Tanker	1941	1942	Ranger	Sunk on Convoy QP14 to Russia
Green Ranger	Tanker	1941	1962	Ranger	
Hickorol	Harbour tanker	1918	1948	*Creosol*	
Ingeborg	Tanker	1940	1946		Small Dutch tanker taken over by Admiralty. In *Navy List* as RFA.
Kimmerol	Harbour tanker	1916	1947	*Creosol*	
King Salvor	Ocean salvage vessel	1942	1954	*King Salvor*	
Larchol	Harbour tanker	1917	1958	*Creosol*	
Limol	Harbour tanker	1917	1959	*Creosol*	
Lucigen	Fuelling hulk	1939	1945		Owned by Admiralty, but managed and manned by former owners. Not in *Navy List* as RFA.
Maine	Hospital ship	1921	1947		Third RFA hospital ship to bear this name
Mixol	Tanker	1916	1948	*Burma*	
Montenol	Tanker	1917	1942	*Belgol*	Torpedoed while in convoy 1941
Nasprite	Spirit tanker	1941	1963	Sprite	
Nora	Coastal stores	1932	1939		
Ocean Salvor	Ocean salvage vessel	1943	1960	King Salvor	
Olcades (ex *British Beacon*)	Tanker	1919	1952	Ol	
Oleander	Tanker	1917	1940	Ol	Attacked by German ships, stranded Harstad Bay, Norway, 1940.
Oligarch (ex *British Lantern*)	Tanker	1919	1946	Ol	Torpedoed 1943, fuel hulk Alexandria until 1946; scuttled with cargo of obselete ammunition.
Olna	Tanker	1921	1941	Ol	Bombed Crete, 1941. Total loss.

Olwen (ex British Light)	Tanker	1919	1946	Ol	Fuelling duties with Eastern Fleet.
Olynthus (ex British Star)	Tanker	1919	1947	Ol	Oiler with South Atlantic Fleet at Battle of River Plate.
Orangeleaf	Tanker	1917	1947	Trinol	On South Atlantic duty 1939, then Gibraltar and Eastern Fleet until sold 1946.
Pearleaf	Tanker	1917	1946	Trinol	Eastern Station
Petrella	Spirit carrier	1918	1946	Pet	
Petrobus	Spirit carrier	1918	1959	Pet	
Petronel	Spirit carrier	1918	1945	Pet	
Philol	Harbour tanker	1916	1949	Creosol	
Plumleaf	Tanker	1917	1942	Trinol	On Mediterranean Station from 1931, until bombed and sunk in Malta Harbour 1942.
Prestol	Tanker	1917	1958	Belgol	
Prince Salvor	Ocean salvage vessel	1943	1966	King Salvor	
Rapidol	Tanker	1917	1948	Belgol	
Red Dragon	Fuel hulk	1918	1946		
Reliant	Stores ship	1933	1948		
Robert Dundas	Coastal stores carrier	1938	1972	Robert	
Robert Middleton	Coastal store carrier	1938	1972	Robert	
Ruthenia	Fuel Hulk	1914	1949		Stationed at Singapore as oil hulk. Scuttled when Japanese invaded.
Salvestor	Ocean salvage vessel	1942	1970	King Salvor	
Salvictor	Ocean salvage vessel	1944	1966	King Salvor	
Scottish American	Tanker	1939	1947		Owned by Admiralty, but managed and manned by

					former owners. Not in *Navy List* as RFA.
Scotol	Harbour tanker	1916	1947	*Creosol*	
Serbol	Tanker	1918	1958	*Belgol*	
Slavol	Tanker	1917	1942		Torpedoed 1942
Spa	Water tanker	1942	1946	Spa	
Spabeck	Water tanker	1943	1966	Spa	
Spabrook	Water tanker	1942	1946	Spa	
Spaburn	Water tanker	1942	1977	Spa	
Succour	Coastal salvage vessel	1944	1973	Kin	
Thermol	Tanker	1916	1947	*Burma*	
Viscol	Tanker	1916	1947	*Creosol*	
War Afridi	Tanker	1921	1958	War	
War Bahadur	Tanker	1921	1946	War	
War Bharata	Tanker	1921	1947	War	
War Brahmin	Tanker	1921	1959	War	
War Diwan	Tanker	1921	1944	War	Mined Scheldt estuary 1944
War Hindoo	Tanker	1921	1958	War	
War Krishna	Tanker	1921	1947	War	
War Mehtar	Tanker	1920	1941	War	Torpedoed off Harwich 1941
War Nawab	Tanker	1921	1946	War	
War Nizam	Tanker	1921	1946	War	
War Pathan	Tanker	1921	1947	War	
War Pindari	Tanker	1921	1947	War	
War Sepoy	Tanker	1937	1940	War	Bombed and sunk Dover harbour. Used as blockship in harbour entrance.
War Sirdar	Tanker	1937	1942	War	
War Sudra	Tanker	1937	1948	War	Bombed and captured by Japanese 1942
Wave Emperor	Tanker	1944	1960	Wave	
Wave Monarch	Tanker	1944	1960	Wave	
Wave Regent	Tanker	1945	1960	Wave	

Notes: In 1939, the RFA fleet consisted of one hospital ship, four store carriers and sixty-three tankers and spirit carriers. Of the tankers, twelve belonged to the elderly *Creosol* class and were only really useful for harbour and coastal work, while the rest, with the exception of the seven new Dale class, were all in the region of 20 years old and so nearing the end of their economic working life. By 1945, both Ranger fleet replenishment tankers and the rest of the Dale class had joined, together with several of the Wave and Fort classes, increasing the number of vessels to 120.

Lighters, tugs and other vessels on yard and harbour craft agreements have been omitted from this list

Chapter 11

Post-war Changes

The first British vessel to anchor in Tokyo Bay after the end of the war was RFA Dingledale. Along with *Wave King*, she was still there, on 2 September, when the Japanese Foreign Affairs Minister, Mamoru Shigemitsu signed the Japanese instrument of surrender aboard USS *Missouri*. The masters and chief engineers from both RFAs were invited aboard *Missouri* by General Douglas MacArthur to witness this event.

Dingledale remained in Japanese waters and soon after the surrender was transferred to Kure, Hiroshima's main port, to help get its oil installation working again. She remained there five months and during that time, some members of her crew were taken to Hiroshima city itself.

Nothing was left of what had been one of the largest cities in Japan, except dust and ash. In one street there was a marble balustrade that seemed intact. When touched, it simply crumbled to nothing. A German missionary, who had been standing halfway through the door of his chapel when the atomic bomb exploded, was found with his right side burned black while his left side, which had been inside the building, was untouched. Surprisingly, he lived to tell his story, unlike the 80,000 people killed in the initial blast and the 10,000 to 50,000 who died of their injuries or radiation poisoning before the end of 1945. One of *Dingledale*'s crew members, who saw Hiroshima at the time, wrote ' ... I shall never forget what one atomic bomb did. If everybody could have seen these things, it surely must put a damper on this maniacal talk of nuclear warfare ...'.

The Ministry of War Transport (MoWT) responsibilities were assumed by the newly created Ministry of Transport in 1946. During the same period, a number of ships in several recently introduced classes also began operation with the RFA fleet, although it is doubtful if the two events were connected, despite MoWT's involvement in wartime tanker deployment.

Most recent and innovative of these new acquisitions were the Wave class tankers, four of which had been in operation with the British Pacific Fleet Train.

Early in the war, it had quickly become clear that convoy losses due to enemy action would soon create a shortage of fast freighting tankers, so plans for a vessel of this type were drawn up. By the time the necessary material had been collected and building space found for them in the yards, these ships were no longer required and so the Admiralty's original, diesel-engined design was abandoned. Unfortunately, the navy was still desperate for a large number of large, fast, reliable tankers, for carrying out replenishment-at-sea operations with the British Pacific Fleet. In order to satisfy this requirement, some of the new 12,000-ton MoWT standard design tankers then being built were fitted with turbine engines, together with several other modifications, and offered to the Admiralty. Eventually, the navy took twenty of these vessels, out of the total twenty-one under construction.

Although many originally had names with an *Empire* prefix, upon transfer to the RFA, they were renamed the Wave class and the first four, *Wave King*, *Wave Emperor*, *Wave Governor* and *Wave Monarch*, were immediately dispatched to Sydney. Before departure, they were fitted on either side with a sixty-foot, two-ton derrick, modified to allow the use of a single refuelling hose. Roller fairleads were installed for astern refuelling, the starboard fitting modified to take two 5-inch hoses. Their port side fairlead only took one, of 3 ninches diameter, specifically for the transfer of petrol or aviation spirit to aircraft carriers.

During 1944–6, nineteen Wave class ships were completed and acquired by the Admiralty. Six went immediately into service with the RFA, while the other thirteen were placed under commercial management until the DoS was ready to assume responsibility for them. When these vessels came back into RFA hands during 1947–8, several were found to have suffered badly at the hands of their managers and crews. Accommodation was described as 'a slum' and several had major engine defects including a cracked and stripped turbine in *Wave Master*. Sigwart (1969), claimed that it was the Wave's construction, engine and boiler room design that also gave rise to excessive repair and operating costs, although he admitted that a captain experienced with the class could significantly reduce the original 50 tons per day fuel consumption.

Along with running and repair costs, the ships' initial design was poorly suited to their role as replenishment tankers. Amongst other problems, the cargo pumps originally fitted were far too small for RAS work and their deck layout also needed extensive modification. Some of the omissions in the original design and later refits were quite significant. A report on the condition of *Wave Sovereign* in 1953, for example, showed that the cast iron deck rollers had never been fitted for lubrication and that one was so badly pitted there was a danger of it tearing the hose.

In the light of experiences during the Korean war, eight of the best Waves were later extensively modified during refit. Larger cargo pumps and bigger derricks were installed, in the hope that this would make them suitable for work with the Royal Navy's increasingly modern fleet. Unfortunately, as a class, they were generally still too slow and were soon superseded by the bigger, faster ships of the early Tide class. These later ships used many of the design features developed during the successive modifications of the Wave class tankers.

Before the Tide class made its appearance, however, the RFA had the use of another tanker of very sophisticated, even innovative design, the turbo-electric *Olna*.

Initially manned by a Royal Navy crew of about 300, *Olna* was the first of two ships that the Admiralty bought, late in the Second World War, for use as fast fleet tankers. Built originally as *Hyalina* for the Anglo-Saxon Petroleum Co Ltd, in 1945, she was purchased before completion by the Admiralty and renamed. Her sister ship, *Helicina*, was also acquired but the war ended before her conversion was complete and she was returned to her original owners.

Olna's British Thomson-Houston turbo-electric machinery was intended to give her a service speed of about 18 knots, although she was usually run at 15–16 knots to conserve fuel. She had nine high-capacity cargo pumps, capable together of delivering 1000 tons/hour, serving sixteen tanks, all with heating coils, containing diesel, lubricating and furnace fuel oil, as well as drinking water. Petrol (or aviation spirit), over 2000 tons for carrier replenishment, was also carried in specially armoured centre and wing tanks.

To deliver this varied cargo, she had eight steam winches, together with four 4-ton derricks and one of 5-tons capacity for abeam replenishment with double hoses. She could also fuel astern by buoyant rubber hose, again either single or double.

Armament was of a comparable standard. Her original fit was intended to be one 4-inch gun aft, four twin, power operated Bofors anti-aircraft guns and eight single, sponson mounted Oerlikons. During building, it was felt that the power operated Bofors might be too complex for the crew's DEMS gunners, so four army type, single Bofors were substituted for them. All guns were served from a single, combined magazine sited in the lower flat of No 1 Hold, with ammunition delivered on an Admiralty ammunition hoist. This magazine had flooding arrangements installed to Royal Navy standard. Deck stowage for depth charges was provided on the port side and the ship had paravane and degaussing equipment. She was originally intended to have smoke-making apparatus, although this was never fitted.

This formidable vessel was completed in time to serve, with an RN crew, during the Pacific Fleet's later operations, where she proved a considerable asset, both her speed and large capacity being comparable to the US Navy *Cimarron* class oilers. She proved capable of refuelling abeam both battleships (HMS *King George V* and *Duke of York* are specifically mentioned in an Admiralty report of the period) and aircraft carriers, using only a marked heaving line to keep station, a practice soon adopted by all RFAs. Simultaneous refuelling of three ships was also found to be a matter of routine and she achieved pumping rates during one trial of over 1000 tons/hour, without loss of speed. Although her rates in service were usually lower, *Olna* still had about three times the pumping capacity of the new Wave class tankers.

This difference in performance so impressed senior Fleet Train officers that, during the Pacific Fleet's fourth fuelling period (31 July–1 and 2 August 1945), *Olna* was ordered to pump over 4000 tons of FFO from *Dingledale* and 2000 tons from *Wave King* because it was felt that then refuelling could be completed in one day, instead of the two originally set aside for it.

Olna was transferred to RFA manning in 1946. Her complement was reduced from 300 naval personnel to 106 RFA officers and men (125 Lascar crew: Lascar (Indian or Pakistani) crews were always slightly larger than UK crews because it was believed, rightly or wrongly, that Lascars were not as well adapted to the hard work demanded of merchant seamen. See ADM 116/5535 where this appears). Sometime later, crew numbers were further reduced to seventy-seven RFA officers and men.

Replenishment-at-sea was still an experimental technique until about 1950 and *Olna* underwent many changes to her RAS gear in order to determine the best and quickest method of fuel transfer. As with the Waves, many of these improvements were later incorporated in the early Tide class fast fleet replenishment tankers.

Olna was not the only Admiralty ship conducting replenishment-at-sea trials after the war.

When Copenhagen was captured by the British in 1945, they found a well-equipped German naval auxiliary vessel there. Originally named *Nordmark*, she had seen some service, having accompanied *Admiral Scheer* during its operations between September 1940 and May 1941.

Nordmark was subsequently taken over by the Admiralty and renamed *Northmark*, whereupon it was suggested that she might be used as an RFA and modified for service with the British Pacific Fleet Train. When in service with the German navy, she had been remarkably well equipped for an auxiliary, especially by contemporary British standards.

Described as a combined tanker and supply ship, she was nearly 550 feet long with two, twin screw, geared turbines which produced a combined horse power at the shaft of 22,000 shp and a top speed of 21 knots. Waves, which were of comparable size, only produced 6800 bhp with an average top speed of 13–15 knots, while the US Navy's best oiler, USS *Cimarron*, produced 16,900 shp with a top speed of 19 knots. She also had a hospital, with six cots and an operating theatre, as well as good officer accommodation, although crew quarters were considered poor by Royal Navy standards. Armament was impressive, too, consisting of three 15-cm (6-inch) L/48 C36 guns, two 37-mm AA guns, four 20-mm AA guns and eight machine guns, these last presumably the excellent MG34 or MG42.

At a meeting held in the Admiralty in April 1945, to discuss her subsequent employment, concerns were expressed by the DoS about the cost of running and conversion so, instead of joining the RFA Fleet, after a period in reserve at Rosyth, *Northmark* was eventually commissioned into the Royal Navy as HMS *Bulawayo*. Excessive running costs were hardly surprising, incidentally, given her performance.

She was involved, along with several of the Ranger class, in an extensive series of replenishment-at-sea trials, commencing in 1946, and which continued intermittently until her sale in 1955.

Her trials in 1947–8 examined a number of aspects of the replenishment process, including hose connector design, pump rates (a maximum of 1200 tons/hour was obtained using two 7-inch hoses), light design and positioning when conducting RAS operations after dark and the best form of approach to the receiving ship by the oiler. Most importantly, she was found to be capable of steaming at 20 knots, while supplying oil at the maximum rate through a 7-inch hose, although this size of hose was later changed to the USN size 6-inch hose. Transfer of stores and casualties were also trialed successful and as a result, it was suggested that loads of up to 1.5 tons could be transferred by jackstay. This seems laughable now, because these days RFAs routinely use heavy jackstay rigs to move loads of up to 5 tons, while even heavier lifts are possible by VERTREP. At the time, though, it was clearly a considerable advance on previous performances.

Never used on active service, HMS *Bulawayo* was decommissioned in 1955 and sold for scrapping.

As *Bulawayo*'s trials make clear, RFA operational requirements during this post-war period were not confined to tankers. Dry stores also had to be issued at sea and this led to the introduction of more ships in a second important class, the early Fort class of stores issuing ships. These vessels were of Canadian Victory ship design, differing from the more familiar Liberty ship, by being of riveted rather than welded construction. Put together with the minimum of delay in US or Canadian shipyards, their quality sometimes suffered because the speed with which they were built, although the RFA Fort class vessels appear to have lasted well, several remaining in service for over twenty years.

With merchant ship losses of both cargo ships and tankers in the Atlantic becoming acute by September 1940, new tonnage was desperately needed from somewhere. British shipyards were full to capacity with warships, so the government organised the British Merchant Shipbuilding Mission, which went to the United States and

Canada to either buy or build new merchant ship tonnage. The Mission was equipped with several sets of plans, supplied by J L Thompson & Son Ltd, Sunderland, for a cargo ship of 10,000 tons deadweight. Orders were placed, based on these drawings, at shipyards in Portland, Maine and Richmond, California, for sixty of these vessels, which were later to become known as the North Sands type. The four Richmond yards at which the Mission placed its orders were to become major centres for Liberty ship production. Between them they produced 747 US Victory (the US Victory ship was substantially different to the Canadian Victory) and Liberty ships during the war years.

Hulls and engines were built to a proscribed design, which meant that all parts were fully interchangeable. Nine ships were eventually taken in to the RFA fleet, all having initially spent periods under commercial management, as stores issuing ships, the two earliest acquisitions serving with the BPF Train. They had single shaft, triple expansion steam engines, which gave them a consumption of 28–30 tons of oil per day at 11 knots. Several of this class served with the RFA until the late 1960s, although their low service speed made them unsuitable for replenishment at sea operations. They were replaced by the larger, faster and considerably more sophisticated ships of the Ness class, which were introduced in 1967. One final acquisition was made in 1948, when a new hospital ship joined the fleet. Registered as *Maine*, like the previous three, she served in Korea, where she received a battle honour, before being sold out of service in 1954.

As well as new acquisitions, post-war operations demanded improvements to older members of the existing fleet and the three Dale class LSGs were among the first lined up for modernisation. Their war service had been rigorous, with much involvement in amphibious operations but, during 1946–7, all three were converted to freighting tankers. Their extra accommodation was retained and they were used for several years freighting oil and carrying passengers between Trinidad and Britain, until new commercial tonnage made up the deficiency in passenger berths. All three returned to normal RFA freighting duties, before eventually being scrapped during 1960–67.

The Ranger class had also seen a good deal of wartime service but because of their good record as replenishment tankers and reliability, they were retained, after also undergoing some modernisation. New, heavy duty RAS equipment was fitted, two 52-foot derrick, with samson posts, taking the place of the 42-foot derricks and the wooden rollers for the astern buoyant hose being replaced with steel rollers. To mark the advent of the modern post-war age, Rangers were also equipped to withstand gas attack. This consisted of nailing rubber strips to all the doors and fitting what were optimistically termed 'Fearnought' curtains to some of them. They also had a cleansing station fitted near the officers' accommodation. It was not very high-tech, but then given the sort of weapons being developed at the time, no-one would probably have known much about it if they had been attacked.

New requirements for replenishment-at-sea brought not only these new additions but also meant that many of the RFA's older vessels were now unsuitable for duty with its fleet and so were sold. This included ships in both the *Belgol* and *Creosol* classes of harbour tankers, most of the elderly War class and all of the First World War Fast Leaf ships. There were several good reasons for disposing of these vessels.

The War class vessels were slow, even by contemporary merchant ship standards, had never been fitted for oiling at sea and would probably have been impossible to adapt to this role. *Belgol*, *Creosol* and Leaf class ships were all at least thirty years old and so were becoming uneconomic to operate. To replace these ships, a new 1500-ton class assumed coastal and harbour duties, while deep sea freighting fell to the few remaining War class vessels and those Wave tankers not fitted for oiling-at-sea. Later, oil freighting and some replenishment was also carried out by the new Leaf class, commercially built freighting tankers acquired by the Admiralty under a new arrangement, termed bareboat charter. This form of charter meant that the Admiralty chartered the tanker, literally as a bare boat, and was then responsible for all aspects of its operation. The RFA freighting tankers still operate under this form of charter, with RFA Leaf names and are included in the *Navy List* as RFAs.

During the Second World War, conditions of service and pay in the RFA had lagged behind what was being offered by the best of the tanker companies. Consequently, with the end of hostilities, RFA personnel were leaving Admiralty service in increasing numbers for the better pay with commercial firms.

Between November 1947 and October 1948, 128 junior officers left the RFA for jobs elsewhere. Clearly, this could not be allowed to continue and in acknowledgment of the need to retain a permanent staff of well motivated, experienced personnel, the DoS improved officer's working conditions and, for the first time, offered a contract to RFA petty officers.

In July 1947, this contract's main features, were:

- continuous pay and employment after a year's continuous service in an RFA vessel;
- higher rates of monthly pay;
- contract men were to be paid when standing by a ship in ports;
- Eastern bonus of 25 per cent was to be paid on top of basic pay, with additional leave entitlement.

Conditions were further improved later with the introduction of sick pay, pensions, the extension of voluntary contracts to all personnel and RAS bonuses for POs and ratings on UK-manned replenishment ships.

This acknowledgment of the need to retain good personnel in the fleet was an important turning point. Clearly, without well-trained, knowledgeable crew, no vessel can perform to its full potential and, with complex vessels like the early Tides now being designed, the RFA were going to need every experienced officer, petty officer and able seaman they could get.

The RFAs did not take part in any armed conflict during this post-war period, although British forces had a role in both the Palestinian and Malayan emergencies. Royal Navy vessels and accompanying RFAs were involved in tasks of a different sort, however, at opposite ends of the planet.

With the USSR now clearly seen as the next potential opponent in any global war, service chiefs became concerned about the performance of British forces in the extreme environments which might be encountered during operations against the Soviet Bloc.

In response to these concerns, British troops began to carry out regular winter exercises in Norway. Additionally, in 1949, trials were also conducted aboard HMS *Vengeance* to establish how well she and her aircraft and crew could operate in conditions of extreme cold.

Along with several Royal Navy vessels and *Wave Premier*, the carrier was sent to the

Arctic. In a voyage lasting six weeks, they tested aircraft and weapon's operation, life saving equipment and the effects of Arctic weather on radio and radar equipment. Most importantly, successful RAS operations were also carried out, with particular attention being paid to the effectiveness of Arctic clothing against frostbite during operations on deck. Even the crew's calorific intake was monitored, with a careful check being kept on how much they ate between meals as well!

December of the same year saw another cold-weather deployment, this time to the Antarctic, when *Gold Ranger* accompanied the relief ship *John Biscoe* to rescue eleven scientists stranded on Stonington Island, in the Antarctic.

A Norseman light aircraft was to be used to rescue the men and had been transported in aboard one of the ships for this purpose. *Gold Ranger* was responsible for supplying fuel and other necessities, but during the time spent preparing the aircraft, the extreme cold meant that the tanker's crew were forced to spend most of their time thawing out the ship's fresh water tanks. Nor was unloading the necessary supplies a normal operation, because the conformation of their anchorage in Whaler's Bay, Deception Island, would not allow the use of boats. Instead, their cargo of 400 drums of aviation spirit and diesel fuel had to be floated ashore. After days of preparation, the scientists were rescued, along with their huskies, and the ships sailed for home, without further mishap.

The Second World War had forced many changes on the Royal Fleet Auxiliary and, after their experiences with the Pacific Fleet Train, replenishment at sea, both liquid and solid, was seen as an essential component of the post-war Royal Navy. Financial considerations, however, meant that the Admiralty was still using ships which had been modified for this operation, rather than specifically designed for it. Even ships in the modern Wave class, some with a top speed of 15 knots, were still too slow and lacking in manoeuvrability for service with the next generation of naval warships.

This situation was not to last very long. Big changes were coming for the Royal Fleet Auxiliary – changes which would result in a vastly different fleet for the second half of the twentieth century.

RFA fleet 1945–50

Name	Type	In service	Left service	Class
Abbeydale	Tanker	1937	1960	Dale
Airsprite	Spirit carrier	1943	1963	Sprite
Appleleaf	Tanker	1917	1946	Trinol
Arndale	Tanker	1937	1960	
Bacchus	Store ship	1936	1962	
Belgol	Tanker	1917	1958	Belgol
Birchol	Coastal tanker	1946	1969	1500-ton
Bishopdale	Tanker	1937	1970	Dale
Black Ranger	Tanker	1941	1973	Ranger
Blue Ranger	Tanker	1941	1971	Ranger
Boxol	Harbour tanker	1917	1948	Cresol
Brambleleaf	Tanker	1917	1946	Trinol
Broomdale	Tanker	1937	1960	Dale
Brown Ranger	Tanker	1941	1975	Ranger
Cedardale	Tanker	1939	1959	Dale
Celerol	Tanker	1917	1958	Belgol
Cherryleaf	Tanker	1917	1946	Trinol
Danmark	Fuel hulk	1942	1946	
Delphinula	Tanker	1915	1946	
Demeter	Stores hulk	1942	1946	
Denbydale	Tanker	1941	1955	Dale
Derwentdale	LSG	1941	1959	Dale
Dewdale	LSG	1941	1959	Dale
Dingledale	Tanker	1942	1959	Dale
Distol	Harbour tanker	1916	1947	Creosol
Eaglesdale	Tanker	1942	1959	Dale
Easedale	Tanker	1942	1960	Dale
Echodale	Tanker	1941	1961	Dale
Elderol	Harbour tanker	1917	1959	Creosol
Elmol	Harbour tanker	1917	1959	Creosol
Empire Salvage	Tanker	1941	1946	
Ennerdale	Tanker	1941	1959	Dale
Fort Beauharnois	Store ship	1948	1962	Fort
Fort Charlotte	Store ship	1947	1967	Fort
Fort Constantine	Store ship	1949	1969	Fort
Fort Duquesne	Store ship	1947	1967	Fort
Fort Rosalie	Store ship	1947	1972	Fort
Fort Sandusky	Store ship	1949	1972	Fort
Fortol	Tanker	1917	1958	Belgol
Freshbrook	Water tanker	1942	1946	Fresh
Freshburn	Water tanker	1944	1945	Fresh
Freshener	Water tanker	1942	1946	Fresh
Freshet	Water tanker	1940	1945	Fresh

Freshford	Water tanker	1944	1946	Fresh
Freshlake	Water tanker	1942	1946	Fresh
Freshmere	Water tanker	1943	1946	Fresh
Freshpond	Water tanker	1945	1945	Fresh
Freshpool	Water tanker	1943	1946	Fresh
Freshtarn	Water tanker	1944	1946	Fresh
Freshwater	Water tanker	1940	1946	Fresh
Freshwell	Water tanker	1943	1946	Fresh
Gold Ranger	Tanker	1941	1973	Ranger
Green Ranger	Tanker	1941	1962	Ranger
Hickorol	Harbour tanker	1918	1948	*Creosol*
Ingeborg	Tanker	1940	1946	
Kimmerol	Harbour tanker	1916	1947	*Creosol*
King Salvor	Ocean salvage vessel	1942	1954	*King Salvor*
Larchol	Harbour tanker	1917	1958	*Creosol*
Limol	Harbour tanker	1917	1959	*Creosol*
Lucigen	Fuelling hulk	1939	1945	
Maine	Hospital ship	1920	1947	
Mixol	Tanker	1916	1948	*Burma*
Nasprite	Spirit tanker	1941	1963	Sprite
Oakol	Harbour Tanker	1946	1959	1500-ton
Ocean Salvor	Ocean salvage vessel	1943	1960	*King Salvor*
Olcades (ex *British Beacon*)	Tanker	1918	1952	Ol
Oligarch (ex *British Lantern*)	Tanker	1922	1946	Ol
Olna	Fast Fleet tanker	1945	1966	
Olwen (ex *British Light*)	Tanker	1922	1948	Ol
Olynthus (ex *British Star*)	Tanker	1922	1947	Ol
Orangeleaf	Tanker	1917	1947	*Trinol*
Pearleaf	Tanker	1917	1946	*Trinol*
Petrella	Spirit carrier	1918	1946	Pet
Petrobus	Spirit carrier	1918	1959	Pet
Petronel	Spirit carrier	1918	1947	Pet
Philol	Harbour tanker	1916	1949	*Creosol*
Prestol	Tanker	1917	1958	*Belgol*
Prince Salvor	Ocean salvage vessel	1943	1966	*King Salvor*
Rapidol	Tanker	1917	1947	*Belgol*
Red Dragon	Fuel hulk	1918	1946	
Reliant	Stores ship	1933	1948	
Robert Dundas	Coastal stores carrier	1938	1972	Robert
Robert Middleton	Coastal store carrier	1938	1975	Robert
Ruthenia	Fuel Hulk	1915	1949	
Rowanol	Harbour tanker	1946	1971	1500-ton
Salvestor	Ocean salvage vessel	1942	1970	*King Salvor*

Salvictor	Ocean salvage vessel	1944	1966	*King Salvor*
Salviola	Ocean salvage vessel	1945	1959	*King Salvor*
Scotol	Harbour tanker	1916	1947	*Creosol*
Scottish American	Tanker	1939	1947	
Sea Salvor	Ocean salvage vessel	1944	1973	*King Salvor*
Serbol	Tanker	1918	1958	*Belgol*
Spa	Water tanker	1942	1970	Spa
Spabeck	Water tanker	1943	1966	Spa
Spabrook	Water tanker	1944	1977	Spa
Spaburn	Water tanker	1946	1971	Spa
Spalake	Water tanker	1946	1947	Spa
Spapool	Water tanker	1946	1976	Spa
Succour	Coastal salvage vessel	1944	1973	Kin
Teakol	Harbour tanker	1946	1969	1500-ton
Thermol	Tanker	1916	1946	*Burma*
Thornol	Tanker	1947	1948	
Viscol	Tanker	1916	1947	*Creosol*
War Afridi	Tanker	1921	1958	War
War Bahadur	Tanker	1921	1946	War
War Bharata	Tanker	1921	1948	War
War Brahmin	Tanker	1921	1959	War
War Diwan	Tanker	1921	1944	War
War Hindoo	Tanker	1921	1958	War
War Krishna	Tanker	1921	1947	War
War Nawab	Tanker	1921	1946	War
War Nizam	Tanker	1921	1946	War
War Pathan	Tanker	1921	1947	War
War Pindari	Tanker	1921	1947	War
War Sudra	Tanker	1921	1948	War
Wave Baron	Fleet tanker	1948	1972	Wave
Wave Chief	Fleet tanker	1946	1972	Wave
Wave Commander	Freighting tanker	1946	1959	Wave
Wave Conqueror	Freighting tanker	1946	1958	Wave
Wave Duke	Freighting tanker	1946	1969	Wave
Wave Emperor	Freighting tanker	1944	1960	Wave
Wave Governor	Freighting tanker	1945	1960	Wave
Wave King	Freighting tanker	1944	1960	Wave
Wave Knight	Fleet tanker	1947	1964	Wave
Wave Laird	Freighting tanker	1946	1970	Wave
Wave Liberator	Freighting tanker	1946	1959	Wave
Wave Master	Fleet tanker	1946	1963	Wave
Wave Monarch	Freighting tanker	1944	1960	Wave
Wave Premier	Freighting tanker	1946	1960	Wave
Wave Prince	Fleet tanker	1947	1971	Wave

Wave Protector	Freighting tanker	1946	1963	Wave
Wave Regent	Freighting tanker	1945	1960	Wave
Wave Ruler	Fleet tanker	1947	1976	Wave
Wave Sovereign	Fleet tanker	1946	1967	Wave
Wave Victor	Fleet tanker	1946	1971	Wave

Note: During 1945–50, the RFA Fleet underwent radical changes. All of the slow, elderly War, class except *War Afridi*, *War Brahmin* and *War Hindoo* were disposed of, along with the six ships of the First World War Fast Leaf class, which were not so fast anymore. Replacing these were the ships of the Wave class, modified for replenishment at sea.

By 1950, the fleet had been reduced to eighty-five ships, excluding tugs and harbour craft, although many of these were in reserve.

Lighters, tugs and other vessels on yard and harbour craft agreements have been omitted from this list.

Ship Data Tables

Miscellaneous vessels that served as RFAs

Kharki
Tonnages: 675 gross, 850 deadweight, 1455 displacement
Registered length: 185.2 ft
Beam: 29.1 ft
Depth: 11.8 ft
Machinery: 1 screw, triple expansion engine by McKie & Baxter, 775 ihp (bunkers 90 tons coal)
Service speed: 10 knots
Complement: 17

Completed in February 1900 by Irvine Shipbuilding & Engineering Co Ltd, she was purchased by Admiralty on 20 March, soon after completion, for £14,650. Converted in 1906–7 to carry lubricating oil to UK dockyards and depots, with her early years based at Portland. Fitted with storage tanks for 27,000 gallons and two Worthington pumps, which had originally been in HMS *Mars*, giving a delivery of 12,000 gallons/hour. Cost of conversion was over £7000.

Initially in UK waters, based at Portland, with occasional Mediterranean voyages, until transferred to the China Station in 1920, where she was badly damaged by a typhoon on 19 August 1923, while in Hong Kong harbour. Sold in July 1931 for breaking up at Hong Kong.

Petroleum
Tonnages: 4686 gross, 6100 deadweight, 9900 displacement
Registered length: 370.8 ft
Beam: 48.7 ft
Depth: 29.3 ft
Draught: 24 ft
Machinery: 1 screw, triple expansion engine by North Eastern Marine Engineering Co Ltd, 2000 ihp (coal or oil fuelled; bunkers 632 tons coal, 668 tons oil fuel)
Service speed: 10.5 knots (13 knots max)
Complement: 45

Built by Swan Hunter & Wigham Richardson Ltd, Newcastle, and completed in May 1903 for the Texas oil trade. Built originally for the Petroleum United Agencies Ltd, Liverpool, and part owned by her builders, she was laid up on completion until purchased by the Admiralty in March 1905, as its first operational RFA tanker.

Employed on fleet attendance during 1906–7, then on oil freighting and RAS trials as. Fleet attendance in Scapa Flow during the First World War. On 20 April 1937 was handed over to T W Ward Ltd, Inverkeithing, for breaking up.

Isla
Tonnages: 518 gross, 348 deadweight, 980 displacement
Registered length: 170 ft
Beam: 26 ft
Depth: 11 ft
Draught: 12 ft
Machinery: 1 screw, compound steam engine by Hutsons & Sons Ltd, 650 ihp (bunkers 75 tons coal)
Service speed: 9 knots
Complement: 15

Built by Garston Graving Dock Co Ltd in 1903 as collier for J Brewster & Sons, Whitehaven and registered as *Thistle*. Bought by Admiralty on 6 March 1907 for use as collier. Later converted to spirit/petrol carrier to supply submarines; fitted with twenty-two rectangular tanks of capacities varying between 2250 and 6400 gallons, four rotary pumps and an unspecified quantity of 2.5-inch, bronze, flexible hose. Sold 9 September 1921 and renamed *Pass of Brander*. After further changes of owner and name, she arrived at Bremerhaven on 14 May 1959 to be broken up as the German-flagged *Ludwig Friederich*.

Mercedes
Tonnage: 4487 gross, 7500 deadweight, 9930 displacement
Registered length: 351 ft
Beam: 50.75 ft
Depth: 28.3 ft
Draught: 23.9 ft with all holds and wing tanks full
Machinery: 1 screw, triple expansion engine by North Eastern Marine Engineering Co Ltd, 2350 ihp (bunkers 753 tons coal)
Service speed: 10.5 knots (12 knots trials)
Complement: 43

Completed in February 1902 by Northumberland Shipbuilding Co Ltd, Howden-on-Tyne, for Christie & Co Ltd, Cardiff and described at the time by the shipping press as 'the finest collier afloat'. She had four large, unobstructed holds, served by two long derricks and Temperley Transporters. These arrangements allowed her to discharge her cargo at a rate of about 400 tons/hour, with her full cargo discharged in about 17 hours. Holds were self trimming, by means of wing, upper ballast tanks, which could also carry cargo.

Purchased by the Admiralty in 1908, she was initially used for an unsuccessful series of CAS trials but with the change to oil fuelling, her ballast tanks were fitted for the transport of fuel oil and she was used for transporting coal between UK naval bases. On the outbreak of the First World War, she was in continual operation for a period of 42 hours with the Home Fleet, moving from ship to ship and discharging her entire 7500-ton cargo. Standard Marconi 1.5 kW W/T system was fitted in 1912.

She was sold in July 1920 to Spanish owner J Olavarriaga and renamed *Juan Olavarriaga*. Subsequently renamed *Iberia* (1923), *Virgen de Bergona* (1925), *Euskera* (1930), and *Elanchove* (1935) by a series of Spanish owners, she foundered in a storm on 7 October 1936, 150 miles off Bilbao when on voyage from Bilbao to Cardiff with iron ore.

Port of London Authority (PLA) oil barges
Built: *Barkol, Battersol* 1898; others 1906–7
Tonnages: *Barkol, Battersol* 704 gross; others 869 gross
Lengths: *Barkol, Battersol* 190.0 ft (registered); others 198 ft (registered), 204 ft (overall)
Beam: *Barkol, Battersol* 30.1 ft; others 32.1 ft
Depth: *Barkol, Battersol* 14.6 ft; others 16.3 ft
Machinery: 1 screw; triple expansion engine (coal fuel)
Speed: Probably about 4 knots
Complement: –

RFA name	PLA name	On charter	Off charter
Barkol	*PLA Hopper No 3*	1.17	1920
Battersol	*PLA Hopper No 4*	16.11.16	1920
Blackol	*PLA Hopper No 5*	9.16	1920
Greenol	*PLA Hopper No 6*	11.16	1920
Purfol	*PLA Hopper No 7*	9.9.16	1920
Silverol	*PLA Hopper No 8*	10.16	1920

Designed as hopper barges to work in conjunction with the PLA fleet of dredgers, these vessels were chartered by the Admiralty in 1916–17, due to a shortage of harbour tankers, and renamed after significant features of the Thames (Barking, Battersea, Blackwall, Greenwich, Purfleet, Silvertown).

They were easily converted for use as tankers by simply plating over the bottom sludge door joints and installing a pump and pipeline, probably the standard Admiralty 5-inch fitting. *Navy Lists* for the relevant years include them as RFAs, with a lieutenant RNR in command and a Lieutenant(E), RNR as chief engineer. A sub-lieutenant RNR served as second officer and on some vessels there was also a sub-lieutenant (E). They were not, however, restricted to service on the Thames, for *Purfol* is reported to have stranded at Killybegs, Ireland, while supporting HMS *Platypus* and its flotilla of submarines.

They were returned to the PLA in 1920, and returned to normal duties on the River Thames. By the mid 1930s, the barges had all been sold, and the last to survive was *Greenol*, which was broken up in Cork in 1982.

Nucula

Tonnages: 4614 gross, 9830 displacement
Registered length: 370 ft
Beam: 48.5 ft
Depth: 28.7 ft
Draught: 24.35 ft
Machinery: 1 screw, triple expansion engine by Wallsend Slipway Co Ltd
Service speed: 10 knots
Complement:

Completed by Armstrong, Whitworth & Co Ltd, Newcastle, in September 1906, as *Hermione* for CT Bowring & Co Ltd. Sold in 1908 to Toyo Kisen Kaisha, Tokyo, she was renamed *Soyo Maru*. Bought by Anglo-Saxon Petroleum Co Ltd in 1917, and renamed *Nucula*, she was acquired by the Admiralty in 1922 and sent to the China Station. In October 1922, took over service from *Pearleaf* at Singapore, and *Pearleaf* returned to UK. Based at Nagasaki as base oiler September to November 1923, during earthquake relief operations. From 27 May 1924 she was on hire to the Royal New Zealand Navy. She was decommissioned on 10 June 1937, and on 5 July was laid up and used as a storage hulk at Shoal Bay, Waitemata harbour. She was scuttled 11 miles east-north-east of Cuvier Island in Hauraki Gulf, New Zealand, on 24 October 1947.

Empire Salvage

Tonnages: 10,746 gross, 15,597 deadweight
Length overall: 496.2 ft
Beam: 73.3 ft
Depth: 35.5 ft
Draught: 28.3 ft
Machinery: 1 screw, 8-cylinder Stork diesel engine
Service speed: 12 knots
Complement: 78

Launched on 17 April 1940 by Rotterdam Dry Dock Co, for Phs van Ommeren, Rotterdam, as *Papendrecht*. Commandeered on 16 May 1941 by German navy during invasion of Holland, renamed *Lothringen*. Served as supply ship to *Bismarck* until captured by HMS *Dunedin* on June 15 1941, following sighting by an aircraft from HMS *Ark Royal*, and taken to Bermuda. Renamed *Empire Salvage* and in Admiralty service, crewed by RFA personnel, her equipment gave much information about German RAS techniques, especially the development of bouyant rubber hose. Served at Halifax, Nova Scotia, and in Eastern waters. She arrived at Portsmouth on 15 May 1946 and the following day was officially returned to her former Netherlands owners and renamed *Papendrecht*. She arrived at Onomichi, Japan, on 15 April 1964 to be broken up.

Northmark

Tonnages: 10,848 gross, 22,000 full load displacement
Length overall: 585 ft
Beam: 72.5
Depth: -
Machinery: 2 screw, steam turbine with double reduction gearing, 21,590 shp; 2 x Wagner boilers
Speed: 21 knots
Armament: 3 x 150-mm guns, AA guns, and machine guns
Complement: 133 German navy, 292 Royal Navy

Built by Schichau, Elbing, as the Kriegsmarine replenishment ship *Westerwald*. Later renamed *Nordmark*. She was captured in Copenhagen on 9 May 1945 and on 8 June arrived at Rosyth. She then went to Palmers', Hebburn, for refit and in January 1946 her name was anglicised to *Northmark* for RFA operation. She was commissioned into the Royal Navy as HMS *Bulawayo* in July 1947, because the DoS thought she would be too expensive to run, she was involved in several RAS trials between 1946 and 1955. These trials were instrumental in deciding many of the design features in the later Admiralty-designed RFA fast fleet replenishment tankers. In October 1950 she was placed in reserve at Gareloch and used as headquarters for

Reserve Fleet Clyde Division. Sold to BISCO in 1955 and arrived at Dalmuir on 4 October to be broken up.

Characteristics of USN *Cimarron* class, RN Wave class, *Olna* and *Northmark*

Characteristic	*Cimarron* class	Wave class	*Olna*	*Northmark*
Length overall	553 ft	492.4–493.8 ft	583.4 ft	550 ft
Breadth	75 ft	64.1–64.3 ft	70.2 ft	72.5 ft
Deadweight tons	18,300	11,900	17,520	22,000
Cargo capacity	150,000 barrels	9680 tons	14,600 tons	12,000 tons
Trial speed/ horsepower	19.5 kts/16,900 shp	13–15 kts/6800 bhp	19 kts/13,000 shp	21 kts/22,000 shp
Armament	1 x 5-in LA/HA gun, 4 x 3-in AA guns, 4 x 40-mm Bofors, 8 x 20-mm Oerlikon	1 x 4-in LA/HA, 4 x 20-mm Oerlikons, 2 x machine guns	1 x 4-in LA/HA, 4 x single 40-mm Bofors, 8 x 20-mm Oerlikon	3 x 6-in guns, AA guns and smaller calibre machine guns

Note: Trials speed of 17.9–18.2 knots was attained by *Wave Ruler* for a short period. None of the other vessels in this class appeared to match this.

Hospital ships

Maine is the traditional name for the Royal Navy hospital ship and has been so since the first ship entered service in 1905. The line ended when *Maine* (V) was cancelled in 1952.

Name	Builder	Completed/acquired	Out of service
Maine (I)	Wm Gray & Co Ltd, West Hartlepool	1887/1900	1914
Maine (II)	D & W Henderson & Co Ltd, Glasgow	1906/1913	1916
Maine (III)	Fairfield Shipbuilding & Engineering Co Ltd, Glasgow	1902/1920	1947
Maine (IV)	Ansaldo San Giorgio, Spezia	1925/1948	1954
Maine (V)	Barclay Curle & Co Ltd, Glasgow	Cancelled	–

Maine (I)
2816 tons gross, 4540 displacement. Dimensions (Length, beam, depth) 315.2 ft x 41 ft x 25.6 ft. Single screw, triple expansion engine by Central Marine Engineering Works Ltd, giving a top speed of 11 knots.

Completed as *Swansea* in July 1887, a cattle and cargo ship, she was renamed *Maine* in 1888.

During the First Boer War, in 1900, a group of American ladies, headed by Lady Randolph Churchill, tried to raise funds to equip a hospital ship. Their fund raising activities did not produce enough money to finance the venture, so instead, the president of the Atlantic Transport Line agreed to lend one of his subsidiary company ships, *Maine*, and its crew, to the army for six months. He also paid for her conversion. *Maine* never saw service in South Africa, being more urgently required to deal with casualties from the Boxer Rebellion. After her China service, she was presented to the Royal Navy on 29 June 1901, becoming its first permanent hospital ship, and was taken over by the RFA upon its formation in 1905.

She ran aground in thick fog on the small island of Eilean Straide Eun, Mull, on 17 June 1914, although all her patients and most of her equipment were safely landed. The wreck was sold on 6 July 1914, and in 1969 it was located by divers in deep water, broken up and spread over a wide area.

Maine (II)
4688 tons gross, 8785 displacement. Dimensions 390 ft x 52.7 ft x 27.1 ft. Triple expansion engine, speed 12 knots.

Completed in 1905 as *Heliopolis* for London owners, she was acquired for conversion to a hospital ship by the Admiralty in February 1913. She was renamed *Mediator* but with the loss of *Maine* (I), she became *Maine* (II). Her conversion proceeded slowly during the First World War and it was eventually decided that her conformation made her unsuitable for service as a hospital ship and she reverted to her previous owners in March 1916 with the name *Heliopolis*. She was sold to Canadian Pacific Railway Co in 1917 and renamed *Methven*. She was renamed *Borden* in 1923. Sold out of the Canadian Pacific fleet in 1926, she became the Greek-owned *Perseus*, under which name she arrived at Genoa on 24 August 1932 to be broken up.

Maine (III)

5981 tons gross, 10,100 displacement. Dimensions 401.2 ft x 52.3 ft x 33.6 ft. Twin screw, triple expansion engines, 4100 ihp, speed 13 knots.

Completed in May 1902 as the liner *Panama* for Pacific Steam Navigation Co, Liverpool, this vessel was chartered by the Admiralty for use as a hospital ship during the First World War, being purchased in August 1920, and converted fully in 1921. She was always RFA manned, with additional naval medical personnel. Most of her service was with the Mediterranean Fleet, based on Malta, although in 1926, she was transferred to the China Station for some months, until November 1927. Later, during 1936–7, she transported and cared for refugees from the Spanish civil war, usually based in Marseilles. She also assisted at Smyrna, in the Greco-Turkish war and participated in relief work during the Corinth earthquake.

During the Jubilee Review of July 1935, her Red Cross markings were removed and she served as government guest hotel ship. Her distinguished guests ran into some problems with her NAAFI organised catering while she was in this role and questions were actually asked in the House of Commons about the standard of hospitality provided. It seems nobody got anything to eat at all!

In 1936, she was based at Alexandria during the Italo-Abyssinian conflict, and then went to Haifa during the Palestine troubles. Her next duty was during the Spanish visit war, when she steamed 20,996 miles and mevacuated 6574 refugees of 41 nationalities.

Internationally numbered '1', as the oldest hospital ship afloat, during the Second World War, she was mainly in Alexandria, receiving over 13,500 patients during this period and narrowly escaping damage when she suffered a near-miss on 6 September 1941, during an air raid on the harbour. No patients were injured, but, unfortunately, four members of her crew were killed and twelve injured during this incident. Between October 1944 and February 1945 she served in Greek waters.

On 22 october 1946, when the British destroyers *Saumarez* and *Volage* struck Albanian mines in the Corfu channel, and killing forty-five, Maine went to the scene, grounding as she did so. She paid off at Rosyth on 21 February 1947. She was sold in 1948 for breaking up and arrived at the Bo'ness yard of P & W MacLellan Ltd on 8 July.

Maine (IV)

7515 tons gross. Dimensions 447 ft (overall) x 52.2 ft x 36 ft. Twin screw, steam turbine engines by builders, Ansaldo. Cots for 420 patients and RFA crew of 200 (147 Indian ratings).

Completed by Ansaldo, Muggiano, in May 1925 as the passenger liner *Leonardo Da Vinci* for the Società di Navigazione Transatlantica Italiana, Genoa. Captured by British forces at Mogadiscio, Somaliland, (in 1942) while trying to escape capture. First renamed *Empire Clyde* in 1943 after refitting in the Baltimore Naval Yard as a army hospital ship, she served mainly in eastern waters until October 1945, when she became the naval base hospital ship in Hong Kong. She had arrived at Hong Kong on 27 October 1945 from Shanghai. She left on 5 July 1946 for Singapore, and returned to Hong Kong, from where she again sailed, on 16 November 1946, for Malta, arriving there on 23 January 1947. She was taken over as the Royal Navy hospital ship RFA *Empire Clyde* on 1 January 1947, and was renamed *Maine* in 1948. She served in Korea where she was the only hospital ship in the theatre. During the war, she carried nearly 2000 casualties to Japan, and the medical staff treated 2115 US personnel and carried out over 1000 cases of surgery. Sold on 26 April 1954 and broken up at Hong Kong.

Maine (V)

10,000 displacement tons.

Laid down in February 1952. Contract cancelled in June 1952 after tank top, keel and part of framing were laid. Money and material allocated used for construction of Royal Yacht *Britannia*, which was originally designed for use, secondarily, as a wartime hospital ship.

Several vessels were chartered for use as hospital ships during the two world wars, but these were not included in the *Navy List* as RFAs.

Colour scheme

Hospital ships are protected from attack by the Geneva Convention and their colour scheme was proscribed by the Third and Tenth Hague Convention of 1907.

Before 1947, instructions were that they should be painted white overall with a broad green hull band and Red Cross markings around the upper part of the hull. In 1940, they were further identified by red crosses painted from fore to aft on the upper deck to facillitate identification by aircraft.

At night, they were to be clearly illuminated, with an additional horizontal row of green lights around the hull. Requirement for the broad, green hull band was discontinued by the Geneva Convention 1947.

Burma Class

Although similar in size, these tankers differed considerably in specification and were thus not all sisterships.

Burma
Tonnages: 1832 gross, c2500 cargo
Registered length: 270.5 ft
Beam: 36.6 ft
Depth: 22 ft
Machinery: 1 screw, J & G Kincaid triple expansion engine
Service speed: 10–11 knots; maximum 12 knots

Name	Builder	Laid down	Launched	Completed	Out of service
Burma	Greenock & Grangemouth Dockyard Co Ltd, Greenock	1911	3.3.11	1.6.11	1935

First of her class, she was also the first oil tanker constructed to Admiralty order. Innovations included electric lighting, steam heating, and a steam fan for clearing the tanks of vapour. The estimated cost for the construction of *Burma* was £40,107, but upon completion this had risen to £43,854. On 20 October 1917, *Burma* was attacked by a submarine in the Mediterranean, but the torpedo missed.

Unfortunately, OAS trials were disappointing and she served as a freighting tanker until placed in reserve at Rosyth from 1926 to 1935. Offered for sale on 21 May 1935, she was sold for scrap to P & W McLellan Ltd for £3715. She arrived at Bo'ness on 28 June 1935 to be broken up.

Mixol and *Thermol*
Tonnages: 1977/1902 gross, 2000 cargo, 4326 displacement (full load)
Length overall: 280 ft
Beam: 38.7 ft
Draught: 21 ft
Depth: 21.9 ft
Machinery: 1 screw, triple expansion engine, 1200 ihp; engines by Caledon (*Mixol*), J & G Kincaid (*Thermol*) (bunkers 150 tons fuel oil)
Service speed: 10.5 knots

Name	Builder	Laid down	Launched	Completed	Out of service
Mixol	Caledon Shipbuilding & Engineering Co Ltd, Dundee	–	17.6.1916	10.16	1947
Thermol	Greenock & Grangemouth Dockyard Co Ltd, Greenock	–	29.4.16	8.16	1946

Mixol
Built as a prototype for the Admiralty class of 2000-ton tankers, her stability was so unsatisfactory that she carried 200 tons of oil in her Nos 1 and 3 tanks, which were never pumped out.

Her RFA service was indifferent, to say the least. From 1922 to 1935 she was laid up, with *Thermol*, in Gibraltar's large dry dock. During the spring cruise of the combined Home and Mediterranean fleets, the two ships were towed to the North Mole, only to be returned when the warships departed!

She went to Abyssinia in 1935, during the Italian war, but performed badly and was returned to the UK and once again placed in reserve. With the outbreak of war in 1939, when in reserve at Devonport, some 300 tons of steel was stripped from her superstructure. Her stability was now satisfactory, although her appearance was not improved and she was able to operate with a full cargo. On 13 September 1939, she sailed Rosyth for Scapa Flow under the escort of HMS *Matabele*, and later she was making voyages between Loch Ewe, Methil, Scapa Flow and the River Clyde. Sold in 1948 to a subsidiary of Counties Ship Management Co Ltd, London, and renamed *Whitebrook*. She was sold again, in 1951, to Marcou & Sons, Ltd, London and renamed, *Irene M*. She arrived at Antwerp on 27 December 1952 to be broken up.

Thermol
Similar in specification to *Mixol*, her superstructure was also lightened in 1940. Only 100 tons had to be removed to give her satisfactory stability. *Thermol* was transferred to the Ministry of Transport on 8

November 1946. Sold to Harker (Coasters) Ltd, Knottingley, in May 1947, she was renamed *Brocodale H*, and in the following year sold to Mirupanu Steam Ship Co Ltd and renamed *Julia C*. She arrived at Savona on 22 July 1954 to be broken up.

Trefoil and *Turmoil*
Tonnages: 2070 gross, 2100 cargo, 4060 displacement (full load)
Length overall: 278.8 ft
Beam: 39.1 ft
Depth: 22.1 ft
Machinery: 2 screw; *Trefoil*: 2 x 6-cylinder Vickers diesel, 1500 bhp (bunkers 200 tons fuel oil); *Turmoil*: 2 x triple expansion engines by Ross & Duncan, Glasgow
Service speed: 11–12 knots

Name	Builder	Laid down	Launched	Completed	Out of service
Trefoil	Pembroke Dockyard	15.1.13	28.8.13	1917	1935
Turmoil	Pembroke Dockyard	3.11.13	7.3.17	1917	1935

Trefoil
Begun at H.M Pembroke Dockyard, but completed at the Barrow-in-Furness shipyard of Vickers Ltd. In reserve at Rosyth from January 1929. Offered for sale on 21 May 1935 lying Rosyth. Sold on 28 June 1935 to P & W McLellan Ltd for breaking up, and arrived at Bo'ness on 30 July. Sale price was £5865.

Turmoil
Originally intended to be fitted with Vickers diesels, but these were requisitioned for fitting in the monitor *Marshal Soult*. In another innovation, her tanks were fitted with steam pipes to reduce the viscosity of the oil to facilitate pumping in cold weather.

This ship and *Trefoil* were both found to be mechanically unreliable and were not used very much. Kept in reserve at Rosyth from 1923 until 1935, she was also sold as scrap to P & W McLellan Ltd, Bo'ness, for £4905.

First 1000-ton class harbour tankers
Tonnages: 1016–1054 gross, 1025 cargo, *Attendant* 1935 displacement, others 2178 displacement
Length overall: 200 ft
Beam: 34.2 ft
Draught: 15 ft
Depth: 15.2 ft
Machinery: 1 screw; *Attendant* triple expansion engine by Chatham Dockyard, 450 ihp (bunkers 60 tons coal); others 2 x 4-cylinder Bolinder diesel engines, 450 bhp (bunkers 29 tons oil)
Service speed: *Attendant* 8 knots; others 7 knots
Complement: 17

Name	Builder	Laid down	Launched	Completed	Out of service
Attendant	Chatham Dockyard	7.10.12	5.7.13	8.14	1935
Carol	Devonport Dockyard	1913	6.11.13	8.14	1935
Ferol	Devonport Dockyard	14.11.13	3.10.14	1.15	1920
Servitor	Chatham Dockyard	1913	26.5.14	5.15	1922

These first four 1000-ton tankers were really little more than powered barges and were employed exclusively on coastal voyages. Engines were in the aft section of the ship with crew accomadation forward. Ships were usually harbour based, with the crews on yard craft agreements and so living ashore.

Attendant
1016 tons gross. After a period spent fuelling in dockyards, placed in reserve at Rosyth from 1929 to 1935. Offered for sale on 21 May 1935. Sold to P & W MacLellan Ltd, Bo'ness, for breaking up, but resold to Hemsley Bell Ltd, Southampton. Chartered by Admiralty 1939–45, serving mainly in Scapa Flow. She was damaged when she struck a mine off Sheerness on 1 January 1941, but made port for repairs. Returned to owners in 1945, who used her on the south coast and in the Thames as a refuelling ship. Sold to British-Mexican Petroleum Co Ltd in 1948. Arrived Queenborough 8 October 1964 for breaking up.

Carol
1054 tons gross. The early diesel engines fitted to this ship were very unreliable and *Carol*'s maiden voyage, from Devonport to Liverpool took three months, because of constant engine breakdowns. After a period of dockyard work, she was placed in reserve at Rosyth from 6 January 1928 until 1935, when she was sold for £2722 to P & W McLellan Ltd, Bo'ness, for breaking up.

Ferol
1020 tons gross. *Ferol* suffered similar problems of engine reliability to those of *Carol*. Consequently, when sold on 29 January 1920 to Anglo-American Oil Co Ltd, London, she was re-engined by J Pollock & Sons Ltd, at Faversham. Renamed *Osage*, she now had a deadweight of 1125 tons and a shallower draught of 13 ft 7 in. Bombed by German aircraft and sunk on 18 December 1940, 4 miles north-east of Arklow light vessel.

Servitor
1023 tons gross. After dockyard service, being based on the First of Forth from September 1916, she was sold at Sheerness in September 1922 for £5000. She had a long and eventful career. She was renamed *Puloe Brani* for service on the Great Lakes, and after two unsuccessful attempts to cross the Atlantic under her own power, she was towed to Montreal. Subsequent owners renamed her *B B McColl* (1927), *A J Patmore* (1929), USS *Rotary* (1942), *A J Patmore* (1946), *Peggy Reinauer* (1946) and *Detroit* (1955). As *B B McColl* she was seriously damaged by fire in 1928 at Buffalo and rebuilt, and in 1932 as *A J Patmore* she was damaged by an explosion while unloading petrol at Toronto. On 13 November 1942 she was acquired by the UN Navy and commissioned as USS *Rotary* for service on at Casco, Maine, under operational command of Destroyers, US Atlantic Fleet.. She decommissioend in December 1945 and was transferred to the US Maritime Commission for disposal, reverting to her previous name *A J Patmore*. She was sold later in 1946 and renamed *Peggy Reinauer* and in 1955 became *Detroit*, owned by Michigan Tankers Inc, Detroit. *Detroit* operated on the Great Lakes until 1975 and was reported broken up at South Chicago in 1982. Her partially dismantled hull was abandoned in 1985 in the backwaters of Lake Calumet.

Lane & Macandrew Leaf Group

The ships in this group were all of emergency wartime construction, modification or purchase. Although these were managed by London shipping company Lane & Macandrew Ltd, the Director of Stores was concerned in their maintenance and repair and the Director of Transports was responsible for overseeing manning and the issue of sailing orders.

They were by no means a homogenous collection. Some were old liners, previously in use as dummy battleships, converted by the insertion of cylindrical tanks in the holds. Others were bought on the stocks and converted, while several were under construction as tankers when taken over. Their -ol-suffixed names are included here.

Most were sold at the end of the First World War to commercial operators to help make good wartime losses. Evidence from Admiralty documents reveals that the Royal Navy wanted to dispose of those built under the stringencies of wartime construction because riveting and general construction were of doubtful quality.

Name	Builder	Completed	Into service	Out of service
Ashleaf	Ropner & Sons Ltd, Stockton-on-Tees	1916	1916	1917
Aspenleaf	Barclay, Curle & Co Ltd, Glasgow	1900	10.16	1919
Bayleaf	Harland & Wolff Ltd, Belfast	1894	1916	1920
Beechleaf	Richardson, Duck & Co Ltd, Stockton-on-Tees	1917	3.17	1919
Birchleaf	Short Bros Ltd, Sunderland	1916	12.16	1919
Boxleaf	Barclay, Curle & Co Ltd, Glasgow	1916	2.17	1919
Briarleaf	J Readhead & Sons Ltd, South Shields	1916	12.16	1919
Dockleaf	Bartram & Sons Ltd, Sunderland	1917	4.17	1919
Elmleaf	Earle's Shipbuilding Co Ltd, Hull	1917	3.17	1920
Fernleaf	Napier & Miller Ltd, Glasgow	1917	1.17	1920
Hollyleaf	Wm Hamilton & Co Ltd, Port Glasgow	1917	3.17	1919
Laurelleaf	Craig Taylor & Co Ltd , Stockton-on-Tees	1916	12.16	1919
Limeleaf	Barclay, Curle & Co Ltd, Glasgow	1916	12.16	1919
Mapleleaf	C S Swan & Hunter Ltd, Newcastle	1898	7.15	1919
Oakleaf	A Stephen & Sons Ltd, Glasgow	1899	7.7.15	1917

Palmleaf	Irvine's Shipbuilding & Dry Docks Co Ltd, West Hartlepool	1916	11.16	1917
Roseleaf	Sir Raylton Dixon & Co Ltd, Middlesbrough	1916	8.16	1920
Vineleaf	C S Swan & Hunter Ltd, Newcastle	1901	1917	1919

Ashleaf
5768 tons gross. Under construction as cargo ship *Olga*. Completed as tanker *Ashleaf*. Torpedoed by *U88* and sunk 29 May 1917 in 48 54N 10 08W when on voyage from Trinidad to Falmouth with petrol.

Aspenleaf
6124 tons gross. Built for Elder Dempster & Co, Liverpool, as *Lake Erie*. Sold to Canadian Pacific Railway 1903. Renamed *Tyrolia* on 29 March 1913. After service as a BEF transport, hired by Admiralty on 28 October 1914 and converted at Belfast to dummy battleship *Centurion*, based at Loch Ewe. During February to June 1915 she was based in the Aegean and then became a stores carrier. Converted to tanker and renamed *Saxol* on 9 June 1916. On 27 June 1916 she was purchased by the Admiralty for service as a fleet oiler, and on 7 October 1916 she was renamed *Aspenleaf*, with base port Portsmouth, upon commencement of management by Lane & Macandrew Ltd. While on passage from Sabine, Texas to the UK, on 30 December 1916 she was mined in the English Channel off the Owers light vessel. The mine had been laid by *UC16*. There were no fatalities and *Aspenleaf* was towed into port for repairs. She was out of service until June 1917. On 7 November 1917 registered ownership was transferred to the Shipping Controller. Sold 12 September 1919 to Anglo-Saxon Petroleum Co Ltd; renamed *Prygona* on 11 January 1921, when she became a floating oil depot at Southampton. Sold to Danish breakers and arrived Copenhagen on 6 February 1925 to be broken up.

Bayleaf
8455 tons gross. Built as Oceanic Steam Navigation Co (White Star Line) cargo and passenger vessel *Cevic*. Hired by the Admiralty in October 1914 and converted at Belfast to dummy battleship *Queen Mary*. She sailed Belfast on completion of conversion on 11 February 1915 but hit rocks two days later and had to return to Belfast for repairs. She again sailed Belfast on 10 April 1915 but grounded on Rathlin Island in fog the following day. She was refloated on 12 April and arrived at Loch Ewe, sailing almost immediately again to commence her patrol of the North Atlantic. On 25 April 1915 she arrived off New York on the same day as the German liner *Kronprinz Wilhelm*, which was interned the following day. After this she was based in the Aegean, until June 1915, and paid off at Belfast in September 1915. Purchased on 8 September 1915, converted to tanker and renamed *Bayol* in 1916. Renamed *Bayleaf* in 1917 upon transfer to the Shipping Controller and management of Lane & Macandrew Ltd. She was at first sold in 1920 to British Tanker Co Ltd, but promptly resold, on 9 June 1920, to Anglo-Saxon Petroleum Co Ltd; renamed *Pyrula*. After a few years as a bunkers hulk at Curaçao, she arrived at Genoa in October 1933 to be broken up.

Beechleaf
5861 tons gross. Under construction and launched as *Olmos*. Completed in March 1917 following conversion to tanker *Beechleaf*. On 3 January 1918, attacked by submarine in the Mediterranean – the torpedo missed. Sold 1919 to Anglo-Saxon Petroleum Co Ltd; renamed *Limicana* 1921. Sold 1927 to Naptha Industrie und Tankanlagen AG Nitag, renamed *Ch N Kahan*. Sold again to J Billmeir Co Ltd, London 1937, and renamed *Stanbridge*. Sold to Europaische Tankreederei GmbH, Hamburg, 1939, and renamed *Eurofeld*. Taken over by Kriegsmarine and acted as tanker for the battlecruiser *Admiral Scheer*. On 12 November 1940 with *Nordmark* (later to become RFA *Northmark*), *Eurofeld* undertook RAS with *Admiral Scheer* – fuel, ammunition and provisions – in the Atlantic at 25N 45W. On 11 September 1944 scuttled at St Nazaire when Allied forces were approaching the city; after the war, recovered and broken up in 1950.

Birchleaf
5873 tons gross. Laid down as cargo ship *Oldbury*; completed December 1916 as tanker *Birchleaf*. On 23 February 1918 attacked and damaged by *U91* about 20 miles from the Skerries when in ballast from Milford Haven to Oran. The submarine fired a torpedo and with gunfire hit the submarine. Two crewmen killed and the master was taken prisoner. Sold 1919 to British Tanker Co Ltd; renamed *British Birch* 1920. Arrived Port Glasgow 23 December 1931 to be broken up.

Boxleaf
7388 tons gross. Under construction for the British India Steam Navigation Co Ltd as cargo ship *Margha*. Contract requisitioned October 1915 and construction changed to fleet oiler as *Olinda*; entered service in February 1917 as *Boxleaf*. Sold 26 August 1919 to Oliefabriken Insulinde 'India', Amsterdam, and renamed

India. Sold in 1924 to British Molasses Co Ltd, and renamed *Atheltarn*, and sold again, in 1929, to Nippon Tanker Co Ltd, Tokyo, and renamed *Zuiyo Maru*. On 1 October 1944 torpedoed by submarine USS *Cabrilla* and sunk in Lingayen Gulf.

Briarleaf

5882 tons gross. Laid down as cargo ship *Oletta* and completed in December 1916 as tanker *Briarleaf*. On 17 October 1918 attacked in the North Atlantic by a submarine. The torpedo exploded prematurely and a shot fired from the submarine's gun missed. Sold 1919 to Anglo-Saxon Petroleum Co Ltd; renamed *Lacuna* 1921. Sold 1927 to Olsen & Ugelstad, Oslo, renamed *Dovrefjell*. Sold again in 1938 To Naptha Tankers Ltd, London, and renamed *Naptha Shipper*. Seized by Germany on 3 September 1939, taken over by the Kriegsmarine on 7 October, and renamed *Altengamme* in 1940. On 4 May 1945 bombed by Russian aircraft and sunk at Neu Mukran, Rugen Island, Germany

Dockleaf

5311 tons gross. Under construction as cargo ship *Oleary*; completed April 1917 as tanker *Dockleaf*. On 3 June 1917 mined and damaged off Genoa while on a voyage from Port Arthur to Spezia with a cargo of oil. The mine had been laid by *UC35*. None of the crew were killed or injured. Sold 1919 to Anglo Saxon Petroleum Co Ltd; renamed *Litiopa* 1921 (intended new name *Placuna* not proceeded with). On 22 October 1943, attacked by *U68* and sunk by torpedo and gunfire about 185 miles south-east of Freetown. The escort, HMS *Orfasy*, was also torpedoed and sunk with the loss of the entire crew.

Elmleaf

5948 tons gross. Under construction as cargo ship *Olivet* and completed in March 1917 as tanker *Elmleaf*. On 24 December 1917, torpedoed by *U91* and damaged north of the North Minch when on voyage from Port Arthur to the UK with a cargo of oil. Towed to port and repaired. Sold 1920 to Anglo Saxon Petroleum Co Ltd; renamed *Melona* 1921. Sold 1924 to British Molasses Co Ltd, renamed *Athelcrest*. Depot hulk at Flushing 1935 for NV Vlissingsche Mineraalolie & Asphalt Raffinaderij, renamed *Vlismar II*, and became a depot hulk at Vlissingen. On 8 February 1983 towed from Vlissingen to Burcht, Belgium, for breaking up.

Fernleaf

5938 tons gross. Under construction as cargo ship *Oleander*. Converted to tanker completed as *Fernleaf* in January 1917. In June 1917, off south-west Ireland, *Fernleaf* attempted to ram an attacking German submarine and later maintained sustained fire from the ship's gun so that the submarine's attempted renewed attack was abandoned. On 10 January 1918 in a collision with tanker *San Gregorio* inside the gate of the first boom defence of the Cromarty Firth. Sold 1920 to British Tanker Co Ltd, renamed *British Fern*. Broken up at Osaka, where she arrived on 13 September 1931.

Hollyleaf

5162 tons gross. Under construction as cargo ship *Oleaster*. Converted to tanker and completed as *Hollyleaf* in March 1917. On 30 April 1918 attacked by a submarine in the Mediterranean, but the torpedo missed. Sold 8 September 1919 to British Tanker Co Ltd; renamed *British Holly* 26 November 1920. Broken up Osaka, Japan, 1931.

Laurelleaf

5631 tons gross. Under construction as cargo ship Olalla and completed in December 1916 as tanker *Laurelleaf*. Sold 1919 Anglo-Saxon Petroleum Co Ltd; renamed *Lampas* 1921. In 1939 she was sold to Greece and renamed *Loida*. On 5 September 1952, when owned by Foundation Shipping Corp, Honduras, and named *Foundation Star*, broke in two in a hurricane and sank five days later off North Carolina with the loss of eleven of her crew of thirty.

Limeleaf

7339 tons gross. Under construction for British India Steam Navigation Co Ltd as cargo ship *Masula*. Contract requisitioned by the Admiralty and construction changed to fleet oiler as *Oligarch*; entered service in December 1916 as *Limeleaf*. On 19 April 1917 torpedoed by *UB40* and damaged near the Owers light vessel in the English Channel with the loss of seven crew. Sold 1919 to 'California' Oliefabricken Insulinde, Amsterdam, and renamed *California*. Sold 1924 to British Molasses Co Ltd, renamed *Athelrill*. Sold, again, in 1926 to Nippon Tanker KK, Tokyo, and renamed *Koyo Maru*, and changed hands again to become *Ogura Maru No 3*, owned by Ogura Sekiyu KK. On 24 March 1942 requisitioned by the Imperial Japanese Navy and on 23 February 1944 torpedoed and sunk by submarine USS *Cod* in the South China Sea.

Mapleleaf

8039 tons gross. Originally named *Mount Royal*, built in 1898 by Swan, Hunter & Wigham Richardson Ltd, Newcastle, for Elder Dempster Line. Subsequently, she became a Canadian Pacific liner, before being hired by the Admiralty on 28 October 1914 and converted to dummy battleship *Marlborough*. Based at Loch Ewe. Converted to oiler, renamed *Rangol*, and entered RFA service on 6 July 1915. She was transferred to Lane & Macandrew management on 17 November 1916 and renamed *Mapleleaf*. During war service, she was narrowly missed by a torpedo in the north Atlantic on 21 October 1917. *Mapleleaf* was transferred to the Shipping Controller on 7 November 1917, and on 4 October 1919 was sold to British Tanker Co Ltd and renamed *British Maple*. Breaking up began at Rosyth on 25 January 1933 and on 12 May that year the remaining hulk was transferred to Charlestown to hold oil residues. She was transferred back to Rosyth the following year and demolition was completed on 6 March 1935.

Oakleaf

7345 tons gross. Built in 1899 as the Elder Dempster liner *Montezuma*. Sold to Canadian pacific Railway 1903. Hired by the Admiralty on 12 September 1914 to ferry part of the Canadian Expeditionary Force to Britain. On 20 December 1914 completed conversion to dummy battleship *Iron Duke*. Purchased by the Admiralty 7 July 1915 and converted to tanker *Abadol*. Renamed *Oakleaf* 7 February 1917 upon transfer to management of Lane & Macandrew Ltd. Torpedoed by *UC41* and sunk 25 July 1917 about 64 miles NW of Butt of Lewis (voyage Invergordon to Port Arthur, Texas).

Palmleaf

5489 tons gross. Under construction as cargo ship *Oliphant*, and completed in November 1916 as tanker *Palmleaf*. On 4 February 1917 torpedoed by *U54* and sunk about 230 miles west of Fastnet when on voyage from Sabine Pass, Texas. There were no fatalities. The master and chief engineer were taken prisoner.

Roseleaf

6572 tons gross. Laid down as cargo ship *Rona*; renamed *Califol* while under construction. Acquired by Admiralty in 1916 and converted to tanker. Renamed *Roseleaf* 1917. On 27 April 1917 was attacked by gunfire from an unidentified submarine. She fought off the attacker using her own gun. While refitting at Cardiff on 16 July 1919, twelve people were killed in a gas explosion on *Roseleaf* (the number killed reported in some sources is twenty six). She was sold on 5 January 1920 to British Tanker Co Ltd and renamed *British Rose*. Sold 1930 to La Riviera SA de Nav of Genoa, a subsidiary of A Lauro, Naples, and renamed *Portofino*. On 6 November 1942, while under the control of the Italian navy, attacked by aircraft of the Royal Air Force while in Benghazi, bombed and sunk.

Vineleaf

7678 tons gross. Originally *Patrician*. Built for T & J Harrison, Liverpool. Hired by the Admiralty on 30 November 1914, and converted to dummy battlecruiser *Invincible*. Upon conversion she was based at Loch Ewe and was in the Aegean during February–June 1915. On 6 July 1915 she was purchased by the Admiralty, converted to a tanker, and entered service as RFA *Teakol*. Renamed *Vineleaf* 1917 upon transfer to management of Lane & Macandrew Ltd. Sold 1919 to British Tanker Co Ltd, becoming *British Vine* on 20 April 1920. Sold to H Borge, Tønsberg, Norway, and became the whaling tanker *Busen* on 29 August 1923. Arrived at Genoa 29 July 1935 to be broken up.

Admiralty store ships *Bacchus* (1915, 1936), *Reliant* (1933)

Name	Builder	Launched	Completed	Out of service
Bacchus	Wm Hamilton & Co Ltd, Port Glasgow	10.5.15	7.15	1936
Bacchus	Caledon Shipbuilding & Engineering Co Ltd, Dundee	15.7.36	9.36	1962

Bacchus (1915)
Tonnages: 2343 gross, 3656 displacement
Registered length: 295.1 ft
Beam: 44.1 ft
Depth: 12.5 ft
Draught: 20.65 ft

Machinery: 2 screws, triple expansion engines (bunkers 873 tons coal)
Speed: 10 knots
Complement: 52

Ordered by Indo-China Steam Navigation Co Ltd, London, and similar to two vessels under construction for the company in Hong Kong. Purchased by the Admiralty while under construction. Operated by the Director of Stores from the beginning, with an RFA crew (*ie* crew paid by DoS). Entered service as a tender to HMS *Blenheim*, 19 April 1916. Sent to Port Said for army service as distilling ship. Allocated to North Russia Expedition 1919, as tender to HMS *Cyclops*. Involved in collision on 4 May 1928, resulting in sinking of Greek steamer *Ioannis Fafalios* about 30 miles S of St Alban's Head. *Bacchus* held to be at fault, proceeding too fast in fog. Served on Chatham–Gibraltar–Malta run until 1936. Under the named *Bacchus II*, she was damaged as a bombing target in November 1938, and sunk by gunfire from cruiser HMS *Dunedin* on 15 November in the Hurd Deep, about 10 miles off Alderney.

Bacchus (1936)
Tonnages: 3154 gross, 2856 deadweight, 5150 displacement (stdd), 5790 displacement (full load)
Length overall: 338.5 ft
Beam: 49 ft
Depth: 23ft
Draught 18.0 ft
Machinery: 1 screw, North Eastern Marine Engineering Co Ltd triple expansion engine, 2100 ihp (bunkers 643 tons oil fuel)
Service speed: 12 knots
Complement: 49

Built to Admiralty design to replace *Bacchus* (1915), this vessel was ordered on 17 November 1935, and laid down on 14 February 1936. Commissioned on 20 September 1936, she took over Chatham–Gibraltar–Malta run 1937 until 1939. Engagement with U-boat September 1939 in Bay of Biscay. Served Clyde and Scapa Flow until 1941; converted to naval stores issuing ship. East Indies Station 1942, Persian Gulf 1944–5; Pacific Fleet Train 1945. Reconverted to store carrier at Hong Kong 1946, operating UK–Mediterranean–Far East. *Bacchus* took part in the Suez operations in 1956. Decommissioned on 13 April 1962, she was sold soon after to Chip Hwa Shipping & Trading Co, Singapore, and renamed *Pulau Bali*. Delivered to breakers at Singapore on 12 August 1964.

Name	Builder	Laid down	Launched	Completed	Out of service
Reliant	Furness Shipbuilding Co Ltd, Haverton Hill-on-Tees	30.10.20	25.11.22	12.23	1945

Reliant (1933)
Tonnages: 7938 gross, 11,357 deadweight, 17,000 full load displacement after refit
Length overall: 471.5 ft
Beam: 58 ft
Depth: 38 ft
Draught: 30 ft
Machinery: 1 screw, 2 x Brown Curtis/Richardsons, Westgarth geared turbines, 5000 shp (bunkers 2170 tons oil fuel)
Speed: 14 knots
Complement: 143

Ordered as *Bay State*, while under construction renamed *Indiana*, but launched as *London Importer* for Furness, Withy & Co Ltd, London, for UK–North Pacific service. Sold to the Admiralty on 24 March 1933, for £46,000. On purchase, converted to naval and victualling store ship, which included addition of considerable refrigerated storage. Defensively equipped in 1937. Accompanied the Mediterranean Fleet until 1939 and acted as a victualling supply depot for destroyers and submarines at Malta. Service during Second World War included spells at Mombasa and Singapore. She became surplus in October 1945 and was transferred to the MoWT/MoT. Sold to Malta Cross Steamship Co Ltd in April 1948, renamed *Anthony G.* Sold 1949 to East & West Steamship Co Ltd, Karachi, renamed *Firdausa*. Broken up at Gadani Beach, Karachi in April 1963.

Fast Leaf class tankers

Tonnages: 5891–5927 gross, 5400 deadweight, 12,270–12,370 displacement
Length overall: 425.7 ft
Beam: 54.5 ft
Depth: 32.6 ft
Draught: 27.6–27.8 ft
Machinery: 2 screws, 2 x triple expansion engines, 6750 ihp, 6 Scotch boilers, oil burning
Speed: 16 knots (trials maximum), 14 knots (service). Fuel consumption 90 tons/day. After 1918, class reduced to running on 3 boilers; speed in this conformation 12 knots at 33 tons/day
Complement: 66 European, 90 Lascar

Name	Launched	Completed	Out of service
Appleleaf (launched as *Texol*)	28.11.16	2.17	1946
Brambleleaf (*Rumol*)	28.12.16	4.17	1942
Cherryleaf (*Persol*)	9.11.16	4.17	1946
Orangeleaf (*Bornol*)	26.10.16	4.17	1947
Pearleaf (*Gypol*)	12.9.16	3.17	1946
Plumleaf (*Trinol*)	4.8.16	2.17	1942

Appleleaf
Built and engined by Workman Clark & Co Ltd, Belfast, at a cost of £287,234. On North Atlantic convoy and Mediterranean duties until 1922, when placed in reserve at Rosyth. Chartered 1926–30 to Anglo-Saxon Petroleum Co Ltd. Returned to Admiralty service and in 1934 went to the China station with *Pearleaf*, relieving *Belgol* and *Fortol*. Returning to the UK in 1946, she was mainly idle at various locations in western Scotland. *Appleleaf* was broken up at Troon, where she arrived on 15 December 1947.

Brambleleaf
Built by Russell & Co Ltd, Port Glasgow, with engines by D Rowan & Co Ltd. Served as a North Atlantic escort tanker before transfer to the Dardanelles between 1919 and 1922. In reserve until 1925, when she began service with the Mediterranean Fleet, based on Malta, She was torpedoed by *U 559* on 10 June 1942, one day out of Alexandria, bound for Tobruk. Among her crew of sixty, there were eight fatalities. The crew abandoned ship, but reboarded her and she was towed to Alexandria, where she served as a fuelling hulk. She developed a leak in January 1951, but although this was stopped, it was decided that she should be scrapped. *Brambleleaf* arrived at Spezia in 2 April 1953 for breaking up.

Cherryleaf
Built by Sir Raylton Dixon & Co Ltd, Middlesbrough, with engines by Richardsons, Westgarth & Co Ltd. North Atlantic convoy duties until end of war, then Bermuda oiler until in reserve. On charter to Anglo-Saxon Petroleum Co Ltd between 1925 and 1930, then station oiler at Malta, relieving *Montenol* until 1945. Postwar she saw service east of Suez, but came back to the UK, and was laid up at Sheerness. Sold to Stevinson, Hardy & Co Ltd, London, in January 1947, she did a few voyages for her new owners still with the name *Cherryleaf*. She was renamed *Alan Clore* later in the year. She was sold for breaking up in 1950 after a long period of lay-up at Falmouth brought about by serious boiler and engine trouble, and arrived at the breakers yard in Troon on 29 January 1951.

Orangeleaf
Built by Joseph L Thompson & Sons Ltd, Sunderland, with engines from George Clark & Co Ltd. Wartime convoy escort duties were followed by a period in reserve. This was followed by charter to Anglo-Saxon Petroleum Co Ltd until 1932, when she relieved *Serbol* as Bermuda Station oiler. Postwar, *Orangeleaf* was east of Suez, but came back to the UK for lay up at Methil (arrived 18 April 1947). She arrived at Briton Ferry on 25 January 1948 to be broken up.

Pearleaf
Built by Wm Gray & Co Ltd, West Hartlepool, with engines by Central Marine Engineering Works Ltd. Duties similar to *Orangeleaf* until 1930, when she undertook Admiralty freighting until assignment to the China Station in 1934, and serving there for most of the Second World War. Following the war she came back to the UK, made a few voyages between Scotland and Norway, and was laid up at Leith on 2 September 1946. *Pearleaf* was sold for breaking up at Blyth, and arrived there on 23 December 1947.

Plumleaf

Built by Swan, Hunter & Wigham Richardson Ltd, Wallsend-on-Tyne, which was also engines supplier. Similar duties to other members of the class until 1931, when she relieved *Dredgol* as station oiler at Malta. She was bombed by enemy aircraft at Parlatario Wharf, Malta, on 26 March 1942 and sank in about 40 feet of water. Raised in 1947, she arrived at Catania on 11 October to be broken up.

Second 2000-ton class harbour tankers

Tonnages: 2607–2669 gross, approx. 2226 deadweight (2150 oil cargo), 5049–5620 full load displacement
Length overall: 342.5 ft
Beam: 41.5 ft
Depth: 23.1 ft
Draught: 22.5 ft (max)
Machinery: 1 screw, triple expansion engine by various makers, 3 x Scotch boilers (bunkers 320 tons fuel)
Service speed: 11–12 knots (operating two boilers, at 75 rpm; fuel consumption 38 tons/day); maximum speed: 15 knots (operating three boilers, at 103 rpm; fuel consumption 48 tons/day)
Complement: 42 UK (55 Lascar)

Name	Builder	Launched	Completed	Out of service
Belgol	Irvine's Shipbuilding & Dry Docks Co Ltd, West Hartlepool	23.4.17	10.17	1958
Celerol	Short Bros & Co Ltd, Sunderland	23.5.17	10.9.17	1958
Fortol	A McMillan & Son Ltd, Dumbarton	21.5.17	31.8.17	1958
Francol	Earle's Shipbuilding & Engineering Co Ltd, Hull	18.10.17	18.12.17	1942
Montenol	Wm Gray & Co Ltd, West Hartlepool	5.7.17	20.11.17	1942
Prestol	Napier & Miller Ltd, Glasgow	4.9.17	12.17	1958
Rapidol	Wm Gray & Co Ltd, West Hartlepool	23.4.17	28.8.17	1946
Serbol	Caledon Shipbuilding & Engineering Co Ltd, Dundee	7.7.17	1.18	1958
Slavol	Greenock & Grangemouth Dockyard Co Ltd, Greenock	21.4.17	1.11.17	1941
Vitol	Greenock & Grangemouth Dockyard Co Ltd, Greenock	24.5.17	10.17	1918

Entirely different from any vessels previously constructed for the Admiralty, these looked most unlike a conventional tanker. With the bridge and funnel amidships, they more closely resembled the cargo boats of the period. They were fast, being capable of over 15 knots when operating on all three boilers, although this caused high fuel consumption.

Their high speed may have reflected the Admiralty's previous preoccupation with RAS, and the need for a faster than average replenishment fleet. During this period, the fastest US commercial tankers only had a design speed of 13 knots, which made for considerable difficulties when the US Navy introduced its National Defense Features scheme.

As well as their oil cargo, this class had stowage for 5000 gallons of lubricating oil, in bulk. They were a long serving class, some members remaining in service for over forty years.

Belgol

2648 tons gross. Navigating bridge fitted with armour plate while in China. Served on Home, Mediterranean and China stations. In reserve at Rosyth in 1935, and during 1938–9 at Devonport. In the earlier months of the war was at Scapa Flow, and remained in Scotland, with occasional voyages to Iceland, until 1943. Arrived at Trincomalee in April 1944. Came under fire while supplying Royal Navy ships on the Yangtze river, China, during the early troubles there. In reserve from 1953. Sold to BISCO and arrived at Charlestown, Fife, on 22 June 1958 for breaking up by Shipbreaking Industries Ltd.

Celerol

2649 tons gross. Began operations with Grand Fleet, in Baltic, during 1918–22, and with her deep draught caused her to run aground on several ocassions. Placed in reserve at Rosyth from January 1926 to 1935, when she was surveyed and sent to relieve *Orangeleaf* on the Bermuda Station. When war broke out in 1939, she was in reserve at Devonport. She then was involved in UK voyages, until 1943 when she was in the Mediterranean. She was at Gibraltar in May 1947 and was laid up in reserve at Rosyth on 29 March 1953. Sold to BISCO and arrived at Rosyth on 9 July 1958, but was transferred to Bo'ness, where she arrived on 17 July to be broken up by P & W MacLellan Ltd.

Fortol
2629 tons gross. Home, Mediterranean and China stations. In reserve at Rosyth July 1932. Converted to white oil carrier 1935, serving in that capacity in Gulf of Suez. Was in reserve at Devonport upon the outbreak of war in 1939, and saw service at Mauritius and southern and west Africa during 1940–42. During 1943 was escort oiler to convoys from UK to West Africa and in 1944 involved with Iceland convoys. On 8 May 1945 was in the Skagerrak with other British ships for the surrender of the German fleet. Postwar, was at Rosyth and east coast of Scotland, and on 17 January 1950 was laid up at Devonport. Sold to BISCO and arrived at Rosyth on 6 August 1958 for breaking up by Shipbreaking Industries Ltd.

Francol
2607 tons gross.
Served whole of career on China Station, Hong Kong in winter and Wei Hai Wei during summer. Involved in target towing and RAS trials during this period. Sunk by air attack gunfire from Japanese warships 3 March 1942, 300 miles south of Java, in 11 30S 109 03E, and her crew subsequently interned at Macassar, Celebes. She was on voyage from Batavia to Fremantle.

Montenol
2646 tons gross. Fleet attendance in Black Sea and Dardanelles during 1921–3, then based at Malta, as station oiler, until 1932, when *Cherryleaf* replaced her, at the same time exchanging crews. In reserve at Rosyth until 1936, when she saw service during Spanish Civil War, based at La Rochelle. Later served at Haifa and Alexandria. At the outbreak of war was based at Scapa Flow, and for a few weeks in 1940 was based on the Clyde as a fuel oil depot ship; she then returned to Scapa. Torpedoed by *U159* on 21 May 1942, in 36 41N 22 45W, en route to Freetown and Table Bay in convoy OS28, which had left Liverpool on 12 May. Subsequently sunk by gunfire from accompanying escorts.

Prestol
2629 tons gross.
Based at Portsmouth for most of her career. On 29 November 1920 in collision at Danzig with the steamer *Susquehanna*, which was subsequently found to be responsible. At the time *Prestol* was supplying oil to the British naval squadron operating in the Baltic. *Prestol* went to Rosyth for repairs and *Belgol* took over in the Baltic. Involved in early RAS trials with *Carol* in 1923 and paravane trials in 1935-6 in Spithead. In 1936, at La Coruna, Spain, oiling British destroyers that were involved in policing the blockade of Bilbao during the Spanish civil war. In the Mediterranean in 1944 and the Far East by 1949, where, on 15 November she was struck by gunfire when bound from Shanghai to Hong Kong. *Prestol* collided at Gibraltar with the frigate *Loch Scavaig*, which needed docking for repairs. Sold to BISCO and broken up by James A White & Co Ltd, St David's, where she arrived on 8 June 1958.

Rapidol
2649 tons gross. At Colombo 4 July 1922 as oiler to East Indies Squadron, and then based Trincomalee 1925–7; South Atlantic Station 1928–32; laid up Simonstown July 1933. Subsequently, undertook duties during Italo-Abyssinian war (1935–6) and in early part of the Second World War was voyaging from the UK to West Africa. Supported convoys from Iceland to UK in 1943–4, and ran aground briefly in Reykjavik harbour on 3 May 1943. Served off Normandy beachhead as part of Operation 'Neptune'. Transferred to Pacific Fleet Train and arrived Hong Kong 19 September 1945. Sold March 1948 to Mollers (Hong Kong) Ltd, and renamed *Louise Moller* in August 1948 for Moller Line Ltd. Changed hands again in November 1951 and renamed *Mount Cameron*. Scrapped Hong Kong 1955.

Serbol
2668 tons gross. Mediterranean station until 1924, then West Indies Station oiler, at Bermuda. Malta 1935–6, then back to UK. In reserve at Gibraltar 3 September 1939, but sailed in convoy for Liverpool before the end of the month. Service in Colombo, 1945, Manus, 1945, Hong Kong, 1945–7, then in UK waters. Laid up at malta 26 August 1953. Sold to BISCO and arrived Blyth on 30 June 1958 for breaking up by Hughes Bolckow Ltd.

Slavol
2623 tons gross. Served as oiler with 1919 Archangel River Expedition, then eastern Mediterranean until 1921. With Home Fleet until 1926, at Plymouth. Oiler for 4th Cruiser Squadron, Trincomalee, 1927–39. She transported a party of Royal Marines to deal with stowaways aboard the liner *Jervis Bay* on 23 June 1928 in the India Ocean. Transferred to Port Said 1939. Torpedoed by *U205* and sunk 26 March 1942 off Sidi Barrani, Egypt, in 32 01N 25 55E on passage Alexandria to Tobruk with fuel oil.

Vitol
2639 tons gross. Torpedoed by *U110* and sunk, 7 March 1918, in 52 37 55N 05 04 07W, while on voyage from Liverpool to Queenstown.

Second class of 1000-ton harbour tankers

Tonnages: 1115–1179 gross, 1070 cargo, 1430 deadweight
Length overall: 220–221 ft
Beam: 34.5–34.8 ft
Depth: 13.5 ft
Draught: 16.2 ft
Machinery: 1 screw;
Steam: 1 screw, triple expansion engine, 700 ihp, by variety of makers (bunkers 40 tons fuel oil; 12 tons/day)
Diesel (*Oakol, Palmol, Sprucol, Teakol*): 2 screw, 2 x 4-cylinder diesels by J & CG Bolinders Co Ltd, Stockholm, 640 bhp (bunkers 40 tons)
Service speed: Steam: 11.5 knots; diesel: 9.5 knots
Complement: 19 (European)

Name	Builder	Launched	Completed	Out of service
Birchol	Barclay, Curle & Co Ltd, Glasgow	16.6.17	12.9.17	1939
Boxol	Barclay, Curle & Co Ltd, Glasgow	12.7.17	9.17	1948
Creosol	Short Bros Ltd, Sunderland	5.2.16	22.8.16	1918
Distol	W Dobson & Co Ltd, Newcastle	4.3.16	7.16	1947
Ebonol	Clyde Shipbuilding Co Ltd, Port Glasgow	16.10.17	12.12.17	1941
Elderol	Swan, Hunter & Wigham Richardson Ltd, Newcastle	10.5.17	23.6.17	1959
Elmol	Swan, Hunter & Wigham Richardson Ltd, Newcastle	23.7.17	27.8.17	1959
Hickorol	A McMillan & Son Ltd, Dumbarton	30.11.17	3.18	1947
Kimmerol	Craig, Taylor & Co Ltd, Stockton-on-Tees	4.4.16	10.16	1947
Larchol	Lobnitz & Co Ltd, Renfrew	19.6.17	9.8.17	1954
Limol	Lobnitz & Co Ltd, Renfrew	18.10.17	18.12.17	1959
Oakol	Wm Gray & Co Ltd, West Hartlepool	19.9.17	9.3.18	1920
Palmol	Wm Gray & Co Ltd, West Hartlepool	14.11.17	5.18	1920
Philol	Tyne Iron Shipbuilding Co Ltd, Newcastle	5.4.16	8.16	1956
Scotol	Tyne Iron Shipbuilding Co Ltd, Newcastle	23.6.16	11.16	1948
Sprucol	Short Bros Ltd, Sunderland	4.7.17	1.18	1920
Teakol	Short Bros Ltd, Sunderland	17.8.17	1.18	1920
Viscol	Craig, Taylor & Co Ltd, Stockton-on-Tees	21.2.16	8.16	1947

Costing in the region of £66,000 each, these small tankers were among the most useful and long serving of the RFA early fleet, with the exception of the four diesel-engined vessels, which were sold soon after the Armistice. Although not very pretty to look at and originally designed as coastal tankers, many actually voyaged as far as Hong Kong and the Great Lakes.

Birchol
1115 tons gross, 2407 displacement. Dockyard service. Stranded during fog 29 November 1939 on Uist, Hebrides, in 57 05N 07 13 44W and became a total loss. On 9 October 1970 the wreck was sold to Elliott & Co.

Boxol
1115 tons gross, 2200 displacement. Dockyard duties initially then fleet oiler at Malta 1921–48, surviving

wartime service without incurring any but minor damage. This was helped by keeping her empty until needed then refuelling from protected, underground tanks. Was at Malta during 1944–5. Sold to Oscar Shipping Co Ltd, London, in 1948 and renamed *Portnall*. Re-acquired by Admiralty in 1951 during Korean war, renamed *Boxol* in 1952 and stationed at Gibraltar. Arrived at Llanelly on 2 September 1959 to be broken up by Rees on behalf of BISCO.

Creosol
1179 tons gross, 1920 displacement. Torpedoed by *UC17* and sunk on 7 February 1918 north-east of Seaham in 54 52N 01 11W.

Distol
1174 tons gross, 1920 displacement. On fleet attendance at several UK dockyards, with her crew usually signed on under yard craft agreements, allowing them to sleep ashore because such ships would rarely leave harbour. In reserve at Rosyth January 1929 to January 1935 and at Devonport June 1938 to December 1939. On 19 July 1941 involved in collision. Sailed in convoy OS109 from Milford Haven on 6 February 1945 and into convoy KMS82 and arrived at Gibraltar on 12 February. She then proceeded to Port Said, Calcutta and Colombo, and after some service at Trincomalee, arrived at Bombay on 26 January 1946. She remained at Bombay and on 23 April 1947 was handed over to STO Bombay for disposal. Sold in 1948 to Kuwait Oil Co Ltd, she was renamed *Akhawi* and used as a fresh water carrier between Abadan and Mena-al-Ahmadi. Broken up at Bombay, where she arrived in April 1954.

Ebonol
1158 tons gross 2200 displacement. Fuelling duties at Portsmouth and south coast yards until transferred to Hong Kong in 1931. Scuttled at Hong Kong 19 December 1941, to avoid capture by Japanese. Raised and placed in service by Japanese under name *Enoshima Maru*. Recovered at Batavia in September 1945 and towed to Singapore where she resumed duty as *Ebonol* as a depot ship in 1945. She was sold on 15 August 1947 to Singapore interests, Chin Ah Co Ltd, without change of name. In the following year sold to Yap Kah Hoe, Singapore, and reverted to her then previous owner in 1949. Purchased by Great Southern Steamship Co Ltd, Hong Kong, on 14 November 1949, she struck a mine, presumably laid by Chinese nationalists, and sank in bad weather off Sugar Loaf Island, on 24 May 1950, when on voyage from Swatow to Hong Kong with passengers and a cargo of sugar.

Elderol
1170 tons gross. 2200 displacement. On UK dockyard duty, and in the Second World War, between 2 march 1940 and 25 February 1945 primarily served Falmouth, Devonport, Dartmouth, Portland, Southampton and Portsmouth. She was laid up at Portsmouth on 21 May 1954. Sold 1959 to BISCO and broken up by Rees, Llanelly, where she arrived on 1 September.

Elmol
1170 tons gross, 2200 displacement. Dockyard duty in UK ports. During the Second World War, spent much time in service on the English and Scottish east coast, and was later at Portsmouth. In 1956 on charter to Enid Shipping Co Ltd, London, until sold to that company in 1959. She was sold to breakers Haulbowline Industries Ltd, Cork, in 1961, but resold to AG Weser, Bremen, for use as a slops storage vessel. She was broken up by AG Weser and breaking up commenced on 17 July 1978.

Hickorol
1176 tons gross, 2200 displacement. During July and August 1919 involved as oiler with British and US minesweepers removing the Northern Barrage – the series of minefields laid across the northern North Sea to restrict the passage of German U-boats. Served in UK dockyards 1920–32 as port oiler. Chartered to Sun Oil Co for use in Great Lakes and Canadian ports, and during this period she is reported to have broken the speed record for the class when she went down the St Lawrence rapids at 18 knots. In reserve 1936–8. After dockyard service during the Second World War, she was sold in 1947 to Hemsley, Bell & Co Ltd, Southampton, and renamed *Hemsley II* in 1948. Sold to N T Papadatos of Piræus and renamed *Grammos* in 1950, then sold again, in 1956, to D'Alesio & Castaldi of Leghorn, and renamed *Ardenza*. In 1967 she was sold to Ottavio Novella, Genoa, and renamed *Pannesi*. She was a breaker's yard at Spezia in July 1978 awaiting scrapping.

Kimmerol
1172 tons gross, 2400 displacement. Portsmouth port oiler on yard craft agreement January 1921 until transferred to RFA in November 1939. For much of the Second World War, saw service on the English south

coast. Port oiler at Colombo and Trincomalee from 6 March 1945 until laid up at Trincomalee on 10 January 1947. She had been transferred to the Ministry of Transport in December 1946. Sold to Centaur Shipping Co Ltd, London, 1947, without change of name. In 1949 changed hands again, and became *Lanka Bahu*, owned by Ocean Freighters (Ceylon) Ltd, Colombo. In 1950 she was purchased by Wallem & Co, Hong Kong, transferred the Panamanian flag and in the following year was renamed *Tenena*. She changed hands again under Panamanian registry and in December 1953 her owners were blacklisted by the Panamanian authorities. She became Chinese owned in early 1954 and reported as scrapped.

Larchol
1097 tons gross, 2200 displacement. Port oiler at Sheerness 1920–52, with some voyages on the east coast. She was laid up in reserve at Pembroke Dock on 13 July 1954. Sold to R S Hayes, Pembroke, June 1958, and arrived Antwerp on 23 August 1959 en route to be broken up at Boom.

Limol
1159 tons gross, 2200 displacement. Port oiler at various UK dockyards, and during the Second World War spent much time on the English east coast. In reserve at Pembroke Dock from 30 June 1953. Sold to BISCO and broken up by T W Ward Ltd, Briton Ferry, where she arrived on 23 August 1959.

Oakol
1144 tons gross, 1925 displacement. Sold 29 January 1920 to Anglo-Saxon Petroleum Co Ltd and renamed *Orthis*, and in 1925 transferred to its subsidiary, Rising Sun Petroleum Co Ltd (Teikoku Sempaku KK), Yokohama, as *Orthis Maru*. Scrapped in 1934.

Palmol
1144 tons gross, 1925 displacement. Sold 1920 to British-Mexican Petroleum Co Ltd (manager Andrew Weir & Co Ltd), and renamed *Invercorrie*. Transferred to Weir later in the same year. She was fitted with two McKie & Baxter triple expansion engines. Back to British-Mexican registered ownership in 1923. In 1925 sold to Lago Shipping Co Ltd (manager remained Weir), and in 1931 sold to Lago Petroleum Corporation, Venezuela. Dismantled and scuttled near Maracaibo 1938.

Philol
1178 tons gross, 2200 displacement. Port oiler in various UK dockyards, ending her career as stationary tank and sullage barge at Chatham from 1956. She was sold in 1967 and arrived at Burcht in June to be broken up.

Scotol
1177 tons gross, 2200 displacement. Port oiler at Dover and Portland. On 28 December 1944 was in collison with a trawler and was holed in the area of the port anchor. Sold 21 April 1948 to Hemsley, Bell & Co Ltd, Southampton, and renamed *Hemsley 1*. Ran aground in fog 12 May 1969 off Portcothan, 6 nm south of Padstow, when on voyage from Liverpool to Antwerp in ballast. She was dismantled *in situ*.

Sprucol
1137 tons gross, 1925 displacement. On 10 July 1918 torpedoed by *UB110* in the North Sea; she was damaged, but made port and was repaired. Sold 29 January 1920 to Anglo-American Oil Co Ltd, London, and renamed *Juniata*. Sold in July 1934 to Société Auxiliare de Transports, Paris, and taken back by Anglo-American in 1936. She was requisitioned by the Royal Navy and on 17 April 1940 scuttled at Water Sound, Scapa Flow, east of the Churchill Barrier linking the islands of South Ronaldsay and Burray. In July 1949 was raised for scrapping. It was found that her condition would not allow tow to a shipbreaking yard, so she was towed to Inganess Bay, Orkney and beached. Some scrapping work seems to have been carried out there, as the stern section has been separated from the wreck, leaving only the bow section still visible above the surface, a short distance out from the sandy beach off the end of the main runway at Kirkwall airport.

Teakol
1137 tons gross, 1925 displacement. Sold 29 January 1920 to Eagle Oil Transport Co Ltd, London, and renamed *San Dario*. The Ailsa Shipbuilding & Engineering Co Ltd, Troon, fitted her with two triple expansion engines in 1922. In 1931 she was transferred to Eagle Oil & Shipping Co Ltd. Sold to BISCO and broken up by T W Ward Ltd, Grays, Essex, where she arrived on 30 September 1957.

Viscol
1163 tons gross, 2400 displacement. Port oiler at Gibraltar from 1918–45. Used as oil hulk at Gibraltar from

June 1945 to 4 May 1946, when she resumed service as fleet attendant oiler. Left Gibraltar on 30 August 1947 in tow of *War Bharata* and arrived at Devonport on 5 September. Sold 1947 to Risdon, Beasley & Co Ltd, Southampton, name unchanged. Sold in 1950 Ottavio Novella, Genoa, and renamed *Frecciamare*, she had three more changes of registered owner until the Italian flag before arriving at Brindisi on 24 November 1982 for breaking up.

War class

Tonnages: 5502–5730 gross, 8450 deadweight, 7400 cargo, 11,400 displacement
Length overall: 412 ft
Beam: 52.2–52.5 ft
Depth: 31 ft
Draught: 25.1 ft
Machinery: 1 screw, triple expansion engine by various makers, 2500 ihp (bunkers for both oil (1050 tons) and coal (1393 tons), although coal never used)
Speed: 11 knots (fuel consumption of 22 tons/day at 67 rpm)
Complement: 44

Name	Builder	Launched	Completed	Out of service
War Afridi	R Duncan & Co Ltd, Port Glasgow	11.11.19	29.1.20	1949
War Bahadur	Armstrong, Whitworth & Co Ltd, Newcastle	4.11.18	12.18	1946
War Bharata	Palmers' Shipbuilding & Iron Co Ltd, Jarrow	24.11.19	30.3.20	1948
War Brahmin	Lithgows Ltd, Port Glasgow	28.11.19	2.20	1949
War Diwan	Lithgows Ltd, Port Glasgow	28.6.19	21.8.19	1944
War Hindoo	Wm Hamilton & Co Ltd, Port Glasgow	30.9.19	10.19	1952
War Krishna	Swan, Hunter & Wigham Richardson Ltd, Newcastle	24.10.19	26.11.19	1946
War Mehtar	Armstrong, Whitworth & Co Ltd, Newcastle	9.10.19	2.3.20	1941
War Nawab	Palmers' Shipbuilding & Iron Co Ltd, Jarrow	13.6.19	8.19	1946
War Nizam	Palmers' Shipbuilding & Iron Co Ltd, Jarrow	5.9.18	10.18	1947
War Pathan	Sir James Laing & Sons Ltd, Sunderland	19.3.19	5.19	1947
War Pindari	Lithgows Ltd, Port Glasgow	29.12.19	16.3.20	1947
War Sepoy	W Gray & Co Ltd, West Hartlepool	5.12.18	6.2.19	1940
War Sirdar	Sir James Laing & Sons Ltd, Sunderland	6.12.19	2.20	1942
War Sudra	Palmers' Shipbuilding & Iron Co Ltd, Jarrow	18.3.20	5.20	1946

These ships, owned by Shipping Controller upon completion, were modified versions of A and B class wartime standard dry cargo ships. Known as the Z class, the first six were fitted with five cargo tanks. These modifications were unsatisfactory, having resulted in excessive rivet leakage. Consequently, the last group of nine was strengthened with extra bulkheads. Despite these changes, they still leaked. The ships were transferred to the Admiralty in 1921. The commercial managers of the vessels were inherited from the Shipping Controller.

Thirty-eight other vessels of this type were built, although none served as RFAs.

Group 1: Five cargo tanks

War Bahadur
5565 tons gross. Managed until 1931 by C T Bowring & Co Ltd, London; in reserve at Rosyth from September 1931 to 1936; returned to Director of Stores (DoS). Badly damaged in an Atlantic storm on 14 January 1938, but through use of emergency steering made Devonport. Used as fuelling hulk at Devonport dockyard. She was handed over to the MoT on 7 August 1946 and soon after sold to BISCO. She arrived in tow at Hughes Bolckow & Co Ltd, Blyth, on 22 September for scrapping.

War Diwan
5551 tons gross. Managed until 1936 by C T Bowring & Co Ltd; returned to DoS. During 1938–9 in reserve at Devonport. Her service during the war was mainly in the UK. While on passage from Southend to Antwerp in convoy TAM19, struck mine and broke in two in the Schelde estuary on 16 December 1944. Both parts sank and the vessel was declared a total loss shortly after. The forepart was raised on 4 May 1952 and taken to Vlissingen for breaking up.

War Nawab
5577 tons gross. Managed until 1936 by British Tanker Co Ltd, London; returned to DoS. Freighting duties and various charters. In September 1940 was to be used as a fire ship in the abandonded attack on Calais harbour (Operation 'Lucid'). Used as a fuel hulk at Devonport from November 1946. Sold to BISCO and arrived Troon on 26 July 1958 to be broken up by West of Scotland Shipbreaking Co Ltd.

War Nizam
5592 tons gross. Managed until 1937 by British Tanker Co Ltd; returned to DoS. During earlier months of the war, was in service on UK east coast from Scapa Flow to Sheerness. In September–October 1940, was fire ship in the abandoned Operation 'Lucid'. She then continued service on the UK east coast and on 11 November 1941 was attacked by German aircraft and damaged off Aldeburgh. She was sold in 1947 to Basinghall Shipping Co Ltd, London, and renamed *Basinghall*, and two years later sold to breakers in Antwerp, where she arrived in July 1949.

War Pathan
5581 tons gross. Managed until 1936 by Andrew Weir & Co Ltd, London; returned to DoS. Sold on 16 October 1947 to Bulk Storage Co Ltd, London, and renamed *Basingbank*. Arrived Antwerp in July 1949 to be broken up.

War Sepoy
5557 tons gross. Managed upon completion by Anglo-Mexican Petroleum Co Ltd and from 1921 to 1936 by Hunting & Son Ltd, Newcastle; returned to DoS. Bombed by German aircraft 19 July 1940 and beached in Dover harbour. On 7 September, with holds full of concrete, she was scuttled as a blockship, together with two other vessels, at the western entrance to the harbour. Removal of the blockships started in 1950 and was not completed until July 1962.

Group 2: Seven cargo tanks

War Afridi
5551 tons gross. Managed until 1937 by C T Bowring & Co Ltd; returned to DoS. Freighting duties and occasional charter; storage hulk in Hong Kong from January 1949. Sold in August 1958 to breakers at Hong Kong.

War Bharata
5600 tons gross. Entered service for the RFA on 20 March 1920. Managed until 1934 by British Tanker Co Ltd; returned to DoS. Freighting duties and occasional charter; in reserve at Rosyth from August 1931 to 1934. Normal RFA service, and during the war was involved in UK service. In the immediate post-war period, she was at Yokohama, and Palestine in 1947. Sold in 1948 to Verano Steamship Co Ltd, London, and renamed *Wolf Rock*. Sold to BISCO and arrived at Troon on 15 May 1953 for breaking up by West of Scotland Shipbreaking Co Ltd.

War Brahmin
5551 tons gross. Managed until 1937 by C T Bowring & Co Ltd; returned to DoS. Only member of class built with patent davits. Normal service until 1945, then period spent as storage hulk at Gibraltar. Later, water carrier Augusta–Malta and Casablanca–Gibraltar. Arrived at Spezia on 5 February 1960 to be broken up.

War Hindoo
5565 tons gross. Managed until 1936 by Gow, Harrison & Co Ltd, Glasgow; returned to DoS. Normal RFA freighting duties, with an occasional charter, until 1939 when she became harbour oiler at Milford Haven until transfer to Singapore, in 1944, then Hong Kong. In April 1950 hired by Shell Oil for use as a storage hulk at Gibraltar. Upon completion of hire, she went back to freighting, and then Malta from 1952 as fuelling hulk following a series of repairs. Sold to BISCO and arrived at Hughes Bolckow Ltd, Blyth, on 9 May 1958 to be broken up.

War Krishna
5730 tons gross. Only vessel of this class with engines installed aft. Managed upon completion by Lane & Macandrew Ltd and from 1923 to 1936 by Davies & Newman Ltd, London; returned to DoS. For most of the war in Europe saw service in the Mediterranean and in June 1945 arrived at Trincomalee. She was sold in 1946 to Bulk Storage Co Ltd, London, and in 1948 transferred to Basinghall Shipping Co Ltd, without change of name. She left Trincomalee in tow on 11 February 1949 and arrived at Karachi on 2 March to be broken up.

War Mehtar
5502 tons gross. Managed until 1937 by Hunting & Son Ltd; returned to DoS. Accompanied HMS *Repulse* to South Atlantic, with the then Prince of Wales. Freighting duties and occasional charter. While in convoy FS650 on passage from Grangemouth to Harwich with a cargo of fuel oil, on 20 November 1941 torpedoed by German E-boat *S104* and sunk off Great Yarmouth.

War Pindari
5551 tons gross. Managed until 1937 by C T Bowring & Co Ltd; returned to DoS. In reserve at Rosyth from August 1931 to 1936. In April 1940 supported Royal Navy ships in Operation 'Maurice', the Allied landings at Namsos, Norway. Normal freighting service, mainly on Scottish east coast, until sold to Wentbridge Shipping Ltd (manager John Harker Ltd, Knottingley), in 1947 and renamed *Deepdale H*. Sold 1952 to Società di Navigazione Ligure-Toscana, Genoa, and renamed *Carignano*. Sold to BISCO and arrived at Hughes Bolckow Ltd, Blyth, on 4 February 1954 for breaking up.

War Sirdar
5518 tons gross. Managed upon completion by Anglo-American Oil Co Ltd and from 1923 to 1937 by Hunting & Son Ltd; returned to DoS. During February 1942 was bombed by Japanese aircraft at Tanjong Priok, Netherlands East Indies. On 28 February she stranded on the Jong Reef, Batavia, and following unsuccessful attempts at refloating, she was declared a total loss on 1 March. Salved by the Japanese, she was renamed *Honan Maru*, and was torpedoed and by the submarine USS *Bluegill* on 28 March 1945 off Nha Trang, French Indo-China. She was beached at Cape Varella, and following another attack by *Bluegill* on 29 March, was finally destroyed by demolition charges placed on her on 5 April by a landing party from the US submarine.

War Sudra
5599 tons gross. Managed until 1937 by British Tanker Co Ltd; returned to DoS. Served in Scapa Flow and Iceland as fuel depot ship from July 1940 to April 1942. She was then based in Scotland. Sent to Hong Kong for use in harbour as floating storage in April 1946, where she was listed for sale later in the same year. Sold in 1948 to Oak Shipping Co Ltd, London, but not renamed. Resold to Compania Maritima Iguana SA, Panama, and renamed *Germaine*. Broken up at Hendrik-Ido-Ambacht, Netherlands, where she was delivered in December 1954.

Pet class spirit carriers

Tonnages: 475 gross, 300 deadweight, 747 displacement (stdd), 1024 displacement (full load)
Length overall: 164.2 ft
Beam: 28.1 ft
Depth: 11.2 ft
Draught: 11.4 ft
Machinery: 1 screw, Dunlop Bremner triple expansion engine, 500 ihp (bunkers 50 tons oil)
Speed: 9–10 knots
Complement: 16

Name	Builder	Launched	Completed	Out of service
Petrella	Dunlop, Bremner & Co Ltd, Port Glasgow	16.2.18	4.18	1946
Petrobus	Dunlop, Bremner & Co Ltd, Port Glasgow	8.11.17	2.18	1959
Petronel	Dunlop, Bremner & Co Ltd, Port Glasgow	27.4.18	6.18	1947

All served in UK waters, *Petrella* and *Petrobus* as spirit carriers, while *Petronel* was with the Atlantic Fleet as its water boat until sold in 1947.

Petrella
Sold out of service in 1946 and renamed *Captain Mikes*. After further changes of owner and name, she was broken up in Greece in 1976.

Petrobus
Sold to Thomas Ward Ltd and arrived Grays, Essex, on 24 February 1959 to be broken up.

Petronel
In 1947 was sold to Bulk Oil Steamship Co Ltd, London, and renamed *Pass of Glencoe*. Sold again in 1949, she became *Athelglen*, and after a further sale in 1954, broken up as *Molaglen* in 1958 in the Demerara River.

Ol class

British group
Tonnages: gross: 6891 (*Olcades*), 6897 (*Oligarch*), 6688 (*Olynthus*), 6470 (*Olwen*); deadweight: 10,730 (*Olcades, Oligarch*), 10,683 (*Olynthus*), 9760 (*Olwen*); approx. 13,700 displacement (full load)
Length overall: 444.1 ft (*Olwen* registered length 419.7 ft)
Beam: 57 ft (*Olwen* 54.5 ft)
Depth: 33 ft (*Olwen* 32.5 ft)
Draught: 27.2 ft (*Olwen* 27 ft)
Machinery: 1 screw, triple expansion engine, made by respective builders, 3100 ihp; 3 Scotch boilers
Speed: 10–11 knots
Complement: 43

Name	Builder	Launched	Completed	Out of service
Olcades	Workman, Clark & Co Ltd, Belfast	7.9.18	9.10.19	1953
Oligarch	Workman, Clark & Co Ltd, Belfast	11.6.18	8.18	1946
Olynthus	Swan,Hunter & Wigham Richardson Ltd, Newcastle	14.2.18	3.18	1947
Olwen	Palmers' Shipbuilding & Iron Co Ltd, Jarrow	3.10.17	12.17	1948

The four ships in this first group were built as conventional commercial tankers. Acquired by the Admiralty between 1918 and 1922, they were all placed under the management of the British Tanker Co Ltd, painted in its livery and retaining their British prefixed names. Crews, unusually, were also paid by the management company, instead of by the Director of Stores, which was said to be more usual. During this period, they were used mainly for commercial freighting. When they were taken over by the Director of Stores, in 1936, and renamed, their role was similar, in that they spent most of their time filling fuel tanks at the various Royal Navy bases worldwide.

Olcades
Built as *British Beacon*. Acquired by Admiralty 1918. Commercial freighting service until 1936, when was handed over to the Admiralty and renamed *Olcades*. Freighting service for DoS until 1942, when following shaft trouble she became a hulk at Bombay. Repaired in 1943, she joined the replenishment group of Eastern Fleet, becoming jetty and pumping station at Woodlands in 1946. Sold to breakers, having suffered a serious fire at Singapore in 1952. She left Singapore in tow of the tug *Englishman* on 29 October 1952 and arrived at Blyth on 18 April 1953 to be broken up. However, even this voyage was not without incident, because on 31 January the tow broke in heavy weather and she went ashore at Bacton, Norfolk.

Oligarch
Built as *British Lantern*. Acquired by Admiralty 1922. Commercial freighting service until 1936, when was handed over to the Admiralty and renamed *Oligarch* in the following year. Torpedoed 1943, and towed to Alexandria and used as fuel hulk. On 14 April 1946, she was scuttled with load of obsolete ammunition at the southern end of the Red Sea.

Olynthus
Built as *British Star*. Acquired by Admiralty 1922. Commercial freighting service until 1936, when was handed over to the Admiralty. She was renamed *Olynthus* in 1937. Service during the Second World War included refuelling off Argentina HMS *Ajax* (15 December 1939) and HMNZS *Achilles* (17 December), which were ships of the squadron hunting the German pocket battleship *Admiral Graf Spee*. She was an escort oiler in 1941 and with Eastern Fleet during 1942–5. *Olynthus* was sold in 1947 to Stevinson, Hardy & Co Ltd, London, then two years later to Luigi Pittaluga, Genoa, and renamed *Pensilvania*. In 1960 she was broken up at Savona, Italy.

Olwen
This tanker was slightly smaller than the three preceding ships. Built as *British Light* at a cost of £191,789.

Acquired by Admiralty 1922. Commercial freighting service until 1936, when was handed over to the Admiralty and was renamed *Olwen* in the following year. On 22 September 1939, she was at Montevideo with defects, which were repaired, and she left three weeks later to join Force G and to give support, with other RFAs, to the RN units involved in the search for the German pocket battleship *Admiral Graf Spee*. She was transferred on fuelling duties with the Eastern Fleet, during 1942–6. She was sold in 1948 and renamed *Mushtari*, and following further changes of owner she was broken up at Karachi in 1957.

Dockyard group
Tonnages: gross: 7023 (*Olna*), 7045 (*Oleander*); deadweight: 10,160 (*Olna*), 10,210 (*Oleander*); approx. 13,700 displacement (full load)
Registered length: 430 ft
Beam: 57 ft
Depth: 33.7 ft
Draught: 27.4 ft
Machinery: 1 screw, triple expansion engine, made by respective builders, 3100 shp; 3 Scotch boilers
Speed: 11 knots
Complement: 43

Name	Builder	Laid down	Launched	Completed	Out of service
Olna	HM Dockyard, Devonport	14.6.20	21.6.21	10.10.21	1941
Oleander	HM Dockyard, Pembroke	1.12.20	26.4.22	20.10.22	1940

Built as the result of a post-war government decision to keep the naval dockyards employed by building tankers, despite the excess of tanker tonnage at that time.

Two well-built ships, *Murex* and *Nassa*, were produced as part of this scheme at Portsmouth and Devonport for Anglo-Saxon Petroleum but then finance appears to have run out. Consequently, the two ships built for the RFA, which were based on the *British Isles* class (10,240 tons deadweight), were constructed of spare or out-of-date fittings and auxiliaries taken from obsolete warships. The resulting maintenance bills, perhaps not unexpectedly, were heavy and both ships spent much of their working lives on charter to pay for the excessive running costs. The orders for the tankers were placed by the Shipping Controller and they were delivered to the Admiralty upon completion. Both were managed by Davies & Newman Ltd, London, although in this case crews were RFA, *ie* wages, recruitment, etc was the responsibility of the Admiralty, through the DoS.

Olna
Managed commercially by Davies & Newman Ltd. Returned to Admiralty service in 1936. Badly damaged when she ran aground near Batticaloa, Ceylon in 1939. Bombed by German aircraft and set on fire at Suda Bay, Crete, on 18 May 1941 during the German invasion. She was beached, and burnt out. She was refloated by German salvors and was found derelict at Skaramanga in September 1944. She was sold for scrap.

Oleander
Managed commercially by Davies & Newman Ltd. Returned to Admiralty service in 1936, she took the first cargo for Royal Australian naval tanks to Sydney in 1937. Attacked by German aircraft and badly damaged by a near miss at Harstad Bay, Norway, on 26 May 1940 and beached; she was declared a total loss on 8 June 1940.

Early Dale class

Tonnages:
Diesel group: 8129–8402 gross, 12,235 deadweight, 17,210–17,357 displacement
Steam group: 8032–8219 gross, 12,040 deadweight, 16,820–17,000 displacement
Length overall: 479.3–483 ft (diesel), 479–483.1 ft (steam)
Beam: 59.4–61.9 ft (diesel), 59.4–61.2 ft (steam)
Draught: 27.0–27.5 ft (diesel), 27.1–27.5 ft (steam)
Depth: 33.1–34.0 ft (diesel), 33.0–33.8 ft (steam)
Machinery: 1 screw
Diesel:
4-cylinder Doxford diesel, 2850 bhp (Abbeydale, Aldersdale, Arndale)
6-cylinder J G Kincaid/Burmeister & Wain diesel engine, 2850 bhp (*Bishopdale, Boardale, Broomdale,*

Darkdale, Denbydale, Derwentdale – as re-engined 1946)
8-cylinder J G Kincaid/Burmeister & Wain diesel engine, 3500 bhp (*Cedardale*)
8-cylinder Harland & Wolff/Burmeister & Wain diesel engine, 3500 bhp (*Cairndale, Derwentdale* (as built),
Dewdale, Dingledale, Dinsdale, Echodale) (bunkers c850 tons fuel oil; 12.5 tons/day at 12 knots)
Steam:
Triple expansion engine by shipbuilders (*Ennerdale*), Richardsons, Westgarth & Co Ltd (*Eaglesdale,
Easedale*), 3650 ihp
Service speed: 11.5–12 knots
Complement (diesel/steam): 44 (70 Lascars); LSGs: 70 and 16 DEMS gunners/accommodation for 260+
Weapons: Variable.In 1943, 1 x 4-in LA or HA/LA, 2 x 12-pdr HA/LA or 1 x 3-in LA, 4–6 x 20-mm Oerlikon,
2 x Colt/Browning 0.5-in (50 calibre) machine guns

Although there were similarities in design and construction, these vessels were not all sisterships.

1937 Dale class (BTC 3 Twelves)

Name	Builder	Laid down	Launched	Completed	Out of service
Abbeydale	Swan, Hunter & Wigham Richardson Ltd, Newcastle	–	28.12.36	3.37	1960
Aldersdale	Cammell Laird & Co Ltd, Birkenhead	9.36	7.7.37	17.9.37	1942
Boardale	Harland & Wolff Ltd, Glasgow	–	22.2.37	7.6.37	1940
Arndale	Swan, Hunter & Wigham Richardson Ltd, Newcastle	–	5.8.37	9.37	1960
Broomdale	Harland & Wolff Ltd, Belfast	–	2.9.37	3.11.37	1960
Bishopdale	Lithgows Ltd, Port Glasgow	–	31.3.37	6.37	1970

This class of vessels was bought from the British Tanker Co Ltd (BTC), while they were building, primarily
at the insistence of Sir William Gick, who was concerned about the age of the RFA fleet and the number of
ships it contained that were over twenty years old and approaching the end of their working lives.

Primarily, it seems they were intended as freighting tankers and so were not fitted for RAS while building,
although three later vessels were converted on the slips into Landing Ships Gantry (LSG) for delivery of
landing craft LCM Mk1 during amphibious operations. A number were later fitted for fuelling at sea under
the Admiralty's escort oiler programme. Similar ships in the BTC fleet were designated 'three twelves'
because their deadweight tonnage was 12,000, speed 12 knots, running on 12 tons of fuel per day.

Abbeydale
8402 tons gross, 12,235 deadweight. Saw service on West Indies convoys and in Mediterranean. While in
convoy XTG2, torpedoed by *U73* off Algeria on 27 June 1943 and broken in two. One half towed to Taranto,
other to Bizerta. Second half later also towed to Taranto where parts was rejoined early 1947 and returned
to service. Laid up at Devonport on 18 September 1959 and offered for sale on 5 July 1960. Sold to British
Iron & Steel Corp (BISCO) in August 1960 and arrived at Barrow-in-Furness on 4 September to be broken
up by Thomas Ward Ltd.

Aldersdale
8402 tons gross, 12,235 deadweight. While returning from service as escort oiler to Reykjavik–Murmansk
convoy PQ14, suffered heavy weather damage and was on the Clyde from 23 April 1942 to June 4, repairing.
Dispersed from convoy PQ17 (Hvalfjord, Iceland–Archangel) on Admiralty orders due to the belief that
German heavy units were putting to sea. On 5 July 1942, bombed by German aircraft and abandoned by
the crew of fifty-four, which was picked up by HMS *Salamander*; two days later, *Aldersdale* was torpedoed
by *U457* and sank in 75N 45E.

Boardale
8334 tons gross, 12,160 deadweight. Struck reef in Assund Fjord, near Narvik, while following a destroyer
and a store ship into that anchorage during the Norwegian campaign; crew rescued by Polish destroyer
Burza. Broke in two and sank on 30 April 1940.

Arndale
8296 tons gross, 12,180 deadweight. Saw service with Pacific Fleet train, in particular, against Okinawa, in
which *Arndale* and six other RFAs were attached to Operation 'Iceberg'. In August 1945, damaged by fire,

and repaired at Brisbane. Normal RFA freighting service after war. Radioed she was in need of assistance in heavy weather on 20 January 1952, while off eastern Scotland but when a destroyer reached her she reported she was out of danger. For sale 4 December 1959 at Rosyth. *Arndale* was sold for scrap in March 1960 and arrived at the breaker's yard at Willebroek on 12 April 1960.

Broomdale
8334 tons gross, 12,160 deadweight. First RFA tanker to be fitted with gantry king posts and net defence derricks for OAS trials and conical heating coils in cargo tanks. War service included Norwegian campaign, and during this, on 16 May 1940, she was bombed by German aircraft and sustained damage. On 1 August 1942 left Trincomalee as part of one of three dummy convoys used in Operation 'Stab' – a diversionary operation to invade the Andaman Islands and take attention away from the US invasion of Guadalcanal. While at Bombay on 14 April 1944, was damaged when the ammunition ship *Fort Stikine* blew up in the harbour, and later in the same year, on 28 August, was damaged when accidentally torpedoed by HMS *Severn* in Trincomalee harbour. Offered for sale at Devonport on 20 October 1959 and arrived at Bruges on 2 January 1960 for breaking up.

Bishopdale
8406 tons gross, 12,160 deadweight. War service spent Pacific, with earlier deployment to South Atlantic.
On 5 August 1942, en route to Brisbane from Noumea, struck a mine in an Allied minefield and had damaged repaired at Sydney. *Bishopdale* was damaged by a kamikaze bomber in Leyte Gulf on 14 December 1944 and in the following moth was involved in supporting Allied forces in the liberation of the Philippines as part of Task Group 77.10. Laid up at Devonport on 8 October 1959, and just over ten years later offered for sale. Sold to Spanish breakers, 28 January 1970 and arrived at Bilbao on 17 February.

1939 Dale class (Shell type)

Name	Builder	Laid down	Launched	Completed	Out of service
Cairndale	Harland & Wolff Ltd, Glasgow	–	25.10.38	26.1.39	1941
Cedardale	Blythswood Shipbuilding Co Ltd, Glasgow	–	25.3.39	25.5.39	1959

In 1939, the Admiralty bought two Anglo-Saxon Oil Co Ltd tankers, which were similar in many ways to the 'three twelves', to compare the performance of the two classes. Similar in dimensions to the BTC ships, they differed considerably in appearance. Forehold had two tanks designed for 75 tons of cargo lubricating oil, operated on a separate system, while two of the main cargo tanks were also separated from the main cargo pump line, so as to allow the carriage of 1000 tons of petrol.
Trials speed at maximum load was 13.25 knots at 121 rpm, although service speed was 11.5 knots.

Cairndale
8129 tons gross, 11,875 deadweight. Building as *Erato*, she was taken over by the Admiralty after her running trials as *Cairndale*. Initial war service was as harbour oiler in Freetown, Sierra Leone, before transfer to Gibraltar as Force H oiler. She sailed from Gibraltar on 25 May 1941 to join Force H, the Gibraltar-based contingent of the group chasing *Bismarck* but was torpedoed and sunk in the eastern Atlantic on the 30th by the Italian submarine *Guglielmo Marconi*, with the loss of two officers and two ratings killed and four ratings injured.

Cedardale
8132 tons gross, 11,857 deadweight. Had uneventful war service, at Okinawa operation then remained in Eastern waters until 1946. Stranded near Mena-al-Ahmadi in 1952, but refloated without major damage. Laid up at Hong Kong on 15 November 1959, and arrived at a local breaker's yard on 2 February 1960 for scrapping.

1941 Dale class (MoWT war construction programme tankers)

Name	Builder	Laid down	Launched	Completed	Out of service
Derwentdale	Harland & Wolff Ltd, Belfast	14.11.39	12.4.41	30.8.41	1959
Denbydale	Blythswood Shipbuilding Co Ltd, Glasgow	26.12.39	19.10.40	30.1.41	1955

Dingledale	Harland & Wolff Ltd, Belfast	11.12.39	27.3.41	10.9.41	1959
Dewdale	Cammell Laird & Co Ltd, Birkenhead	29.12.39	17.2.41	14.6.41	1959
Darkdale	Blythswood Shipbuilding Co Ltd, Glasgow	10.39	23.7.40	15.11.40	1941
Dinsdale	Harland & Wolff Ltd, Belfast	–	21.10.41	11.4.42	1942
Echodale	Hawthorn Leslie & Co Ltd, Newcastle	8.1.40	29.11.40	4.3.41	1961

Built for the MoWT, some were launched under 'Empire' names, but taken over by the Admiralty after launch. Three were subsequently completed as LSGs.

Derwentdale

8398 tons gross, 11,387 deadweight. Taken over by Admiralty and completed as LSG. Her maiden voyage was in convoy ON19, which left the Clyde on 22 September 1941 for Halifax. Present at Madagascar, North Africa, Sicily and Italian landings. Dive bombed and badly damaged at Salerno on 3 September 1943, and left there for Malta and then for UK in tow. Re-engined with *Denbydale*'s machinery in February 1946 and returned to normal freighting after removal of gantry gear. Laid up at Rosyth 19 May 1959, and offered for sale on 20 October. Sold to Kent Line, Canada, December 1959, renamed *Irvingdale 1*. Arrived Ferrol, Spain, on 23 July 1966 to be broken up.

Denbydale

8145 tons gross. Launched as *Empire Silver* for MoWT. Taken over by Admiralty, and her maiden voyage was from the Clyde to join Liverpool convoy OB287, after dispersal of which she arrived at Trinidad on 10 March. Served as escort oiler, Gibraltar. Damaged by Italian frogmen at Gibraltar on 19 September 1942. Machinery removed and used to re-engine *Derwentdale*. Fuelling and accommodation hulk, Gibraltar. Sold to BISCO and arrived at Hughes Bolckow Ltd, Blyth, on 27 July 1955 to be broken up.

Dingledale

8186 tons gross, 11,953 deadweight. Following acquisition by the Admiralty, her maiden voyage was from the Clyde, on 18 September 1941, from where she joined convoy ON17, and after dispersal arrived at Curaçao on 9 October 1941. Based at Gibraltar, serving as escort oiler on several Malta convoys, in company with *Brown Ranger*. On 13 November 1942, she was attacked by *U431* in 37 21N 02 10E, but the torpedo missed. Served with Pacific Fleet Train and present in Tokyo Bay at Japanese formal surrender on 2 September 1945. Normal RFA freighting until laid up at Devonport and subsequently offered for sale on 20 October 1959. Sold to Compagnie d'Armament Maritime SA, Djibouti, 9 December 1959, by which she was renamed *Royaumont* and in service as a storage hulk. Arrived at Santander on 23 January 1967 for breaking up.

Dewdale

8265 tons gross, 11,500 deadweight. MoWT wartime construction, finished as a LSG. Wartime service included Bougie (Operation 'Torch'). Bombed in Algiers harbour, 12 November 1942 and severely damaged. Returned UK for repair 15 October 1944. With squadron off Piræus during Allied re-occupation of Greece and at Malaya landings. On 25 September 1945, *Dewdale* was the first RFA to enter Singapore following its liberation. Converted to freighting tanker at Portsmouth 1946–7. Laid up at Portland on 6 May 1959, and on 20 October offered for sale. Arrived Antwerp on 23 December 1959 to be broken up.

Darkdale

8145 tons gross. Launched for MoWT as *Empire Oil*, before being taken over by the Admiralty. Her maiden voyage was from the Clyde and Liverpool, in convoy OB246, and she arrived at Curaçao on 11 December 1940 to load gasoline on charter to Anglo-Saxon Oil Co Ltd. During the war, served as convoy escort oiler and fleet oiler at Freetown. Torpedoed by *U68* on 22 October 1941, while anchored off St Helena. Lost with all hands, except master, chief engineer and one rating, who were ashore.

Dinsdale

8254 tons gross. Launched as *Empire Norseman* for MoWT and completed as *Dinsdale*. On maiden voyage, torpedoed by Italian submarine *Comandante Cappelli* on 31 May 1942, north-east of Pernambuco, Brazil, while on voyage from Trinidad to Port Elizabeth with a cargo of petrol; she sank the following day.

Echodale
8150 tons gross, 11,810 deadweight. Laid down as *Empire Granite* for MoWT; completed as *Echodale*.
She sailed from Liverpool on 24 March 1941 on her maiden voyage in convoy OB302, and arrived at Aruba on 17 April to load. War service included Burma landings and with Eastern Fleet, and then normal RFA freighting. Laid up at Devonport on 12 April 1959. Arrived Spezia 20 September 1961 to be broken up.

1941–2 Steam group

Name	Builder	Laid down	Launched	Completed	Out of service
Eaglesdale	Furness Shipbuilding Co Ltd, Haverton Hill-on-Tees	19.12.40	18.11.41	10.1.42	1959
Easedale	Furness Shipbuilding Co Ltd, Haverton Hill-on-Tees	15.2.41	18.12.41	12.2.42	1960
Ennerdale	Swan, Hunter & Wigham Richardson Ltd, Newcastle	–	27.1.41	11.7.41	1959
Eppingdale	See note below				

As a whole, the steam group were unsatisfactory ships, heavy on fuel and with vibration problems which resulted in heavy repair bills for cracked frames and leaking rivets. Perhaps surprisingly, vibration disappeared completely when the ships were run at full speed!

Eaglesdale
8032 tons gross, 12,040 deadweight. Launched as *Empire Metal* for MoWT; completed as *Eaglesdale*. Her first ocean voyage was delayed due to a collision in Tees Bay on 19 January 1942, when she received damage above the water line. Repairs were completed in time for her to join convoy OS23 from Liverpool (left 24 March 1942) for Freetown, from where she proceeded to Curaçao to load her first cargo. Fleet oiler with Eastern Fleet and at Cape Town during 1943–6. Laid up on the River Tyne on 21 July 1958. Sold November 1959 to MISR Tankers, Egypt, renamed *N Tisar*. Broken up shortly afterwards at Hamburg, where she arrived on 29 November.

Easedale
8032 tons gross, 12,040 deadweight. Following her maiden voyage from Belfast Lough in convoy ON71, and from which she arrived at Curaçao in March, her war service included operations with Eastern and Pacific fleets, against Madagascar (May 1942) and Sumatra (August 1943). Laid up at Devonport 5 February 1959, offered for sale on 7 May, and on 7 March 1960 arrived at Willebroek to be broken up.

Ennerdale
8150 tons gross, 11,428 deadweight. Completed as LSG. War service included landings in North Africa, Italy and Far East. On 5 December 1945, hit a stray mine while on passage in the Malacca Strait between Penang and Port Swettenham. Suffered damage but made her way to Singapore for temporary repairs before return to the UK. Returned to normal freighting after repair and removal of LSG equipment. Laid up March 1958. Sold to BISCO for scrap, and arrived Faslane on 14 April 1959.

Eppingdale
8028 tons gross, 12,040 deadweight. This ship was launched on 4 October 1940 by Furness Shipbuilding Co Ltd, Haverton Hill-on-Tees as *Empire Gold* and completed in January 1941. The name *Eppingdale* had been allocated to her but the ship was not taken by the Admiralty, although some RFA officers had been nominally appointed to her. She entered service for the MoWT in February 1941. On 18 April 1945, while part of convoy HX348 and from Philadelphia and New York to Antwerp loaded with 10,278 tons of petrol, she was torpedoed by *U1107* and sunk about 70 miles west of Brest.

Coastal store ships

Tonnages: 1125 gross (*Robert Dundas*), 1124 gross (*Robert Middleton*)
Length overall: 222.5 ft
Beam: 35.2 ft
Depth: 18 ft
Draught: 13.5 ft
Machinery: 1 screw, 6-cylinder diesel engine by British Auxiliaries Ltd, 960 bhp

Service speed: 10.5 knots
Complement: 5 officers, 15 ratings

Name	Builder	Launched	Completed	Out of service
Robert Dundas	Grangemouth Dockyard Co Ltd, Grangemouth	28.7.38	11.38	8.12.71
Robert Middleton	Grangemouth Dockyard Co Ltd, Grangemouth	29.6.38	25.8.38	1975

Both ships were coastal store carriers, visiting a number of UK ports, with the occasional trip overseas. Extremely adaptable craft, No 2 Hatch was 72 ft x 34 ft, which meant anything used in the RFA service could be carried there, including landing craft.

Robert Dundas
Named after Robert Dundas, Storekeeper General to the Navy, 1832–69. On yard craft agreement (*ie* dockyard manned) until 1940, then transferred to RFA manning. Service included Malta and D-Day landings.
   Was for sale at Chatham Dockyard on 18 March 1972. Sold to Thomas Ward Ltd and arrived Grays, Essex, on 7 May 1972 to be broken up.

Robert Middleton
Named after Captain Robert C Middleton, first Storekeeper General to the Navy, 1729–32. On yard craft agreement (*ie* dockyard manned) until 1940, then transferred to RFA manning. On 16 September 1974 started planned refit at Chatham Dockyard – the first RFA to do so. Sold 1975 and renamed *Myrina*. Broken up at Keratsini during 1982–3.

Sprite Class Spirit Tankers

Tonnages: *Airsprite* 970 gross, *Nasprite* 965 gross; 848 deadweight, 950 displacement (stdd), 1900 displacement (full load)
Length overall: 214.0 ft
Beam: 33.2 ft
Depth: 13.5 ft
Draught: 12.8 ft
Machinery: 1 screw, triple expansion engine by D Rowan, 900 ihp
Service speed: 10 knots
Builder: Blythswood Shipbuilding Co Ltd, Scotstoun, Glasgow

Name	Ordered	Laid down	Launched	Completed	Out of service
Airsprite (A 115)	2.7.41	9.41	22.12.42	16.2.43	1963
Nasprite (A 252)	9.10.39	7.3.40	28.11.40	11.2.41	1954

These spirit carriers served mainly in UK ports and in the Mediterranean.

Airsprite
On her first voyage, *Airsprite* joined convoy WN398, which left Loch Ewe on 24 February 1943, and arrived at Methil two days later, and then proceeded to Scapa Flow. On 19 February 1951, involved in a tactical exercise with HMS *Bleasdale*, six RN fast patrol boats, RAF units of Coastal Command, RAF and Danish ships in the North Sea. Laid up in reserve at Devonport October 1963, and offered for sale on 12 January 1965. Arrived at Antwerp on 14 March 1965 to be broken up.

Nasprite
Served in UK ports during 1941–2, and left River Clyde on 18 October 1942 in convoy KX2, arriving at Gibraltar on 29 October. On 21 June 1943 left Gibraltar in convoy GTX3 in company with twenty-six other ships, including *Celerol*, *Cherryleaf* and *Oligarch*, and arrived at Malta on 28 June. She later served in Italy, and in November 1945 was at Venice, Ancona and Bari. Decommissioned 31 August 1954 and laid up in reserve at Devonport. *Nasprite* was put up for sale in August 1963 and on 5 February 1964 arrived at Willebroek for breaking up.

Spa class water tankers

Tonnages: gross: 719 (*Spa*), 702 (*Spabeck*), 718 (*Spabrook, Spaburn*), 672 (*Spapool, Spalake*); deadweight: 615; 630 (*Spalake, Spapool*); displacement 1219 (stdd)
Length overall: 172 ft
Beam: 30 ft
Depth: 14.1 ft
Draught: 12.0 ft
Machinery: 1 screw, triple expansion engine, 675 ihp (bunkers 90 tons coal/120 tonnes oil); engine makers Plenty & Son Ltd, Newbury; C D Holmes & Co Ltd, Hull (*Spalake, Spapool*)
Service speed: 9 knots
Complement: Originally RFA manned during the Second World War; transferred 1946–7 to dockyard manning, becoming part of the Port Auxiliary Service.

The first four built by Philip & Son Ltd, Dartmouth; *Spalake, Spapool* built by Charles Hill & Sons Ltd, Bristol

Name	Laid down	Launched	Completed	Out of service
Spa	26.9.40	11.10.41	24.4.42	1946
Spabeck	14.5.43	21.6.43	3.9.43	1947
Spabrook	16.9.43	24.8.44	12.12.44	1946
Spaburn	7.10.44	5.1.46	12.4.46	1947
Spalake	13.8.45	10.8.46	28.11.46	1947
Spapool	13.8.45	28.2.46	14.6.46	1947

Water tankers in service at ports around UK and abroad and occasionally used by the army in locations where water supply was difficult. *Spabeck* was extensively modified to carry high test peroxide, when the Royal Navy was conducting trials of this fuel for both submarines and torpedoes.

Spa
Arrived Passage West, Cork, 9 October 1970, to be broken up.

Spabeck
This tanker was launched as *Rivulet*, but completed as *Spabeck*. Converted at Barrow-in-Furness to carry HTP (111 tons HTP, 17 tons Avcat) for E class submarines. She was decommissioned in March 1966 and laid up at Devonport, where she was offered for sale on 29 March 1966. *Spabeck* arrived at Willebroek on 14 May 1966 to be broken up.

Spabrook
This tanker was decommissioned in 1977, and on 13 September that year arrived at Briton Ferry to be broken up.

Spaburn
This tanker was station at Sheerness 1950–56, at Malta 1956–63, on the River Clyde 1963–71, and was in reserve from 1971. She was sold to West of Scotland Shipbreaking Co Ltd and was broken up at Troon in 1977.

Spalake
This tanker was transferred to the Royal Army Service Corps in 1947. She was sold to West of Scotland Shipbreaking Co Ltd in 1977 and broken up at Troon in 1978.

Spapool
Left Bristol on 23 July 1946 and arrived Devonport two days later. In 1967 commissioned under White Ensign for voyage from Singapore to Mombasa, where she was then based. Broken up at Mombasa; breaking up commenced in July 1976.

Ranger class fleet replenishment tankers

Tonnages: B group: 3417 gross, 3435–3631 deadweight; G group: 3313 gross, 3943 deadweight
Length overall: B group: 365.8 ft; G group: 355.35 ft
Beam: B group: 47 ft; G group: 48.35 ft
Depth: 22.5 ft
Draught: 20.2 ft
Machinery: B group: 1 screw, six-cylinder Harland & Wolff/Burmeister & Wain diesel engine, 3500 bhp; G group: 1 screw, four-cylinder Doxford diesel engine, 2800 bhp
Speed: 14 knots at 110 rpm; consumption 14 tons/day (bunkers 300 tons)
Complement: 40 RFA, plus DEMS gunners (number dependent upon armament)
Armament: 1 x 4-in low angle (LA), 1 x 12-pdr HA/LA , 4 x Lewis machine guns; changed later in Second World War to 1 x 4-in LA, 1 x 40-mm Bofors, 4 x single 20-mm Oerlikon

B group

Name	Builder	Laid down	Launched	Completed	Left service
Black Ranger	Harland & Wolff Ltd, Govan	12.10.39	22.8.40	28.1.41	1973
Blue Ranger	Harland & Wolff Ltd, Govan	26.10.39	29.1.41	5.6.41	1971
Brown Ranger	Harland & Wolff Ltd, Govan	28.10.39	12.12.40	10.4.41	1975

G group

Name	Builder	Laid down	Launched	Completed	Left service
Gold Ranger	Caledon Shipbuilding & Engineering Co Ltd, Dundee	14.5.40	12.3.41	4.7.41	1973
Gray Ranger	Caledon Shipbuilding & Engineering Co Ltd, Dundee	24.6.40	27.5.41	25.9.41	1942
Green Ranger	Caledon Shipbuilding & Engineering Co Ltd, Dundee	23.9.40	21.8.41	4.12.41	1962

These were the first Admiralty-designed classes since the First World War, and intended to replace 2000-ton *Belgol* class. Well protected with steel armour over petrol tanks and 4-in plastic armour around bridge. Originally fitted for RAS by stirrup method, but this was replaced with buoyant hose astern, 40-ft derricks fitted for abeam replenishment, initially using Admiralty bronze hose, later replaced by rubber hose.

Black Ranger
Served as escort oiler to all of the Russian convoys, except the last. After war service, she was mainly based at Portland as training oiler for ships 'working up', although she also had a variety of other roles. She was sold commercially to Greece in 1973 and renamed *Petrola XIV*, and renamed again in 1976 to *Petrola 14*. She was broken up in Greece in 1983.

Blue Ranger
Served as escort oiler to Russian convoys. Peacetime role mostly with Mediterannean Squadron based on Malta. Largely in reserve after Malta base run down. She was sold in 1971 and renamed *Korytsa*, and arrived at Aliaga on 8 September 1987 to be broken up.

Brown Ranger
Served as escort oiler to Malta convoys, based on Gibraltar. Then oiler to North Africa invasion force. Service at Bone and Algiers before assignment to Pacific Fleet Train as water tanker at Leyte. Also took part in re-occupation of Hong Kong and Shanghai, and remained in Japan for several months. Peacetime duties included accompanying HMS *Vanguard* on the Royal Family's South Africa tour and operations on both Mediterranean and Home stations. She was sold to Spanish breakers in 1975 and arrived at Gijon on 28 May to be scrapped.

Gold Ranger
All of war and peacetime service in Indian Ocean and China stations, when usually based Singapore. Accompanied survey ship *John Biscoe* to Deception Island in Antarctic, 1949. Sold to Singapore interestes in 1973 and broken up at Hong Kong in 1977.

Gray Ranger
Fitted with first successful self-tensioning RAS winch. Entered service 1941 as escort oiler on Arctic convoys, torpedoed by *U 435* on 22 September 1942, when in convoy QP14 on voyage from Murmansk to Reykjavik; sunk by naval gunfire.

Green Ranger
Used as navy's first large spirit carrier, transporting white oil. War and peacetime service on China Station, although initially based at Mombasa. Later, in reserve at Plymouth and while being towed by tug *Caswell* from there to Cardiff for refit, blown ashore at Sennen Cover, near Hartland Point on 17 November 1962.

Fresh class water tankers

Tonnages: 283 gross (except *Freshbrook, Freshener, Freshlake*, 278; *Freshet, Freshwater*, 264; *Freshspray* 289); all 236 deadweight; 594 displacement
Length overall: 126 ft
Beam: 25.35 ft
Depth: 11.5 ft
Machinery: 1 screw, triple expansion engine made by Lytham Shipbuilding & Engineering Co Ltd, 450 ihp. Coal burning (later oil fuel)
Service speed: 9.5 knots
Complement: Partly manned by RFA personnel during the Second World War; transferred 1945–6 to Port Auxiliary Service.
Builder: Lytham Shipbuilding & Engineering Co Ltd, Lytham

Name	Laid down	Launched	Completed	Out of service
Freshbrook	19.6.41	5.11.41	17.4.42	2.1.46
Freshburn	7.7.43	29.10.43	1.4.44	5.11.45
Freshener	8.11.41	16.3.42	22.7.42	1946
Freshet	26.3.40	6.7.40	10.12.40	9.11.45
Freshford	11.43	23.3.44	18.7.44	1946
Freshlake	18.3.42	15.7.42	14.11.42	1946
Freshmere	16.7.42	23.11.42	22.3.43	1946
Freshpond	–	28.8.45	22.12.45	1945
Freshpool	26.11.42	11.3.43	3.7.43	1946
Freshspray	4.9.45	5.3.46	7.8.46	(1946)
Freshspring	12.9.45	15.8.46	10.2.47	(1947)
Freshtarn	3.44	22.8.44	22.12.44	1946
Freshwater	29.11.39	23.3.40	10.9.40	1946
Freshwell	18.3.43	2.7.43	30.10.43	1946

Small water tankers, usually in service in UK ports. Short RFA service; later became part of Port Auxiliary Service. *Freshspray* and *Freshspring* were not in RFA service, but are included here for completeness.

Freshbrook sold to Netherlands breakers October 1963; *Freshburn* sold to Netherlands breakers March 1982; *Freshener* stricken 1971; *Freshet* sold 1963; *Freshford* sold 1967 and arrived Antwerp 16 August for breaking up; *Freshlake* sold to breakers 1988; *Freshmere* in collision with HMS *Gurkha* in harbour on 11 February 1967. Sold December 1975 and broken up 1976; *Freshpond* sold October 1977 and renamed *Dunkmouse*; *Freshpool* sunk as target 1975; *Freshspray* sold 1969; *Freshspring* in service at Malta, River Clyde and Portsmouth. Sold 1972. In 2006 at Newnham, Gloucestershire, awaiting restoration; *Freshtarn* sold 1969; *Freshwater* sold 1968 and renamed *Porto Grande*. Still in service 2010 at Mindelo, Cape Verde Islands; *Freshwell* sold Haulbowline Industries Ltd; arrived Passage West, Cork, 29 January 1968 for breaking up.

First Wave class

Tonnages: 8141–8199 gross, 4545–4664 net, 11,600–11,955 deadweight, 16,650 full load displacement as designed
Cargo capacity – 8000 tons FFO, 750 tons diesel, 950 tons aviation fuel/petrol, drinking water. Limited stores capability
Length: 492ft 8in

Beam: 64ft 4in
Draught: 28ft 6in
Depth: 35ft 6in
Machinery: 1 screw, 2 geared steam turbines, 6800shp, water tube boilers.
Speed: 14.5–15 knots; oil consumption of 50 tons/day
Complement: 60 RFA

Name	Builder	Laid down	Launched	Completed	Left Service
Wave Baron (A242)	Furness	1.9.44	19.2.46	6.46	1972
Wave Chief (A265)	Harland & Wolff	–	4.4.46	27.8.46	1974
Wave Knight (A249)	Laing	–	22.10.45	5.46	1964
Wave Master (A193)	Laing	1943	25.5.44	12.44	1963
Wave Prince (A207)	Laing	1945	27.7.45	3.46	1971
Wave Ruler (A212)	Furness	27.10.44	17.1.46	4.46	1976
Wave Sovereign (A211)	Furness	10.5.44	20.11.45	2.46	1967
Wave Victor (A220)	Furness	16.11.42	30.9.43	2.44	1971
Wave Commander (A244)	Furness	1.4.43	21.4.44	8.44	1959
Wave Conqueror (A245)	Furness	16.12.42	27.11.43	3.44	1958
Wave Duke (A246)	Laing	–	16.11.44	4.45	1969
Wave Emperor (A100)	Furness	15.9.43	16.10.44	20.12.44	1960
Wave Governor (A247)	Furness	30.11.43	30.11.44	8.3.45	1960
Wave King (A182)	Harland & Wolff	23.3.43	6.4.44	21.7.44	1960
Wave Laird (A119)	Laing	1945	3.4.46	10.9.46	1970
Wave Liberator (A248)	Furness	1.3.43	9.2.44	6.44	1959
Wave Monarch (A108)	Harland & Wolff	17.6.43	6.7.44	3.11.44	1960
Wave Premier (A129)	Furness	6.7.45	27.6.46	12.46	1960
Wave Protector (A215)	Furness	15.6.43	20.7.44	10.44	1963
Wave Regent (A210)	Furness	28.4.44	29.3.45	31.5.45	1960

Originally standard Ministry of War Transport 12,000-ton tankers, many with 'Empire' prefixed name. Taken over by the Admiralty and became the Wave class, with RN buying twenty out of whole class of twenty one. *Wave King, Wave Emperor, Wave Governor* and *Wave Monarch* served with the British Pacific Fleet, the rest being managed commercially until under control of Director of Stores (DoS)

Eight of the class were modified as fast fleet tankers, with the rest used as freighting tankers with some replenishment capability. The ships in this class differed from one another in some respects – *Wave Baron, Wave Chief, Wave Commander, Wave Conqueror, Wave Duke* and *Wave Laird* all had Metrovick geared turbines; the rest had Parsons geared turbines. *Wave Liberator* had a slightly different bridge to the other ships in the class. Quite unsatisfactory ships, although some of the lessons learned during their subsequent modifications were employed in the early Tide class.

The following ships were modified to perform fast fleet replenishment duties:

Wave Baron
8174 gross. Originally *Empire Flodden*. Built by Furness Shipbuilding Co Ltd, Haverton Hill-on-Tees. Metrovick turbines by Richardsons, Westgarth. Managed by Gow, Harrison & Co Ltd, Glasgow. Modernised in refit during 1961–2 and at Swansea 1966. Laid up, Devonport, December 1969; for sale, Plymouth, February 1972. Sold to Dutch trading house for scrapping; resold Spanish breakers. Arrived Bilbao 23 April 1972 for scrapping.

Wave Chief
8097 gross. Originally *Empire Edgehill*. Built by Harland & Wolff Ltd, Glasgow. Metrovick turbines by Metropolitan Vickers Ltd. Entered RFA service 30 August 1946. Only vessel in class with a complete foremast and topmast. Extensively modernised for RAS early 1960s. Served in Korean War (1950–53; Battle Honour) and in the first Cod War 1958–61. Escorted Sir Alec Rose around Cape Horn in his yacht in April 1968. Out of service August 1974, laid up at Rosyth; arrived Inverkeithing on 13 November 1974 for breaking up.

Wave Knight
8187 gross. Originally *Empire Naseby*. Built by Sir J Laing & Sons Ltd, Sunderland. Parsons turbines by North Eastern Marine Engineering Co Ltd. Managed initially by Tankers Ltd, associate company of Athel

Line Ltd. Taken over by DoS, May 1946. Served in Korea and first Cod War. Laid up Plymouth 1964. Sold to Belgian breakers, arriving Willebroek in tow 19 October 1964 for breaking up.

Wave Master
8199 gross. Originally *Empire Salisbury*. Built by Sir J Laing & Sons Ltd, Sunderland. Parsons turbines by North Eastern Marine Engineering Co Ltd. Managed initially by Eagle Oil & Shipping Co Ltd, beginning RFA service 1947. Laid up Singapore 23 September 1962. Sold April 1963, towed to Jurong for breaking.

Wave Prince
8175 gross. Originally *Empire Herald*. Built by Sir J Laing & Sons Ltd, Sunderland. Parsons turbines by Barclay, Curle & Co Ltd. Managed initially by Athel Line Ltd, entering RFA fleet 12 February 1947. Refitted and modernised 1961–2; part of fleet visiting British Trade Fair, Stockholm same year. Escort oiler for Royal Yacht on numerous occasions including Queen's visit to Australia 1953. Laid up Plymouth August 1965; for sale from May 1971. Towed from Plymouth 5 December 1971, arrived Burriana, Spain, 16 December for scrapping.

Wave Ruler
8138 gross. Originally *Empire Evesham*. Built by Furness Shipbuilding Co Ltd, Haverton Hill-on-Tees. Parsons turbines by Richardsons, Westgarth. Managed initially by Eagle Oil & Shipping Co Ltd. During initial trials, she attained 18 knots, making her potentially one of the fastest in the class. Present at Christmas Island nuclear tests, served in first Cod War and relieved *Wave Victor* as Air Ministry fuel hulk at Gan Island in October 1970. Sold January 1976 'as lies' for scrapping and towed to Singapore. Off Johore, Malaysia, September 1976. Towed to Taiwan 1977 for breaking.

Wave Sovereign
8122 gross. Built by Furness Shipbuilding Co Ltd, Haverton Hill-on-Tees. Parsons turbines by Richardsons, Westgarth. Into RFA service 28 February 1946. Present at Christmas Island tests and first Cod War. Out of service 1966, Singapore. Sold locally in June 1967 for scrap.

Wave Victor
8128 gross. Originally *Empire Bounty*. Built by Furness Shipbuilding Co Ltd, Haverton Hill-on-Tees. Parsons turbines by Richardsons, Westgarth. Entered RFA service 1946 as *Wave Victor*. Served during first Cod War, then Air Ministry fuel hulk at Gan 1960–71; replaced by *Wave Ruler*. Towed to Singapore for scrapping. Reported as hulk, Manila Bay, March 1975. Scrapped 1981.

The following ships of the class were used mainly as freighting tankers, although they also had some RAS capability:

Wave Commander
8141 gross. Managed by Athel Line Ltd, London, upon completion as *Empire Paladin* by Furness Shipbuilding Co Ltd, and in 1947 was taken into RFA service as *Wave Commander*. Metrovick turbines by Richardsons, Westgarth. Apart from a collision in the Strait of Gibraltar in 1954, *Wave Commander* had a relatively uneventful career, and was for sale at Devonport, where she had arrived on 22 October 1958. She arrived at Inverkeithing in tow on 9 May 1959 for breaking up by Thomas W Ward Ltd.

Wave Conqueror
8128 gross. Completed as *Empire Law* by Furness Shipbuilding Co Ltd, and placed under management of Anglo-Saxon Petroleum Co Ltd, London; acquired by Admiralty 1947 as *Wave Conqueror*. Metrovick turbines by Richardsons, Westgarth. Arrived Sheerness 31 December 1957, laid up and sold to H G Pounds, Portsmouth, 1958. *Wave Conqueror* became a fuel hulk at Le Havre in 1959 and was broken up at La Spezia, where she arrived in tow on 23 April 1960.

Wave Duke
8199 gross. Managed by British Tanker Co Ltd upon completion as *Empire Mars* by Sir J Laing & Sons Ltd. Metrovick turbines by Metropolitan Vickers Ltd. Sold to Admiralty 10 January 1946, and managed by Hadley Shipping Co Ltd until 27 January 1948 as *Wave Duke*. Accepted into RFA service on 16 November 1946. On 25 March 1957, *Wave Duke* left Houston for the UK with a full cargo of oil and struck a submerged wreck in the Houston Channel and sustained damage. She was still in the Channel two weeks later and had transshipped cargo to *Derwentdale*. Out of service and laid up Devonport, 30 April 1960; for sale at Plymouth in October 1969. Left Plymouth in tow and arrived at Bilbao on 25 December 1969 for scrapping and work began the following month.

Wave Emperor
8196 gross. Ordered 3 February 1943 from Furness Shipbuilding Co Ltd. Parsons turbines by Richardsons, Westgarth. Served with the British Pacific Fleet Train (pennant number B523). For sale 'as lies' Portland, 1959; sold BISCO, and arrived Barrow-in-Furness 19 June 1960 for breaking by Thomas W Ward Ltd.

Wave Governor
8196 gross. Launched as *Empire Trinidad* by Furness Shipbuilding Co Ltd; Parsons turbines by Richardsons, Westgarth. Served with the British Pacific Fleet Train (pennant number B524). Laid up Rosyth 30 April 1959, and sold for breaking to BISCO, and arrived Faslane 9 August 1959 for breaking up by Shipbreaking Industries Ltd.

Wave King
8159 gross. First of class acquired by the Admiralty. Under construction as *Empire Sheba* by Harland & Wolff Ltd Glasgow, and acquired upon completion. Parsons turbines by Parsons Marine Steam Turbine Co Ltd. Refuelled force deployed for Operation 'Outflank', the attack on the Palembang refineries and served with the British Pacific Fleet Train (pennant number B525). Out of service 1956 and laid up Portsmouth; sold March 1960 to H G Pounds, Portsmouth. Resold to BISCO for breaking by Thomas W Ward Ltd, and arrived at Barrow-in-Furness on 16 April 1960.

Wave Laird
8187 gross. Launched as *Empire Dunbar* and completed by Sir J Laing & Sons Ltd for RFA service. Metrovick turbines by Metropolitan Vickers Ltd. Supply ship to HMS *Protector* in the Antarctic and the Falkland Islands, and support ship in the first Cod War. Out of service 1961; laid up Plymouth. Sold October 1969 to Spanish breakers, arriving Gandia February 1970 for breaking up.

Wave Liberator
8135 gross. Managed by British Tanker Co Ltd, London, on completion as *Empire Milner* by Furness Shipbuilding Co Ltd. Parsons turbines by Richardsons, Westgarth. Sold to Admiralty, 10 January 1946, and managed by Hadley Shipping Co Ltd until 10 January 1948 as *Wave Liberator*. At Bombay, 1958 for sale 'as lies' with unrepaired collision damage. Sold to Hong Kong Towing & Salvage Co, left Bombay in tow on 5 April 1959, arriving Hong Kong 4 May for breaking.

Wave Monarch
8159 gross. Laid down by Harland & Wolff Ltd, Glasgow, as *Empire Venus*; subsequently completed for Admiralty service. Parsons turbines by Barclay Curle & Co Ltd. Served with the British Pacific Fleet Train (pennant number B526). Sold March 1960 to H G Pounds, Portsmouth; became storage hulk at Le Havre, replacing *Wave Conqueror*. Resold 1960 to Société Mirolene, renamed *Noema*. Arrived Bilbao 8 April 1964 for breaking up.

Wave Premier
8182 gross. Laid down as *Empire Marston* by Furness Shipbuilding Co Ltd and acquired by Admiralty upon completion. Parsons turbines by Richardsons, Westgarth. Out of service Rosyth, June 1959 and laid up. Sold BISCO, June 1960 and broken up on its behalf by Shipbreaking Industries Ltd, Faslane, June 1960.

Wave Protector
8148 gross. Launched as *Empire Protector*. Managed by Anglo-Saxon Petroleum Co Ltd upon completion by Furness Shipbuilding Co Ltd as *Empire Protector*. Acquired by Admiralty 1946 and renamed *Wave Protector*. Parsons turbines by Richardsons, Westgarth. Replaced *War Hindoo* as oiling store hulk at Grand Harbour, Malta, March 1958. For sale at Malta 'as lies'; sold for scrap to Italian interests, arriving Le Grazie for breaking, August 1963.

Wave Regent
8184 gross. Under construction as *Empire Regent* by Furness Shipbuilding Co Ltd, and completed as *Wave Regent*. Parsons turbines by Richardsons, Westgarth. Normal RFA freighting service after acquisition by Admiralty. Arrived Devonport May 1959, laid up. Sold to BISCO and arrived Faslane 29 June 1960 for breaking up by Shipbreaking Industries Ltd.

Fort class (1944–5)

Tonnages: 7201–7332 gross, 3771–4184 net; *Fort Rosalie, Fort Sandusky*: 6391 deadweight, others: 7720–9520 deadweight; 9790 displacement
Length overall: *Fort Beauharnois, Fort Duquesne*: 439ft 2in; others: 441ft 6in
Beam: 57ft 2in
Draught: 26ft 11in–27ft
Machinery: 1 screw, triple expansion engine by various makers, 2500ihp
Speed: 10.5–11 knots
Range: 11,000 nm/10 knots
Complement: 115

Name	Builder	Laid down	Launched	Completed	Out of service
Fort Beauharnois (A285)	West Coast	–	29.10.44	29.10.44	1969
Fort Charlotte (A236)	West Coast	–	5.4.44	5.4.44	1967
Fort Constantine (A237)	Burrard	–	11.3.44	25.4.44	1969
Fort Dunvegan (A160)	Burrard	–	28.2.44	14.4.44	1968
Fort Duquesne (A229)	West Coast	–	28.9.44	25.11.44	1967
Fort Langley (A230)	Victoria	–	31.10.44	18.5.45	1970
Fort Rosalie (A186)	United SY	29.8.44	28.11.44	7.7.45	1972
Fort Sandusky (A316)	United SY	11.9.44	25.11.44	1.8.45	1972

Built in Canada as part of the Emergency War Tonnage Programme, these were of a riveted construction, unlike the welded Liberty ships. Ships in this class were all managed by commercial interests on behalf of th MoWT during and after the Second World War, before transfer to the RFA.

Ships were constructed to three designs:

The North Sands design conformed to the original design supplied to Canada by J L Thompson & Sons, Sunderland. Designed as coal burners, they had three Scotch boilers and were shelter-deck type ships.

The Victory design also had a shelter deck, although these ships had only two oil burning water tube boilers to reduce running costs and crew numbers.

The Canadian design was similar to the Victory except the Scotch boilers installed in these ships used either coal or oil.

Fort Beauharnois, Fort Charlotte, Fort Constantine, Fort Dunvegan, Fort Duquesne, Fort Langley were Victory design, while *Fort Rosalie* and *Fort Sandusky* were Canadian. All were named after early Canadian forts, a tradition that has continued with other RFA store and victualling vessels.

Fort Beauharnois
7253 gross. Launched *as Fort Grand Rapids*, completed as *Cornish Park*, and renamed *Fort Beauharnois* in May 1945. Managed by Alfred Holt & Co, Liverpool, for MoWT/MoT, before joining the RFA in 1950, as a stores issuing ship. Present at the Christmas Island nuclear tests, she arrived at Leith on 22 January 1959 for refit, and while at the shipyard there was a fire on board. Employed on freighting duties between the UK and the Far East during 1960–2, including the Chatham–Gibraltar–Malta run. Offered for sale 'as lies' Malta 1962, she arrived at Spezia on 8 November 1962 for breaking up.

Fort Charlotte
7214 gross. Completed as *Buffalo Park*; renamed in 1945. Managed by Eastern & Australian Steam Ship Co Ltd, London, for MoWT/MoT until acquired by Admiralty on 11 June 1948, as a stores issuing ship. Served in Korea and present at the 1957 Christmas Island nuclear tests. Employed on the UK–Malta run from 1960; later transferred to Hong Kong. Out of service 1967, Singapore. Sold to local breakers January 1968.

Fort Constantine
7221 gross. Completed as a stores issuing ship (air), to operate with aircraft carriers and forward air bases in the Pacific. In addition to her merchant navy crew, she carried a unit from the Admiralty Victualling Division. Managed by Ellerman & Bucknall Steamship Co Ltd, London, for MoWT/MoT, management changed to W H Seager & Co Ltd, Cardiff upon joining RFA in 1948. Initially on Mediterranean–Far East freighting run, also present at Christmas Island nuclear tests; later on Chatham–Gibraltar–Malta run. Laid up Plymouth 1965, Arrived Hamburg 24 October 1969 for breaking up.

Fort Dunvegan
7225 gross. Managed by Ellerman & Bucknall Steamship Co Ltd for MoWT/MoT, joining RFA on 19 March 1951, as stores issuing ship. First employed on freighting runs UK–Malta, she was the first RFA ship to fly a commodore's burgee. Transferred to the Far East in 1960, remaining there until 1968, when she left the service. Broken up Kaohsiung 1968.

Fort Duquesne
7220 gross. Launched as *Queensborough Park* and completed as *Fort Duquesne* with manager Alfred Holt & Co, Liverpool, for MoWT/MoT. Joined RFA on 16 September 1947, as stores issuing ship, attached to the Mediterranean fleet. Fitted with experimental flight deck in 1951; used for VERTREP trials with RN Dragonfly helicopters; at Suez 1956. Out of service, April 1967 at Chatham. Sold for scrap, and arrived Tamise, Belgium, 29 June 1967 for breaking up.

Fort Langley
7285 gross. Launched as *Montebello Park*, completed as *Fort Langley* with manager Alfred Holt & Co, Liverpool, for MoWT/MoT. Management transferred to G Nisbet & Co, Glasgow, 1948, until entering Admiralty service as armament stores ship in May 1954. Later fitted with a small helicopter landing platform aft. Out of service February 1970, Plymouth and officially returned to the Canadian government. Sold to Marine Salvage Co Ltd, of Port Colbourne, Ontario. Resold for breaking at Bilbao, arriving there July 1970.

Fort Rosalie
7374 gross. First of class allocated to Admiralty and completed to is requirements; operated under Ellerman Lines Ltd management as MFA with British Pacific Fleet Train. Acquired by Admiralty, November 1947; converted to an armaments store ship. Served on Far East Station during 1949–51, and made several voyages to Australia and South Africa, loading ammunition stored in both countries during the war. Present at the Christmas Island nuclear tests in 1957. Fitted with cargo lifts during 1959–60. In autumn 1962, *Fort Rosalie* left the Mediterranean for the UK for refit by Henry Robb Ltd, Leith. Out of service 1 May 1972, laid up Rosyth before official return to the Canadian government. Sold to Spanish breakers, left Rosyth in tow on 24 January 1973, arrived Castellon 10 February for breaking.

Fort Sandusky
7374 gross. Managed by Ellerman Lines Ltd, London, for MoWT/MoT. Management transferred to W H Seager & Co, Cardiff in 1948. Acquired by Admiralty January 1949, converted to an armament store ship and assigned to the Far East Station, from where she made voyages to Australia and South Africa with her sister *Fort Rosalie* to return ammunition stored in these countries from the Second World War. Took part in operations during the Suez crisis of 1956. Laid up Rosyth 13 February 1972, before official return to Canadian government. Sold to Spanish breakers, leaving Rosyth in tow, 24 January 1973, arriving Castellon 10 February for breaking.

Fleet oiler *Olna*

Tonnages: 12,660 gross, 7412 net, 17,500 deadweight, 17,000 displacement
Length overall: 583ft 5in
Beam: 70ft 2in
Depth: 40ft 6in
Draught: 31ft 8in
Machinery: 2 BTH steam turbines, 11,000 shp, driving two generators 4200 kW/3000 V ac, connected to electric motor
Service speed: 16.5 knots
Complement: 300+ RN, 106 RFA (later reduced to 77) (125 Lascar)
Weapons: 1 x 4-in gun aft, 4 x single Bofors, 8 x single Oerlikon; paravane and degaussing equipment

Name	Builder	Launched	Completed	Out of service
Olna (A216)	Swan, Hunter & Wigham Richardson Ltd, Newcastle	28.12.44	8.5.45	1966

Built as *Hyalina* for Anglo-Saxon Petroleum Co Ltd, London (Shell), and first of two sisterships with turbo-electric drive. She was taken over by the MoWT before completion in early 1945 and originally commissioned as HMS *Olna*, with a Devonport crew and a lieutenant commander RNR in command. She entered service with the RFA as *Olna* on 20 March 1946. It was also planned to take over *Olna's* sister ship *Helicina* and, after similar modifications commission her as HMS *Oleander*. Hostilities ceased before conversion and she was returned to Anglo-Saxon, re-assuming her original name.

Nineteen-forty-six was not a good year for *Olna* – on 13 May, she caused damage to the Commission Quay, North Shields, while berthing, and on 29 August she ran aground in the river at Abadan. She was refloated four days later. She took part in the Coronation fleet review on 15 June 1953, and in Operation 'Grapple', the nuclear bomb tests in 1953. In 1956, she was involved in Operation 'Musketeer', the Suez crisis campaign. *Olna* was sold for scrap in December 1966, for £100,000. She left Plymouth in tow on 6 January 1967, arriving at Castellon, Spain, on 19 January for breaking up.

1500-ton class harbour tankers (1946)

Tonnages: 1440 gross, 1638 deadweight, 2670 displacement
Length overall: 231.4 ft
Beam: 38.2 ft
Depth: 17 ft
Draught: 15.7 ft
Machinery: 1 screw, triple expansion engine, 1140 ihp
Service speed: 10.5–11 knots; range 4000 nm, consumption 18 tons/day (bunkers 240 tons oil)
Complement: 26

Name	Builder	Laid down	Launched	Completed	Out of service
Birchol	Lobnitz & Co Ltd, Renfrew	25.5.45	19.2.46	12.6.46	1969
Oakol	Lobnitz & Co Ltd, Renfrew	12.12.45	28.8.46	1.11.46	1965
Rowanol	Lobnitz & Co Ltd, Renfrew	27.9.45	15.5.46	21.8.46	1971
Teakol	Lobnitz & Co Ltd, Renfrew	27.5.46	14.11.46	14.1.47	1969

Birchol
Left Renfrew on 5 August 1946, and in what was not a good start to her career, put into Gibraltar on 11 August with condenser trouble. This was repaired and she proceeded to Hong Kong, where she was stationed as harbour tanker. She was part of the RN Fleet Train deployed during the Korean war. *Birchol* was offered for sale on 12 July 1969 'as lies' Devonport, at the same time as *Oakol* and *Teakol*, and arrived at Antwerp on 18 September on her way to breaker's yard.

Oakol
Harbour tanker Singapore, where she arrived on 23 March 1947 after a voyage from Portland, calling at Gibraltar and Abadan. She was decommissioned in February 1965 and laid up at Devonport; put up for sale four years later. She arrived at the breakers in Ghent on 26 September 1969, and breaking up commenced on 14 November.

Rowanol
Rowanol was laid down as *Ebonol*, but after the original ship of this name was recovered from the Japanese, the new ship was renamed *Cedarol*. However, this caused some confusion with correspondence wrongly sent to *Cedardale* and vice-versa, so in 1947 the ship was renamed *Rowanol*. She was harbour tanker at Malta. She was laid up at Devonport on 3 December 1970 and one year later was sold to Belgian breakers. *Rowanol* arrived at Bruges on 10 December 1971 for scrapping.

Teakol
Service in home waters, and her first base was Rosyth, where she arrived on 29 January 1947 from Glasgow. Sold 1969 to breakers and arrived at Antwerp 22 September on way to the breaker's yard.

Appendix 1

Chronology of World Events and RFA Involvement 1905–50

1900s

1900 Launched: *Aquarius* (as *Hampstead*); completed: *Kharki* (as collier); transferred or taken over by Admiralty: *Kharki*.

1901 Launched: *Petroleum*.

1902 Transferred or taken over by Admiralty: *Kharki* (converted to oil tank vessel 1905); *Aquarius* (water tanker).

1904 Sir John (Jackie) Fisher appointed First Sea Lord.

1905 Admiralty owned fleet auxiliaries now designated Royal Fleet Auxiliaries.
Launched: *Heliopolis*; transferred or taken over by Admiralty: *Petroleum* (converted from oil to coal burning; crew initially employed on yard craft agreement despite sailing for Gibraltar in August); first vessel named as an RFA: *Maine*.
Oiling-at-sea (OAS) experiments begun (Admiralty Instructions issued by Naval Stores Circular)

1906 Launched: *Nucula* (as *Hermione*), *Argo* (as *Argo*); completed: *Nucula*, *Argo*; transferred or taken over by Admiralty: *Mercedes* (collier), *Aquarius* (commissioned for service under White Ensign as repair and distilling ship).
Petroleum: Naval Stores Coal memo ordering testing OAS arrangements with HMS *Victorious*; succession of OAS trials between Feb and June.
Coaling-at-sea (CAS): Metcalfe apparatus developed. Collier *Torridge* chartered and fitted with CAS rig for trials with Channel Fleet.
OAS: Conference at Admiralty agrees procedure with destroyers; 3.5-inch flexible bronze hose ordered as consequence.

1907 Transferred, converted or taken over by Admiralty: *Isla* (as *Thistle*, for conversion to petrol carrier for submarines) (note: *Isla* apparently so named as corruption of *Oiler*); *Aquarius* (converted to depot ship).

1908 Launched: *Industry* (as *Tay and Tyne*); completed: *Delphinula* (as *Bayu Maru*); taken over by Admiralty: *Mercedes*.

1909 Launched: *Berbice* (hospital ship: as *Berbice* for Royal Mail Lines).

1910s

1910 Launched and completed: *Reliance* (as *Knight Companion*).
Petroleum and *Kharki* fitted out for OAS experiments.
Mercedes: fitted with modified Metcalfe rig for CAS.
Fisher leaves Admiralty.

1911 Launched and completed: *Burma* (first Admiralty constructed 2000-ton tanker: fitted for OAS)
OAS trials: Relatively unsuccessful and C-in-C Home Fleet reports '... use of tanker vessels for oiling destroyers at sea was unlikely to be of service and further trials are unnecessary'.
Admiralty Committee on the use of Oil Fuel in the Navy (1911–12): '... ultimately more economical for Navy to freight its own fuel'.
Admiralty order in council for the Regulation of Naval Service No 121 (Statutory rules and order 1911 No 338): RFAs registered as British merchant ships under the Merchant Shipping Acts and as government vessels in the service of the Admiralty not forming part of the Royal Navy.
Tenders invited for new 4590-ton hospital ship

1912 Building started: *Attendant, Carol*; transferred or taken over by Admiralty: *Reliance* (as *Knight Companion*).
Royal Fleet Auxiliary appears in *Navy List* for first time.
Mercedes fitted with Marconi W/T installation.
Inconclusive CAS trial with HMS *Dominion*.
Royal Commission on Fuel and Engines (1912, 1913, 1914); Chairman Admiral Lord Fisher: 'Oil preferred over coal'.

1913 Building started: *Trefoil, Santa Margherita* (as *Olympia*), *Turmoil, Ferol*; launched: *Attendant, Carol, Trefoil*; transferred or taken over by Admiralty: *Heliopolis* (to be renamed *Maine*: originally intended to be renamed *Mediator*).

1914 Launched: *Servitor, Ferol*; completed: *Attendant* (first of 1000-ton group of tankers); purchased, transferred or taken over by Admiralty: *Industry, Isla* (re-rated as tankers: Admiralty's first spirit carrier) *Ruthenia* (requisitioned as BEF transport), *Aro* (for conversion to submarine depot ship), *Perthshire* (as dummy battleship HMS *Vanguard*); lost at sea: *Maine*.
Pennant numbers: first allocation to auxiliaries D, N (terminated 1916), P: Y3 (colliers), Y7 (tankers/transports).
Maine: *Heliopolis* renamed *Maine*; *Ruthenia*: arrived Belfast for conversion to dummy battleship; *Petroleum*: rescued crew of Norwegian barque *Charla*, during hurricane while on passage from Port Arthur, Texas to Portsmouth (2 February).
First World War commences (4 August: declaration of war against Germany)

1915 Ordered/building started: *Viscol, Plumleaf, Orangeleaf, Appleleaf, Brambleleaf, Cherryleaf, Pearleaf;* launched: *Bacchus, Innisfree, Innisinver, Innisjura, Innisulva, Santa Margherita;* completed: *Servitor, Bacchus;* purchased, transferred or taken over by Admiralty: *Ruthenia* (purchased for conversion to store ship and water carrier), *Delphinula* (as *Buyo Maru*), *Nucula* (as *Soyo Maru*), *Tarakol* (as *Patrician,* ex dummy battleship HMS *Invincible*), *Canning* (as kite balloon ship/depot ship), *Rangol* (as *Mount Royal,* ex dummy battleship HMS *Marlborough*), *Abadol* (as *Montezuma,* ex dummy battleship HMS *Iron Duke*); damaged or lost at sea: *Innistrahull.*

Pensions: Order in council approves scheme of pensions, grants and allowances for officers and ratings injured or disabled while serving on auxiliaries. Scheme also provides for dependants.

1916 Launched: *Viscol, Kimmerol, Philol, Scotol, Thermol, Mixol, Roseleaf* (as *Califol*), *Innistrahull, Scotol, Plumleaf* (as *Trinol*), *Oliphant* (as *Palmleaf*), *Oldbury* (as *Birchleaf*), *Olalla* (as *Laureleaf*), *Pearleaf* (as *Gypol*), *Olga* (as *Ashleaf*), *Kurumba, Orangeleaf* (as *Bornol*), *Olmos* (as *Beechleaf*), *Oligarch* (as *Limeleaf*), *Cherryleaf* (as *Persol*), *Oleary* (as *Dockleaf*), *Appleleaf* (as *Texol*), *Brambleleaf* (as *Rumol*); completed: *Mixol, Santa Margherita, Distol, Viscol, Thermol, Philol, Roseleaf, Creosol, Kimmerol, Scotol, Palmleaf, Oligarch* (as *Limeleaf*) *Olinda* (as *Boxleaf*); purchased, transferred or taken over by Admiralty: *Bayol* (converted to tanker from Admiralty-owned *Cevic*), *Reliance* (mixed crew: RFA, RNR and dockyard staff), *Saxol* (converted from store carrier as fleet tanker, renamed *Aspenleaf*), *Rangol* (renamed *Mapleleaf*); *Barkol, Battersol, Blackol, Greenol, Purfol, Silverol,* converted to tanker from *PLA Hopper No 3, No 4, No 5, No 6, No 7, No 8,* respectively; laid up or sold: *Maine* (ex *Heliopolis*: not completed; hull sold).

Pennant numbers: flag superior X allocated to RFAs until 1947, replaced by flag superior A.

Ministry of Shipping (Shipping Controller) starts operation.

1917 Building started: *British Star* (renamed *Olynthus* 1937); launched: *Belgol, Birchol, Boxol, British Light* (renamed *Olwen* 1937), *Celerol, Cherryleaf* (as *Persol*), *Ebonol, Elderol, Elmol, Fortol, Francol, Hickerol, Larchol, Limol, Montenol, Oakol, Palmol, Petrobus, Prestol, Rapidol, Rumol, Serbol, Slavol, Sprucol, Teakol, Turmoil* (experimental ship: mechanically poor and little used), *Vitol;* completed: *British Light* (under British Tanker Co Ltd management; renamed *Olwen* 1937), *Appleleaf* (as *Texol,* first Admiralty-designed Fast Leaf ex *Trinol* class), *Boxleaf, Kurumba; Elmleaf* (under Lane & Macandrew Ltd (L&M) management), *Hollyleaf* (L&M), *Plumleaf* (as *Trinol;* L&M), *Pearleaf* (as *Gypol:* L&M), *Dockleaf* (L&M), *Cherryleaf, Brambleleaf* (as *Rumol;* L&M), *Orangeleaf* (as *Bornol;* L&M), *Belgol, Birchol, Boxol, Celerol, Ebanol, Elderol, Elmol, Fortol, Francol, Larchol, Limol, Montenol, Prestol, Rapidol, Slavol, Vitol;* transferred or taken over by Admiralty: *Oakleaf* (originally as *Abadol,* transferred L&M management), *Argo* (chartered for Q ship, later purchased as coastal stores carrier), *Tyne and Tay* (chartered as Q ship: served as *Cheriton* and *Dundreay,* later purchased as store ship), *Mercedes* (transferred Rees Jones management); damaged or lost at sea: *Limeleaf* (damaged; returned to service December 1918), *Ashleaf* (lost), *Dockleaf* (damaged; returned to service June 1918), *Appleleaf* (damaged; returned to service April 1918), *Elmleaf* (damaged).

Director of Transports (Admiralty official) transferred into Ministry of Shipping.

1918 Launched: *British Beacon* (renamed *Olcades* 1937), *British Lantern* (renamed *Oligarch* 1937), *British Star*, *Dredgol*, *Petrella*, *Petronel*, *War Bahadur*, *War Nizam*, *War Sepoy*; completed: *British Beacon*, *British Lantern*, *British Star* (all under British Tanker Co Ltd management), *Dredgol*, *Hickorol*, *Oakol*, *Palmol*, *Petrella*, *Petrobus*, *Petronel*, *Serbol*, *Sprucol*, *Teakol*; transferred or taken over by Admiralty: *Aro* (converted to troopship); *Dredgol* (from Calcutta Port Commissioners ownership); damaged or lost at sea: *Appleleaf* (damaged; returned to service September 1918), *Bayleaf* (damaged; returned to service May 1918), *Birchleaf* (damaged; returned to service May 1918), *British Star* (damaged; returned to service September 1918), *Creosol* (lost), *Fernleaf* (damaged; returned to service March 1918), *Industry* (torpedoed), *Sprucol* (damaged July 1918: returned to service November/December 1918), *Vitol* (lost).

Management: Admiralty ships under commercial management to be controlled by Director of Transports (this department was incorporated into Ministry of Shipping).

First World War ended on 11 November 1918.

1919 Launched: *War Afridi*, *War Bharata*, *War Brahmin*, *War Diwan*, *War Hindoo*, *War Krishna*, *War Mehtar*, *War Nawab*, *War Pathan*, *War Pindari*, *War Sirdar*; completed: *War Diwan* (under C T Bowring & Co Ltd management), *War Hindoo* (under Gow, Harrison & Co Ltd management), *War Krishna* (under Davies & Newman Ltd management), *War Nawab* (under British Tanker Co Ltd management), *War Nizam* (under British Tanker Co Ltd management), *War Pathan*, *War Sepoy* (Hunting & Sons management); transferred or taken over by Admiralty: *Perthshire* (converted to oiler; Malta fuel hulk), *Ruthenia* (converted to oiler); laid up or sold: *Industry*, *Kurumba*, *Reliance* (repair ship); *Santa Margherita*; lost or damaged: *Appleleaf* (aground), *Roseleaf* (explosion in boiler room while undergoing repairs at Cardiff).

Treaty of Versailles: Official end of First World War.

1920s

1920 Building started: Oleander, *Olna*; launched: *War Sudra*; completed: *War Afridi*, *War Bharata*, *War Brahmin*, *War Mehtar*, *War Pindari*, *War Sirdar*, *War Sudra* (*note*: War class tankers owned by Shipping Controller and under commercial management from completion); transferred or taken over by the Admiralty: *Berbice*, *British Beacon*, *Maine*; sold: *Aro*, *Canning*, *Teakol*, *Oakol*, *Palmol*, *Innisjura*, *Sprucol*, *Innisulva*, *Aquarius*, *Innisinver*, *Mercedes*, *Innisshannon*, *Innisfree*; charter ended: *Barkol*, *Battersol*, *Blackol*, *Greenol*, *Purfol*, *Silverol* (all returned to owner); damaged at sea: *War Bahadur*; renaming: *Tay and Tyne* to *Industry*.

First technical adviser (later marine superintendent) appointed to Director of Stores.

Naval Estimates make provision for two naval hospital ships.

1921 Launched and completed: *Olna*; transferred or taken over by Admiralty: *War Afridi, War Brahmin, War Diwan, War Krishna, War Hindoo, War Nawab, War Nizam, War Pathan, War Sepoy, War Sirdar, War Pindari, War Bharata, War Sudra* (all preceding remained under commercial management), *Perthshire* (converted to stores ship); laid up or sold: *Ferol*; damaged or lost at sea: *Pearleaf, Olcades, War Afridi*.

Management of RFAs: Transferred to Director of Stores (Head of Naval Stores Department) from Ministry of Shipping (Shipping Controller), including adoption of working practices.

1922 Launched: *Oleander, Reliant* (as *London Importer*): completed: *Oleander*; transferred or taken over by Admiralty: *Nucula* (from Anglo Saxon Petroleum Co Ltd), *British Lantern, British Light, British Star*; laid up or sold: *Appleleaf, Brambleleaf, Cherryleaf, Mixol, Orangeleaf, Pearleaf, Plumleaf, Servitor, War Sepoy*: First cargo of oil to Singapore.

1923 Completed: *Reliant* (as *London Importer*); laid up: *Trefoil, Turmoil* (both mechanically poor); damaged or lost at sea: *War Mehtar, Kharki, War Brahmin, British Lantern*.

Petroleum: Freighting and fleet attendant duties at Gibraltar and Malta.

OAS: *Prestol* towing *Carol*.

Disaster relief: *Nucula* to Nagasaki for Yokohama earthquake relief.

1924 Sold: *Nucula* (hired to RNZN), *Industry*.

Petroleum: Towed oil barge to Port Stanley, Falklands, carrying first cargo of oil fuel (Stanley previously coaling station).

Perthshire: Reconditioned as Mediterranean Fleet refrigerated supply ship.

Armament: Admiralty Conference (Trade Division; Naval Staff).

1925 Oil Board: Established March as a subcommittee of the Committee of Imperial Defence (CID).

1926 Launched: *William Scoresby* (Falkland Islands research ship); transferred or taken over by the Admiralty: *Appleaf, Cherryleaf, Pearleaf, Plumleaf, Orangeleaf*; laid up or sold: *Attendant, Celerol*; damaged or lost at sea: *War Pathan*.

OAS trials: *Brambleleaf*/HMS *Ramillies* by hose hawser, *Belgol* with trough method.

1927 Launched and completed: *Berta*; laid up or sold: *Ruthenia*.

Prestol: Received ship's library

1928 Sold: *Racer*; damaged: *Bacchus* (collision with Greek steamer *Ioannis Fafalios*).

Slavol: Transport of armed Royal Marines group to liner *Jervis Bay*.

Disaster relief: *Perthshire* relief supplies to Corinth earthquake.

1929 Launched: RRS *Discovery*; transferred or taken over by Admiralty: *Nora* (as renamed *C65* coaling craft); laid up: *Burma*.
Serbol: Deployed to transport party of divers and attached personnel to raise wreck of *Balabac* in Port of Spain.
Pensions: Scheme of retiring allowances introduced for certain RFA officers (PRO ref 1927–35 T162/358).

1930s

1930 Laid up or sold: *Petroleum* (care and maintenance status).
Brambleleaf: Modified to carry aviation spirit.
earleaf: Modified to carry aviation spirit and explosives.
Rescue at Sea: *Pearleaf* rescued crew of 18 from Japanese trawler *Ibuki Maru* in China Sea.

1931 Sold: *Kharki* (July); laid up: *British Beacon*, *Dredgol*; laid up Rosyth: *War Bahadur* (28 September), *War Bharata* (18 August), *War Pindari* (19 August).
Naval manning of RFAs: Admiralty examined.

1932 Laid up: *British Lantern* (Sheerness 30 June), *Fortol*, *Montenol*.
OAS: Extended series of trials resulting in adoption of stirrup method, abandonment of hose-hawser, trough in use for destroyers.
Station allowances: paid to RFA crews on fleet attendances duties on foreign station for first time.

1933 Transferred or taken over by Admiralty: *War Bharata* (under DoS management), *Reliant* (as *London Importer* before conversion and duty as Mediterranean Fleet supply ship); laid up or sold: *Rapidol*.

1934 Laid up or sold: *Perthshire*.

1935 Launched: *Amherst* (as *Fort Amherst*); transferred or taken over by the Admiralty: *Mixol* (reactivated after lay up), *Bacchus*, *Rapidol* (reactivated after lay up); laid up or sold: *Burma*, *Turmoil*, *Carol*, *Trefoil*, *Attendant*, *Dredgol*.
Maine: Silver Jubilee Fleet Review, Spithead.
Armament: *Prestol* conducted paravane experiments
OAS: Exercise ZL; first successful use of trough method. Admiralty orders further trials with both stirrup and trough methods.
Tanker Tonnage committee: set up to consider tanker supply in wartime.
Spitfire prototype built: RAF to be trebled in size.
Radar: First report made available.

1936 Building started: *Bacchus*, *Abbeydale*, *Aldersdale*, *Boardale*; launched: *Bacchus*, *Abbeydale*; completed: *Bacchus*; transferred or taken over by Admiralty: *British Beacon*, *British Lantern*, *British Light*, *British Star*, *War Krishna*, *War Nawab*, *War*

Nizam, War Pathan, War Pindari, War Sepoy (all under DoS management); laid up or sold:
Delphinula (hulk), *Petroleum, Bacchus, Fortol*.
Company Service Contracts (CSC): Introduced for officers *only*.
OAS: Discussion about standard method for 2000- and 5000-ton tankers. Admiralty adopt trough method for oiling destroyers from capital ships.
Supply Ships Committee: Set up to consider ship requirements (except oilers) in emergency situations.
Spanish Civil War begins.
Maine: Hospital support from base in Malta.
Palestine: Arab revolt.
George V dies. Edward VIII succeeds then abdicates in December.

1937 Building started: *Arndale, Broomdale*; launched: *Bishopdale, Boardale, Aldersdale, Arndale, Broomdale*; completed: *Abbeydale, Bishopdale, Boardale, Aldersdale, Arndale, Broomdale*; transferred or taken over by Admiralty: *War Afridi, War Sirdar* (all transferred from commercial to DoS management); renamed: *British Beacon* to *Olcades, British Lantern* to *Oligarch, British Light* to *Olwen, British Star* to *Olynthus*; laid up or sold: *Nucula* (reduced to hulk), *Bacchus* (renamed *Bacchus II*) used as bombing target, sunk over the Hurd Deep, off Alderney, 1938.
Colour scheme: Uniform colour scheme adopted for RFAs.
Circular letters: Introduced as means of communicating instructions to RFAs.
Merchant Navy Training Board: Began operation. Responsible for all aspects of training and working conditions of Merchant Navy personnel.
Spain: *Plumleaf* and *Cherryleaf* at Barcelona; *Celerol, Prestol* and *Montenol* at Gibraltar and La Pallice. *Maine* to Valencia to evacuate refugees.

1938 Launched: *Robert Middleton, Robert Dundas, Cairndale*; completed: *Robert Middleton, Robert Dundas*; transferred or taken over by the Admiralty: *Hickorol* (re-enters service); laid up or sold: *War Bahadur* (storm damage; became fuel hulk), *Argo* (munitions hulk).
Armaments: DEMS and anti gas training for RFA personnel introduced.
Merchant Navy Pensions: Officers' fund introduced.
RFA Handbook: First edition of BR 875, *Regulations and Instructions Related to Registered Royal Fleet Auxiliaries* published.
Singapore: Naval base opens.
Munich Agreement: Chamberlain 'Peace in our time …'.
Germany: Hitler's troops invade Sudetenland.

1939 Building started: *Black Ranger, Blue Ranger, Brown Ranger, Derwentdale, Denbydale* (as *Empire Silver*); launched: *Cedardale, British Lady*; completed: *Cairndale, Cedardale*; transferred or taken over by the Admiralty: *Fortol* (re-enters service); laid up or sold: *Berta* (transferred to Anglo-Saxon Petroleum Co Ltd, renamed *Shell Dezoito*), *Nora, War Mehtar, War Nawab, War Sepoy, War Nizam*; lost at sea: *Birchol* (stranded in fog).
Armament: *Oleander* and *War Krishna* involved in paravane trials.
OAS: *Prestol* in trials with HMS *Fury* off Scapa Flow.

CB 4029 (B) (39) Vol 2: *Instructions Concerning the Supply of Fuel in War; Details of RFAs*, published.
Spanish Civil War: Ends in victory for the Fascists, led by Franco.
Arab revolt: Ends, although talks on future of Palestine fail to reach agreement.
Second World War begins: 3 September: 11am war declared: to begin at 5pm
Poland: Germany invades; Poles poorly equipped and quickly defeated.
Convoy system and DEMS introduced.
Liner *Athenia* torpedoed off Ireland.
October: HMS *Royal Oak* torpedoed in Scapa Flow.
December: Battle of the River Plate: *Graf Spee* scuttled off Montevideo.
As part of propaganda war, German newspaper *Bremer Zeitung* claims *Abbeydale* sunk. *Abbeydale* is, in fact, undamaged.

1940s

1940 Building started: *Eaglesdale*, *Echodale* (as *Empire Granite*), *Ennerdale* (as MOS9), *Nasprite*, *Freshet*, *Gold Ranger*, *Gray Ranger*, *Green Ranger*, *Spa*; launched: *Freshwater*, *Freshet*, *Darkdale* (as *Empire Oil*), *Black Ranger*, *Denbydale* (as *Empire Silver*), *Nasprite*, *Echodale* (as *Empire Granite*), *Brown Ranger*; completed: *Empire Salvage* (as *Papendrecht*), *Freshwater*, *Freshet*, *Darkdale* (as *Empire Oil*); transferred or taken over by Admiralty: *Ingeborg* (Dutch motor tanker), *Papendrecht*; damaged/destroyed by enemy action or lost at sea: *Aldersdale* (collision with HMS *Exeter*), *Cherryleaf* (collision with *Oxfordshire*), *Boardale* (abandoned after grounding), *Broomdale* (bombed), *Olcades* (aground), *Oleander* (bomb damage), *War Sepoy* (bombed in Dover Harbour; wreck later filled with concrete and used as block ship), *Scotol*.
Olwen: Assigned to oil Force G. Discontent among crew.
Arndale: Fleet attendance South Atlantic and Falkland Islands.
War Nawab: Shot down enemy aircraft.
Olna and *Brambleleaf*: Established fuelling base at Suda Bay, Crete.
OAS: *Arndale* in trials with HMS *Hawkins* and *Cumberland*.
Seaman's Welfare Board: Established October and supported by Port Welfare Committees.
Tanker Tonnage Allocation Committee: replaces Tanker Tonnage Committee. TTAC responsible for overseeing service requirements.
Winston Churchill forms a National Government (10 May).
Operation 'Puma': Plans for taking Azores and Cape Verde Islands.
Operation 'Sackbutt': Proposed occupation of Cape Verde Islands; *Olwen* allocated.
Dunkirk: (17 May–4 June).
Battle of Britain: (May-September) Luftwaffe is heavily defeated; planned invasion of Britain (Operation 'Sealion') called off.

1941 Building started: *Easedale*, *Freshbrook*, *Airsprite*, *Freshener*; launched: *Easedale*, *Ennerdale*, *Dewdale*, *Blue Ranger*, *Gold Ranger*, *Dingledale*, *Derwentdale*, *Grey Ranger*, *Green Ranger*, *Dinsdale* (as *Empire Norseman*), *Freshbrook*, *Spa*, *Eaglesdale* (as *Empire Metal*); completed: *Black Ranger*, *Blue Ranger*, *Nasprite*, *Echodale* (as

Empire Granite), Brown Ranger, Denbydale, Dewdale, Gold Ranger, Ennerdale, Derwentdale, Dingledale, Gray Ranger, Green Ranger; transferred or taken over by Admiralty: *Denbydale* (as *Empire Silver*); attacked/damaged/ destroyed by enemy action or lost by marine hazard: *Olna* (bombed, wrecked, Suda Bay, Crete), *Denbydale* (bombed, Liverpool), *Cairndale* (torpedoed, sunk, W of Gibraltar), *War Pindari* (bombed, Norway), *Blue Ranger* (collision, off Clyde), *Maine* (bombed, Alexandria), *Petrella* (bombed, Mediterranean), *Berta, Denbydale, Darkdale* (torpedoed, St Helena), *War Mehtar* (torpedoed, sunk, off Great Yarmouth), *Ebanol.*

Degaussing: Procedure introduced for all British ships (March).

OAS: Director Plans (Admiralty) recommends development of floating hose; Admiralty meeting 'Oiling of Capital Ships and Cruisers at Sea'; preliminary trials ordered (C-in-C Home Fleet) and carried out.

Lothringen: German tanker captured with RAS gear intact; temporarily registered as *Empire Salvage.*

Gedania: German oiler captured, renamed *Empire Garden.*

Ranger class: Declared unsuitable for oiling in Atlantic.

War is costing Britain £11 million per day (February estimate).

Pearl Harbor: Attacked by Japanese carrier force (7 December).

Britain and United States declare war on Japan (7–8 December).

Germany declares war on United States (8 December).

Operation 'Exce': Convoy to Piræus and Malta. Force A with *Brambleleaf.*

Operation 'Puma': Recapture of Azores and Cape Verde Islands, becomes Operation 'Pilgrim': *Olwen, Abbeydale, Dewdale, Ennerdale* placed on alert.

Operation 'Sackbutt': Recapture of Cape Verde Islands.

Bismarck: Cairndale deployed with Force H

Operation 'FB/Gauntlet': Force A destruction of Spitzbergen facilities; *Oligarch* and *War Sudra* supporting.

Operation 'Halberd': Supply convoy to Malta; *Brown Ranger* as oiler.

Operation 'Anklet': Commando raid on Lofoten Islands from Scapa Flow.

1942 Building started: *Freshlake, Freshmere, Freshpool;* launched: *Freshener, Freshlake, Freshmere, Airsprite;* completed: *Eaglesdale, Easdale, Dinsdale* (as *Empire Norseman*), *Freshbrook, Spa, Freshener, Freshlake;* transferred or taken over by the Admiralty: *Empire Salvage;* attacked/damaged/destroyed by enemy action or lost at sea: *Orangeleaf* (collision; with *Botnia* no damage), *Ruthenia* (captured), *War Sirdar* (bombed; Java), *Francol* (bombed; Java), *Plumleaf* (bombed, sunk), *Slavol* (torpedoed, sunk, on passage to Tobruk), *Montenol* (torpedoed, sunk, Azores), *Dinsdale* (torpedoed, sunk, South Atlantic), *Brambleleaf* (torpedoed, towed to Alexandria; used as fuel hulk), *Aldersdale* (bombed, sunk, Barents Sea), *Bishopdale* (struck mine), *Spa* (collision HMS *Howe*), *Dingledale* (fire; arson suspected), *Gray Ranger* (torpedoed, sunk, Arctic), *Spa* (collision HMS *King George V*), *War Sudra* (collision *Prestol*), *Ennerdale, Dewdale* (bombed Port d'Alger), *Thermol* (collision), *Dewdale* (mine damage).

OAS: Canvas hose used in place of rubber until sufficient rubber hose available.

Operation 'Ironclad': Occupation of Diego Suarez, Madagascar; *Derwentdale* (carrying 12 LCMs) and *Easdale* (as convoy oiler) deployed.

Operation 'Vigorous'/'Harpoon': Supply convoys from Alexandria to Malta and Gibraltar to Malta simultaneously.

Operation 'Pedestal': Malta convoy.

Operation 'Torch': Allied landings in French North Africa; *Derwentdale, Ennerdale, Brown Ranger* and *Dingledale* deployed.

Singapore: Surrender to Japanese.

1943 Building started: *Freshwell, Wave King* (as *Empire Sheba*), *Spabeck, Wave Emperor, Wave Monarch* (as *Empire Venus*), *Freshburn, Wave Governor, Spabrook, Freshford, Seafox*; launched: *Freshburn, Freshpool, Freshwell, Spabeck, Wave Conqueror* (as *Empire Law*), *Wave Victor* (as *Empire Bounty*);

completed: *Airsprite, Freshmere, Freshpool, Spabeck* (as *Rivulet*), *Freshwell*; attacked/damaged/lost by enemy action or lost by marine hazard: *Celerol* (collision), *Dewdale* (bombed), *War Bharata* (collision), *Belgol* (bombed), *Oligarch* (torpedoed), *Ennerdale* (bombed Sicily), *Derwentdale* (bombed Salerno), *Dingledale* (collision Freetown HMS *Stork*).

Empire Salvage: Defensive armament upgraded.

Operation 'Husky' (Sicily invasion): *Derwentdale, Ennerdale*, supported by *Cedardale, Nasprite*.

Operation 'Pilgrim' (Azores invasion): Plans for invasion abandoned.

Operation 'Avalanche' (Salerno landings): *Derwentdale* deployed as part of southern attack force.

Atlantic convoy war: Begins to turn in favour of Royal Navy.

Italy surrenders (8 September).

1944 Building started: *Empire Gull* (as LST3), *Fort Rosalie, Fort Sandusky, Freshpond, Spaburn*; launched: *Wave Liberator* (as *Empire Milner*), *Fort Charlotte* (as *Buffalo Park*), *Fort Dunvegan, Fort Constantine, Freshford, Wave Commander* (as *Empire Paladin*), *Wave Master* (as *Empire Salisbury*), *Wave Monarch, Wave Regent* (as *Empire Protector*), *Freshtarn, Spabrook, Fort Beauharnois* (as *Fort Grand Rapids*), *Fort Duquesne* (as *Queensborough Park*), *Wave Emperor, Wave Duke* (as *Empire Mars*), *Fort Rosalie, Fort Sandusky, Wave Governor, Olna*; completed: *Wave Victor* (as *Empire Bounty*), *Wave Conqueror* (as *Empire Law*), *Wave King* (as *Empire Sheba*), *Wave Monarch* (as *Empire Venus*), *Freshburn, Buffalo Park, Fort Dunvegan, Fort Constantine, Wave Liberator* (as *Empire Milner*), *Freshford, Wave King, Wave Commander* (as *Empire Paladin*), *Wave Victor* (as *Empire Bounty*), *Fort Grand Rapids* (as *Cornish Park*), *Fort Langley* (as *Montebello Park*), *Fort Duquesne* (as *Queensborough Park*), *Wave Master* (as *Empire Salisbury*), *Spabrook, Freshtarn*; transferred or taken over by Admiralty: *Wave King, Wave Monarch*; attacked/ damaged/destroyed by enemy action or lost at sea: *War Nizam* (air raid (undamaged), Southend), *Broomdale* (explosion, Bombay harbour), *Abbeydale* (torpedoed; later repaired), *Derwentdale* (reduced to care and maintainance; later repaired using *Denbydale*'s engines), *Rapidol* (Cherbourg), *Broomdale* (torpedoed by submarine HMS *Severn*), *Boxleaf* (as Japanese *Zuiyo Maru*), *Bishopdale* (bombed, San Pedro Bay, Philippines), *War Diwan* (mined River Scheldt estuary). RADAR: Introduced into RFAs (September); tankers deployed to eastern waters had priority.

Operation 'Tungsten': attack on *Tirpitz*; carriers launched attack supported by *Blue Ranger* and *Black Ranger*.
Operation 'Neptune': Normandy invasion.
RFA officers and Naval Stores Department staff involved in planning fuel requirements.
Rapidol and *Robert Dundas* were only RFAs directly involved.
Operation 'Dragoon'; Allied invasion of South of France.
Dewdale, Ennerdale, Celerol involved in amphibious operations.
Operation 'Outflank'.

1945 Building started: *Birchol, Rowanol, Spalake, Spapool, Ebanol, Oakol*; launched: *Empire Gull* (as LST3), *Wave Prince* (as *Empire Herald*), *Freshpond, Wave Knight* (as *Empire Naseby*), *Wave Sovereign* (as *Empire Sovereign*), *Rippledyke* (as *Empire Tesbury*); completed: *Olna, Wave Governor, Wave Duke* (as *Empire Mars*), *Fort Rosalie, Fort Langley, Wave Regent, Fort Sandusky*; transferred or taken over by Admiralty: HMS *Olna* (transferred to RFA 1946), *Nordmark* (subsequently *Northmark*); laid up or sold: *Appleleaf*; attacked/damaged/destroyed by enemy action or lost at sea: *War Sirdar* (as Japanese tanker *Honan Maru*), *Ennerdale* (mined Malacca Strait).
Dewdale: First RFA into Singapore after re-occupation.
British Pacific Fleet: 16 January: Departs Trincomalee; *Arndale, Wave King* as part of underway RAS group (URG).
15 March: retitled Task Force 57 (as USN) for Operation 'Iceberg'; URG was *Arndale, Cedardale, Dingledale*.
British Pacific Fleet Train: Task Force 112; includes *Wave King, Wave Monarch, Arndale, Cedardale, Dingledale*.
Operation 'Meridian': RFAs as part of Task Force 69.
Operation 'Lentil': Pangkalan Brabdon, air strike on oil refineries.
Carriers HMS *Indomitable, Victorious, Indefatigable* and escorts supported by RFA URG.
Operation 'Iceberg': Invasion of Okinawa.
Operation 'Sunfish': Malayan reconnaissance and anti-shipping sweep; *Easedale* attached.
Operation 'Judgement': Attack on U-boat depot ship at Kilbotn; *Blue Ranger* attached.
Operation 'Dracula': Entry into Rangoon, *Echodale* and *Gold Ranger* deployed in support.
Operation 'Dukedom'; Attack on Japanese heavy cruiser *Haguro*.
Second World War ends.
German surrender 7 May.
Japanese surrender 14–15 August.
Palestine emergency.

1946 Building started: *Teakol*; launched: *Teakol, Rowanol, Wave Ruler, Ebonol, Oakol, Wave Baron, Wave Chief, Wave Laird, Wave Premier, Spapool, Spalake*; completed: *Birchol, Ebonol, Oakol, Rowanol, Rippledyke* (as *Empire Tesbury*), *Wave Chief, Wave Conqueror* (as *Empire Law*), *Wave Knight* (as *Empire Naseby*), *Wave Laird, Wave*

Premier, Wave Prince (as *Empire Herald*), *Wave Baron, Wave Sovereign, Spaburn, Spapool, Spalake*; transferred or taken over by Admiralty: *Wave Chief, Wave Commander* (as *Empire Paladin*), *Wave Duke* (as *Empire Mars*), *Wave Liberator* (as *Empire Milner*), *Wave Master* (as *Empire Salisbury*), *Wave Protector* (as *Empire Protector*), *Wave Ruler* (as *Empire Evesham*), HMS *Olna* registered as *Olna* after conversion work; laid up or sold: *Petrella, War Bahadur, Brambleleaf, Pearleaf, Cherryleaf, War Nizam, Thermol, War Nawab, War Krishna, Olwen*.
Note: Several ships were still under commercial management although owned by Admiralty (*eg Wave Baron*, after completion for Admiralty placed under commercial management of Gow, Harrison & Co Ltd, Glasgow).
Ranger class: Building of new 3500-ton Ranger class oilers discussed.
Ministry of War Transport responsibilities transferred to newly formed Ministry of Transport.

1947 Completed: *Teakol*; transferred or taken over by Admiralty: *Maine* (as *Empire Clyde*), *Fort Duquesne, Fort Charlotte, Fort Rosalie*; laid up or sold: *Distol, Ebonol, Nucula, Kimmerol, War Pathan, War Pindari, Hickorol, Viscol, Petronel, Spapool, War Nizam*.
Petty officers offered improved employment conditions, including contracts after one year satisfactory service aboard an RFA freighter.
Northmark: Moved to Portsmouth for conversion for RAS, incorporating ideas from British Pacific Fleet experience.
Cederol: renamed *Rowanol*.

1948 Building started: *Retainer* (as *Chungking*); transferred or taken over by Admiralty: *Fort Beauharnois, Fort Charlotte, Fort Dunvegan, Wave Baron, Wave Commander*; laid up or sold: *Boxol, Mixol, Nimble* (ferry: on yard craft agreement), *Rapidol, Reliant, Scotol, Thornol, War Bharata*.
Merchant Navy Welfare Board established.
Revised pension regulations for personnel employed since 1938.
Palestine emergency: Ends with creation of new state of Israel.
Malayan emergency: Britain involved until 1960.
Britain warns Argentina to stay off the Falklands.
Berlin airlift begins (1 July).

1949 Building started: *Resurgent* (as *Chungchow*); transferred or taken over by Admiralty: *Fort Constantine, Fort Sandusky*, RRS *William Scoresby* (manned and managed by DoS); laid up or sold: *Ruthenia, Argo, War Afridi, War Brahmin*; refit: *Bulawayo*

Appendix 2

RFA Colour Schemes

Before 1937, there was no uniform colour scheme for Royal Fleet Auxiliary vessels, although they were frequently painted partly in the colour schemes used by their management companies. In addition, ships on some stations were painted according to the C-in-C's preference. On the Eastern Station, in the early 1920s, for example, ships had light grey hulls with dark funnels and upperworks. Later, this was changed to an overall covering of light grey.

The following ships had the following colour schemes while under management:

Ship	Management company	Colour scheme
Olcades,	British Tanker Co Ltd 1918–36	Black hull, black funnel, white upperworks
Oligarch		
Olynthus, Olwen		
War Pathan	Andrew Weir & Co Ltd 1919–37	Not known
War Mehtar	Hunting & Son Ltd 1920–26	Not known
War Sudra	British Tanker Co Ltd 1920–36	Black hull, black funnel, white upperworks
War Nawab	British Tanker Co Ltd 1919–36	Black hull, black funnel, white upperworks
War Nizam	British Tanker Co Ltd 1919–36	Black hull, black funnel, white upperworks

During the Spanish Civil War, vessels operating in those waters were painted with two vertical coloured stripes amidships as a protective measure, in line with the Nyon Agreement.

A uniform colour scheme was introduced in 1937 for freighting tankers, fleet attendant tankers, supply ships and store vessels. The scheme applied to vessels in Home waters and the Mediterranean Station, although on other stations the scheme was left to the C-in-C's discretion. During the Second World War, the scheme was changed again.

1937 colour scheme, including variants

Structure	Home and Mediterranean 1937	Hong Kong and East Indies 1920s	Hong Kong and East Indies 1937–9	Wartime scheme, 1939–45
Bottom	Red	Light grey	White	Black
Hull	Black	Light grey	White	Red
Upperworks	Mediterranean grey	Dark grey	Buff	Grey
Funnel	Grey, black band	Dark grey	Buff	Grey, black band
Boats/spars	Grey	Not specified	Buff	Not specified

Pacific Fleet Service

Funnels of RFA oilers serving with the Pacific Fleet were each colour coded for identification :

- *Wave Governor* – yellow funnel, one black band
- *Wave King* – red funnel, black top
- *Wave Monarch* – yellow funnel, black top
- *Arndale* – two white bands
- *Dingledale* – three white bands
- *Eaglesdale* – two red bands

During 1950–70, three different colour schemes were in use. In 1982, a reduced visibility scheme was introduced for RFA vessels serving in the Falklands War. This scheme has been retained to the present (2010).

RFA colour schemes 1950–2010

Structure	1950	1959	1969	2010 (Falklands)
Bottom	Red	Light grey	Red	Light grey
Hull	Black	Light grey	Light grey	Light grey
Superstructure	Light grey	Light grey	Light grey	Light grey
Spars/boats	Light grey	Light grey	Grey or white (boats)	Light grey (spars)
Funnels	Light grey/ black band	Light grey/ black band	Grey/black band	Light grey
Decks	Light grey	Light grey	Green	Grey
Flight deck	–	–	Black	Grey
Aluminium lifeboats	–	–	–	Light grey
GRP lifeboats upperworks	–	–	–	White, orange
Internal boat surfaces	–	–	–	Day-Glo orange
Lifeboats/survival aids	–	–	–	Day-Glo orange
GRP liferaft containers	–	–	–	White

Ammunition ships and victualling ships had function bands on their funnels, between 1950 and 1969–70, red bands denoting ammunition ships, white bands, victualling ships. For reasons unknown, some tankers also had a white funnel band.

Variations from this scheme include:
- RFAs serving with Mediterranean Fleet in 1950, were light grey overall; some supply and ammunition ships had black funnel bands, with function bands below.
- *Empire Gull* and the reserve tanker *Dewdale* retained their black hulls.
- Sir class LSLs, while under British India Steam Navigation Co Ltd management, had the 'Blue Band Margarine' livery of peacetime British troopships: White hull with blue band, white superstructure, buff funnel.
- Point class ro-ro strategic-lift ships, *Sea Crusader* and *Sea Centurion* had grey hull with white upperworks, with lifeboats in Day-Glo orange, in line with Safety of Life at Sea (SOLAS) requirements.

Appendix 3

Service, Honours and Awards

It would be impossible to list all of the honours and awards for individual RFA men from 1905 to the present. Shown here are several sources that may be used to locate a relative who served in the RFA and/or Merchant Navy, which will include their decorations, war service and other personal details.

National Archives, Kew
Website: www.nationalarchives.gov.uk
Crew agreements and official logs are held here for the period 1913–72 in a collection called 'Merchant Seaman: Sea Service Records 1913-1972'. Deaths at sea are listed in 'The Marine Register Book, Deaths 1837–1965'.

National Maritime Museum Caird Library
• *The Roll of Honour of the Merchant Navy and Fishing Fleets; 1939–1945*, three volumes; published 1958 by London Ministry of Transport and Civil Aviation.

• This publication lists ship, date of loss and memorial of over 33,000 merchant seaman lost at sea between 1939 and 1945. Their names also appear on either the Merchant Navy Memorial, Tower Hill or one of the other memorial world-wide.

• *Seedie's Roll of Naval Honours and Awards 1939–1945*; published 1989.
Single, alphabetical list by name, including merchant seamen, giving name, award, rating, ship the action for which the award was made and the date of the relevant *London Gazette* entry.

Guildhall Library
• *Lloyd's List*: this holds citations for some medals awarded to merchant seamen.

• Voyage record cards: these hold details of ship voyages as well as some other details (also available on-line from National Archives).

• *Lloyd's Captains Register* – some awards to masters.

• *Lloyd's Medals; 1876–1989*
(author Jim Gawler), published 1989 by Hart Publishing Co, Toronto.

• The *London Gazette* holds records of awards to merchant seaman, as well as other British citizens. Available at this location, with indexes.

Appendix 4

Battle Honours
Awarded to RFA Ships 1905–50

Battle Honours have been awarded to Royal Navy ships since Elizabethan times. The Navy Board makes these awards on the recommendation of the Battle Honours Committee.

Since its inception in 1905, the Royal Fleet Auxiliary has been awarded Battle Honours for a number of actions, beginning in the Second World War.

North Africa
Dingledale (1942–3)

North Africa (Operation 'Torch')
Abbeydale, Brown Ranger, Derwentdale, Ennerdale, Nasprite (1942)

Salerno
Derwentdale (1943)

Sicily
Cedardale, Derwentdale, Ennerdale, Pearleaf (1943)

Appendix 5

Refuelling at Sea 1905–50

During the 1920s and the 1930s, the RFA's predominant task logistically had consisted of transporting fuel and dry stores to Royal Navy shore bases. Replenishment-at-sea (RAS) was still an unreliable, slow and largely experimental technique.

Prior to 1936 and the Supply Ships Committee, financial constraints and short sighted thinking had forced the Admiralty to shelve any programme that might have allowed the development of an efficient rig for refuelling at sea. In a meeting at the Admiralty, as late as 1938: 'Their Lordships decided that, generally speaking, the larger ships (author's note: *ie*, bigger than destroyers), would not require to oil underway.'

It was further considered that battleships and most other warships would *always* be able to refuel in harbour or at 'an exposed anchorage'.

Few RFA tankers were even equipped for refuelling-at-sea, the predominant pre-war method of refuelling warships involving the tanker being alongside the receiving vessel in a sheltered anchorage. Incidentally, many of the world's navies still use this method as their preferred technique, only the Royal Navy, the US Navy and a couple of European services having developed sophisticated RAS techniques. This is a field in which British superiority has become a marked feature, so much so that many foreign navies send their ships to Portland for training in RAS techniques with RFA vessels.

Wartime pressures and the loss of bases like Singapore accelerated technological development in RAS techniques, as in many other fields, and by 1945, with the help of captured German equipment, oiling-at-sea was becoming almost routine, while significant progress had been made on techniques for jackstay transfer of both dry stores and ammunition.

Petroleum was the first RFA tanker to be modified for refuelling-at-sea (RAS). Bought from her builders in 1906, the purchase price included 600 feet of Admiralty hose and several modifications to her pumping arrangements. This included a 5-inch deck connector which could be used to draw excess oil out of the hose, after refuelling was finished. She was fitted for refuelling by the stirrup method, which was to be the predominant technique until the early 1930s. *Burma*, accepted into the RFA fleet in 1911, was similarly equipped.

The First World War was dissimilar in many respect to the later conflict and no more so than in the nature of naval logistic operations. Most engagements took place in the North Sea or Atlantic, well within reach of port refuelling facilities. So there was no pressure on the Royal Navy to perfect RAS techniques, unlike their counterparts in the US Navy. Importantly, RAS development was not helped by the many warships on both sides being coal burners.

One of the first serious British attempts at improving fuel replenishment, after the First World War, was conducted in 1924, using what was called the 'hose hawser' method.

This technique employed a hawser, by which the receiving ship was towed, passed through the fuel hose. It proved extremely unreliable and the service soon reverted to the stirrup method, whereby a 3.5-inch metal hose was suspended from the towing hawser by a series of brass stirrups mounted on rollers, the practice now being for the tanker to tow the receiving ship.

The system was dangerous and time-consuming, since each stirrup on the fuelling hose had to be transferred from the stirrup rail to the towing hawser by a crew member. The whole complex arrangement was then passed out of a special stern chute and along the hawser to the receiving ship. Adding to the difficulty was the need to secure a cork lifebelt around the hose, halfway between each stirrup, to keep it afloat in the event of a breakage, an all too common occurrence with this particular rig. Having secured the hose, pumping could begin, and rates of about 120 tons per hour usually were achieved. The high pressures needed to achieve even this rate in the long and tortuously coiled metal hose resulted in frequent bursts, which delayed fuel transfer even more.

Needless to say, the RFA men who were called upon to operate it were not very keen on the system, either, their usual advice to newcomers being '... keep a bucket handy for spare thumbs', because of the danger inherent in transferring the stirrups while the hose was moving down the stern chute.

Despite its fairly obvious shortcomings, the stirrup method remained in service until the Second World War, although, by 1937, trials had begun with the 'trough' system.

This technique involved the tanker and the receiving ship steaming abeam of each other, some 70 yards apart, secured by a towing hawser and a breast rope.

While maintaining the required distance by station keeping and adjustment of the breast rope, the tanker lowered a derrick from which was suspended a single trough containing two 5-inch flexible bronze hoses, through which fuel oil could be pumped at rates of about 500 tons per hour. Burst hoses were still a problem, however, until the next major breakthrough.

This came in 1941, when two German support tankers, *Lothringren* and *Gedania,* were captured and found to be using buoyant rubber hoses for refuelling. British trials quickly resulted in the production of a successful 5-inch buoyant rubber hose, which could be filled with compressed air and simply hauled across to the receiving ship, vastly simplifying the stern replenishment process. Stirrup rails and stern chutes were now dispensed with, the hose being simply laid out on a set of wooden or cast iron rollers, before being attached to a wire rope and then passed through a roller fair lead, usually 5 inch, situated in the stern of the vessel. The wire rope was transferred to the warship by means of a thin 'messenger', which was either attached to a float, to be grappled by the warship, or fired across by a service rifle fitted with a special adapter. This messenger was then hauled across with the wire rope attached (or 'seized on'), followed in turn by the inflated rubber fuelling hose.

Since it was both simple to install and effective in operation, this was the preferred method for both RFAs and the escort oilers which accompanied many Second World War convoys, especially as it cut down replenishment times considerably. Connecting up, in particular, was considerably simplified. HMCS *Athabaskan* set a record for this operation, during the Korean War, when she managed it, from line hitting the deck to coupled fuel hoses, in one minute forty seconds. Not bad when one considers that during the RFA's first refuelling trials with bronze hose, between *Petroleum* and HMS *Victorious*, connecting up took five hours, including a break for meals! Admittedly, disconnecting was quicker. It only took three hours!

Rubber now replaced the bronze and canvas hoses previously in use for the trough method as well. Together with the fitting of experimental gantry-type 'King' posts and long net-defence derricks to *Broomdale*, this began the development of the sophisticated RAS equipment in use by today's RFAs.

Advances were not just being made in liquid replenishment (RAS(L)), however. Warships needed victualling stores and ammunition as well, which also had to be provided at sea.

During the Pacific war, the US Navy developed sound techniques for jack-stay transfer of ammunition and dry stores and the Royal Navy were not slow to follow their lead, having previously used an unsatisfactory 'whip and inhaul' method for stores transfer. Modern jackstay techniques grew out of these early beginnings, with loads of up to five tons now being routinely transferred between ships. The development of what is termed 'vertical replenishment' (VERTREP) by helicopters has, of course, added a whole new dimension to the RFA's ability to replenish warships at seas.

Who knows what new techniques will appear during the twenty-first century? Whatever they are, the RFA is sure to be, as usual, in the forefront of any developments which make their job of replenishing the Royal Navy's warships more efficient.

References

General
Adams, Thomas A, and James R Smit, *The Royal Fleet Auxiliary: A century of service* (London: Chatham Publishing, 2005).
Jordan, Roger, *The World's Merchant Fleets 1939* (London: Chatham Publishing, 2000).
Sigwart, Captain E E, *Royal Fleet Auxiliary* (London: Adlard Coles Ltd, 1969).

National Archives of the United Kingdom

Wikipedia
This online encyclopedia has details of almost every topic mentioned in this book. Experience has shown, however, that when using any website, corroboration should also be obtained from other sources, because such sites do not usually operate a system of peer review.

Chapter 1
Gaman, P M, *The Science of Food* (2nd edn, Oxford: Pergamon, 1981). Macdonald, Janet, *Feeding Nelson's Navy: The true story of food at sea in the Georgian era* (London: Chatham Publishing, 2006).
Website
www.pbenyon1.plus.com/KR&AI/Victualling.html – This site contains detailed information about King's Regulations and Admiralty Instructions.

Chapter 2
Padfield, Peter, *The Great Naval Race: Anglo-German Naval Rivalry 1900–1914* (Edinburgh: Birlinn, 1974).
Wildenberg, *Thomas, Gray Steel and Black Oil: Fast tankers and the Replenishment at Sea in the US Navy, 1912-1995* (Annapolis: Naval Institute Press, 1996).
Website
www.American Global Security.org – Contains detailed information about American trials of coaling at sea apparatus.

Chapter 3
Ditmar, F J, and J J Colledge, *British Warships 1914–1919* (London: Ian Allen, 1972).
Hampshire, A Cecil, *The Phantom Fleet* (London: William Kimber, 1962).
Janes Fighting Ships 1919 (London: Janes Publishing, 1919).

Chapter 4
National Maritime Museum. Ship covers department – original papers on ship construction.

Chapter 5
National Archives documents from Admiralty departments.

Chapter 6
Forster, Mark Arnold, *The World at War* (London: Collins, 1973).

Chapter 7
Forster, Mark Arnold, *The World at War* (London: Collins, 1973).
Lovering, Tristan (ed.), *Amphibious Assault: maneuver from the sea* (Rendlesham: Seafarer Books, 2007).

Chapter 8
Forster, Mark Arnold, *The World at War* (London: Collins, 1973).
Website
www.pows-of-japan.net/index.html – Prisoners of War of the Japanese 1942–1945.

Chapter 9
National Archives. *History of the Fleet Train.* Document ADM 116/5535
Puddefoot, Geoff, *The Fourth Force* (London: Seaforth Publishing, 2010).
Sarantakes, Nicholas E, *The Short but Brilliant Life of the British Pacific Fleet*, Joint Force Quarterly, 40, First Quarter 2006, pp. 85–91.
Smith, Peter C, *Task Force 57* (London: William Kimber, 1969).
Winton, John, *The Forgotten Fleet* (London: Michael Joseph, 1969).

Chapter 10
Kershaw, Robert, *The Tank Men* (London: Hodder & Stoughton, 2008).
Sigwart, Captain EE, *Royal Fleet Auxiliary* (London: Adlard Coles Ltd, 1969), Ch 5, 'Fuelling at Sea'.
Website
www.naval-history.net – Thames dumb barge conversions.

Chapter 11
Sigwart, Captain E E, *Royal Fleet Auxiliary* (London: Adlard Coles Ltd, 1969).

Index